Research Methods for Medical Graduates

Research Methods for Medical Graduates

Abhaya Indrayan

CRC Press
Taylor & Francis Group
Boca Raton London New York

CRC Press is an imprint of the
Taylor & Francis Group, an **informa** business

CRC Press
Taylor & Francis Group
6000 Broken Sound Parkway NW, Suite 300
Boca Raton, FL 33487-2742

First issued in paperback 2021

ISBN-13: 978-1-138-35181-3 (hbk)
ISBN-13: 978-1-03-208725-2 (pbk)

This book contains information obtained from authentic and highly regarded sources. While all reasonable efforts have been made to publish reliable data and information, neither the author nor the publisher can accept any legal responsibility or liability for any errors or omissions that may be made. The publishers wish to make clear that any views or opinions expressed in this book by individual editors, authors or contributors are personal to them and do not necessarily reflect the views/opinions of the publishers. The information or guidance contained in this book is intended for use by medical, scientific, or health-care professionals and is provided strictly as a supplement to the medical or other professional's own judgment, their knowledge of the patient's medical history, relevant manufacturer's instructions, and the appropriate best practice guidelines. Because of the rapid advances in medical science, any information or advice on dosages, procedures, or diagnoses should be independently verified. The reader is strongly urged to consult the relevant national drug formulary and the drug companies' and device or material manufacturers' printed instructions, and their websites, before administering or utilizing any of the drugs, devices, or materials mentioned in this book. This book does not indicate whether a particular treatment is appropriate or suitable for a particular individual. Ultimately it is the sole responsibility of the medical professional to make his or her own professional judgments, so as to advise and treat patients appropriately. The authors and publishers have also attempted to trace the copyright holders of all material reproduced in this publication and apologize to copyright holders if permission to publish in this form has not been obtained. If any copyright material has not been acknowledged please write and let us know so we may rectify in any future reprint.

Library of Congress Cataloging-in-Publication Data
Names: Indrayan, Abhaya, 1945– author.
Title: Research methods for medical graduates / by Dr. Abhaya Indrayan.
Description: Boca Raton : CRC Press, [2020] |
Includes bibliographical references and index. |
Summary: "This book discusses the why and how of each step of data-based medical research that can provide basic information to emerging researchers and medical graduate students who write theses or publish articles. The chapters are arranged in the sequence of steps for data-based research. – Provided by publisher.
Identifiers: LCCN 2019034459 (print) | LCCN 2019034460 (ebook) |
 ISBN 9781138351813 (hardback ; alk. paper) | ISBN 9780429435034 (ebook)
Subjects: MESH: Research Design | Education, Medical, Graduate |
Research–education
Classification: LCC R834 (print) | LCC R834 (ebook) |
NLM W 20.5 | DDC 610.71/1–dc23
LC record available at https://lccn.loc.gov/2019034459
LC ebook record available at https://lccn.loc.gov/2019034460

Visit the Taylor & Francis Web site at
www.taylorandfrancis.com

and the CRC Press Web site at
www.crcpress.com

Contents

Preface

Medical research endeavors have enormously increased over the past few decades, but the awareness about proper methods has not kept pace. Thus, the number of publications has steeply increased without much improvement in their quality. This is more so with theses that medical graduates around the world are required to write as part of their curriculum of doctorate degree. No elementary book is available that comprehensively describes the basic methods of research for medical graduates in a simple language. This book covers all aspects of medical research from searching a topic for research to reporting of results, including planning, execution, and analysis – thus fulfilling this need. A wide spectrum of essentials for the initiators is presented to cover almost the entire process of research and its management from the beginning to the end. The book can serve as a useful reference for all clinical and health care research.

Devoid of polemics and intricacies, the text is designed for delightful reading with features such as boxes for explaining important concepts for special attention of the reader, and clearly demarcated examples from current literature to demonstrate the relevance and to illustrate the methods. References are provided at the end of each chapter with their web link wherever relevant. These links would be of definite help in the electronic version of the book. The intricacies of medical research are explained by a clear step-by-step procedure that appeals to conscience. The book discusses the why and how of each step of medical research and strives to provide basic information to emerging researchers. A wide breadth of the essential aspects of empirical methods as required by an initiator is described. The text is tailored to improve the precision and credibility of medical research by framing precise questions, minimizing sampling and nonsampling errors through the development of appropriate design, eliciting quality information, performing adequate statistical analysis that provides correct answers to the questions earlier framed, drawing valid conclusions, and preparing a worthwhile report based on evidence. It also describes the tools which are used to conduct robust research studies. All the essentials of how to conduct various research-related tasks have been discussed without over-burdening a graduate student.

The book comprehensively covers all aspects of primary medical research comprising descriptive and analytical data-based studies including clinical trials, but excludes qualitative research such as focus group discussion, as well as secondary research such as cost–benefit analysis, operations research, decision analysis, health system analysis, and meta-analysis.

The chapters are arranged in the sequence of the steps required to conduct data-based research in medicine and health. The contents of this book can be divided into five broad categories. The first two chapters explain what medical research is all about, its various types, and the broad steps, such as how to select a topic and how to set up the objectives and hypotheses. The second part (Chapters 3, 4, and 5) is on research designs such as for clinical trials and observational studies. Chapters 6 through 9 are on strategies for collection of valid and reliable data – how to assess medical factors in a research setting, methodology of data collection, and sampling methods and determination of sample size. All this culminates into developing and framing a credible protocol that could pass peer scrutiny. The next two chapters (Chapters 10 and 11) are on data processing and analysis. These chapters describe only the essentials without going into the details as a large number of books are available on this aspect. The last broad section, comprising Chapters 12, 13, and 14, is on the presentation of the results as a thesis, a paper, or a report, including the details of the reporting guidelines and reporting ethics. One of these chapters covers the fraud and misconduct that inflict some of our research endeavors. There is a separate chapter on reporting guidelines such as CONSORT for clinical trials, STROBE for observational studies, STARD for diagnostic accuracy studies, and SAMPL for statistical methods in publications.

Much of the material in this book is based on my interaction with medical graduates, their supervisors, and other faculty members while providing guidance on medical research methodology. I am grateful to my students, colleagues, and critics for their useful inputs during these interactions. This has been enriched by my assignments with agencies such as WHO, World Bank, and UNAIDS for their health projects from time to time.

Abhaya Indrayan

Author

Abhaya Indrayan, PhD, obtained a PhD from the Ohio State University and was bestowed with distinguished honors such as FRSS, FAMS, and FASc. He has been the Professor and Head of the Department of Biostatistics at Delhi University College of Medical Sciences with 30 years of experience guiding the research of graduate medical students. He has also conducted online courses for medical professionals around the world for the past 15 years. Dr. Indrayan has more than 230 publications including his flagship book *Medical Biostatistics*, now in its fourth edition, published by Chapman & Hall/CRC Press, and has presented papers at nearly 20 international conferences. He has completed more than 40 projects for WHO, the World Bank, and UNAIDS; and has been Visiting Faculty at the Ohio State University and a Visiting Research Scientist at the University of Massachusetts.

1

Basics of Medical Research

Research in any field is an enterprise that carries its own risks and benefits. One may make a heavy investment in terms of time, money, and expertise, yet the returns are not ensured in this endeavor. This is particularly so for medical research where we deal with unpredictable human beings and vitals such as health and life are at stake. First-time research is daunting anyway, but more so in medicine. Let us first understand what medical research is and what it is about in our context, so that the contents of this book are properly demarcated. This chapter gives an overview of medical research endeavors, including the pre-eminent role of empiricism, the dominance of uncertainties, broad steps, and the essential ingredients of good research. This would help in maintaining high standards in the research process so that the findings are believable and replicable. Details of all these aspects are provided in the subsequent chapters.

1.1 What Is Medical Research?

Research is discovery of new facts, enunciation of new principles, or fresh interpretation of the known facts or principles. It is an attempt to reveal to the world something that was either never thought of, or was in the domain of the conjectures – at best being looked at with suspicion. It is a systematic investigation to develop or contribute to generalizable knowledge. Research is a step in the relentless search for truth – it is an organized and systematic approach to finding answers to the intriguing questions. The basic function of research is to answer the why and how of a phenomenon, but searching for answers to questions such as what, when, how much, is also part of research endeavors. All these questions have relevance to any discipline, but medicine seems to have special appetite for such enquiries. The purpose of medical research is to learn how systems in the human body work, why we get sick, and how to get back to health and stay fit. It is a logical process to better understand the etiology, pathophysiology, diagnosis, therapy, and prognosis of health and diseases. Research is the very foundation of improved medical care. It can also provide evidence for policies and decisions on health development at the community level.

Besides the core activities just mentioned, sometimes an established regimen is used in a new setting or on a new kind of subject to test its applicability to the new environment. This kind of confirmatory work is not hard-core research, but is accepted for graduate thesis because the objective there is training in research methodology and new results if any are considered bonus. A large number of medical theses are based on such confirmatory research.

Much of human biology is still speculative, and its interaction with the environment is intricate. Thus, medical science has enormous potential for useful research. At the same time it has its own risks. This is illustrated by the reports questioning established modalities. Tamoxifen, a selective estrogen-modifying agent and a popular breast cancer therapy for women, was found to carry an increased risk of endometrial cancer. Menopausal women who took estrogen for a long time were found to be at higher risk of getting ovarian cancer. Arthroscopic surgery for osteoarthritis of the knee was found to be a useless procedure. A high level of cholesterol is no longer considered as much a risk as it used to be. These are not isolated examples. There are many instances when established medical practices were overturned. Some recent advances have indeed been bivalent – potentially useful as well as potentially harmful. As discussed later in this chapter, this happens because most of modern medical research is empirical. It depends on the interpretation of what we observe, and neither observations nor their interpretation are infallible.

1.1.1 Medical Research and Empiricism

Medicine is a delicate science because it is concerned with vitalities of life such as health, disease, and death. Thus, it brooks no error. Ironically, no theories are available that can make it infallible. There are no lemmas and no theorems, and it must depend on evidence provided by observations and experience. Medicine is largely an inductive science and has very little space, if any, for deductive methods. It is individualized yet participatory. If a treatment regimen has worked in Mr. Somebody and nine others of his clan, there is a high likelihood that it would also work in the 11th person of that type. The past experience and present evidence provide an insight into the future. Such empiricism (Box 1.1) is the backbone of medical science. In dealing with a new case, or an old case with a new set of conditions, past knowledge and experience are applied, and it is hoped that they will also work in the new setup. Often they do, but sometimes not. There is no assurance. Miscues cited earlier are examples of such errors.

Empiricism is often contrasted with rationalism. Rational knowledge comes from the exploration of concepts, deduction, intuition, and revelation. For these, sensual experience is not necessary. However, it can be argued that all these also initially come from primary experiences. Empiricists argue that the knowledge we cannot sense does not exist – it could be just a guess or a presumption.

Without entering further into this debate, let us emphasize that empiricism and rationalism are complementary to each other for expansion of knowledge. This is more so in the context of medical research because much of it is on cause and effect. Mental illumination stipulated in theories may provide a clue to what may be really going on, but this needs support from actual observations. Only then can you hope to convince colleagues to accept your theory. Thus, most medical research has no escape from evidence base and empirical process. This book is restricted to the data-based research that is tangible and based on experience rather than intuition.

1.1.2 Types of Medical Research and the Scope of This Book

Medical research encompasses a whole gamut of endeavors that ultimately help to improve the health of people. Although nomenclature exists, such as qualitative and quantitative research, and public health and clinical research, functionally it can be divided into

BOX 1.1   EMPIRICISM AND RATIONALISM

Two basic forms of expansion of knowledge are empiricism and rationalism. Empiricism is based on induction from sensual learning: it is based on observations and experience as these arise from our senses. These observations and experience form what we call the evidence, and require that we do our best with whatever we have. Empirical evidence could arise from experiments, trials, natural occurrences, experiences, records, and such other sources. It refers to the actual facts as currently present or occurred in the past. You can see that empiricism emphasizes the tentative and probabilistic nature of knowledge. In contrast, mathematics and some other physical sciences are based on theories and theorems that are considered rational. For example, we postulate that the numbers that do not divide by any other number except 1 and themselves are prime, and deduce that 3 and 7 are two prime numbers less than 8. Such arguments are deductive and not empirical. Deductive science holds that the mind can directly perceive truth without going through the process of sensual experience.

Empiricism has no conflict with rationalism. The observations must stand up to the reason, and should have an adequate rational explanation. After all, it is the logic of reasoning that separates humans from other species. Research results are more acceptable when the accompanying evidence is compelling, stands to reason, and inspires confidence. Without logic, research is reduced to storytelling.

BOX 1.2   EVIDENCE ANALYSIS AND SYNTHESIS

The kind of medical research discussed in this book depends mostly on the analysis of evidence from various sources. The objective of this analysis is to identify clear signals emanating from the varying and sometimes conflicting evidence from the study subjects. When these signals conform with one another, clear conclusions can be drawn.

There is another type of medical research that is very popular and very effective. This is collecting diverse evidence from various studies (not individual subjects) and synthesizing it to get a holistic picture after resolving any conflicts. Review articles and meta-analyses appearing in medical journals are of this type. The discussion section of a master's thesis, doctoral dissertation, or a research paper also tries to do such synthesis, although this is limited to integrating your findings with the results of others. Methods for research synthesis are not included in this text.

basic and applied types. **Basic research**, also sometimes termed "pure research," involves advancing the knowledge base without any specific focus on its application. The results of such research are utilized sometime in the future when that new knowledge is required. In medicine, basic research is generally done at the cellular level for studying various biological processes. Although this kind of research can provide a radical breakthrough, this book is not adequate for this kind of research. **Applied research**, on the other hand, is oriented to an existing problem. Applied medical research could be on the diagnostic and therapeutic modalities, agent–host–environment interactions, or health assessments, whether based on evidence analysis or synthesis (Box 1.2).

Primary and Secondary Research

Applied medical research can be classified into two major categories, although this is not a universally accepted classification. The first category can be called primary research and includes analytical studies such as case–control studies, laboratory experiments, and clinical trials. It also includes descriptive studies such as surveys, case series, and census. The second category is secondary research, which is quite common these days, and includes meta-analysis, decision analysis (risk analysis and decision theory), operations research (prioritization, optimization, simulation, etc.), evaluation of health systems (assessment of achievements and shortcomings), economic analysis (cost–benefit, cost-effectiveness, etc.), and qualitative research (focus group discussion). This text is confined to the methods used in primary research (Figure 1.1), but does not contain specialized methods required for pharmacokinetic and toxicological studies.

This book is designed to provide a holistic picture of the methodology of primary research that still forms the bulk of modern medical research. The text is for basic methods only and would be adequate for most research that is required to be collated as a master's thesis or doctoral dissertation, and for other such small-scale endeavors. Advanced methods would be different for, say, cancer research than for tuberculosis research and for a drug trial than for behavioral research. For such focused research, particularly if it is on a large scale, consult other relevant reference books and material.

The book describes all steps of primary medical research in simple language. We hope that this will help emerging scientists to learn the concepts and principles of designing and conducting such a research project with precision. It describes methods for formulating a research problem and setting objectives, for reviewing the existing literature and data, for identifying uncertainties, for designing the study to handle these uncertainties, for collection and collation of evidence, for measuring uncertainties, for assessing the antecedents and outcomes, for statistical analysis of data including significance and

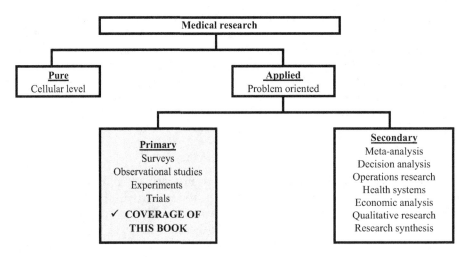

FIGURE 1.1
Types of medical research and coverage of this book.

relationships, and for preparing a manuscript for dissemination of the results, including graduate theses and papers for publication in scientific journals.

Not many who undertake medical research are fully trained in research methodology. This tends to limit the quality of their effort. This limitation has lately attracted attention, but research methodology still is "what is not taught in a medical school." This book may fulfill the need of a text required to impart training in the basics of medical research methods.

Interdisciplinary Research

Increasing numbers of medical graduates all over the world are opting for interdisciplinary research. The need for such research in health and medicine is indeed widely felt, and a positive attitude is advocated to encourage interdisciplinary research. This kind of research can be highly relevant and can have immensely useful application. Remember that the heart and soul of health care are interdisciplinary. Such research provides a unique opportunity for professional growth and can be very satisfying, but has potential risks as well. Embracing the relevance of multiple disciplines and integrating this into focus for the problem in hand is not easy. An expanded frontier and increased breadth of knowledge of theory and practice are required for interdisciplinary research to be successful. The process of bridging disciplines is challenging although it could be exciting as well. In case you plan to go interdisciplinary, adopt abundant caution as there may be a lack of respect for each other among basic, clinical, applied, and public health researchers. Team work is important for successful interdisciplinary research, but individuals should also shine and flourish [1].

Translational Research

A new paradigm of translational research is fast coming up that intends to serve as a bridge between pure and applied research. It promotes multidisciplinary collaboration so that efficiency from bench to bedside increases and the applied process is accelerated. This has now become feasible as most research data are available in electronic form that can be quickly shared and immediately analyzed. The contents of this book may not be sufficient to address this kind of research although some of the methods we describe may be applicable.

1.1.3 Levels of Medical Research

Medical research can be an individual effort with hardly any assistance from anyone except probably guidance from advisers, and can also be the collaborative effort of several institutions and agencies that require enormous funding and diverse expertise. These different "levels of research" have their unique benefits and challenges, and can have a serious impact on the quality of conclusions. Box 1.3 provides details of various levels of research and specifies their contents.

Graduate Thesis

Most universities awarding master's degrees in medicine require students to devote part of their time to conducting small-scale research, involving planning, collecting, collating, and presenting results as a thesis. This is very different from a doctoral dissertation (Box 1.3)

BOX 1.3   LEVELS OF PRIMARY MEDICAL RESEARCH

First Level of Research – Master's Thesis

- Generally a small-scale investigation that puts forward a hypothesis to be tested by further study.
- The student can select the topic of research, but the fine-tuning mostly depends on the supervisor.
- The thesis must be completed strictly within a time frame not extending beyond 3 years – mostly only 1 or 2 years.
- The objective is to provide training to the student in research methodology including in scientific and critical thinking – thus the process is more important than the outcome.
- The thesis seldom provides results that can be immediately implemented in medical care.
- The thesis is generally in part fulfillment of the degree.
- The guide is generally called the supervisor and the supervisor's intellectual resources are extensively utilized.
- The supervisor may or may not be chosen by the student. Sometimes the supervisor is assigned by the department.
- A master's thesis is almost invariably based on institutional resources without the support of any funding agency.
- There is no public defense of the findings.
- Volume is nearly 100 pages.

Second Level of Research – Doctoral Dissertation

- A detailed discourse or treatise on a particular topic that provides a new result or new perspective – the results must be capable of publication in a reputed journal.
- It must provide evidence of critical thinking of the candidate on the topic of research.
- Many times a doctoral dissertation provides results that can be immediately implemented in health care.
- Duration is mostly 3–4 years (full time) and mostly the dissertation itself is enough for the award of the degree.
- The guide is generally called an advisor and the work is mostly based on the candidate's own intellectual contribution. The advisor is generally chosen by the candidate on the basis of his or her expertise in the area of research.
- Time is enough for a good research work that can provide satisfaction to the candidate and the advisor.
- Enough time is available to take short-term courses on the topic of research.
- Almost the entire time is devoted to research.
- The candidate can select a topic of interest. Protocol can be revised and resubmitted.
- A doctoral dissertation is mostly based on institutional resources, but can be part of large-scale research funded by some agency.
- It is required to be publicly defended.
- Volume is generally 200 pages or more.

Third Level of Research – Institutional Study

- This is a large-scale investigation that culminates in a fully fledged project report and mostly published in a reputable journal in concise form.
- It is generally conducted in only one location.
- It is expected to provide a path-breaking result that can be immediately implemented in health care.
- Institutional study is mostly based on specially marked funds.

Fourth Level of Research – Multicentric Study

- A multicentric study is conducted in several locations with common protocol to check replicability in a variety of settings, and to provide more reliable results.
- It is necessarily a large-scale investigation for which a fully fledged report is prepared and almost invariably finds a place in a reputable journal in a concise form.
- It attracts attention because of its size, but there is no evidence yet that this level of research produces path-breaking results more often than institutional level research.
- It is invariably based on specially marked funds.

which is expected to be complete research. The primary purpose in a master's thesis is not frank research but only training of the students in research methodology and to inculcate scientific thinking, although an unexpected finding can be a good outcome in some cases. This book occasionally gives tips on doctoral dissertations, but our focus is on master's theses.

There are pros and cons of the provision of a thesis in the graduate medical curriculum. When carried out as intended, a thesis provides training and prepares the student for an academic career. It helps in fine tuning the thought process and inculcates the ability to critically evaluate the evidence, including that available in literature. If students decide to go for teaching, they are better prepared to supervise master's students and to serve as a mentor to give direction to the career of their students and provide effective recommendation for a job. The institution gets credit for research and sometimes humanity benefits by the discovery of improved procedures.

On the down side is the extra time needed to complete the education and the potential hazards of being treated as an assistant to the supervisor. Sometimes, the supervisor is ill-equipped and adds to the confusion instead of providing clarity. They may lack time and the institution may not have the necessary infrastructure in some setups.

There is another downside to some of these theses. Often, there are students that tend to learn how to fudge the data and manipulate results. A new technology called "copy–paste" has emerged as computerology is spreading its tentacles. This malpractice tends to be replicated by the next generation. The ultimate loss is of time and reputation. No wonder that some research is seen through microscopic eyes, sometimes with suspicion and sometimes with contempt, because of such malpractices.

Research at Higher Level

As explained in Box 1.3, most elementary forms of higher-level research are done for doctoral dissertations. This generally requires full-time devotion of the student on a specific topic and is carried out with no or little funding. Next is institutional research that aims at a new result that is perceived to benefit a certain segment of the population. This may be the collaborative effort of several investigators, possibly involving different departments of the same institution. This generally requires sufficient funding. Because of pooling of diverse expertise, this kind of research is generally successful in achieving its objectives. Next to this is multicentric research, where different centers pool their resources to produce high-quality research.

1.2 Uncertainties in Medical Research

All scientific results are susceptible to error, but uncertainty is an integral part of the medical framework. The realization of the enormity of uncertainty in medicine may be recent, but the fact is age-old. No two biological entities have ever been exactly alike; neither will they be so in the future. Our knowledge about biological processes is also still extremely limited. These two aspects – first, variation, and second, limitation of knowledge – throw an apparently indomitable challenge at medicine. Yet, medical science has not only survived but is ticking with full vigor. The silver lining is the ability of some experts to learn quickly from their own and others' experience, and to discern signals from noise, waves from turbulence, trend from chaos. It is due to this learning that death rates have steeply declined in the past 50 years and life expectancy is showing a relentless rise in almost all nations around the world. The burden of disease is steadily but surely declining in most countries.

Management of uncertainty requires a science that understands randomness, instability, and variation. **Biostatistics** is the subject that deals specifically with these aspects. We do mention statistical methods where needed, but deliberately avoid mathematical intricacies in this book. The attempt is to make this text light and enjoyable for the medical community so that medical research is perceived as a delightful experience, and not as a burden. However, appreciation of medical uncertainties is important for meaningful research. For this reason, we describe them in considerable detail in this section, and divide them into epistemic and aleatory categories for easy comprehension. These details will help in providing a right perspective to medical research. For further discussion of aleatory and epistemic uncertainties, see Sandomeer [2], although this is in the context of engineering applications. A brief discussion follows.

1.2.1 Epistemic Uncertainties

Uncertainties arising from our limitations are called epistemic. Knowledge gaps are wider than generally perceived; thus these uncertainties have a dominant role. One paradigm says that what we do not know is more than what we know. Such unfamiliarity breeds uncertainty and gives rise to epistemic bottlenecks. A long way down from the art of healing based on esoteric knowledge, the realization of epistemic gaps in medicine is recent. In the context of health and medicine, this type of uncertainty was first highlighted and explained by Indrayan in 2008 [3].

Besides incomplete knowledge, epistemic uncertainty also includes: (i) ignorance, for example, how to choose one treatment strategy when two or more are equally good or equally bad, such as between amoxicillin and co-trimaxazole in nonresponsive pneumonia; (ii) parameter uncertainty regarding the factors causing or contributing to a particular outcome such as etiological factors of vaginal and vulvar cancer; (iii) speculation about unobserved values such as the effect of extremely high levels of NO_2 in the atmosphere on our health; (iv) nonavailability of the exact quantitative effect of various factors such as diet, exercise, obesity, and stress on raising blood glucose level; and (v) confusion about the definition of various health conditions such as hypertension – that the blood pressure cutoff should be 130/85, 140/90 mmHg, or any other. .

Another kind of epistemic uncertainty arises from nonavailability of the proper instrument. How do you measure blood loss during a surgical operation? Swabs that are used to suck blood are not standardized. In some surgeries blood can even spill on to the floor. Even a simple parameter such as pain is difficult to measure. Visual analog scales and other instruments for this are just approximations. Stress defies measurement and behavior/opinion types of variables present stiff difficulties. If the measurement is tentative, naturally the conclusion too is tentative. The following is a brief description of some sources of epistemic uncertainties that may make you more aware of their dominance in medical research endeavors.

Inadequate Knowledge

Notwithstanding claims of far-reaching advances in medical sciences, many features of the human body and mind, and their interaction with the environment, are not sufficiently well known. How the mind controls physiological and biochemical mechanisms is an area of current research. What specific psychosomatic factors cause women to live longer than men is still shrouded in mystery. Nobody knows yet how to reverse hypertension that can obviate the dependence on drugs. Cancers are treated by therapy or excision because a procedure to regenerate aberrant cells is not known. Treatment for urinary tract infections in patients with impaired renal function is not known. Such gaps in knowledge naturally add to the spectrum of uncertainty.

The preceding paragraph discusses universal epistemic gaps. In addition, there is the incomplete knowledge of a particular physician. This can arise at two levels. First, is that the physician does not know enough although medical science does know. Second, is that the physician knows but is not able to recollect when facing a patient. Both can result in misdiagnosis or missed diagnosis and improper prescriptions.

Incomplete Information on the Patient

Consider the following examples. When a patient arrives in a coma at the casualty department of a hospital, the first steps for management are often taken without considering the medical history of the patient or without waiting for laboratory investigations. An angiography may be highly indicated for a cardiac patient, but initial treatment decisions are taken in its absence if the facility is not available in that health center. Even while interviewing a healthy person, it cannot be ensured that the person is not forgetting or intentionally suppressing some information. Suppression can easily happen in the case of sexually transmitted diseases because of stigma. An uneducated person may even fail to understand the questions or may misinterpret them. Some investigations such as computed tomography (CT) and magnetic resonance imaging (MRI) are expensive, and lack of funds in some countries may sometimes lead to proceeding without these investigations even when they are highly indicated. Thus, the information remains incomplete in many cases despite best efforts. Clinicians are often required to make a decision about treatment on such incomplete information. Such decisions mostly remain tentative and lack the confidence that medical decisions are supposed to have.

Imperfect Tools

A clinician uses various tools during the course of their practice. Examples are signs–symptoms syndrome, physical measurements, laboratory and radiological investigations, and intervention in the form of medical treatment or surgery. Besides the clinician's own skills in optimally using what is available, their efficiency depends on the validity and reliability of the tools they use. **Validity** refers to the ability to measure correctly what a tool is supposed to measure, and **reliability** means consistency in repeated use. Indicators such as sensitivity, specificity, and predictivities are calculated to assess the validity of such a tool. Reliability is evaluated in terms of measures such as Cohen kappa and Cronbach alpha. In practice, no medical tool is 100% perfect, so much so that even a CT scan can give a false-negative or false-positive result. A negative histologic result for a specimen is no guarantee that proliferation is absent, although positive predictivity is nearly 100% in this case. These values of measurements such as creatinine level, platelet count, and total lung capacity are indicative rather than absolute, that is, they mostly estimate the *likelihood* of a disease, and do not establish or deny its existence. Signs and symptoms seldom provide infallible evidence. Because all these tools are imperfect, decisions based on them are also necessarily probabilistic rather than definitive.

Chance Variability

Let us go a little deeper into the factors already listed. Aging is a natural process but its effect is more severe in some than in others. When exposed equally to heavy smoking for a long duration, some people develop lung cancer, whereas others do not. Despite consuming the same water with deficient iodine, some people do not develop goiter, whereas some do – that too in varying degree. The incubation period of a disease differs greatly from person to person after the same exposure. Part of such variation can be traced to factors such as personality traits, lifestyle, nutritional status, and genetic predisposition, but these known factors fail to explain the entire variation. Two apparently similar patients, not just with regard to the disease condition but also for other known factors, can respond differently to the same treatment regimen. Even susceptibility levels sometimes fail to account for all variations. These unknown factors are called **chance**. Sometimes, the known factors that are too complex to comprehend or too many to be individually considered are also included in the chance syndrome. In some situations, chance factors could be very prominent contributors to uncertainties and in some situations they can be minor, but their existence cannot be denied.

Epistemic Gaps in Research Results

Most medical research is an attempt to fill in epistemic gaps. Descriptive studies tell us prevalence rates of health and disease in various segments of the population and their trends which otherwise were not known. The objective of analytical studies is to find the antecedent–outcome relationships. However, realize that only those factors are included in the study that are known or suspected to affect the outcome and others are excluded. For example, blood group could be a contributory factor for a particular health condition but will not be included till such time that some evidence comes forth implying its possible role. Including limited factors in the study is pragmatic too as nobody can include all the factors. Genomic information is not included as it is rarely known for the subjects of research at this point in time. Thus, the research remains incomplete and we wonder why the results are not widely applicable in practical conditions. The search for truth does not relent although the goalposts are continuously shifted upward as new results appear.

Statistical Models

Statistical models are sometimes developed to plug epistemic gaps. But they can also exacerbate the situation because models are always developed under certain strict conditions. This can be easily illustrated for **regression models**. In this case, first is the limited number of independent variables and the rules that govern choice. The most commonly ignored limitation is restriction to the linearity of effect of the factors on the outcome. This is used for simplicity as the study of curvature is not only intricate but the model also loses its parsimony. After all, the purpose of generating models is to explain the phenomenon in an easily understood manner in the hope that the left-out portion is not so high as to cause much damage to the explanation. In some cases, this turns out to be too much to expect. Second is about the measurements. Statistical methods assume that the values of each variable are exactly known without any error. This is hardly ever true. Third, it also assumes that the measurements available are indeed valid markers for the phenomenon under study. For malaria, you may include palpable spleen without considering its false positivity and false negativity. Large numbers of such epistemic gaps can be cited.

1.2.2 Aleatory Uncertainties

Aleatoricism is the incorporation of chance into the process of creation [4]. Aleatory uncertainties can be understood as those arising from factors internal to the system. They are inherent, unpredictable, and stochastic in nature. Aleatory uncertainties are mostly due to biologic, environmental, instrumental, and other factors, and due to biases and errors. These vary from person to person and time to time, and can affect the outcome. We can divide them into the following categories for effective control.

- Biological (nonmodifiable): Age, gender, heredity or genetic make-up, birth order, height, etc.
- Biological (modifiable): Anthropological, physiological, and biochemical parameters
- Socio-economic: income, education, and occupation, as these can affect personal hygiene, nutrition, and self-esteem
- Cultural, behavioral, and psychological: Mental status, family system, faith in prayers, sexual practices, addictions, personality traits, tension/anxiety/stress, etc.
- Observers, instruments, and laboratories that can lead to avoidable variation in measurements
- Environmental: Climate, dust, mosquitoes, flies, pollution, sanitation, water supply, infection load, quality and quantity of health facilities, family and societal support, communication, traffic, laws and their enforcement, etc.
- Multifactorial: Lifestyle, hygiene, nutrition, knowledge/attitude/practices, susceptibility, utilization of health services, etc.; importantly, sampling errors/fluctuations in an empirical setup

Note the enormity of the aleatory uncertainties in an empirical medical research setup. Example 1.1 aptly illustrates both epistemic and aleatory uncertainties and discusses how the inferences can go haywire. This example uses some statistical concepts but should still make sense to those who are not familiar with these concepts.

Example 1.1: Aleatory and Epistemic Uncertainties in Predicting Systolic Blood Pressure by Age and Body Mass Index (BMI)

Consider the possibility of predicting the level of systolic blood pressure (SysBP) in healthy male adult obese residents of hypothetical Townsland. Two important correlates of SysBP are age and obesity. A survey was conducted on a random sample of 200 apparently healthy male adult (age 30–49 years) overweight (BMI $\geq$ 25) residents. No other factor was considered in the selection of subjects.

Suppose the regression (Chapter 11) obtained is as follows.

SysBP = 96.6 + 0.72(age) + 0.26(BMI); 30 $\leq$ age $\leq$ 49 years; BMI $\geq$ 25 kg/m^2

Confidence interval (CI) (Chapter 11) for mean SysBP for a specific age and BMI can be obtained quickly using this equation and properties of the Gaussian distribution in view of a fairly large sample size. For age = 45 years and BMI = 26, suppose 95% CI for mean SysBP is 135.1 to 136.2 mmHg. The prediction interval for an individual of this age and BMI would be relatively large, say, 133.1 to 138.2 mmHg. Statistical theory tells us that the CI would be relatively narrow when age and BMI are close to the respective averages of the group. The regression coefficients are estimates and subject to sampling fluctuation themselves. Simultaneous 95% CI for age coefficient, which is 0.72 in this equation, could be from 0.65 to 0.78, and for BMI coefficient, which is 0.26, it could be from 0.16 to 0.36. The latter is really large in this example, as can happen due to colinearity between age and BMI. When these lower and upper ends are used, the prediction interval for SysBP becomes 128.5 to 142.8 mmHg for an individual of age = 45 years and BMI = 26. Note how quickly the interval has widened in this case when errors in estimates of regression coefficients are considered. This would further enlarge if the possibilities of inadvertent random errors in measurement of age and BMI are admitted. Both may be correctly assessed, but if age is measured as on last birthday and BMI to nearest integer, the implied range already is 40.0–40.9 for age and 29.5–30.4 for BMI. These apparently small-looking variations can also make a difference of 1 mmHg in the predicted SysBP. If inherent variation in measuring SysBP is also admitted, the range could finally be something like 126–145 mmHg. This is the **uncertainty interval** attached to the normal level of SysBP for a person whose age and BMI are known. This interval delineates the aleatory uncertainties. Such a large interval in a way shows a limitation of the conventional CI as well as inadequacy of the statistical model used in this example.

Now consider epistemic uncertainties associated with such prediction. The question at the outset is whether the normal level is person-specific, or there is some absolute normal that is valid for all adults. Later on, we refer to the debate on the definition of hypertension. If various body functions indeed work in synchronization with each other to attain dynamic homeostasis, is it specific to the person? The next question is whether age and BMI are adequate determinants of physiological levels of BP in adult males. Rise in SysBP with age and BMI can partly transgress into the pathological domain. If these two are not adequate, what other variables should be considered? These simple-looking questions do not have simple answers and point to the limitation of knowledge on this aspect. Depending on how these questions are answered, the normal SysBP would change.

Even if age and BMI are considered as largely appropriate determinants, epistemic uncertainties arise because BMI is used as a surrogate for obesity. There are suggestions that waist–hip ratio, skinfold thickness, waist circumference, index of conicity, and weight–height ratio can also be used. There is no universally accepted criterion to measure obesity. On the outcome side, SysBP can be just one reading or can be the average of three readings. Accordingly the results could vary, although the variation may not be large in these instances.

The regression model in this example is linear. This is the most common and most preferred form because of its simplicity. But it is not known what functional form best expresses a normal level of SysBP in terms of age and BMI. Various other forms such as quadratic and logarithmic can be tried and the one that provides the best empirical fit can be adopted. A very large number of options are available and it may not be possible to try all of them. Then it needs to be externally validated. Each model may give different values of normal level of SysBP and different uncertainty intervals.

Because of diurnal variation in SysBP, all measurements for such modeling should be taken at a specific time of the day for all subjects and in a similar posture and surrounding. It is sometimes not possible to adhere to this strictly. Some subjects may not be fully relaxed when measured. There may also be some "white-coat effect" [5] that occurs while facing a doctor.

This survey was intended on a random sample of subjects from an area. If the design actually adopted were different from simple random, an adjustment in the CI would be required. The selection process should be examined to assess whether the sample was indeed random or not. Then there arises the question of cooperation of the subjects. Nonresponse, if any, would also affect the results.

There would be other nonsampling errors. Digit preference in blood pressure readings is known. Hopefully the instruments used for measuring SysBP, height, and weight are standardized and accurate. Errors in recording and in data entry to the computer also have to be ruled out. If a sphygmomanometer is used, the hearing acuity of the observer and the care adopted in deflating the cuff can affect the reading. If there is more than one observer, the interobserver differences may not be negligible. Thus a large variety of sources of uncertainties exist that put a question mark on the results.

Extrapolation of the results requires that the subjects included in the trial are truly representative of the target population and the new patients are also from this target population. Also that there is no dropout, or else the dropout effect is properly adjusted. The possibility of bias in the sample introduces another component to the epistemic uncertainty. The method of analysis of data and their interpretation should be complete and free from bias. In this particular example, the possibilities of these positives are bright but the situation may not so nice in other setups.

The basic message from Example 1.1 is that the uncertainty around an estimate is much more than what is made out by the conventional statistical CI. Consideration of aleatory uncertainties may provide an enormously large uncertainty interval, and epistemic uncertainties put a further question mark on the validity of this interval. Many such uncertainties go unnoticed and uncared for, leading to unexpected results in some cases.

1.2.3 Managing Uncertainties in Empirical Medical Research

Uncertainties are omnipresent, but they are especially prominent in medical situations. As a researcher, you need to be proactive to these uncertainties and manage them. In the initial phase, it may be difficult to determine whether a particular uncertainty should be put in the aleatory category or the epistemic category. It is the job of the researcher to make the distinction so that they can be appropriately managed.

One important feature of aleatory uncertainties is that they are empirical and can be evaluated by probability. The second aspect of aleatory uncertainty, particularly in medical research, is its control. This is achieved by developing a design that can provide evidence largely free of aleatoric variation encumbrances. Because the sources of aleatory uncertainties are known, an appropriate design can indeed be developed that alleviates much of these uncertainties. Uncertainty analysis [6] is one of the tools that helps to delineate aleatory uncertainties by providing intervals within which the results are likely to lie under varying conditions.

Epistemic uncertainties can be reduced by gathering more data on the unknown domain and by using scientific methods to arrive at a conclusion with least error. Some impact of epistemic uncertainties can be studied by sensitivity analyses [6]. These analyses consider alternative scenarios and see how the results are affected. The big question is what, if anything, can we do to reduce the impact of epistemic uncertainties on our medical decisions? Part answers are provided by tools such as etiology diagrams, expert systems, and scoring systems, as discussed by Indrayan [3]. However, these tackle only some specific aspects of epistemic uncertainties and not others. The solution for others is research and to realize that we are in an imperfect world. Epistemic uncertainties can be reduced to a considerable extent by gathering more data or by using advanced scientific principles.

1.3 Broad Steps in Medical Research

Science is known to be a systematic study that follows a discernible pattern and produces testable results. Thus scientific research must follow a step-by-step pathway that fosters clarity and avoids the problem of multiplicity. These steps are much more elaborate for research in medicine than for other disciplines because of enormous uncertainties inherent in the medical field and the implications for human health. Jenicek [7] has provided a layout of a modern argument in medical research involving the processes that go on from what is in your mind to searching external evidence (e.g., literature) for or against, making a qualified claim, then conducting the study, leading to the results with limitations such as probabilities and restricted applicability. Because of the empirical base, investigations are sine qua non for a primary medical research. An outline of the pre-investigation, investigation, and post-investigation steps is given next. The details are in the following chapters.

1.3.1 Pre-Investigation Steps

However, odd as it may sound, the preparation and plan for the investigation would be more critical than possibly the investigation itself. This includes regulatory requirements, but we keep those out of our preview in this book. Other pre-investigation steps are as follows.

Identify the Problem

The first step in research is to identify a problem area to work on. Recognition of the appropriate problem is the first step for solution. As mentioned earlier, one paradigm is that, notwithstanding the knowledge explosion in the past century, the unknown segment of the universe is much larger than the known segment. An alert researcher will find a large number of issues floating around. You may have felt uneasy about how to handle a health problem, deficiency in the evidence base, lack of clarity in the implications of your actions, or any such bottleneck. For selection, match the research area to: (i) the relevance and applicability for improving health in one way or the other; (ii) the interest and expertise of yourself and your collaborators; and (iii) the feasibility of completing the work with available resources, time, subjects, tools, and such other limitations. These three aspects should considerably narrow down the problem area. If the situation permits, select a topic that is in debate or meets a current demand. At the graduate level, do not think that your research will be grand. If it turns out to be so, thank yourself and the environment. For further details, see the next chapter.

Convert the problem to specific questions that require an answer. The questions must pass the "So what?" test. Even when this is done with apparently sufficient specificity, the course of the investigation may reveal that those questions were not so specific after all. Further steps as given below may help to attain focus and clarity.

Collect and Evaluate Existing Information

Collect as much information on the identified problem as possible. We devote a full section in Chapter 2 on critically evaluating the existing information. Although the major source for this is the literature, do not underestimate the potency of other sources. Secondary data might be available in various organizations that can enhance the focus of the problem. Thesis guide and subject experts can provide useful insight that they have imbibed through years of experience of working in that area. Talk to them without inhibition. Do not think that your limited knowledge will be a hindrance. In fact, this limitation will propel you to explore this problem. Experts might lead to the hitherto unexplored literature and, more importantly, to the work other agencies or institutions are doing in that area. Make sure that a reasonable answer to the proposed question is not already available. The objective of all this exercise should be to identify specific information gaps, and to examine how the problem fits into the medical jigsaw puzzle. Assess if the problem is really worth pursuing. If no or very little baseline information is available, consider carrying out an exploratory study as a first step.

Formulate Research Objectives and Hypotheses

Critical evaluation of the literature and other data on the problem will greatly assist in focusing thoughts regarding what exactly to investigate. Translate these to the research objectives. The objectives must match the perceived utility of the results. For example, for interventions, the objectives could be to find efficacy, effectiveness, affordability, efficiency, safety, acceptability, and so forth. Clearly identify the specific aspect to concentrate on and formulate the research objectives accordingly. They should be amenable to evaluation, and should be realistic: clearly phrased and stated in logical sequence. The objectives should be consistent with meaningful decisions taken in actual practice. They should not focus on trivial issues that can be addressed without research. Consider whether you expect to come up with entirely novel findings or just confirm previous work that left some doubt, or would address the present conflict [8].

From objectives emanate hypotheses. A hypothesis is a carefully worded statement regarding the anticipated status of a phenomenon. For example, one may hypothesize that recurrence of eclampsia in pregnant women is more common in those who have a family history of hypertension. The hypothesis should be biologically plausible and supported by reasoning. It should be restricted to the research under plan. Further details about object-ives and hypotheses are described in the next chapter.

Identify the Study Subjects

The definition of the subject of study and the target population should be clearly spelt out. Iodine deficiency can be diagnosed either on the basis of the palpable or visible goiter, or on the basis of urine iodine concentration. Borderline hypertension may be defined to start from 135/85 mmHg or from 140/90 mmHg. Choose a definition that is consistent with the objectives and justify it. State whether only adults are included or only children, or both. Besides inclusion criteria, the exclusion criteria should also be clearly stated so that cases are not excluded midway through the study. For this, anticipate the type of cases that can become ineligible later after inclusion. For example, identify the comorbidities that can confound the results. If there are two or more groups under research, define them.

Think of a Design

Now think of a strategy to get valid and reliable answers to the questions, or to get a solu-tion to the problem. The strategy would be in terms of collection of data in a manner that inspires confidence. This requires identifying all sources of uncertainty, and developing a design that can keep them under control (Chapters 3, 4, and 5). In effect, this means: (i) sample design for survey; (ii) prospective, retrospective, or cross-sectional strategy for observational study; (iii) deciding on the specifics of intervention in the case of a trial or experiment; (iv) determining the antecedent factors and outcome on which the data would be collected: the variables that are valid to provide the correct answer; (v) the methods to obtain valid data on those variables – feasible yet robust methods that can stand scientific scrutiny; (vi) tools such as questionnaires for systematic recording of information; (vii) the strategy to handle any ethical problem that might arise during the course of the investi-gation; (viii) the number of cases or subjects to be included in this kind of investigation; (ix) the method of selection of the subjects of the study; (x) the method of randomization, blinding, matching, and other mechanisms to control bias; and (xi) the method of statistical analysis of data. Most medical professionals do need expert advice from a biostatistician to develop an appropriate design. If needed, catch him or her at the early phase of planning and seek collaboration for all phases of the study. Do not aim at methodological overkill since marginally improved results at a substantially higher cost may not be worthwhile.

Develop the Tools

Tools for medical research are of two types. First is the recording questionnaire, schedule, or proforma that is uniformly followed throughout the investigation. Second are the measurement and investigation tools such as a scoring system and electrocardiogram. The development of tools also includes arranging investigations such as for imaging and those to be done in a laboratory. In some situations, this may require procuring kits with the help of external facilities. Arrangements may also have to be made to procure drugs, including life-saving drugs, to meet any contingency. Work out the modality for getting help from outside agencies when needed in case of exigency. For a large-scale investigation, an instruction manual may be needed. The staff may have to be trained in interview, examination, or laboratory methods so that valid and uniform data are generated. The details are given in Chapters 6 and 7.

Choose the Sampling Plan and Decide about the Sample Size

Even if the target population is precisely defined, it is mostly not possible to include all the subjects in medical research. Some kind of sampling is generally necessary. This may be in terms of restricting the cases to those presenting in a clinic in a defined duration or they may be systematically sampled, such as every eighth in the order the patients come. In case a list of subjects is available, other kinds of random sampling can be done. For details, see Chapter 8.

The other important question is how many subjects should be included in a research. Besides other considerations, the sample size is determined on the basis of margin of error you are prepared to tolerate in the estimates or the statistical power required for detecting a predefined clinically important difference between groups. This is also presented in Chapter 8.

Write the Protocol

All the hard work put into the preceding steps culminates in the draft of a research protocol. It incorporates all the information regarding the plan of research in a concise manner. Developing a protocol is just about the most important step in conducting research. For this reason, we are devoting a full chapter (Chapter 9) to this aspect alone. Protocol states the work plan and identifies the resources required for the project, including the timeline. The latter comprises the time point when each step is to be initiated and how much time this will take to complete. The work on two or more steps of research can go together, and this timeline will also indicate this overlap.

A protocol is a written document and spells out the commitment. It helps in crystallizing and concretizing the thoughts, and in making the objectives and hypotheses more specific, besides improving the strategy to achieve the objectives with minimal resources.

1.3.2 Investigation Steps

Note that pre-investigation steps are complex, and the major component is the thought process. After these steps comes the actual investigation. This also requires some preliminary steps before embarking upon the actual study.

Pretest and Do the Pilot Study

No matter how thoughtful you have been in developing the tools of the investigation, there is always a need to pretest them for their performance in actual conditions on the same kinds of subjects as in the main study. Experience suggests that almost invariably some deficiency is detected, and the tools and their implementation process are found to require some modification. Thus, do not shy away from this exercise. Similarly, a pilot study, which is a small forerunner of the actual investigation, also provides useful inputs regarding changes required in the measurements to be taken, in the interview or examination method, in the laboratory or imaging investigations, in the recording system, and so on. These aspects are discussed in detail in Chapter 7.

Collect the Data

Although the objective of this step is collection of the relevant data, it actually entails administering the intervention, such as a drug if any, and observing the subjects. As always in a medical setup, the data are obtained by inspecting the records, by conducting interviews, by physical examination or laboratory/imaging investigations, or by a combination of these data-eliciting methods. A continuous vigil is maintained to ensure that the data remain of good quality – that is, they are correctly obtained for each subject without favor or fervor, and honestly recorded. The methods earlier decided in the protocol should be strictly followed. If the protocol says that the past history is to be obtained by interview, do not replace it by records available with the patients. The data forms should be legibly filled in, and they should be fully completed. See Chapter 10 for details.

Handle the Nonresponse and Ethical Issues

In a science such as medicine, it is difficult to complete the investigation in all the planned subjects. Some subjects will invariably drop out during the course of the investigation. Anticipate such nonresponse and think of steps to keep it at the minimal level to reduce bias in the results. Make all efforts to extract at least the basic information from each subject that can help in adjusting for any bias.

Then there are ethical issues that need to be constantly monitored, particularly if the research involves an intervention such as a therapeutic maneuver. Even when informed consent is taken, medical ethics requires that the intervention and data generation or collection should not subjugate the interest of the patient.

Scrutinize the Data

Despite all the care exercised at the time of taking a history of patients, at the time of physical examination, and at the time of laboratory/imaging investigation, errors do occur. Most of these can be detected by scrutinizing the data for internal consistency and external validity. For example, if a patient with low hemoglobin has high hematocrit then sufficient reasons for this anomaly should be available within the record. A woman of age 23 years cannot possibly have six singleton children. Such errors look odd but they are practical occurrences, particularly in a large-scale research. Make a distinction between undetectable low values and missing data for some unavailable patients. Sometimes called data cleaning, this step of scrutiny is essential for quality research. The details again are in Chapter 10.

1.3.3 Post-Investigation Steps

After the data are collected, which should be adequate in terms of quality and quantity, they need to be exploited to their full potential to draw conclusions. This requires the following steps.

Analyze the Data

Analysis of data is an umbrella term that incorporates a large number of mini-steps. First is preparing a master chart by tabulating the data in a manner that all the information on one subject constitutes one record. In an Excel format, this really means that there is only one row of data for each person. Also each field (column in Excel) must contain only one piece of information. If an AIDS patient has chronic peritonitis, toxoplasmosis, and Kaposi sarcoma, with codes 7, 12, and 14, respectively, these three should be entered as yes/no in separate fields and not as 7, 12, 14 in one field. Do not write "male" at one place and "Male" at another. Also enter the age as "7" and not as "7 years."

The second step is to use the data for assessing the parameters of health and disease that were outlined in the protocol. Various indicators and indices of health and disease such as waist–hip ratio and scores may have to be calculated to assess risk factors and outcomes of interest. See Chapter 10 for details.

The third step in data analysis is exploring the data for their pattern. Not many researchers appreciate the importance of this preliminary step. For example, pattern in a graphical plot may reveal hidden mysteries in the medical phenomena you are studying, and outliers may reveal new relationships. One-way frequency tables with suitable class intervals may help in examining whether the quantitative variables are really following a Gaussian pattern or not. That may decide whether parametric tests of statistical significance should be used or nonparametric tests. Scatter plots and cross-tabulations can be immensely useful in exploring relationships among various measurements. These will indicate where and what type of relationship should be explored. Such data exploration methods are also discussed in Chapter 10.

The fourth step is to summarize the data. Besides tables, this summarization is done in terms of mean, standard deviation, proportion, rate, and, more importantly in medicine, in terms of medians and percentiles. Such summaries help to grasp the essential features of data. The details are given in Chapter 10. This step sets the tone for statistical analysis.

The next step is grinding the data through the process of statistical analysis. This involves obtaining the CIs, performing statistical tests to assess the significance of differences, obtaining the structure of relationships such as regression and their significance, assessing trends and agreement, estimating the odds ratios and relative risks, and other such indexes. The details are given in Chapter 11.

Wise researchers devote sufficient time to the examination of the data and to their analysis. Collecting quality data is important in itself, but exploiting it fully is even more important. New results are sometimes missed despite the availability of good data because the data are not properly exploited.

If your research involves intricate statistical analysis such as logistic regression, survival analysis, and discriminant functions, enroll a statistician as your partner from the beginning. Statistical consultation after finishing research is like a post-mortem. The statistician can only conjecture what the research died of, but cannot revive it.

Interpret the Results

Whereas statistical analysis is mostly computer based, interpretation of the results requires critical thinking. A series of steps can be suggested:

1. Examine the results in the context of the questions that prompted the research.
2. Verify that various results are consistent with one another and a proper explanation is available for the inconsistent ones.

3. Check that all the potential biases have either been ruled out by design, or the results are properly adjusted for the biases.
4. Assess the reliability of the results.
5. Confirm that a convincing biological explanation is available. For example, make a distinction between a correlation and cause–effect.
6. Show by **sensitivity analysis** and **uncertainty analysis** [6] that the results are robust to the random and systematic variations.
7. Ensure that the final conclusions are indeed a further development and not a repeat of previous knowledge.

In short, not only should you be convinced about the correctness and utility of the conclusions, but there should also be enough reasons to convince others. Results should not be speculative; instead, they should be based on evidence as revealed by the data and other duly established facts.

Write and Disseminate the Report

Report is a generic term that includes a thesis, a dissertation, an article, a paper, and a project report. It should contain all the details in a concise manner. Then disseminate it to the intended audience. Dissemination could be the most fruitful step in a research endeavor. The world is informed about the new conclusions, and feedback is obtained regarding the quality of the conclusions. A clear idea about the users of the results will help to decide how to disseminate findings to the stakeholders.

We devote two full chapters (Chapters 12 and 13) on how to present results effectively to an audience. In brief, the report should be sufficiently detailed to remove any doubt a reader might have about any aspect of the results, and it should be properly worded with a clear demarcation of the evidence-based results from opinions and comments. The report should be adequately illustrated by diagrams to enhance clarity, and numerical results can be summarized in the form of tables. Describe all the limitations candidly in the realization that no result has universal applicability, and the scientific community is fully aware of this fact. Thus the limitations should be stated without inhibition.

The format of the report is geared to meet the expectations of the audience. A scientific paper would concisely state a particular aspect of the research in a paragraph that would take several pages in a thesis or a dissertation. The language for the press release would be very different than for a scientific paper. A report prepared for a funding agency may have a focus that fits their requirement.

Monitor the Reactions

Research is a continuous process. You might want to improve upon it by learning from the reactions of the users of the research. For this, it is necessary that all such reactions are systematically monitored. It is not uncommon in research journals to publish comments and the author's rejoinder. These help to crystallize thoughts, and to improve in a subsequent endeavor, as well as to monitor whether or not the results are being utilized.

This book is written largely to address all these steps. Some steps are discussed at length and others quite briefly depending upon our perception about their relevance for a graduate work. The sequence of presentation in the book is broadly the same as the steps mentioned in the preceding paragraphs, but there are minor alterations in places. We hope this text will help in conducting quality research and in producing a credible report.

1.4 Quality of Medical Research

A large volume of medical research is carried out and reported by individuals, pharmaceutical companies, and other health care organizations, hospitals, government departments, and medical schools, but many fail to make any impact on medical practice. This happens because the results of such research do not really contribute to improvement in health. Thus, a lot of funds and efforts are wasted. The answer to this malady is emphasis on quality of research: an aspect that is seldom taught in our universities and institutions.

1.4.1 What Qualifies Good Research?

Remember that truth is exact and fixed while a lie has no bounds. The objective of research is to reach the truth. Good research will reach close to the truth, if not the absolute truth, and convincingly show that this indeed is so. But that is a tall order for any discipline. How do we know that this is the truth unless we are divine? For a millennium, the "truth" was that sun revolves round the earth, until Copernicus "discovered" another truth. It took almost another century to confirm that this indeed is so. Thus discovery of truth can be a long, drawn-out process.

While reaching the truth may be tantalizing, efforts can easily focus on getting believable and useful results. This can be achieved by ensuring that the research meets the criteria that is given in Box 1.4. These criteria focus on primary empirical research and include steps taken at the planning, execution, and reporting stages.

Quality of research can be assessed by the confidence among the scientists in the findings. This is achieved when the research is carried out openly and honestly, and nothing is concealed. Fanelli [9] reported that 1.97% of scientists admitted in their survey to have fabricated, falsified, or modified data or results at least once, and up to 37.7% admitted other questionable research practices. Many may not have been reported. We all know that known frauds are the tip of the iceberg and many cases are never discovered. Thus, results are seen with suspicion, and no wonder that many results do not work when applied in practice. A full documentation of the methods and limitations can help in gaining the confidence and, in the case of clinical research, a description of side effects and adverse events is also of considerable help. Consider whether the alternative claim made in the research is biologically plausible, and not an improbable result. In short, the scientific reasoning should be sound, convincing, and appealing, and there should be no deception.

1.4.2 Quality of a Good Researcher

A good researcher realizes that they are in a risky occupation with tremendous responsibilities of reaching to a truth that could be elusive. Research is always riddled with uncertainties, and nobody knows for sure what the outcome is going to be. The researcher must feel detached from the results and should be willing to take negative results in stride as much as positive results. While success can be celebrated, failure should be taken sportingly in the realization that uncertainties in this endeavor can be insurmountable. That is easier to say than to practice, but an ideal research worker would be disinterested in the result, and would follow all the steps of good research mentioned in the preceding section without caring for the kind of result that would be finally reached. They must also be prepared to face the situation of no conclusive result either way.

BOX 1.4 QUALITY OF GOOD PRIMARY EMPIRICAL RESEARCH

The main qualities of good research in our context can be listed as follows:

- Research should be on a problem, whose solution can have significant ramifications for the specified section of population or patients, and can improve their health whether in terms of prevention, treatment and disability limitation, or rehabilitation. The results should be of definite help in ameliorating the condition of the specified segment of people. In other words, it must be a relevant problem whose answer matters to humanity, particularly the medical community.
- The research should convert the problem into precise relevant questions and measurable objectives. It must formulate a clear hypothesis that can be examined by generation of data. The antecedent and outcomes should be selected among those that can be directly measured and can be translated to benefit the subjects.
- The research should adopt an appropriate methodology that can provide unbiased, reliable, and verifiable results. This includes selection of the right subjects and appropriate controls where needed, and a design that minimizes effort without compromising the validity and reliability of results, tools that give valid information, collecting right information, and proper analysis of the data.
- The research should be conducted openly, providing full information to all the stakeholders – investigators, participants, and users – regarding each stage of the research so that they are able to assess the worth of the research results. All these must be fully documented for critical review by others. The research must be conducted in an ethical manner and should protect anonymity and confidentiality as needed. Details are discussed in Chapter 14.
- It should be based on a proper assessment of the resources needed, and sufficient resources should be available, not just in terms of funds, time, and equipment, but also in terms of expertise and intellectual input required to visualize the pros and cons of the research and its results.
- It should report truthful results with no deception, admitting the limitations in full without reservations, including side effects and other adverse events.
- The results should be reliable (repeatable) and verifiable.
- It must be conducted by a good-quality researcher as mentioned in the next section.

In addition to the just mentioned philosophical qualities, a good researcher must have sufficient expertise for the topic of research, and should be knowledgeable about the implications of both a positive and negative result as well as of no result. They must have sufficient resources to carry out that research and must be motivated to spend those resources. The researcher must be inquisitive and should have the commitment to discover the truth. A good researcher is able to anticipate the difficulties, and take pre-emptive action. In the end, they must be a good communicator and be willing to answer all the questions that reviewers might raise.

1.4.3 Pleasures and Frustrations of Medical Research

Scientific enquiry is among the most challenging enterprises. As mentioned earlier, any research, more so medical research, is an occupation riddled with uncertainties. If successful in bringing out a path-breaking result, it may be idolized. If it fails to produce expected results, the consequent frustration could be disastrous. Nobody can predict. If the result is predictable, it is not research, after all. The only thing one can do is to take full care of possible biases by developing a good design, and use valid and reliable methods of measurement and analysis. Medical research is becoming increasingly complex and expensive, and the monitoring these days is very close. Because skepticism is accepted as an integral part of all scientific activity, make sure that the results will withstand third-party reviews. The key concern is credibility. The results can be positive or negative, but they must be reliable and valid.

Errors in Research

Three types of errors grip medical research across the world. The first is the honest error. This can occur despite best intentions. Most such errors arise due to limitations of know-ledge about a particular phenomenon. This limitation can be reflected in the study design that fails to address an unforeseen bias, or can be due to the acknowledged reliability and validity of tools that were later found inadequate. Almost nothing can be done to avoid such errors except to take appropriate care in future endeavors.

The second is the negligent error on aspects that are known to affect the results but are not properly accounted for. This can be intentional but is mostly unintentional. Sometimes a particular source of bias is ignored just to come to a positive conclusion. Lilienfeld [10] argued that the asbestos industry in the United States was behind attempts to suppress information on the carcinogenicity of asbestos that affected millions of workers. On the other hand, unintentional errors are due to carelessness. Negligent errors of either type are not excusable, although they sometimes fail to attract attention, as happened for many years for the carcinogenicity of asbestos.

At the bottom is the third type of errors that can be branded as misconduct. This comprises deliberate acts of omission and commission to engineer the findings, and includes plagiarism, which means stealing the results of others. Reporting inflated sample size, stating a methodology that was not actually used, stating results that were not actually obtained, and other such actions come under this category. When a mis-conduct of this nature is detected, some sort of punishment is accorded. The journals blacklist the author; the university forfeits the thesis; and the industry fires the staff. No one should ever indulge in such practices. Misconduct affects the reputation not only of the person concerned but also the institution and the community surrounding that individual.

Flip-flop in medical research results generates concern among the public and erodes con-fidence in health care providers. Intense debate is going on regarding the role of fat in heart disease: it is now emerging that a very low intake of fat, when accompanied by a high-carbohydrate diet to compensate energy requirement, can lower good (high-density lipo-protein) cholesterol. Total cholesterol as a culprit is now being exorcised. Similar concern is expressed about hormone replacement therapy in women. Thus, care should always be exercised so that the results are stable and stand the test of time.

If you are too willing to accept the credit for successful research, be prepared to take the responsibility for failed research as well. You cannot dump it on the head of the laboratory or resources or the statistician, unless they are equal partners as authors. In the present-day environment, correct methodology is over-riding consideration. If you find methodology beyond your comprehension, involve a methodology expert from the beginning.

Fruits of Medical Research

On the bright side are the fruits of medical research when conducted with conscience and dedication. You would be delighted to use your results on your patients, and their use by fellow professionals can give an ecstatic feeling. Sometimes the results can be so useful that they improve the well-being of a large segment of a population. Although research that improves the quality of life of even one patient is worth the efforts, that can be very expensive for society. Thus, efforts should concentrate more on aspects that benefit a large number of persons. This rarely happens. The problems are generally pursued on the basis of a researcher's interest instead of societal interest. Nevertheless, medical research, on the whole, has been very illuminating and has brought abundant cheer to individuals and society. With competition, the time lag between the research and its implementation has considerably reduced.

Considering the major emphasis these days on methodological aspects, it is expected that future research would be more efficient and the benefits would be available to a larger segment of the population at lower cost. You could be an important contributor to these efforts by following the simple rules described in this text.

Fruits and frustration include unexpected findings. It was by chance that Kune et al. [11] found that aspirin may have a protective effect on colorectal cancer. No one knew about it earlier. Subsequent research confirmed that regular and long-term use of aspirin is effective in the prevention of colorectal cancer [12]. Had this accidental finding not been published, further work and confirmation would have been unlikely.

Research also heaps responsibility. Few researchers realize that their result can benefit or imperil life of a large number of people. A mistake on the operating table endangers the life of just one patient, but research results, when wrong and adopted for practice on millions, can threaten hundreds of lives. For surgery, a student is given rigorous training for years, but medical research seems to belong to everyone. No rigorous training is required. Ill-equipped researchers collect data, analyze, and publish. The review process too is slippery in many cases. Thus, substandard research tends to guide the practitioners, and the lives of many are jeopardized. Take care that this does not happen with your research.

References

1. Awasthi S, Beardmore J, Clark J, et al. Five futures for academic medicine. PLoS Med 2005;2:e207. https://doi.org/10.1371/journal.pmed.0020207
2. Sandomeer MK. Aleatoric or epistemic? Does it matter? Swiss Federal Institute of Technology, Zurich, 2009. http://webarchiv.ethz.ch/ibk/emeritus/fa/education/Seminare/Seminar08/PhD_Seminar_Sandomeer.pdf – last accessed 4 April 2019.
3. Indrayan A. Medical Biostatistics, Second Edition. Chapman & Hall/CRC Press, 2008.
4. Nechvatal J. Hyper Noise Aesthetics in Minoy. Punctum Books, 2014.
5. Tanner RM, Shimbo D, Seals SR, et al. White-coat effect among older adults: Data from the Jackson Heart Study. J Clin Hypertens (Greenwich) 2015;18(2):139–145. www.ncbi.nlm.nih.gov/pmc/articles/PMC4742426/
6. Indrayan A, Holt M. Concise Encyclopedia of Biostatistics for Medical Professionals. CRC Press, 2016.
7. Jenicek M. Towards evidence based critical thinking medicine? Uses of best evidence in flawless argumentations. Med Sci Monit 2006;12:RA149–RA153. www.ncbi.nlm.nih.gov/pubmed/16865076

8.   Brand RA. Writing for clinical orthopaedics and related research. Clin Orthop Rel Res 2008;466:239–247. www.medschool.lsuhsc.edu/orthopaedics/docs/writing%20for%20corr.pdf

9.   Fanelli D. How many scientists fabricate and falsify research? A systematic review and meta-analysis of survey data. PLoS One 2009;4(5):e5738. https://doi.org/10.1371/journal.pone.0005738

10. Lilienfeld DE. The silence: The asbestos industry and early occupational cancer research – A case study. Am J Public Health 1991;81:791–800. www.ncbi.nlm.nih.gov/pmc/articles/PMC1405162/pdf/amjph00206-0121.pdf

11. Kune GA, Kune S, Watson LF. Colorectal cancer risk, chronic illnesses, operations and medications: Case-control results from the Melbourne Colorectal Cancer Study. Cancer Res 1988;48:4399–4404. http://cancerres.aacrjournals.org/content/48/15/4399.long

12. Tougeron D, Sha D, Manthravadi S, et al. Aspirin and colorectal cancer: Back to the future. Clin Cancer Res 2014;20(5):1087–1094. http://clincancerres.aacrjournals.org/content/20/5/1087

2

The Topic of Medical Research

The first problem faced by a researcher, particularly at the graduate level, is the selection of an appropriate topic for a thesis. In this chapter, we list the parameters on which the selection can be made after review of the literature and after examining the available resources, and then describe steps that sharpen the topic by precise statement of the objectives and hypothesis.

2.1 Selection of the Topic of Research

It is colloquially said that a research is half done when the problem is clearly visualized. This assertion is not without truth. Thus, do not shy away from devoting time in the beginning to identifying the right problem, understanding thoroughly its various aspects, and choosing the specifics that you would like to investigate.

2.1.1 What Is a Problem?

A problem is a perceived difficulty, a feeling of discomfort about the way things are, the presence of a discrepancy between the existing situation and what it should be, a question about why a discrepancy is present, the existence of two or more plausible answers to the same question, and other such issues [1].

Choosing a Problem for Research

Among countless problems, identifying one suitable for research is not always easy. Researchability, of course, is a prime consideration but rationale, relevance, and feasibility are also important. The other consideration is your interest. Once these are established and the problem area filtered, the next important step is to determine the focus. For this, review the existing information to identify the parameters of the problem and use biological knowledge to refine its focus. Specify exactly what new knowledge the world is likely to gain through this research. This requires the problem to be well-defined and focused. You should have a full grip of the problem. Enormous efforts involving large sums of money and unaccountable hours of work are sometimes wasted in chasing ill-defined concepts that fail to appreciate the nuances.

Choose a topic that is in need of development, verification, or refutation. You may have sufficient reasons to question even an established practice, but the topic should be ethically sound.

Choosing a Thesis Topic

A graduate thesis can be on an extension of existing ideas, or replication with altered focus in a new environment. For example, you can strive to find if the strategy worked out in another country is applicable to your local setup where the underlying conditions can affect the outcome. Exact replication is also permissible if convincing reasons to doubt the existing result are present or if the earlier believable findings that have been questioned have to be confirmed. But do not try to re-invent the wheel.

If all else fails, go to a medical library and browse the last few issues of a journal of your interest. Examine if the results can be extended to another relevant group of subjects, or whether the methods need improvement, or if another explanation is possible, or see the last paragraph of the articles, where authors generally identify new areas of research emerging from their study.

For good research, examine whether the chosen topic has adequate theoretical backup. For example, if the role of a particular form of diet in heart disease is to be investigated, consider why that diet can alter the risk of that heart disease. Biological plausibility gives a definite edge.

For a graduate thesis, it is advisable to consider several topics and choose the one that suits your interest, caliber, and resources. Take guidance from your supervisor. Do not feel shy by selecting another topic if the one you chose earlier does not work out. Finally, believe in yourself, and remind yourself that the human mind has unlimited potential.

Statement of the Problem

The statement of the problem is not just wording the title. It is a comprehensive statement regarding the basis for selecting the problem, details of gaps in knowledge, a reflection on its importance, and comments on its applicability and relevance. The focus should be sharp. For example, if the problem area is the dietary role in cancers, the focus may be on how consumption of meat affects the occurrence of pancreatic cancer in males residing in a particular area. For further focus, the study may be restricted to nonsmoking males to eliminate the effect of smoking. For depth, meat can be specified as red or white. Further depth could be about how much red and how much white meat is consumed, and for how many years. The role of other correlates that promote or inhibit the effect of meat can also be studied. The actual depth would depend on the availability of relevant subjects on the one hand and the availability of time, resources, and expertise on the other. Such a sharp focus is very helpful in specifying the objectives and hypotheses, in developing an appropriate research design, and in conducting the right investigations.

Justification of the problem is crucial to get support from faculty, institution, and other agencies. Explain the rationale of the problem with convincing arguments. Juxtapose it in the context of the local health care framework and convince others that the problem is important for health improvement. Include considerations such as timeliness, the segment of population affected, the relationship with ongoing health care activities or ongoing research, the kind of concern it generates among the medical profession, and so on. All this would require an extensive review of the available information on the chosen topic.

2.1.2 Review of Literature and Databases, and Their Critique

A sound background knowledge of the topic is essential for research to succeed, although that by itself is not enough. You should be thoroughly convinced that the chosen topic requires further investigation, only then can you hope to convince others. It is important to realize what you know and what you don't know about that topic. Review of existing information is a big help in: (i) enhancing understanding of the problem; (ii) identifying the relevant variables; (iii) conceptualizing the relationships that can be investigated; (iv) formulating the objectives and hypotheses; (v) improving methods that can be used in the investigation; (vi) developing an appropriate design; (vii) developing strategies for analysis of data; (viii) learning how to effectively express the implications of your findings; and (ix) evaluating which journal would be appropriate to communicate your results.

The primary purpose is not just to get acquainted with the new developments but also to confirm that what you know is correct. The search for this information should obviously be undertaken at the time of planning the research and not afterward. However, keep track of new developments during the course of the investigations as well.

Two major sources of existing information are literature and data. A brief summary of these is as follows.

Searching Medical Literature

Literature is the best source of knowledge and thus a very effective tool to reduce epistemic bottlenecks. Information explosion has resulted in a cloud with unclear signals. Fortunately, the medical literature is better organized with a host of indexing services, catalogues, and online resources. Thus, searching is relatively easy.

Among the ways to track the latest studies, the easiest is to ask the subject matter expert. If they are really an expert, bet that they know about new methodologies and new regimens, as well as about the unpublished reports and studies currently going on. Beware that publications are biased toward positive findings and mostly provide a skewed picture and cannot be fully relied on. An expert's help in identifying and securing unpublished reports can reduce this risk.

The second easy thing to do is to check books on your own shelf, and possibly journals that you might subscribe to as a member of various academic bodies. The richest resource, however, is the library. Library consultation is a pleasure when the library is properly organized, user friendly, and the library staff are supportive. Do not consider information provided in books and journals as authentic unless you are convinced. A lot of unsubstantiated impressionistic "knowledge" goes into print. Rely on books from established publishers and reputed authors, and landmark books. The latest edition of books with many editions would be mostly free of errors.

For questions pertaining to the research problem, journals are preferable, but medical journals too have enormously proliferated in recent times, and many contain articles of dubious quality. Rely mostly on journals that publish articles after peer review by at least two experts. Internationally reputed journals such as the *New England Journal of Medicine*, *British Medical Journal*, and *Lancet* can always be believed.

Full-length original articles are the best source of the happenings. Some review articles provide an excellent overview of research going on around the world that can provide very good lessons on a particular topic (Box 2.1). Editorials may not be peer reviewed but are written with care, and can be a good source of critical appraisal of the work. Cross-references at the end of each article can provide further information on specific items of

BOX 2.1   SELECT GOOD REVIEW ARTICLES

The best source of comprehensive information is review articles published in reputed journals. These are the most frequently referred to and quoted articles in research presentations. They also generally provide a big list of references of articles on the subject, and discuss their merits and demerits. This list makes it easier for you to select relevant articles. But not all review articles have the same quality. Sieve good articles from not so good ones. One extremely good source for health care interventions is Cochrane Reviews (details at *www.cochrane.org*).

Good reviews are those that efficiently integrate valid information. The reviews must be able to limit the bias that may be present in individual studies and reduce the effect of chance on conclusions. This is generally done with the help of **meta-analysis** – a very effective methodology to combine varying evidence in different reports. Reviews synthesize the research whereas individual studies analyze the data.

interest. Make determined efforts to locate previous studies on the topic of research, but pay special attention to recent developments.

Do not ignore articles on methodology. Credibility of research depends to a large extent on the methodology. Methodological articles can provide important clues on how to improve the quality of the proposed research.

Important resources for recent developments are conference abstracts and proceedings. They may have to be searched manually because popular electronic databases do not capture some of them. Do not forget to consult previous theses on your topic.

Literature is expanding at an exponential rate. Luckily, we are in an era when tracking technology has expanded at an even faster rate. A manual search in a library can be frustrating but it can still be rewarding because it can provide comprehensive information that broadens the horizon. Nevertheless, electronic search is the best mechanism. This is now available almost universally.

The best and the most commonly used source to identify articles of interest is MedLine. It contains citations and abstracts of articles from nearly 20,000 journals published around the world in different languages, and links to other data sources, including the full text in some cases. This database is generally updated daily. MedLine begins from the year 1966 but some articles published earlier are also available. PubMed is the larger database that includes MedLine and incorporates nearly 30 million citations. Because of such a huge collection, it is necessary to acquire skills for searching the relevant articles with minimal effort. You may like to consult various online tutorials for PubMed search.

Another comprehensive literature database is Embase, containing more than 32 million records. This European database is updated daily and is an offshoot of Excerpta Medica (EM). It covers nearly 8500 journals from nearly 95 countries. Embase includes abstracts from more than 7000 conferences in addition to MedLine titles.

A further useful international resource is UK-based BIOSIS Previews, which is concerned with biological sciences in general. This includes data from 1926 to the present, and covers nearly 5000 journals. It processes approximately 75,000 items each year from journals, books, monographs, and conference proceedings. Most of their services require payment.

SciSearch is the paid service of UK-based Clarivate Analytics, which contains all records in their Science Citation Index Expanded and Current Contents series of publications.

SciSearch permits searching by cited references. This is used to find how many times an article has been quoted by others and by whom. This covers 5600 major scientific and technical journals. Current Contents – Clinical Medicine provides access to bibliographic information from more than 1100 leading journals on clinical medicine.

Ovid is another popular platform for searching medical literature. This includes BIOSIS Previews, Current Contents, MedLine, Embase, and Visible Body.

Citation and literature databases are just examples of many electronic resources that can be browsed. Google Scholar is a simple tool to broadly search scholarly literature. It can be used to search across many disciplines and resources, peer-reviewed papers, theses, books, abstracts and articles, websites of professional societies, preprint repositories, and academic publications from universities and other scholarly organizations. Google Scholar helps to locate the most relevant research across the digital world. Engines such as Google and portals such as Bing provide links to a large number of web pages containing the specified terms or phrases. Click the link and get the concerned web page. See if it serves the purpose.

Among other electronic resources are medical dictionaries and encyclopedias. Websites such as MD Consult and Medscape are also useful for research endeavors.

Critique of a Medical Report

After identifying relevant literature comes the question of examining it critically for its use in framing your research. Whereas many reports and other material deserve attention, some are not worth the paper on which they are printed. You must be able to judge on some objective basis that a particular report – article, paper, document, letter, editorial, review – is valuable or not, or what part of it deserves cognizance.

The first aspect is the prestige of the journal. Good journals rarely publish unauthenticated information. For assessing the international acceptability of a journal, one index is the **Impact Factor** developed by ISI. This calculates the number of times an "average" article in a journal is cited by others in their report. This is calculated on the basis of articles published in the previous 2 years. For 2019, citations for articles published in 2017 and 2018 are counted. Good journals may have an impact factor of 3.0 or 4.0, possibly 30 or 40, and poor journals 0.1 or even 0.01. This can be understood as the scale on which the usefulness of journals can be measured, although this has been questioned. The impact factor of each journal is provided by *Journal Citation Reports*.

Before going to the main body of the paper under these headings, critically look at the summary or abstract that almost invariably precedes the text of the paper in all good journals. Many journals provide key messages in short that very succinctly describe the contents of the paper. Guidelines for evaluating the quality of a document are summarized in Box 2.2.

Also examine that the results are stated in a clear and concise manner yet in sufficient detail. Tables, graphs, and charts can provide substantial help in achieving this clarity, but there should not be any contradictions among them. The findings should be evidence-based and opinions should be clearly specified. Statistical associations should not be confused with cause–effect relationships. The methods of statistical analysis should be consistent with the type of data on the one hand and the objectives of the study on the other. Statistical significance should be clearly demarcated from medical significance. Any coincidental findings should be stated as hypotheses and not as conclusive results. The discussion part should clearly resolve any conflicts with the existing literature. It should not be lopsided — promoting one view at the expense of the other. Check that findings have been demonstrated to have adequate reliability and validity, and the conclusions do in fact

BOX 2.2   GUIDELINES FOR EVALUATING THE QUALITY OF A RESEARCH DOCUMENT

- Is the research question sufficiently specific and clearly worded without ambiguity?
- Is the problem really worth investigating? How have the answers from the study advanced knowledge and helped in improving health?
- Did it require setting up a hypothesis, and was it stated in a measurable format?
- Is there any assumption made, and is it sufficiently justified?
- Is the study material (e.g., types of subjects) really appropriate to answer the question posed?
- Were the number of subjects adequate to give enough confidence in the results?
- Are the measurements valid to answer the questions?
- Is the design appropriate to take care of all the confounders and other sources of bias?
- If nonresponse was substantial, were appropriate adjustments to the results made?
- Are the statistical methods appropriate and the interpretation correct?
- Are the results based on evidence provided within the document, focused on the initial question, and meaningful?

emanate from such findings and concomitant knowledge. Also examine if the conclusions really answer the questions or objectives set forth in the introductory part of the paper.

The references provided must be relevant and recent, at least those that are quoted in support of findings. If most citations are more than 10 years old, the study is not likely to be current or mainstream research.

Two other indices have been devised that purport to measure the worth of a scholar as a publisher of articles. The first is called the **h-index** (Hirsch index); it counts the maximum number r of papers of that scholar with at least r citations in other publications. If anybody has a maximum of 4 papers, each with 4 or more citations, the h-index is 4. It tends to improve with time as publications of the scholar increase and are increasingly cited. The second is the **g-index**. This index is r if the top r articles of a scholar are cited together at least r^2 times. If, out of 12 publications, the most cited 3 articles have been cited as least 9 times, the g-index is 3. These 9 citations could be distributed as 5 for the first article, 3 for the second, and 1 for the third.

Caution is required in assessing the validity of the findings reported in a document. The findings must be internally valid within the confines of the study in the sense that they appear consistent with the other findings, methods, and analysis used in the study. They must also be externally valid in the sense that they are generalizable to the target population and consistent with the existing proven knowledge. Try to detect fallacious reasoning that some authors can cleverly camouflage. Exceptions must also be stated. Assess next that the target population matches your setup. Look at any literature with initial suspicion, and leave it to the document to remove that suspicion.

Specific guidelines are available to assess the quality of reports on clinical trials based on the CONSORT statement (Chapter 13) (see, e.g., Li et al. [2]). The criteria include random allocation of subjects, appropriateness of the procedure followed to generate a sequence of randomization, effectiveness of blinding, if any, and appropriate description of withdrawals and dropouts. In addition, other features already mentioned are also considered. Specifically check whether the controversies and differences have been adequately described and resolved, and the generalizations are not too far-fetched for the evidence provided. If a study does not describe them fully to remove any suspicion, consider it a warning sign.

Searching the Existing Data

A search for information on a topic of research is incomplete without peeking into existing resources. Important among them are data, either as disparate records or organized as a database in a predefined structured format (Box 2.3). Much of this information will be numerical rather than textual.

Perhaps the most useful source of clinical data is the records of previous patients of similar types in a clinic, hospital, or health center. Quite often these are computerized. If so, the selected records can be quickly retrieved and analyzed. Electronic records of patients provide a unique opportunity to select large sample sizes and in many cases more complete information can be obtained by linkages with other related databases. However, exercise abundant caution in using such data because they may be biased for specific types of cases. Yet they can provide useful leads.

Cautions in Using Secondary Data

The data available in records and publications are called secondary data. Bias, incompleteness, lack of comparability, and relevance must be considered before using such data for research. Examine how the data were collected and put to use. Selecting the "right data" from the "available data," or collating available data into the right data, is a challenging task that you may have to undertake in this case. Assess whether these data adequately supplement the literature information or if they are in conflict. If in conflict, more in-depth investigation into the quality of secondary data may be required. Use judgment where necessary. In particular, assess: (i) the representativeness of the data; (ii) any relevant group of cases excluded; (iii) that the response rate is adequate; (iv) the method of assessment is valid and reliable; and (v) the data are generated by the methods or instrumentation proposed to be used in your research.

BOX 2.3   EXISTING DATA AS A RESEARCH RESOURCE

Research does not command respect unless all existing avenues of information are explored. Besides the literature, all existing data should be thoroughly searched and examined to avoid duplication, to get clues for research, and to assess the worth of the proposed research. Relevant data for research might exist in:

- Clinic and hospital records
- Disease registries
- Computerized databases on the web
- Reports of national and international health agencies
- Reports of various health surveys

Before using such data for the purpose of research, examine them for uniformity of procedures, completeness, and their relevance to the topic. Sift relevant data from the available mass.

2.2 Feasibility and Resources

After the topic is finalized, there is still some legwork to do to assess if enough resources are available to carry out this research and that it is feasible. Prime considerations for this include ethical requirements and the availability of resources.

2.2.1 Ethical Considerations

Whereas observational studies that do not require any human intervention can be done without worrying much about ethics, ensure that the privacy of the subjects is not being compromised. Experiments and clinical trials often pose more stiff challenges because the subjects are exposed to an unknown regimen. These challenges are best overcome by following the principles enunciated in the Helsinki Declaration.

Helsinki Declaration

Promoted by the World Medical Association, the Helsinki Declaration sets ethical principles for medical research involving humans [3]. The guiding principle is that the duty of a physician is to promote and safeguard the health of the people and to ensure that the health of the subjects is not compromised. Basic features of this Declaration are mostly those as already discussed, such as thorough review of scientific literature and constant monitoring: others are described in Box 2.4.

BOX 2.4   BASIC FEATURES OF THE HELSINKI DECLARATION

- Physicians are bound by "The health of my patient is my first consideration."
- The well-being of individual subjects must precede all other interests.
- The design and performance of each research study involving human subjects must be clearly described in a research protocol.
- Medical research on human subjects must only be conducted by individuals with the appropriate scientific training and qualifications.
- Medical research on vulnerable sections of the population is justified only if it responds to their needs.
- Carry out the research after careful assessment of predictable risk and burdens to the individuals and the concerned community in comparison with foreseeable benefits. Stop the study when the risks outweigh the potential benefits.
- All clinical trials must be registered in a publicly accessible database before recruitment of the first subject.
- Participation must be voluntary.
- Protect the privacy and confidentiality of personal information.
- Obtain informed consent after explaining each aspect of the study.
- Authors, editors, and publishers have ethical obligations for the publication of research results.

The basic requirements of "Do no harm" and individual rights are more important than societal gains unless individuals themselves do not volunteer. Scientific propriety and informed consent are the sheet anchor of this Declaration.

Informed Consent

Of the ethical requirements of medical research involving human subjects, informed consent needs further emphasis. In effect, this means that subjects must be told about the pros and cons of the planned maneuver on themselves as well as about the possible benefits to society in a language and manner that they understand. The purpose of the research, volunteer participation, methods to be followed, alternatives available to the participant, cost implications, and such other aspects should be fully explained. This is a lengthy process but shortcuts are adopted, taking unfair advantage of the vulnerability of subjects, particularly if they are sick and have presented themselves to a hospital or clinic to get relief. The patient should be able to decide whether or not to participate.

2.2.2 Resources

Primary consideration in resources is the sufficient availability of the right kind of subjects and access to facilities for conducting the research on the chosen topic.

Availability of Subjects

Our focus in this text is on medical research on human subjects. Humans are more precious than other species, and their availability for a particular research needs to be properly assessed before embarking on this path. Whereas rare outcomes also need their fair share of research, the priority is generally accorded to more common outcomes that affect a substantial portion of the population. The subjects must be homogeneous as defined by inclusion and exclusion criteria (see Chapter 9), although that can substantially limit the availability of cases. For example, if the research is on nonfatal sequelae of cardiac arrest in patients of age 70 years or more who have had a by-pass, the number of available cases in any hospital may be severely restricted. While the topic is worth investigating, the restricted availability of such cases may render the topic unsuitable for a graduate thesis.

Access to Facilities

A big limitation, particularly in a graduate thesis, is the time available to complete the work. This can considerably restrict the sample size. Also, in other research, time can be a big limiting factor, particularly because there is competition to present a quick result. The topic of research should be selected such that it can be completed within the available time.

The choice of topic also depends on the availability of facilities such as instrumentation and sufficiently equipped laboratory, and their willingness to cooperate. This may require funding or some kind of credit to those facilities. In the case of highly specialized investigations or intricate surgery, availability of expertise also needs to be considered.

Perhaps the most important requisite is the conducive environment that promotes and facilitates research. This is not as easy as it looks because of prejudice and competition. For a graduate thesis, do not select a topic that is already under investigation by a colleague.

2.3 Objectives and Hypotheses

Even the focused area of the problem may have several smaller components. Formulating objectives is breaking down the problem into a parsimonious set of questions to which answers would be sought. These questions are reworded as objectives in a *measurable* format.

2.3.1 Broad and Specific Objectives

A broad objective is generally one that specifies the area of research, and specific objectives delineate specific aspects of the problem. Primary medical research can have two types of broad objectives. One is to describe features of a condition such as clinical profile of a disease, prevalence in various segments of the population, and the levels of medical parameters seen in different types of cases. The second type of objective is to study associations and cause–effect types of relationships. This is called analytical, and involves comparison of two or more groups. The broad objective would determine the methodology to be followed in the proposed research.

A broad objective would generally encompass several dimensions of the problem. These dimensions are spelled out in specific objectives. For example, the broad objective may be to assess whether a new diagnostic modality is better than the existing one. "Better" could be in terms of several aspects that are spelled out in specific objectives. The specific objectives in this case could be: (i) positive and negative predictivity; (ii) safety in case it is an invasive procedure, or there is a risk of side effects; (iii) feasibility under a variety of settings such as field, clinic, and hospital; (iv) acceptability by the medical community and patients; and (v) cost effectiveness. Another specific objective could be to evaluate its efficacy in different age, gender, or disease severity groups so that the kinds of cases where it works well are identified. Specific objectives relate to the specific activities and they identify the key indicators of interest. Do not use umbrella types of terms such as "To study the role of …" Instead, be direct; for example, "To estimate the relative risk of …"

Keep the specific objectives as few and focused as possible. Do not try to answer too many questions in a single study, especially if its size is small, such as a graduate thesis. Too many objectives can render the study difficult to manage. Whatever objectives are set, stick to them all through the study as much as possible. Changing them midway or at the time of report writing signals that not enough thinking was done at the time of protocol development.

In the case of clinical trials, the objective could be to establish the superiority of one regimen over the other, or equivalence, or noninferiority. This objective is different from establishing efficacy, such as that it is at least 70%, or safety that says, for example, that no more than 5% of patients experience significant side effects.

Operationalize the objectives into variables to be studied. If the outcome is recovery, specify that it is in terms of relief in pain, ability to walk, improvement in lung function, and other such aspects. If you can also specify the exact quantity of improvement, the research quality will improve. Also specify the time frame within which this improvement must occur. If the objective is to estimate safety, specify that this will be in terms of side effects, complications, duration of adverse reactions, or whatever is applicable.

2.3.2 Hypotheses

The hypothesis is a precise expression of the expected results regarding the state of a phenomenon in the target population. This converts a question to asserting a position. Research is about replacing the existing "hypotheses" by the new ones that are more plausible. They should not give predictable answers. In medical research, hypotheses could purport to explain the etiology of diseases, prevention strategies, screening and diagnostic modalities, distribution of occurrence in different segments of the population, strategies to treat or manage a disease, to prevent the recurrence or adverse sequelae, or any other. Consider which of these types of hypothesis can be investigated by the proposed research.

Hypotheses are not guesses but reflect the depth of knowledge of the topic of research. Good research begins with a clearly worded, unambiguous set of hypotheses and they must be stated in a manner that can be tested by collecting specific evidence. The hypothesis should be original and should arouse interest in the researchers in that field. The hypothesis that dietary pattern affects the occurrence of cancer is not testable unless the specifics of diet and the type of cancer are specified. Antecedents and outcome variables or other relevant variables should be exactly specified in a hypothesis. Generate a separate hypothesis for each major expected relationship.

The hypotheses must correspond to the general and specific objectives of the study. Thus, carefully examine each objective and assess which of these generates a new hypothesis. Whereas objectives define the key variables of interest, hypotheses are guide to the strategies to analyze the data.

Beware that objectives and hypotheses are governed by the current knowledge. For example, nobody wants to know how music aptitude affects cancer risk, although future endeavor may reveal an association between these.

References

1. Fisher AA, Foreit JR. Designing HIV/AIDS Intervention Studies: An Operational Research Handbook. Population Council, 2002.
2. Li J, Liu Z, Chen R, et al. The quality of reports of randomized clinical trials on traditional Chinese medicine treatments: A systematic review of articles indexed in the China National Knowledge Infrastructure database from 2005 to 2012. BMC Complement Altern Med 2014;14:362. www.ncbi.nlm.nih.gov/pmc/articles/PMC4192762/
3. World Medical Association. Declaration of Helsinki: Ethical Principles for Medical Research Involving Human Subjects. Bull WHO 2001;79:372–374. www.ncbi.nlm.nih.gov/pmc/articles/PMC2566407/pdf/11357217.pdf

3

Study Designs: An Overview

All empirical studies are based on a set of evidence collected from different sources, and this process is expected to follow a design to optimize the resources and to achieve sufficient validity and reliability. This chapter provides an overview of various designs that are generally followed in medical studies: details are in subsequent chapters. We explain what a design of a study is in Section 3.1. The types of design such as descriptive and analytical are explained in Sections 3.2 and 3.3, respectively. Essential features of further classification of analytical studies into interventional and observational are described in Sections 3.4 and 3.5, respectively. Section 3.6 discusses the reliability and validity of a design to give believable results, and Section 3.7 gives a guideline of where to use which design.

3.1 What Is a Design of an Empirical Study?

The design of a study is the pattern, scheme, or plan to collect evidence. The function of a design is to permit justified and unbiased conclusions, and the objective is to get the best out of the efforts. It is the road map by which the credibility of research findings is assessed. In an empirical research setup, a design is formulated in advance after considering the objectives of the study, the kind of target subjects, and the resources available.

The details of design bring in clarity and permit conclusions considering confounding and other such complications that could interfere with the interpretation. Thus, the design is formulated in such a way that it provides not just correct answers to the research questions but also stands in good stead if the study is repeatedly done with the same design. It is mostly due to the holes in a design that allegations such as modern medicine sometimes causes more harm than good.

3.1.1 Elements of a Design

Various elements of design are listed in Box 3.1. Note the wide array of information it contains on how the evidence is proposed to be collected and from whom, including the definition of the target population, specification of intervention if any, and the methods to handle the effects of suspected confounders. It also contains the details of various tools proposed to be used. All these elements will be clear as we continue and give more details in later chapters.

BOX 3.1   ELEMENTS OF A DESIGN OF A STUDY

- Definition of the target population: inclusion and exclusion criteria, area to which the subjects would belong, and their broad background information
- Specification of various groups to be included with their relevance
- Source and number of subjects to be included in each group with justification, including statistical power or precision considerations as applicable
- Method of selection of subjects
- Specification of intervention, if any
- Strategy for eliciting data – animal experiment or human trial, or observational study (prospective, retrospective, or cross-sectional), and the specification of the control group, if any, with justification
- Method of allocation of subjects to different groups if applicable, or matching criteria with justification
- Method of blinding, if applicable, and other strategies to reduce bias
- Definition of the antecedent, outcome, and intermediary characteristics to be assessed along with their relevance for the study objectives
- Identification of various confounders and the methods proposed for their control
- Method of administering various data-collecting devices such as questionnaire, laboratory investigation, and clinical assessment; and the method of various qualitative and quantitative measurements
- Validity and reliability of different devices and measurements
- Time sequence of collecting observations and their frequency (once a day, once a month, etc.), the duration of follow-up, and the duration of the study, with justification
- Methods for assessment of compliance and strategy to tackle ethical problems

3.1.2 Types of Designs

As just stated, the design primarily depends on the objectives of the proposed study. Broadly, primary medical research can have two types of objectives. One is descriptive that seeks to delineate the hitherto unknown levels of one or more parameters in different kinds of subjects, and the other is analytical that seeks explanation of a phenomenon. In the latter case, the factor whose effect is to be studied is called antecedent and the effect itself is called the outcome.

Analytical studies could be experimental where the effect of human intervention is sought to be evaluated, or observational where the naturally occurring events are studied. Observational studies are further divided into prospective, retrospective, and cross-sectional depending on whether the study is moving from antecedent to outcome, from outcome to antecedent, or both are being studied together. All these and their subdivisions are depicted in Figure 3.1 and a summary is given in Box 3.2.

This chapter presents details of descriptive studies and describes only the essentials of other designs. Details of experiments/clinical trials and observational studies are described separately in the next two chapters in view of the intricacy of these designs and their special importance in medical setups.

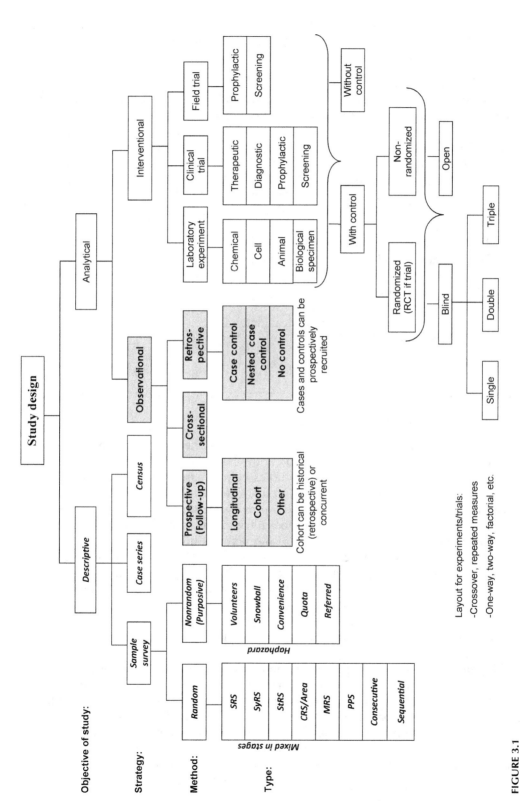

FIGURE 3.1

Types of study designs. CRS, cluster random sampling; MRS, multistage random sampling; PPS, probability proportional to size; RCT, randomized controlled trial; SRS, simple random sampling; StRS, stratified random sampling; SyRS, systematic random sampling.

BOX 3.2   TYPES OF STUDY DESIGNS

DESCRIPTIVE STUDY
For establishing the existing status of a disease or any other condition in a segment of
the population, and associations without cause–effect implications.

ANALYTICAL STUDY
For establishing a relationship, with cause–effect overtones, between two or more
factors – generally antecedents and outcomes:
  By observing the natural course of events (observational study)

- Prospective is from antecedent to outcome
- Retrospective is from outcome to antecedent
- Cross-sectional is when antecedent and outcome are studied together

By human intervention

- Experiments on animals and biological material
- Trials on human beings

3.2 Descriptive Studies

Descriptive studies aim to uncover the distribution part of epidemiology of a disease or
a health condition such as what is common and what is rare, and what is the trend, in
different groups of subjects. Descriptive studies help to assess the extent of health and
the types of diseases prevalent in various groups, and their load in a community. Thus,
for health outcomes, this can also be called a **prevalence study**. But a descriptive study
does not seek explanation or causes, nor does it try to find which group is "better" relative to the other. Evaluation of the level of β_2-microglobulin in cases of HIV/AIDS is
this kind of study. A study on growth parameters of children, or for estimating prevalence of blindness in cataract cases in the elderly, is also descriptive. Unless the existing
status is known, how can one find the cause? Unfortunately, even body temperature
among healthy subjects is not known with precision for many populations. Thus, there
is a considerable scope for carrying out descriptive studies. Such studies can provide
baseline data to launch a program such as the control of breast cancer, and can measure
achievements made.

   A descriptive study can also generate hypotheses regarding the etiology of the health
condition under review when the disease is found to be more common in one group than
the other. In some situations, a descriptive study can be designed to test a hypothesis
regarding the status of a parameter such as whether at least 80% of patients with abdominal tuberculosis come in with the complaints of pain in the abdomen, vomiting, and constipation of long duration, or whether the prevalence of noninsulin-dependent diabetes is
at least 20% among married females of age 50 years or more where the woman's husband
is diabetic. A descriptive study is also good to study relationships such as between systolic

and diastolic blood pressure in patients admitted to an intensive coronary care unit, or between hemoglobin and retinol level in healthy subjects. But this is descriptive only so long as the relationships are viewed as mere incidental association and not cause–effect. A descriptive study generally has only one group because no comparison group is needed for this kind of study, although strata may be present, and compared.

Descriptive studies are mostly undertaken as *sample* surveys, but sometimes complete enumeration of all eligible subjects in the target population, called a census, is done. In addition, particularly in medicine, case studies and case series are reported. The details of these formats are as follows.

3.2.1 Sample Surveys and Their Designs

The term sample survey is generally used for a large-scale descriptive study that is done to estimate the prevalence of certain specified conditions in a segment of the population, although the term is loosely used for many other types of studies as well. Demographic and Health Surveys [1], periodically carried out in many developing countries to obtain a snapshot of health and fertility in the country at a specified point in time, and Global Adult Tobacco Surveys [2] for assessing tobacco use in various segments of the population in different countries, are examples of such surveys. Periodic National Health and Nutrition Examination Surveys in the United States [3] are important sources of information on the health status of the population in that country. These are also sample surveys. Associations or correlations may come out of such investigations as a by-product, but they are not among the main objectives of such surveys.

Surveys generally produce results applicable to one specific area, one specific time, and so on, as opposed to the results of the experimental studies that tend to transcend time and space. When the surveys are periodic, as in the examples just cited, they also provide information on trends. Prevalence in different segments of the population can be statistically compared to find which group has higher prevalence. The reference levels of medical parameters such as cardiac functions in healthy subjects are also obtained by sample surveys, and similarly can also be conducted in diseased subjects to find what and how many aberrations in health occur in different segments of population.

The design of a sample survey is mainly in terms of a sampling plan that we discuss later in Chapter 8. As the main objective in a survey is estimation of the parameters of a population, the sampling methods that can provide a representative sample become especially important. Most large-scale surveys do not use **simple random sampling** because that can provide scattered subjects; instead, they use a **multistage sampling** with appropriate stratification to ensure that no important sections of the population are left out. Some large-scale surveys use **cluster sampling** so that many subjects are available at one place, and this can drastically reduce the cost of the survey, and make it easier to administer. Any other method or a combination of methods can be used, as mentioned in Figure 3.1. Some sections of the population that are not substantial in number but are crucial, such as the elderly, may have to be over-represented in survey sampling so that reliable estimates can also be generated for such segments. Elaborate calculations of sample size are made for the surveys that can provide information on target parameters with desired precision, keeping the sampling methodology in mind and the corresponding **design effect**. Estimation methods too are adjusted to provide **unbiased estimates. Standard errors** of the estimates are a necessary accompaniment of such estimation that provide an assessment of the reliability of the estimates, and sometimes **confidence intervals** are worked out to get a range of not implausible values. (Most of the terms that appear in bold in this paragraph and elsewhere are explained later in this book.)

Descriptive studies conducted at a local level, such as on patients visiting a clinic or a set of clinics, are also called surveys so long as the focus is on prevalence and averages rather than on associations and cause–effect. The profile of cases arriving, say, for kidney stones is technically a survey. Patients are sometimes surveyed to elicit their satisfaction level with the hospital services and sometimes the care givers such as nurses are asked about their perception and practices for managing a particular problem in patients in their care. Example 3.1 briefly describes a survey of kidney transplant clinicians.

> **Example 3.1: A Survey of Kidney Transplant Clinicians for Hepatitis Transmission Risk**
>
> Waller et al. [4] report the results of a survey of 110 kidney transplant clinicians in Australia and New Zealand for hepatitis transmission risk. For a hepatitis B virus surface antigen-positive donor and vaccinated recipient, 44% of clinicians suggested this was unsuitable for transplantation and agreed with the guideline in this respect, but 35% diverged and suggested that this was suitable for prophylaxis. Thus, the transplant suitability decisions varied and often diverged in these clinicians from the guideline.

Among the many examples of sample surveys in health and medicine, a recent one is by Chen et al. [5] in Wuhan (China) comparing the number of men who have sex with men among rural-to-urban migrants. Kenny et al. [6] reported a population-based survey on maternal and child health service utilization in Liberia.

3.2.2 Case Studies and Case Series

A case study, which generally describes features of a new or unusual event, is also descriptive. A series of specific cases of a disease form case series. Both of these can lead to a hypothesis for subsequent investigation.

Case Studies

A case study is a detailed study of an event, its origin, process, and consequences, with the purpose of deriving learning for wider application. Case studies have been found to be effective tools for teaching and learning various aspects of disease such as their management with informatics technology. The primary advantage with this methodology is its flexibility, as case studies do not have to follow a fixed mold, and can be done in a suitable format to study the event. For example, a case study can include results from several studies on that kind of event.

Medical case studies are sometimes confused with **case reports**. Indeed, the terminology has mixed use in the literature. A case report is for a single patient whereas a case study is for a particular event. A case study of a sudden rise in deaths from motor vehicle accidents within the precincts of a particular city would draw information from many sources and would try to reach a reliable conclusion regarding the factors responsible for such a rise. This would not be so in a case report. A case report may include the demographic particulars of a case, etiology of the condition, presenting signs and symptoms, treatment history, diagnosis, disease-related experiences of the patient, timeline, relevant photographs, laboratory and radiological reports, outcome, and prognostic implications.

Case Series

A case series is obviously a series of cases of a specific type and is an extension of case reports. The cases share some common features to be part of a series. For example, they may be suffering from the same disease or they may be undergoing the same regimen of treatment. In medical research, a case series signifies a descriptive study, although here no specific design for selection of cases is formulated. Neither a provision of control nor any protocol for allocation of treatment regimens is made. No cause–effect, not even associations, can be concluded by a case series, but they are capable of generating a hypothesis for planning an analytical study.

There is a question about what is the minimum number of cases to be called a series. An analysis of case series articles appearing in the PubMed database published during 2009 found that the median number of cases reported per series was 7 and the range was 1–6432 [7]. The authors suggest that a case series should contain no less than 4 cases. If they are few, the cases are individually described, but if many, results can be summarized in terms of tables and figures with means, proportions, and rates. Inclusion and exclusion criteria should be specified in any case.

Popular among the case series is the first official documentation in the year 1981 of 5 cases with *Pneumocystis carinii* pneumonia in young gay men in the Los Angeles area who were later identified to have HIV [8].

3.2.3 Census

Opposed to sampling, census is the complete enumeration. The term is usually used for population counts that take place once in 10 years in many countries around the world. For example, the 2011 census in the UK revealed that 9% of people living as a couple were in an interethnic relationship in England and Wales, up 2 percentage points from 2001 [9]. A census can also be done of a specific segment of the population, such as patients visiting a hospital, nurses on critical care duties, and doctors performing a certain type of procedure. This may cover just one hospital or many hospitals.

A population census can be undertaken by any of several methods. In England and Wales, Scotland, and Northern Ireland, the householder receives a questionnaire in the post, completes it, and either submits it online or sends it back in the post. In some other countries, such as Ireland, a large field force visits every household in the land to deliver, and then collect, census questionnaires. The countries of Eastern Europe generally carry out interview censuses where the enumerators collect and record the information on the householder's behalf [10]. Some countries, such as Finland, update their population register online by records of births, deaths, and migration. They can get the complete count and demographic details of the population at any time. In most other countries, a small form is completed for each household in a census. For example, for the U.S. census 2010, the form contained only 10 questions. A sample of households may complete a more detailed questionnaire, which will make this part a sample survey.

For a manual census of the general population in some countries, an enumerator goes from house to house and visits other institutions such as hostels where some people reside, and records the elementary demographic details of each person such as age, sex, and occupation. In India, for example, the count is adjusted to be accurate for sunrise on March 1 of the first year of the decade. The last one was done in the year 2011. This included homeless people who sleep on pavements, at railway stations, and such other locations. Rural and urban areas are divided into census blocks for enumeration purposes and for administrative convenience, and to ensure that nobody is missed. The 2011 census in India also elicited information on the type of drinking water and the types of toilets in households in addition to age, sex, occupation, and housing of the people.

Census data provide useful information for planning health services for different segments of the population, as well as for assessing the impact of the health services. It provides an accurate denominator for many rates such as birth rate and death rate.

A census of out- and inpatients of a hospital can be conducted, although the term census is not used for this population. To be called a census, this will be a complete enumeration and would cover all the target subjects without any sampling. Because of computerization in most parts of the world, this is now easily done. The cases can be analyzed not just for their demographics (and compared with the demographics of the catchment area to identify the kind of people who more commonly visit different departments of the hospital) but also for the diseases they suffer from. Many hospitals may have a database of millions of patients accumulated over time, particularly if they form a consortium. Analysis of such a huge database for meaningful messages has become an important requirement as evidenced by rising science of data analytics and data mining. Similarly, a census of all nurses or all doctors with specific functions can also be done to find their attitudes, difficulties, opinion, and so on, regarding the job they are doing.

3.3 Analytical Studies

The other kind of medical study is analytical, which tries to investigate the etiology of a health condition or cause–effect type of relationship. Determinants of a disease or of a health condition are obtained by this kind of study. Differences between two or more groups are also evaluated by analytical studies. Although the conclusions are associational, the overtones are cause–effect. A properly designed analytical study indeed can provide a conclusion regarding a cause–effect relationship.

Two types of strategies are available for analytical studies – observation and experiment. Observational studies are based on naturally occurring events. There is no human intervention in this setup. Record-based studies are also placed in this group. Observational studies can be further subdivided as shown in Figure 3.1, and briefly explained later in Section 3.5. See Chapter 5 for details. Experimental studies require deliberate human intervention to change the course of events. These include clinical trials. The details of these are presented in the next chapter. The following are the essential features of the analytical studies.

3.3.1 Choice of Strategy for Analytical Studies

A good research strategy provides conclusions with minimal error within the constraints of funds, time, personnel, and equipment. A useful strategy that works in some analytical studies is comparison of characteristics of a population with a high incidence with those of a population with a low incidence. Thus, the factors contributing to the difference can be identified. This is called an **ecological study**. Frequencies and rates in different segments of the population can also be compared. For example, Korkeila et al. [10] compared the frequency of use of antidepressants and the suicide rate in the population of Finland, and found an inverse relationship in the two. You can see that, in an ecological study, only the group characteristics are studied and individuals as such have no role.

While most analytical studies require human intervention to alter the course of events, in some situations the required intervention is not feasible. For investigating the relationship between smoking and colon cancer, intervention in terms of exposing some people to smoking is not an option. Observation of those who are already smoking is the only choice. On the other hand, for establishing efficacy and safety of a drug, intervention in terms of administering the drug is a must. In this case, observational strategy is not an option. The role of potentially harmful factors is generally studied by observations, but potentially beneficial factors can be studied by either strategy. The effect of garlic on cholesterol level can be evaluated by studying people naturally ingesting garlic in various quantities; and also by asking people who almost never consumed garlic to consume it for a while in a specified quantity. Experiments have the edge in providing convincing results. They can also be carried out in controlled conditions – thus, a relatively small sample could be enough. But they raise questions of ethics and feasibility. Guidelines for choosing a strategy for analytical studies can be listed as follows.

- The strategy should be ethically sound, causing least interference in the routine life of the subjects.
- Generally it should be consistent with the approach of other workers in the field. If not, the new approach should be fully justified.
- The strategy should clearly isolate the effect of the factor under investigation from the effect of other factors in operation.
- It should be easy to implement and acceptable to the system within which the research is being planned.
- Confirm that the subjects would sufficiently cooperate during the entire course of the study, and would provide correct responses.
- The strategy should be sustainable so that it can be replicated if required.

3.3.2 Some Useful Terms and Concepts for Analytical Studies

The following terms may help in better understanding the nuances of various designs of analytical studies.

Antecedent and Outcome

Study of the effect of pre-existing maternal anemia on birthweight of their babies can be done in various ways. To understand these, note first that maternal anemia is an antecedent factor in this example and birthweight is the outcome. An antecedent is a precursor such as an exposure (e.g., sex with a subject with sexually transmitted disease) or a risk factor (e.g., high homocysteine level) suspected to affect the disease. The other names for antecedent are cause, predisposing factor, and determinant.

An outcome can be a health state, recovery, side effect, death, or any other event of interest. This is the consequence and must necessarily occur after the antecedent. Other terms for this include effect and result. Note that an outcome of interest can be positive, such as a recovery to full health, or negative, such as death.

Interaction

In the context of design, we are interested in the statistical interaction between different factors under study. It is neither a pharmacological interaction between drugs nor something like host–environment interaction. Statistical interaction is the altered effect of a factor when one or more of the others are also present. It is similar to biological inter-action, which is generally understood to occur when two or more factors are simultan-eously needed to produce or enhance (or retard) the effect. See Box 3.3 for details.

BOX 3.3   WHAT IS AN INTERACTION?

Statistical interaction in the context of designs means that the simultaneous effect of two factors is different from the sum total of their individual effects.

Some factors work more effectively when other conducive factors are also present. Iron supplementation is more effective in raising hemoglobin level in anemic subjects when folic acid is also given. Their combined presence is much more effective than the sum total of their individual effects. This is a positive interaction and is called **synergism**. Because aspirin can reduce the beneficial effect of angiotensin-converting enzyme inhibitors in patients with heart failure, they possibly have negative inter-action. This is called **antagonism**. Most interactions cannot be classified into any of these two categories. Osteoporosis is more severe in older women than older men (Figure 3.2a). Thus, age and gender interact for severity of osteoporosis. Perhaps age and gender have no interaction for total lung capacity (TLC) as the decline in TLC with age runs almost parallel in men and women (Figure 3.2b). A similar pattern of response for various levels of factors, except for a nearly constant difference, indicates absence of interaction. If the responses are not parallel, interaction is said to be pre-sent. Epidemiologically, interaction is called **effect modification**.

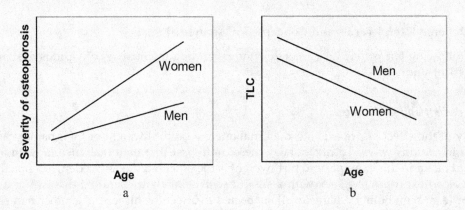

FIGURE 3.2

(a) Age and sex interact to produce a differential effect on severity of osteoporosis; (b) age and sex do not interact for effect on total lung capacity (TLC).

In the sense just described, the term interaction is used for the product of two or more antecedent factors and not for the relationship between an antecedent and an outcome. The differential effect of various levels of an antecedent on outcome is not called an interaction.

You can see that at least two antecedent factors are needed to explore whether inter-action is present or not. When interaction is absent, the factor effects are called **additive**. Also note that when interaction is present, the average effect (called the **main effect**) of the factors can give a misleading picture. The interaction could be such that the factor has negative effect when it is <*a* and positive effect when it is ≥*a*, which could produce an average close to zero. Thus, the main effects have to be carefully interpreted in case the interaction is present. If more than two factors are present, say *A*, *B*, and *C*, you can study the interaction between *A* and *B*, between *A* and *C*, and between *B* and *C*. You can also study higher-order interaction, in this case among factors *A*, *B*, and *C* combined, although this will be difficult to interpret. If you have two quantitative factors such as age and body mass index, these can interact in the sense that higher body mass index in older age can be more harmful for health than the sum total of these two effects individually.

Confounding

Among prominent designs for medical studies is the case–control format, where a case is a subject with disease and the control is without that disease, or a case receives the test regimen and the control receives placebo. To draw valid conclusions from a case–control study, it is easy to understand that the cases and controls should be matched with respect to all those factors that do not fall into the set of hypothesized risk factors. Such extraneous factors are called confounders (Box 3.4).

Obviously, confounders should be identified before the data are collected so that they can be considered for developing an appropriate design that can minimize, if not elim-inate, their effect. Previous research, clinical insight, and clarity about the disease pro-cess can help in this identification. For finding whether sexually transmitted disease per se has a role in acquiring HIV infection, cases are HIV-positives and controls are HIV-negatives, but they should be of the same age, same gender, same sexual behavior (such as having sex with multiple partners), same exposure to injectables, and so forth. These are the confounding factors in this study. Finding controls with so many matching characteristics is an uphill task – thus, some factors may have to be adjusted at the time of analysis.

Age and sex are potential confounders in almost all medical setups. One easy method of identifying other confounders is to draw a list of all possible factors that might influence the outcome of interest. The list may be based on your own knowledge, wisdom of seniors, or review of literature. Out of this list, choose the ones that would be studied as risk factors or antecedents for their role in the outcome. Whatever remains in the list are confounders for that outcome. Note, however, that the confounders so identified would be restricted to those that are known. The knowledge could be incomplete and the list may not be compre-hensive. If so, **epistemic uncertainties** would remain in the results. Nothing can be done to remove this lacuna except to expand the horizon and to look for factors that are not in the conventional domain.

The effect of confounders on the results can be eliminated either by developing a proper design or by performing a suitable statistical analysis. Any one of the following specific steps will help in controlling the effect of confounders.

- Stratify the subjects by the level of the confounder. In our example on smoking and hypertension with obesity as a confounder (Box 3.4), stratify the subjects by levels of obesity. This will tell you the relationship between smoking and hypertension in obese subjects and in nonobese subjects separately. If needed, you can also stratify obesity

BOX 3.4   WHAT IS A CONFOUNDER?

A confounder or a confounding factor is an antecedent characteristic that can be described as a possible explanation of the outcome in addition to the "exposure" under investigation. Thus, it is an extraneous factor that plays spoilsport. It can also be understood as one that is related to the outcome but is not in the causal chain under consideration. It mixes the association of disinterest with that of interest and blurs the causal pathway. Necessary but not sufficient criteria for a factor being a confounder are: (i) it alters the outcome; (ii) it is suspected to be related to the other antecedents under consideration; and (iii) it is not a descendent of exposure or outcome. One simple way to identify a confounder is to imagine that if there is no exposure under the study, the association between the suspected factor and the outcome can remain or will vanish. If any degree of association still remains, the factor is a confounder. If it is in a causal chain, it is called a **mediator** and not a confounder.

In a study on smoking and hypertension, one confounder is obesity (Figure 3.3). Smokers tend to be obese and hypertension is also related to obesity. In other

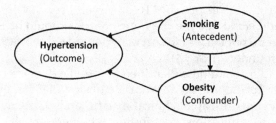

FIGURE 3.3
Obesity as a confounding factor for smoking and hypertension.

words, obesity can also be at least a partial explanation for hypertension in addition to smoking, and it is not in the causal chain under study because smoking per se does not cause obesity. The effect of smoking and obesity on hypertension cannot be disaggregated unless obese and nonobese subjects are separately studied, or unless a suitable statistical model is applied that can disaggregate the effects. The second confounding factor in this example is age. As age increases, the lifelong burden of smoking increases for smokers, and the chance of developing hypertension also increases because of age-related arterial changes. Thus, again, age as a possible explanation should be ruled out to find the net effect of smoking on hypertension.

  into more than two categories, such as normal, overweight, obese, and super-obese subjects.
- Limit the study to one particular group of confounder, such as only obese subjects in our example. At least for this group, you will have clear results.
- Use multivariable analysis such as ordinary and logistic regression (Chapter 11). In our example, when obesity is also entered as a regressor along with smoking, the effect of smoking will be automatically adjusted for any effect of obesity.
- As already noted, these strategies can be adopted only when information on the confounding factor is available. In fact, the first two strategies require that this

information should be available at the planning stage before the data are collected. When stratification is done, it should be sufficiently fine so that the strata are homogeneous. For example, categorizing age as <45 and ≥45 years may not be fully effective for some diseases. Also, in the case of stratification, the result would be available separately for each stratum while the objective could be to get a combined result. The third strategy of regression can be adopted when the data on confounding factor are collected along with the other data. Statistical methods are available to get a pooled estimate of the effect that gives larger weight to the bigger stratum, but this does not work if interactions are present. In that case, do not pool the strata but present the results separately for each stratum. In this strategy, substantial difference between crude and adjusted effect implies that the factor is indeed a confounder, and then the adjusted effect will be the valid estimate as it removes the effect of the confounders.

Example 3.2: Interaction and Confounding in the Relation between Distance to High-Voltage Power Lines and Risk of Childhood Leukemia

The risk of childhood leukemia can be affected by the distance from residence at birth to the nearest power line, but several other factors can also interfere in this relation. In a study reported by Pedersen et al. [11], a statistically significant interaction was observed between this distance and domestic radon concentration at address at birth (when distance was small and radon was high, the risk was much higher), but no interaction was found with traffic-related air pollution. Socio-economic status, urban/rural area, maternal age, and birth order were also investigated as potential confounders. All these can affect the risk of childhood leukemia. Adjusting for these factors had practically no effect on the relationship between the distance and risk of childhood leukemia in this study.

3.4 Essentials of Intervention Studies

As mentioned earlier, two strategies are generally adopted for analytical studies. One is the observation of events when they occur as a consequence of natural intervention, such as iodine deficiency in water, and smoking by some individuals. A brief explanation of this is given later in this chapter, and the details are given in Chapter 5. The other is intentional human interference, where something is deliberately done to subjects to see its effect. This gives rise to intervention studies. By exercising control on the extraneous factors that can affect the outcome in this setup, intervention is the most direct method to study the cause–effect relationship. Such evidence is generally more compelling than that available from observational studies. Science is mostly achieved by intervention studies. In health and medicine, these are divided into experiments when done on animals or biological specimens, and trials when done on humans.

3.4.1 Medical Experiments

Essential ingredients of an experiment are a purported manipulable cause and an anticipated effect. The relationship is speculative – if already confirmed, there is no need for an experiment. An experiment is a procedure to verify or falsify a causal relationship by introducing the purported cause and observing the effect. This definition requires that a cause must be hypothesized and its possible outcomes visualized in advance. Observations are geared to measure this anticipated outcome.

Experiments tend to provide results that transcend time and space, and in many cases beyond the population under study. Observational studies lack such generalization. A medical experiment can be carried out in a laboratory, clinic, or community. The subjects for experiment in the clinic or community are generally human beings, and such an experiment is generally termed a trial. Laboratory experiment, on the other hand, may involve inanimate entities such as physical forces or chemicals; in the context of medicine, laboratory experiments are generally conducted on biological material or animals. Laboratory experiments often provide important clues to the potential of the intervention for formulating a therapeutic agent. When successful, they pave the way for human studies. Thus, experiments have a special place in medical research.

Several different designs of intervention studies are available, and some are mentioned in Figure 3.1. We do not discuss laboratory experiments in this text as our focus is on clinical trials. For experimental studies, see Indrayan and Holt [12].

3.4.2 Clinical Trials

More for convention than semantics, medical experiments on human beings are called trials. A trial necessarily has at least two groups for comparison – one receiving the regimen under test, called the **treatment group**, and the other not receiving it, called the **control group**. The control group can receive either the existing regimen or an inactive substance, called **placebo**. The objective is to study the cause–effect relationship between a medical intervention and a health outcome in human subjects. Because the subjects are human, a large number of issues crop up, ranging from stricter ethics to profound variations. Thus, trials do need extra care.

Clinical trials are mostly done to investigate new modes of therapy. Research on new diagnostic procedures also falls into this category. Most clinical trials are carried out involving heavy investment – thus, extra care is imperative. Because variation between and within subjects occurs due to a large number of factors, it is quite often a challenge to take full care of all of them in this setup. Epistemic uncertainties also play a significant role. It is necessary in this situation that the rules of empiricism are rigorously followed, and the trial is conducted under controlled conditions so that the influence of extraneous factors is minimized, if not ruled out. Also, the trials should be conducted with a sufficient number of patients so that a trend, if any, can be successfully detected. Most clinical trials are done in ideal conditions as much as possible to provide an uncontaminated estimate of the efficacy. For estimating effectiveness in practical conditions, **pragmatic trials** are favored. The details are given in Chapter 4.

By their very nature, all trials are prospective studies where the antecedent is the intervention and the efficacy and safety are the outcomes. A follow-up is built into all trials. Thus, many ideas discussed later in Chapter 5 under observational prospective studies apply to the trial setup as well. All trials involve careful consideration of issues such as selection of subjects and controls, **randomization** and **matching**, and **blinding**, **masking**, and **concealment of allocation**. All these are presented in a separate chapter. Briefly, a double-blind randomized controlled trial (RCT), where one group receives the regimen under test and the other equivalent group receives placebo or the existing regimen after random allocation, and the subjects and assessors are kept blind regarding who is receiving what, is considered the best strategy to reach a valid cause–effect conclusion.

3.5 Essentials of Observational Studies

Nature is a great experimenter. Many interventions or changes occur naturally and require no human intervention. Some people are naturally exposed to contaminated water, and some women naturally have low hemoglobin levels. The study of such naturally occurring events can provide invaluable help in studying antecedent-outcome relationship. Such a study can be based on records or on actual observations, or a combination of both. This is generally categorized as an observational study, and is also sometimes referred to as an **epidemiological study**. As there is no deliberate human intervention (such as a drug) in this setup, such studies carry little risk of harm to the subjects or society. However, such a study is generally conducted for specific groups such as those with high disease prevalence – thus, extrapolation to the general population is not immediate. Many observational studies are done in a hospital setup rather than in a community.

As mentioned earlier, three different ways that an observational study can be carried out are prospective, retrospective, and cross-sectional, depending on whether the starting point is the antecedent or outcome, or none at all, respectively. A schematic depiction of these three methods is given in Figure 3.4. A brief description of each is given next. Details are given in Chapter 5.

3.5.1 Prospective Studies

The most desirable format for studying the relationship between maternal anemia and birthweight is that antenatal women with different levels of hemoglobin are selected and

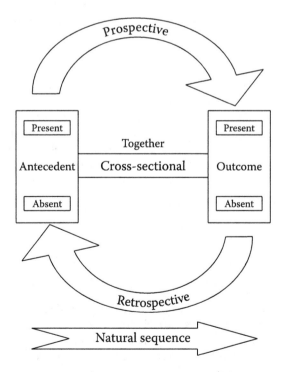

FIGURE 3.4
Schematic depiction of prospective, retrospective, and cross-sectional studies.

followed for birthweight of their babies. Because anemia is the antecedent in this study and birthweight is the outcome, note that antecedents are assessed prior to the outcome in this format in the sequence in which they naturally occur. A study following such a format is called a prospective study. Because any outcome occurs after the antecedent, some follow-up is essential in this format, although it can be short in some situations. Thus, this is also called a **follow-up study**. As discussed later, among the formats in which a prospective study can be carried out is cohort study, longitudinal study, and repeated measures study. A comparison group without the antecedent under study can also be included in this design.

3.5.2 Retrospective Studies

The second format for examining birthweight in relation to maternal anemia is that babies with different birthweights are chosen and anemia status of their mother during the antenatal period is retrieved from records. The first assessment in this format is the outcome and antecedents are subsequently assessed for each type of known outcome. This is a retrospective study because it moves from outcome to antecedent. Note the quickness with which a study in this format can be carried out. There is no need to wait for the outcome to develop or not develop. The outcome is already known and the antecedent is obtained either from records or enquiry. The cases and, in most studies, controls are assembled, and information regarding their past exposure or risk factors is collected. The cases can arise or can be recruited in future, such as cases of breast cancer coming to a clinic from now on, yet the study is technically retrospective so long as it investigates antecedents for known outcome. The retrospective method is especially suitable for rare outcomes because the study can start after enough numbers of cases have been assembled.

3.5.3 Cross-Sectional Studies

The third format for the birthweight–anaemia study is that a group of deliveries is chosen irrespective of maternal anemia and birthweight, and both are elicited. This is a cross-sectional study because both antecedent and outcome are observed at the same time. The presence or absence of either antecedent or outcome is not a consideration at the time of selection of subjects in this kind of design, but the objective still is to investigate the association. Although this kind of format is more appropriate for descriptive studies, such as for estimating the prevalence of a health outcome, it is also appropriate to investigate a hypothesis regarding etiology.

3.6 Reliability and Validity of Designs, and Biases

One of the important functions of a design is to be able to reach reliable and valid results. These concepts have relevance to all medical studies, but are more prominent in descriptive studies than in analytical studies. They are also useful in several other steps of medical studies. The following discussion is restricted to the design aspects. The reliability and validity of other aspects will be discussed in detail in subsequent chapters.

3.6.1 Reliability of a Design

Reliability is the property of giving the same result when the study is repeated under identical conditions. This property generates confidence because you know that the result would not be any different if the study was done again. This depends on many factors, such as reliable measurements, reliable instruments, reliable estimates, and other such factors, but, as just mentioned, we are restricting our discussion to the design aspects for the time being.

In the context of design, reliability mostly depends on the adequacy of the sample, given that the data are correct and analyzed properly. This is ensured by a sufficiently large sample drawn in a manner that is likely to make it representative of all segments of the population. Thus, proper sample size as determined by the desired precision considerations and a good sampling method must be adopted to get a representative sample. The sampling methods are presented in detail in Chapter 8, but note now that when these are scrupulously followed, consistent results in repeat studies can be expected.

Nonresponse in medical studies has an adverse impact on the reliability of results: the ultimate sample size available to draw conclusions is reduced, and that does affect the reliability of the results. This deficiency can be remedied by increasing the sample size corresponding to the anticipated nonresponse, but this does not remedy the bias in case the nonresponse is selective by those who are critically sick, or have more robust health, or any such condition that can affect the outcome.

Whereas most large-scale sample surveys are designed to give reliable results, this cannot be stated for some other formats such as small-scale studies, case studies, and case series. Their results are for specific situations and may not be repeated in other similar cases.

3.6.2 Validity of a Design

A valid design is one that would rightly answer the question the study is intended to answer. Wrong design can provide erroneous or incomplete information, which cannot lead to right answers, and may render the results of a study invalid. Although this can happen due to many factors, faulty design is one among them. The design of the study should be able to anticipate such fallacies and provide for steps to control them. For example, for finding the risk factors for a disease, a survey or a cross-sectional study may not give valid results. A usual clinical trial may not give the actual performance of the regimen in practical conditions because such trials are done in ideal conditions. A case–control study would not give an estimate of the incidence of a disease because that requires a follow-up. A nonrandomized trial is less likely to provide valid results than a randomized trial. Blinding may also be required to enhance the validity of the design. Framing a valid design is important to get valid results.

There is some confusion in the literature about the terms validity and reliability. The difference between the two is aptly illustrated in Figure 3.5. Reliability is hitting the same point on repeated attempts, although this may be far from the target (see third panel). Validity is hitting around the target (second panel). If hits are close together and near the target every time, both reliability and validity are high (fourth panel).

Lack of validity can be due to systematic bias or for any other reason. If the bias is small, we say that the study has high validity and if the bias is large we say that the validity is low. Because all biases are artefacts and not true causes, they are amenable to control by careful planning and meticulous execution. The next section gives a comprehensive list of such biases.

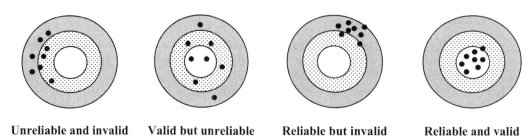

Unreliable and invalid   **Valid but unreliable**   **Reliable but invalid**   **Reliable and valid**

FIGURE 3.5
Dartboards illustrating the difference between validity and reliability.

Example 3.3: Valid Design

Meta-analysis is a method by which the results of different studies on the same outcome are integrated to come up with a more reliable conclusion. A prerequisite for this to succeed is that the studies chosen to be included in the analysis have a valid design. Descatha et al. [13] conducted a meta-analysis of studies on lateral epicondylitis and physical exposure at work and listed their criteria for judging the validity of the design. These are: (i) inclusion and exclusion criteria described; (ii) complete information given and considered for analysis of dropouts; and (iii) the sample is representative of the target population.

The authors limited their analysis to the prospective studies – thus, there was no need to mention the appropriateness of the interventional or observational strategy and prospective/retrospective/cross-sectional nature. There was no need to mention randomization and blinding either as these were not clinical trials. Control of possible biases was relevant for the studies included in their meta-analysis, but was not mentioned. This may be because when such strict criteria are used, the number of studies with valid design may be substantially reduced and that could severely truncate the utility of the meta-analysis.

3.6.3 Biases in Medical Studies and Their Control

The results of a medical study become clouded when some bias is detected after the results are available. Therefore, it is important that all sources of bias are considered while planning a study, and all efforts are made to avoid or control them.

List of Possible Biases in Medical Studies

Because bias can occur at every step of research (planning, execution, analysis, and reporting), a large number of sources of bias exist in a medical research setup. The following list describes those that are most common and most important at some stage of a study, and is not restricted to the design aspects. These biases are not mutually exclusive and the overlap is substantial. Also, some of the biases in this list are collections of biases of similar types. If all these were stated separately, the list might become unmanageable. These are described in brief here in the order in which studies are done, that is, planning, execution, analysis, and reporting.

1. *Bias in concepts*: This bias occurs when there is a lack of clarity about the concepts to be used in the proposed study. This gives an opportunity to the investigators to

use subjective interpretation that can vary from person to person. This bias can also occur when the logic used is faulty: sometimes the premise of the logic itself can be incorrect.

2. *Definition bias*: The study subjects and medical condition under study should be sharply defined so that there is no room for ambiguity. For example, a study on tuberculosis cases should specify that these would be sputum-positive, Mantoux-positive, radiologically established, or some combination. A blurred definition is open to subjective interpretation, and this can affect the validity of the study.

3. *Bias in design*: This bias occurs when the case group and the control group are not equivalent at baseline, and differentials in prognostic factors are not properly accounted for at the time of analysis. Design bias also depends on the structure of the study. For example, an ecological study has more chance of bias in results than a double-blind RCT. Random allocation and blinding tend to minimize this type of bias.

4. *Bias in the selection of subjects*: The subjects included in a study may not truly represent the target population. This can happen when the sample is not randomly selected, or when the sample size is too small. In both these instances, the sample may fail to represent the entire spectrum of subjects in the target population. Studies on volunteers and clinic subjects always have this kind of bias. Selection bias can also occur because the serious cases have already died and are not available with the same frequency as the mild cases (also called *survival bias*). Similar bias can occur in selection of cases with diseases that have highly variable incubation periods such as AIDS. (See also *length bias*.) Bias due to self-selection or volunteers is obvious since those not consenting are excluded.

5. *Bias due to concurrent medication or comorbidities*: Selected patients may suffer from other apparently unrelated conditions but their response might differ either because of the condition itself or because of medication given concurrently for that condition. This can be controlled by appropriate restrictions on concurrent diseases in the **inclusion and exclusion criteria** and by strict restriction of concurrent medications where feasible. Comorbidities may provide biased outcome due to the additionally compromised health of the subjects. This can happen with subclinical conditions such as low hemoglobin levels and high blood sugar levels.

6. *Instruction bias*: When there are no instructions or when unclear instructions are prepared for conducting a study, the investigators use discretion and this can vary from person to person, and from time to time. Modern clinical trial protocols and associated guidelines usually give very clear and detailed instructions regarding each stage of a trial.

7. *Length bias*: Case–control studies are generally based on prevalent cases rather than incident cases. Prevalence is dominated by those who survive for a longer duration, and these patients may be qualitatively different from those who die early. Thus, the sample would include disproportionately more of those who are healthier and survive longer. The conclusions cannot be generalized to those who died earlier. The disease profile can also differ because there would be more cases in whom disease progression is slow. Those suffering from an aggressive form of the disease would be missed because of the early death of some of them.

8. *Bias in detection of cases*: Error can occur in diagnostic or screening criteria. For example, in a prostate cancer detection study, if prostate biopsies are not performed on men with normal results after screening, the true sensitivity and specificity of the test cannot be determined. Also, a laboratory investigation done properly in

a hospital setting is less prone to error in the detection of cases compared to one carried out in a field setting. Detection bias also occurs when cases with mild disease do not report or are difficult to detect. If this is inadvertent, the results would be biased without anybody knowing that such a bias was present.

9. *Lead time bias*: Not all cases are detected at the same stage of the disease. With regard to cancers, some may be detected by screening before they are clinically apparent, for example by Pap smear, whereas some may not be detected until clinical manifestations of the disease start appearing. In some cases detection occurs when the disease is already in an advanced stage, but the follow-up is generally from the time of detection. This difference in "lead time" can cause a systematic error in the results. These issues can be partly addressed by strictly defining inclusion criteria in terms of stage of disease at detection and/or by stratifying subjects according to the stage of disease at detection.

10. *Bias due to unaccounted confounder*: This bias occurs when confounders are not dealt with adequately. If that happens, any difference or association cannot be fully ascribed to the antecedent factors under study. For this, identify the confounders after a thorough review of the literature and devise a strategy to deal with them.

11. *Bias due to epistemic factors*: Efforts can be made to control only those factors that are known, but there may be many unknown factors that could affect the results. These epistemic factors can bias the results in very unpredictable ways. There is nothing specific that can be done for the unknown factors, but randomization and adequate sample size seem helpful for minimizing this type of bias.

12. *Contamination in controls*: Control subjects are generally those who receive placebo or regular therapy. If these subjects are in their homes, it is difficult to know if they have received some other therapy that can affect their status as controls. In a field situation, contamination in a control group can occur if this group is in close proximity to an unblinded test group and learns from the experience of the latter. In a hospital situation, patients from another department may be chosen to serve as controls, but some other program may be going on there that has a spill-over effect on the control subjects.

13. *Berkson bias*: Comparison of hospital cases with hospital controls can be biased if exposure increases the chance of admission. This can lead to an over-representation of subjects with that exposure. Cases of injury in motor vehicle accidents can suffer from this kind of bias.

14. *Bias in ascertainment or assessment*: This bias occurs in unblinded studies when, unknowingly or deliberately, the investigators are more thorough with cases than with controls. A similar problem can also occur when subjects belonging to a particular social group have records but others have to depend on recall. Sometimes this is also called *information bias*.

15. *Interviewer bias or observer bias*: Interviewer bias occurs when one is able to elicit better responses from one group of patients (say, those who are better educated) relative to the other kind (such as illiterate people). Observer bias occurs when the observer unwittingly (or even intentionally) exercises more care about one type of response or measurement such as those supporting a particular hypothesis than those opposing the hypothesis. Observer bias can also occur if, for example, the observer is not fully alert when listening to Korotkoff sounds while measuring blood pressure or is not able to properly rotate the endoscope to get an all-round view of the duodenum in a suspected case of peptic ulcer.

16. *Instrument bias*: This occurs when the measuring instrument is not properly calibrated. For example, a weighing machine that does not show zero when resting will give inaccurate measurement of weight. Another kind of instrument bias occurs when a device does not provide a complete picture of the target organ, thereby giving false or incomplete information. For example, an endoscope might not reach the site of interest. Another example is the **Likert scale** assessment where +3 may be a more frequent response on a –5 to +5 scale than +8 on a 0–10 scale, although both are the same. A third kind of instrument bias occurs when an instrument is considered **gold standard** because this is acknowledged as the best, while forgetting that the best may still be imperfect. Errors can occur even with this gold standard. The fourth kind of instrument bias is when the **predictivity** of an instrument is used in a new setup without considering that different prevalence in this new setup would affect the predictivity.

17. *Hawthorne effect*: When subjects know that they are being observed or investigated, they often alter their behavior and response. In fact, this is the basis for including a placebo group in a trial. The usual responses of subjects are not the same as when they are under a scanner. Such effects may not bias the results of a trial in favor of one treatment as both the groups are under observation, but can affect the results where only one group is under observation in a study.

18. *Recall bias*: There are two types of recall bias. One arises from better recall of recent events than those that occurred a long time ago. Also, serious episodes are easier to recall than mild episodes. The second type of recall bias occurs when cases suffering from a disease are able to recall events much more easily than healthy controls. Thorough probing can possibly help to reduce this bias.

19. *Response bias*: Cases with serious illness are likely to give more correct responses regarding history and current ailments compared with controls. This is not just because of recall, but also because patients with serious illness tend to keep meticulous records. Patients with serious ailments tend to observe themselves more carefully. Some patients, such as those suffering from sexually trans-mitted diseases, may intentionally suppress sexual history and other informa-tion because of the stigma attached to these diseases. Injury history may be distorted to avoid legal consequences. If the subjects are able to exchange notes, the response to questions might alter, and in some cases might even become nearly uniform. An unsuspecting illness, death in the family, or any such drastic event may produce an extreme response. Response bias can also be regarded as a type of *information bias*.

20. *Bias due to protocol violation*: It is not uncommon in a clinical trial that some subjects do not receive the full intervention or the correct intervention, or some ineligible subjects are randomly allocated in error. This occurs when the study **protocol** is not faithfully followed.

21. *Repeat testing bias*: In a pretest–posttest situation, the subjects tend to remember some of the previous questions and they may remove previous errors in posttest – thus doing better for reasons other than the intervention. The observer may acquire expertise to elicit the correct response on the second or third occasion. Conversely, fatigue may set in with repeat testing that could alter the response. Moreover, many biological measurements have a strong tendency toward the mean: extremely high scorers tend to score lower in subsequent testing, and extremely low scorers tend to do better in a subsequent test, whereas midrange scores remain similar.

22. *Clustering bias*: This is related to repeat testing bias. When the subjects belong to an affinity group, they tend to give similar responses. For example, people in one profession, people living close together, family members, etc., are such affinity groups. When members of such groups are study subjects by design, use design effect to minimize the effect of clustering. If clustering occurs by chance, you may not even know that it is there, and the results would be biased.

23. *Mid-course bias*: Sometimes after enrollment, the subjects have to be excluded if they develop an unrelated condition such as an injury, or become so seriously ill that their continuation in the trial is no longer in their best interest. If a new facility such as robotics surgery is started or closed for the subjects being observed for a study, the response may be altered. If two independent trials are going on in the same hospital, one may contaminate the other. An unexpected event such as a nosocomial infection can alter the response of even those who are not affected.

24. *Self-improvement effect*: Many diseases are self-limiting. Improvement over time occurs irrespective of the intervention, and it may be partially or fully incorrectly ascribed to the intervention. Diseases such as arthritis and asthma have natural periods of remission that may look like the effect of therapy. The use of proper controls and random allocation may address this source of bias.

25. *Bias due to digit preference*: It is well known that most people have a special love for the digits 0 and 5. A person aged 69 or 71 is likely to report their age as 70 years. Another manifestation of digit preference is in forming intervals for quantitative data. Blood glucose level categories would be commonly chosen as 70–79, 80–89, 90–99, etc., and not 64–71, 72–79, etc. If digit 0 is preferred, 88, 89, 90, 91, and 92 can be recorded as 90. Thus, intervals such as 88–92, 93–97, and 98–102 may be better to ameliorate the effect of digit preference rather than the conventional 85–89, 90–94, 95–99, etc.

26. *Bias due to nonresponse*: In most medical studies, particularly those requiring follow-up, some subjects refuse to cooperate, suffer an injury, die, or become untraceable. Nonrespondents have two types of effects on the results. First, they are generally different from those who respond, and their exclusion can lead to biased results. Second, nonresponse reduces the sample size and can result in substantial differences between the numbers in different groups, both of which can decrease the power of the study to detect specified differences or associations.

27. *Attrition bias*: The pattern of nonresponse can differ between subgroups in the sense that in one subgroup more severe cases drop out, whereas in another group mostly mild cases drop out. In a rheumatoid arthritis databank study, attrition during follow-up was high in patients of young age, who were less educated, and were non-Whites [14]. Everything possible should be done to convince the subjects to respond and not drop out.

28. *Bias in handling outliers*: No objective rule is generally followed to define a value as outlier other than that the value must be far away from the mainstream values. If the duration of hospital stay after a particular surgery is mostly between 6 and 10 days, some researchers would call 18 days an outlier and may exclude it on the suspicion of being an incorrect recording or transcription, and some would consider it correct and include it in their calculation. In view of this subjective and essentially arbitrary definition of an outlier, many would not exclude any extreme value, howsoever different it might be. Thus, the results would vary depending on the researcher's approach to detecting and handling outliers. Generally speaking,

do not exclude a suspected outlier from analysis unless there is a convincing reason to label it as an outlier. When an analysis with such exclusions is performed, then an analysis without any exclusions should also normally be performed.

29. *Recording bias*: At least two types of errors can occur in recording data. The first arises due to the inability to properly decipher the writing on case sheets, particularly because physicians are notorious for illegible writing. This can happen particularly with similar-looking digits such as 1 and 7, and 3 and 5. Thus, the entry of data may be in error. The second arises due to the carelessness of the investigator. A diastolic level of 87 can be wrongly recorded as 78, or a code 4 entered as 6 when remembered incorrectly. Some errors may also be typographical because wrong pressing of adjacent keys on the keyboard is common. Errors can also occur when data are manually transcribed from one document to another.

30. *Bias in analysis*: In some situations, the statistical analysis of data can be geared to get the results that were anticipated. This can be done by overlooking the underlying conditions of various statistical methods, using class intervals of quantitative measurements that suit the findings, ignoring under- or over-fitting of models, excluding particular variables or particular subjects, using means where proportions are more appropriate or vice versa, and such other mechanisms. Sometimes, the data are overanalyzed (tortured until it confesses!).

31. *Bias due to competing cofactors*: Some factors influence results synergistically or antagonistically when relevant cofactors are present. If this is not properly taken into account, the effect of an intervention can be under- or over-estimated. It is therefore important to identify as many such factors as possible and take them into account during analysis.

32. *Prevalence–incidence bias*: This occurs when the effects of risk factors on prevalence could be a function of the duration of the disease and can be mistaken for effects on disease occurrence when not properly accounted for.

33. *Interpretation bias*: This arises from the tendency among some researchers to interpret the results in favor of a particular hypothesis, ignoring the opposite evidence. This would be mostly unintentional, but can also be intentional in rare cases.

34. *Reporting bias*: Researchers may have conscious or subconscious preconceptions and expectations of results, and this may result in them writing reports that are not really consistent with the data available. For example, it is easy to suppress contradictory evidence by not talking about it.

35. *Bias in presentation of results*: Scales in graphs can be chosen such that a small change looks like a big change, or vice versa [15]. Also the researcher may merely state the inconvenient findings that contradict the main conclusion but not highlight them in the same way as done with the findings that support the main conclusion.

For more details on biases, see Delgado-Rodriguez and Llorca [16].

Steps to Control Bias in Medical Studies

The purpose of describing various types of biases in so much detail is to create an awareness of the need to avoid or at least minimize them, particularly at the time of design. Everything possible should be done to keep them under control so that you do not have to give an explanation such as "hand of God" in a soccer game. In the context of a medical study, bias in results and conclusions is mostly a function of the study design and its implementation.

The following steps can be suggested to minimize bias in the results in a research setup, in addition to those already mentioned in the list of biases. Not all steps apply to all situations: adopt the ones that apply to your setup.

1. Develop an unbiased scientific temperament by realizing that you are in the occupation of a relentless search for truth.
2. Specify the problem and the objectives to the minutest detail.
3. Assess the validity of the identified target population, and the groups to be included in the study in the context of the objectives and methodology. The inclusion and exclusion criteria should be precisely worded to address this problem.
4. Assess the validity of antecedents and outcomes for providing the correct answer to your questions.
5. Beware of epistemic uncertainties arising from the limitation of scientific knowledge. The use of double-blind RCTs goes a long way toward minimizing this bias.
6. Evaluate the reliability and validity of the measurements required to assess the antecedents and outcomes, as well as of the other tools you plan to deploy.
7. Where appropriate, consider undertaking a pilot study and pretest the tools. Make changes as needed.
8. Try to identify all possible confounding factors and other sources of bias, and develop an appropriate design that can take care of most of these biases, if not all.
9. Choose a representative sample, preferably by a random method as and when possible.
10. Choose an adequate size of sample in each group.
11. Rigorously train yourself and your co-workers in making correct assessments prior to beginning a study.
12. Use matching, blinding, masking, and random allocation as needed.
13. Monitor each stage of research, including periodic checking of data.
14. Make determined efforts to minimize nonresponse and partial response.
15. Double check the data and rectify errors in recording, entries, etc.
16. Analyze the data with proper statistical methods. Use **standardized** or **adjusted rates** where needed, perform the **stratified analysis**, or use **mathematical models** such as regression to take care of those confounders that could not be ruled out by design.
17. Report only the evidence-based results, enthusiastically but dispassionately. Interpret the results in an objective manner, based only on the evidence at hand.
18. Exercise extreme care in drafting the report and keep comments or opinions clearly separate from evidence-based results.

Bias and other aspects of design can be very adequately taken care of if you imagine yourself presenting the results a couple of years hence to a critical but friendly audience [17]. Consider what your colleagues would question or advise at that time, and their reaction when you conclude that the results are significant or if you conclude that the results are not significant: might there be alternative explanations of the results, are there any confounding factors that have been missed, or could **chance** or **sampling error** be an explanation? Such considerations will help in developing a proper design, and to conduct the study in a conscientious manner. A word of caution in the end. Do not try to control or eliminate all the sources of bias at the time of planning because that may affect the proper execution of the study and may limit the practical utility of the results. Control the effect of some sources at the time of analysis. Others that remain after adequate design and proper analysis can be acknowledged as limitations of the study. This is appreciated much more than the claim of completely unbiased results.

3.7 Where to Use Which Design?

Different designs have different applications, which are mostly dependent on the objectives of the study, feasibility of the design, and the resources available. In case the objective is to explore a cause–effect relationship, the design dictates the level of validity of the evidence available from the study.

3.7.1 Recommended Designs for Different Types of Research Questions

See Table 3.1 for recommended designs for different objectives. The objectives are listed in a question format for easy comprehension. The table may give you a clear picture of where a particular design may be appropriate. This is not an exhaustive list, though it does cover many types of research questions.

3.7.2 Levels of Evidence for Cause–Effect Relationships

While exploring antecedent–outcome relationships that may have cause–effect implications, it is essential to consider whether the study will provide infallible evidence. For this feature, double-blind RCTs outscore all other designs. An RCT, when properly conducted, tends to provide results that can be hardly questioned for methodology. Ecological studies and case reports are least valid for this purpose. The details are given in Table 3.2.

TABLE 3.1
Recommended Designs for Different Types of Research Questions

Research Question	Recommended Design
1. What is the prevalence or distribution of disease or a measurement, or what is the pathological, microbiological, and clinical profile of certain types of cases?	Sample survey
2. Are two or more factors related to one another (with possible implications of cause–effect)?	Cross-sectional study
3. Do two or more methods agree with one another?	Cross-sectional study
4. What is the inherent goodness of a medical test in correctly detecting the presence or absence of disease (sensitivity and specificity)?	Retrospective study
5. What are the risk factors for a given outcome, or what is their relative importance?	Retrospective study
6. How good is a test or a procedure in predicting a disease or any other outcome?	Prospective study
7. What is the incidence of a disease, or what is its risk in a specified group or the relative risk?	Prospective study
8. What are the sequels of a pathological condition? And how much or how does a factor affect the outcome?	Prospective study
• If the factor under study is potentially harmful	Prospective study in humans; in rare situations animal experiment
• If the factor under study is potentially beneficial	Randomized controlled trial for humans, and experiment for animals or biological material
9. Is an intervention really as effective as or more effective than the other?	Randomized controlled trial for humans, and experiment for animals or biological material

TABLE 3.2
Hierarchy of Study Designs by Level of Evidence (From Best to Worst) for Cause–Effect Relationships

Level of Evidence	Type of Design	Advantages	Disadvantages
Level 1	RCT – double blind	Able to establish cause–effect and efficacy	Assumes ideal conditions
		Internally valid results	Can be done only for potentially beneficial regimen
			Difficult to implement
			Expensive
Level 2	RCT – nonblind but with a control group	Can be used in situations where blinding is not feasible	Biases are more common – thus, caution is required
		Easy to execute	
Level 3	Unblinded trial with no control/not randomized	Can indicate cause–effect when biases are under control	Cause–effect is only indicated but not established
		Effectiveness under practical conditions can be evaluated	Can be done only for a potentially beneficial regimen
		Relatively easy to do	Outcome assessment can be blurred because of bias
Level 4	Prospective observational study	Establishes sequence of events	Requires a big sample
		Antecedents are adequately assessed	Limited to one set of antecedents
		Yields incidence	Follow-up can be expensive and time lag can be huge
	Retrospective observational study – case–control	Outcome is predefined, so no ambiguity	Antecedent assessment can be blurred
		Quick results obtained	Sequence of events not established
		Small sample can be sufficient	High likelihood of survival bias and recall bias
Level 5	Cross-sectional study	Appropriate when distinction between outcome and antecedent is not clear	Does not provide any indication of cause–effect – only the relationship is indicated
		When done on representative sample, same study can evaluate both sensitivity/specificity and predictivity of a medical test	
Level 6	Ecological study and case series	Easy to do	Fallacies are common
Level 7	Case reports and expert opinion	Help in formulating hypothesis	Many biases can occur
			Do not reflect cause–effect

RCT, randomized controlled trial.
Note: Laboratory experiments excluded.

The chance of bias in different designs of analytical studies is represented in Figure 3.6. Expert opinion and case reports can be highly biased. A double-blind RCT has the least bias, although it does not eliminate bias completely. There is no design that can eliminate all kinds of bias: biases can only be minimized and not eliminated. That possibly is the limitation of all empirical studies.

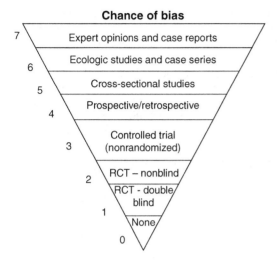

FIGURE 3.6

Chance of bias in different designs of analytical studies. RCT, randomized controlled trial.

References

1. USAID. The DHS Program. www.dhsprogram.com/ – last accessed 9 May 2019.
2. WHO. GATS (Global Adult Tobacco Survey). www.who.int/tobacco/surveillance/gats/en/ – last accessed 9 May 2019.
3. CDC. National Health and Nutrition Examination Survey. www.cdc.gov/nchs/nhanes.htm – last accessed 9 May 2019.
4. Waller KMJ, Wyburn KR, Shackel NA, et al. Hepatitis transmission risk in kidney transplantation (the HINT study): A cross-sectional survey of transplant clinicians in Australian and New Zealand. Transplantation 2018;102(1): 146–153. www.ncbi.nlm.nih.gov/pubmed/28731903
5. Chen X, Yu B, Zhou D, et al. A comparison of the number of men who have sex with men among rural-to-urban migrants with non-migrant rural and urban residents in Wuhan, China: A GIS/GPS-assisted random sample survey study. PLoS One 2015 Aug 4;10(8):e0134712. www.ncbi.nlm.nih.gov/pmc/articles/PMC4524597/
6. Kenny A, Basu G, Ballard M, et al. Remoteness and maternal and child health service utilization in rural Liberia: A population-based survey. J Glob Health 2015 Dec;5(2):020401. www.ncbi.nlm.nih.gov/pmc/articles/PMC4512264/
7. Abu-Zidan FM, Abbas AK, Hefny AF. Clinical "case series": A concept analysis. Afr Health Sci 2012;12:557–562. www.ncbi.nlm.nih.gov/pmc/articles/PMC3598300/
8. Canadian Foundation for AIDS Research. HIV & AIDS History. https://canfar.com/hiv-and-aids/history-of-hiv/ – last accessed 12 May 2019.
9. UK Census. Method of Census Taking. www.ons.gov.uk/ons/guide-method/census/2011/how-our-census-works/about-censuses/methods-of-census-taking/index.html – last accessed 9 May 2019.
10. Korkeila J, Salminen JK, Hiekkanen H, et al. Use of antidepressants and suicide rate in Finland: An ecological study. J Clin Psychiatry 2007;68:505–511. www.ncbi.nlm.nih.gov/pubmed/17474804
11. Pedersen C, Bräuner EV, Rod NH, et al. Distance to high-voltage power lines and risk of childhood leukemia – An analysis of confounding by and interaction with other potential risk factors. PLoS One 2014;9(9):e107096. www.ncbi.nlm.nih.gov/pmc/articles/PMC4178021/
12. Indrayan A, Holt M. Concise Encyclopedia of Biostatistics for Medical Professionals. CRC Press, 2016.

13. Descatha A, Albo F, Lederic A, et al. Lateral epicondylitis and physical exposure at work? A review of prospective studies and meta-analysis. Arthritis Care Res 2016;68(11):1681–1687. https://onlinelibrary.wiley.com/doi/full/10.1002/acr.22874 Supplementary Material at acr22874-sup-0001-suppinfo1.docx

14. Krishnan E, Murtagh K, Bruce B, et al. Attrition bias in rheumatoid arthritis databanks: A case study of 6346 patients in 11 databanks and 65,649 administrations of the Health Assessment Questionnaire. J Rheumatol 2004;31:1320–1326. www.ncbi.nlm.nih.gov/pubmed/15229950

15. Indrayan A, Malhotra RK. Medical Biostatistics, Fourth Edition. CRC Press, 2018.

16. Delgado-Rodriguez M, Llorca J. Bias. J Epidemiol Community Health 2004;58:635–641. http://jech.bmj.com/content/58/8/635.full

17. Elwood M. Forward projection – using critical appraisal in the design of studies. Int J Epidemiol 2002;31:1071–1073. http://ije.oxfordjournals.org/content/31/5/1071.full.pdf

4

Clinical Trials

Medical experiments on human beings are called trials. The objective is to discover or verify the clinical or pharmacological effect of an intervention and to identify its adverse effects. The endpoint could be safety and/or efficacy [1]. The intervention must be potentially beneficial and not harmful. This could be a drug, a surgical procedure, a medical device, some behavioral change, a process of care, or any such intervention.

The regimen research environment is rapidly changing. Safety is increasingly gaining precedence over efficacy. Aspirin, with its marvelous use in cardiac problems, may not have made it to the market today with its side effects of gastric problems. The current paradigm seems to be that a new regimen should be free of toxicity while also efficacious. Perhaps risk–benefit has taken a back seat for daily drugs, but for special drugs such as against cancer, side effects are tolerated and risk–benefit consideration becomes more relevant.

When carefully conducted, clinical trials are the fastest and safest way as of today of evaluating the efficacy and safety of a new regimen under controlled conditions. Although clinical trials have attained central place in product development, many breakthroughs in medicine have occurred without such trials. A recent example is the demonstration of the bacterial origin of gastric ulcer by Marshall, who infected himself with *Helicobacter pylori* and developed gastritis.

Because the subjects are humans in clinical trials, a large number of issues crop up, ranging from ethics to profound variations. Human experimentation cannot be conducted unless sufficient reasons for doing so are present. Ethical considerations, as mentioned in Chapter 2, are more strictly applied to a clinical trial setup than other types of studies. The problems arising from variations and uncertainties were also discussed earlier. This chapter describes various types of clinical trials, their basics, and the conditions under which they provide valid results. The chapter ends with tips for choosing the right design of trial depending on the resources. For further details on how to conduct a clinical trial, see Friedman et al. [2].

4.1 Types of Clinical Trials

From an etiological point of view, clinical trials can be divided into six broad categories: therapeutic trials, diagnostic trials, screening trials, prophylactic trials, preventive and promotive trials in the community, and vaccine trials. Clinical trials are a huge concern and several books have been devoted to this topic. Our description here is brief and introductory. For details see, for example, Chow and Liu [3].

Trials can be done on patients coming to a clinic, or on a community in the field at large. Although clinical trials are mostly for therapeutic modality, they can also be for a prophylactic regimen, such as for amnioinfusion for meconium-stained amniotic fluid at the time of childbirth, or for a diagnostic procedure such as comparison of prostate-specific antigen levels and ultrasound images for prostate cancer. A trial for a screening procedure can also be conducted in a clinic setup, although it is generally conducted in a community. The intervention in the case of diagnostic trials is generally not an external agent but a procedure that can change the diagnosis and thus the course of treatment. A noninvasive procedure does not cause much anxiety except for time and cost, but an invasive procedure has the potential to cause harm to the health of the patient. Field trials are generally done as preventive and promotive regimens. The details of various types of trials are given below.

4.1.1 Therapeutic Trials – Efficacy and Safety

The primary objective of a therapeutic clinical trial usually is to evaluate the safety and efficacy of a treatment regimen in individuals with different levels of severity of disease and of various backgrounds, such as different age, gender, and nutrition status. Extreme care is required because therapeutic trials generally involve exogenous material that may have side effects and may not be beneficial at all relative to the existing modes of therapy. For this reason, before a therapeutic trial is undertaken, it is necessary to be sufficiently convinced regarding nontoxicity and potentiality as a beneficial regimen. Clinical trials are indeed precarious, and they are pursued in humans in phases as described later, particularly for a new formulation or substance such as for drug development. Thus, the previous phases must have provided unequivocal results. The first of them, of course, is a laboratory phase to examine the biochemical properties of the test regimen, and second is an experiment on a suitable animal model that can simulate human conditions. A clinical trial is embarked upon only after success has been achieved in these phases. For research on a therapeutic regimen, make sure that these phases are conducted with convincing success. This requirement is sometimes waived when the therapy or its variation is already in use for some other condition and the trial is to examine its use in a new set of conditions.

Specification of Outcome for Measuring Efficacy

Efficacy is always related to a particular outcome. Terms such as recovery and discharge are vague for the outcomes and they must be clearly specified either in terms of measurements such as glomerular filtration rate for kidney disease, in terms of images such as X-ray for dislocated joint, or in terms of any such objective criterion. Also, the duration after which the outcome is to be assessed should be specified – within a day, within a week, or whatever. This also applies to death. Everybody dies, but if a death occurs 3 months after surgery, should this be ascribed to the surgery? The follow-up period for different outcomes of interest must also be fully specified.

There are other issues as well relating to the outcomes. The actual interest may be in cardiovascular outcomes but, for expediency, change in blood pressure level can be considered as a surrogate endpoint in some cases. Large cohorts and long follow-up are expensive – and surrogates tend to make them expedient. For example, microalbuminuria is a promising surrogate of renal protection in many cases. However, do not use surrogates indiscriminately. Examine first whether they are indeed valid markers for the hard endpoint you are looking for. The surrogate should accurately assess not only the benefit or the lack of it but also the harm. A strong correlate is not necessarily a suitable surrogate.

Safety

A regimen should not be assessed only in terms of its benefits or efficacy. With the possible exception of those that alter lifestyle, no intervention is without risk of side effects and toxicity. Thus, the benefit must be seen in relation to the possible risk. This has special relevance to potentially hazardous regimens. In some situations, safety is more important than efficacy. Some of the side effects, now generally termed as **adverse events**, may be pre-existing or may occur in any case in a person or even a group of persons, but some could be attributed to the regimen. For an account of benefit–risk assessment of various regimens, see Korting and Schafer-Korting [4].

> **Example 4.1: A Therapeutic Trial Comparing Spa and Nonthermal Rehabilitation in the Treatment of Knee Osteoarthritis**
>
> Fazaa et al. [5] randomly divided patients with knee osteoarthritis into two groups. One group received spa therapy consisting of underwater shower, massage jet showers, hydromassage, pool rehabilitation, and peloid therapy. The other group received nonthermal rehabilitation consisting of analgesic physiotherapy, muscle strengthening, and group physical rehabilitation. A blinded evaluation was carried out at day 21 and 12 months following treatment based on the visual analog scale (VAS) of pain, which represented the primary endpoint.
>
> Significant improvement was noted in the spa group at 12 months, but not in the nonthermal group. At day 21, comparison of the two groups revealed no significant difference on the VAS.

4.1.2 Clinical Trials for Diagnostic and Prophylactic Modalities

Whereas most modern trials in clinics are done for therapeutic modalities, many are conducted for other types of medical interventions. The most common of these are trials to assess the efficacy and safety of a new diagnostic procedure and some are conducted to assess the efficacy of prophylactic measures.

Diagnostic Trials

Diagnostic trials are for modalities that help in diagnosis rather than in therapeutics. They are almost invariably conducted in clinics. The intervention in a diagnostic trial is generally a procedure that can change the diagnosis and thus the course of the treatment. Thus, they have the potential to improve decision making and patient management.

From the ethics point of view, noninvasive procedures such as measuring blood pressure and weight do not cause much anxiety except for time, cost, and inconvenience to the patient, but an invasive procedure such as endoscopy has the potential to cause harm to the health of the patient. More care is required for a trial on an invasive diagnostic procedure.

> **Example 4.2: A Diagnostic Trial for Prostate Cancer**
>
> Hartenbach et al. [6] report a prospective diagnostic trial on positron emission tomography (PET)/magnetic resonance imaging (MRI) for the detection of dominant malignant lesions of the prostate. They included 128 prostate lesions and found that PET/MRI has patient-based sensitivity of 95% against postoperative histology.

Prophylactic Trials

Prophylaxis is a procedure that promotes health or controls primordial factors that adversely affect health. As discussed in the next section, a prophylactic trial is generally conducted in the field where a community is involved, although it can also be conducted in a clinical setup. An example of a clinical setup is prophylactic nasal continuous positive airway pressure after major vascular surgery. Amnioinfusion for meconium-stained amniotic fluid in labor at the time of childbirth is also a prophylactic procedure that can be tried for specific types of births. As with all other trials, prophylactic trials are also restricted to a particular segment of the subjects. For example, for a prophylactic drug such as aspirin to reduce cardiovascular events, the participants may be vulnerable people of age 50 years or more.

The principles of clinic-based prophylactic trials are the same as for therapeutic trials. Perhaps a prophylactic procedure is somewhat insulated against harmful effects, thus slight relaxation in ethics may allow stricter control over confounding factors. Community-based trials in the field have a different setup, whether for therapeutic modality, for a prophylactic agent, or for a screening procedure. These are discussed next.

4.1.3 Field Trials for Screening, Prophylaxis, and Vaccines

Field conditions, where a segment of the general population is involved, are different from clinical conditions. Many confounders such as the severity of the patient's condition can be controlled in the clinic but would be difficult to control in the field. In any case, field trials are done for modalities that can be used on a mass scale on the general population or its segment. Thus, they can have wider health policy implications than clinical trials.

In public health, field trials are sometimes done with the health facility as the unit of experiment. The intervention could be training for peripheral workers (such as for Pap smear) to find out whether that improves the case detection rate against a control area where no such training was given. Issues in such trials may be slightly different from those that were discussed earlier in this section for individual-based trials.

Screening Trials

Screening is quite in vogue for cancers. The prostate, lung, colorectal, and ovarian cancer screening trial initiated in 1992 in the United States has enrolled more than 150,000 participants [7]. Nearly half were randomly assigned to the intervention (screening) and the other half remained as control. Whether screening helps in reducing cancer mortality is not certain. Many collateral benefits emerged, though. For example, it was found that chest radiograph abnormalities not suspicious for lung cancer are common, and prostate volume and age are independently associated with increased prostate-specific antigens in men undergoing screening. A second example is a randomized mass screening trial for abdominal aortic aneurysm. Ten-year results show a 73% reduction in mortality by this aneurysm in those screened compared with those not screened [8].

Note how screening trials look like they are based on mass screening, but the procedures used are hospital based. Sankaranarayanan et al. [9] report a community-based trial wherein all persons aged 35 years or older were screened for oral cancer in intervention villages and not screened in the control villages. The screening was done three times at 3-year intervals for signs of oral cancer. There were nearly 60,000 eligible subjects in the intervention group and nearly 55,000 in the control group. The villages were **cluster randomized** rather than individual randomized to receive or not receive the intervention.

The difficulty was, as in most field trials, low compliance when referred for confirmatory examination that has to be done in a hospital. In this trial, compliance was lower than 70%.

Prophylactic Trials in the Field

A prophylactic trial in the field could be for a strategy such as lifestyle changes for coronary disease or could be for vitamin intake – even drugs that are stipulated to prevent the occurrence or recurrence of adverse events. Giving vitamin A supplements to infants and young children to improve their retinol level is an example of such an intervention. Although there is a fine distinction between preventive and prophylactic measures, we are including both in the prophylactic category. Such trials have tremendous value in policy formulation, in saving lives, and in improving health, but they do not receive that kind of attention.

A prophylactic trial is not necessarily conducted in the general population. The vitamin A trial cited in the preceding paragraph is for children. A trial on an educational campaign for responsible sexual behavior may target adolescents. Another trial on hematinic supplementation may target antenatal women of low socio-economic stratum.

Vaccine Trials

The intervention in this case is a potential vaccine to prevent the occurrence or progression of a disease. Vaccine trials are conducted in phases just as therapeutic trials are done but need even more precaution. The need for extra care arises from the applicability of vaccines to a large segment of the populations who are not sick but are at risk, as opposed to therapeutics that is applied only to patients and administered under close supervision. A feature of vaccines is immunogenicity, which might be an important consideration in some diseases, in addition to protective efficacy. In some others, duration of protection may be important. The quality and quantity of immune responses required for protection against infection and against development of disease are scientific challenges. In the case of HIV, for example, there could be a vaccine that inhibits HIV infection, and there could be a vaccine that inhibits or retards the development of disease – AIDS – in those already infected.

In view of the complexities involved in vaccine trials, an additional phase called phase IIB (see phases of a clinical trial later in this chapter) is sometimes advocated. This is also called the "test of concept" phase. The aim of phase IIA could be to establish the schedule of administration for different age groups as it would be most likely a factorial experiment with dose level as one factor and age group as the second factor. Thus, four phases are required for vaccine trials instead of the usual three. The objective of phase IIB is to evaluate whether the vaccine has any (>0%) efficacy at all. In a phase III trial for vaccines, this objective shifts generally to at least 30% efficacy. The participants in phase IIB are not necessarily representative of the target population. For phase III, a representative sample is indicated. Phase IIB also assesses operational efficiency, whereas the objective of phase III is to produce compelling evidence of efficacy for licensure from regulatory agencies.

A phase III trial for the protective efficacy of a vaccine has to be a large-scale trial so that adequate numbers developing the disease, particularly in the control group, are available. The total number of subjects may run into thousands and the follow-up too may go up to several years. Because phase III is an expensive trial for vaccines, phase IIB becomes a highly desirable proposition to indicate whether or not to proceed to phase III. Phase IIB, however, increases the time frame because this too can take at least a couple of years. If the endpoint is not protective efficacy but only immunogenicity level, the trials could be expeditious in reaching a conclusion as immunogenicity can be assessed relatively quickly.

4.1.4 Superiority, Equivalence, and Noninferiority Trials

Regular clinical trials generally have the objective of showing that the test regimen has reasonable efficacy so that it can be adopted for wider use. In this case, the comparison could be with placebo or an existing regimen, but the objective generally is not to demonstrate superiority. A regimen is considered superior to the existing regimen if its performance exceeds it by at least a pre-specified margin. For example, if the existing regimen has 78% efficacy, you can specify that the new regimen must be at least 3% better and must have efficacy of 81% or more to be called superior. If the efficacy is 80%, statistically significant or not, the test regimen is not considered superior under this scheme.

Similarly, equivalence is different from statistically not significant difference. This also requires setting up a margin of clinical indifference within which the new regimen will be considered equivalent to the existing regimen. If the equivalence margin is ±2%, and the comparison is with a regimen with 78% efficacy, the new regimen should have efficacy between 76% and 80%. Such equivalence is called a **therapeutic equivalence**, and this is different from bioequivalence as the latter is for the entire course of the disease progression from one stage to another. Therapeutic equivalence considers only the outcome in the end and not the course of the disease.

More important these days is a noninferiority trial. This also requires a preset margin within which noninferiority is concluded. If you set this margin as 1%, a regimen with efficacy of at least 77% would be considered noninferior to a regimen with 78% efficacy. This kind of trial is done for a regimen which otherwise is less expensive or more convenient, or safer. If noninferiority is established, the noninferior regimen can be recommended for adoption because it is less expensive or more convenient or safer.

There are two challenges in these kinds of trials. First is setting up the margin of clinical indifference. This could be based on your expectation of random variations beyond human control, which could occur anyway, or your clinical assessment of what margin can be allowed without affecting patient management. If the features of the new regimen are highly desirable, a bigger margin may be acceptable both to the physicians and to the patients.

The second challenge is statistical in nature of three types:

1. The analysis of such trials is in reverse gear where the null hypothesis is of inequivalence instead of generally equal performance. This puts the onus on the trial to show equivalence, superiority, or noninferiority.
2. Such trials require a larger sample because the margin of clinical indifference is generally small.
3. More care is required in conducting such trials because a careless trial may unsuspectingly provide equivalence. Also, the existing regimen under comparison must have established good efficacy. Equivalence can occur easily if both have poor performance. The same is true for superiority and noninferiority.

Example 4.3: A Noninferiority Trial of Ibuprofen versus Pivmecillinam for Uncomplicated Urinary Tract Infection (UTI) in Women

Vik et al. [10] assessed whether treatment of uncomplicated UTI with ibuprofen was noninferior to pivmecillinam in achieving symptomatic resolution with a noninferiority margin of 10% (note the large noninferiority margin in this case).

Nonpregnant women aged 18–60 years presenting with symptoms of uncomplicated UTI were screened for eligibility. Patients with informed consent were randomized (1:1 ratio) to treatment with either 600 mg ibuprofen or 200 mg pivmecillinam three times a day for 3 days. Note that blinding may not be effective in this case because of varying dose although the patient, treating physician, and study personnel were blinded to treatment allocation. The primary outcome was the proportion of patients who felt cured by day 4 as assessed from the patient diary. Secondary outcomes included the proportion of patients in need of ancillary treatment with antibiotics and cases of pyelonephritis. A total of 383 women were randomly assigned to treatment with either ibuprofen (n = 194, 181 analyzed) or pivmecillinam (n = 189, 178 analyzed). By day 4, 38.7% of the patients in the ibuprofen group felt cured versus 73.6% in the pivmecillinam group. At 4-weeks follow-up, 53% of patients in the ibuprofen group recovered without antibiotic treatment. Seven cases of pyelonephritis occurred, all in the ibuprofen group. A limitation of the study was the extensive list of exclusion criteria, eliminating almost half of the patients screened.

Ibuprofen was found inferior to pivmecillinam for treating uncomplicated UTIs. The study concluded that ibuprofen alone cannot be recommended as initial treatment to women with uncomplicated UTIs until those women who will develop complications are identified.

4.1.5 Other Types of Clinical Trials

Besides those discussed so far, there are many other types of trials that do not strictly fall into the traditional groups. The main ones include pragmatic trials, multicentric trials, and adaptive trials.

Pragmatic Trials

Regular clinical trials (sometimes called **explanatory trials**) are generally done in ideal conditions that do not exist in practice. The subjects are carefully chosen with strict inclusion and exclusion criteria, administration is done in standard conditions, efforts are made for full compliance, patients get full attention, the results are adjusted for dropouts and other missing observations, and the response is carefully assessed by experts. These steps help to draw a *causal inference* and establish the efficacy of the regimen under trial. However, the actual performance of the regimen in practice may differ. **Efficacy** of a treatment is what is achieved in a trial that simulates optimal conditions, and **effectiveness** is what is achieved in practical conditions when the treatment is actually prescribed. For clarity, the latter is sometimes called **use effectiveness**. Effectiveness could be lower than efficacy because of lack of compliance of the regimen due to cost or inconvenience, inadequate care, nonavailability of the drugs, and so forth, and a mix of cases. These deficiencies are not expected to occur in a regular trial. Experience suggests that nearly three-fourths of patients in general practice do not adhere to or persist with their prescriptions. Thus, patients and maneuvers adopted during a regular trial may not translate their results into patients at large. Generally, such external validity of the trial results is not high, but regular clinical trials do establish the potency of a regimen to effect a change. Effectiveness as obtained by pragmatic trials, on the other hand, is a suitable indicator to decide whether or not to adopt that regimen in practice, or what to expect.

Pragmatic trials are those trials that give high importance to the practical feasibility of the regimen. A regimen may have 90% efficacy but what is that worth if it is extremely difficult to implement? Effectiveness under practical conditions has brought pragmatic trials into focus. The patients recruited for this kind of trial are not homogeneous as in a regular clinical trial, but reflect variations that occur in real clinical practice. Strategies such as **randomization** and **control** are also not structured in this trial. Instead, patients receiving an existing regimen or not receiving any treatment serve as controls. Because of a large number of intervening factors in this setup, interpretation could be difficult. Statistically, the standard deviation could be relatively large. For details of pragmatic trials, see Roland and Torgerson [11].

In the absence of blinding and placebos in a pragmatic trial, the results could be biased because of the **Hawthorne effect**. The expectation of participants could be favorable or unfavorable and that will determine the actual bias. If patients are allowed to choose a treatment, as could occur in practice, a further bias may creep in. Causal inference, which says that the effect is due to a certain regimen, suffers. Thus, a better approach would be to do a pragmatic trial to assess usefulness in real-life situations *after* efficacy in ideal conditions has been established by regular clinical trials.

Example 4.4: A Pragmatic Trial on Amantadine in Patients with Early Parkinson's Disease

Kim et al. [12] examined whether amantadine can prevent the development of dyskinesia in patients with early Parkinson's disease using a pragmatic trial strategy. They recruited drug-naïve patients younger than 70 years of age. The exclusion criteria included the previous use of antiparkinsonian medication, the presence of dyskinesia, significant psychological disorders, and previous history of a hypersensitivity reaction. Patients were consecutively assigned to one of three treatment groups in an open-label fashion: group A-1 ($n = 27$), amantadine first and then levodopa when needed; group A-2 ($n = 27$), amantadine first, dopamine agonist when needed, and then levodopa; and group B ($n = 26$), dopamine agonist first and then levodopa when needed. The primary endpoint was the development of dyskinesia. Twenty-four patients were excluded from the analysis due to various reasons. After exclusion, 5 of the 56 (8.93%) patients developed dyskinesia. Patients in groups A-1 and A-2 tended to develop dyskinesia less often than those in group B, although the differences were not statistically significant.

Note that, because of the open-label design and large exclusions that substantially reduced the size of the groups, and the statistically nonsignificant results, the conclusions drawn in this study may have limited utility.

Multicentric Trials

As the name implies, these are clinical trials that are simultaneously conducted at several centers following a common protocol. The purpose is: (i) to get more cases as one center may not have sufficient cases; (ii) to have a better cross-section of cases as different centers can have different patient profiles; (iii) to study the impact on efficacy and side effects of the varying environments prevailing in different centers; and (iv) to make a more realistic assessment of the reliability of results not just because of more accrual of cases but also by checking that different centers provide consistent results despite each being based on a relatively small sample. All these can help us to be more confident in the results and provide better generalizability.

Multicentric trials pose tough challenges. Most prominent among them is to devise a common protocol – different centers may have different opinions and different problems. Protocol development for a multicentric trial is a long and arduous task, and requires extensive consultation with the investigators at different centers. The collaborators must have a flexible attitude and should come to a consensus to realize a common goal. The second problem is its uniform execution. Some centers may experience unforeseen problems that require deviation from the agreed protocol and investigators at some centers may want deviation after initially agreeing to participate with a common protocol. Patient interest is commonly cited to justify such deviations. Some of these deviations can be so serious as to contaminate the results. The third problem is in arranging the huge funds that a multicentric trial needs. The fourth problem is in analysis of the data. The data from different centers are sent to one place where the data are scrutinized again for inconsistent entries even if already checked at each center. Pooling can be done only after ensuring that the data from different centers are not heterogeneous. This means that center-wise data are analyzed separately and checked for consistency in results for all the centers. A method of stratified analysis such as Mantel–Haenszel chi-square may be used for analyzing data from multicentric trials. If the results differ despite sticking to the uniform protocol, perhaps a new hypothesis can be introduced to explain the differences.

Although varying conditions is an essential ingredient of multicentric trials, they tend to exacerbate due to varying interpretations of the protocol requirements. The difficulty arises when such variations are not acknowledged and go on inadvertently, finally damaging comparability. Thus, these trials need periodic review – much more than single-center trials do. Reviews such as by a **Data Safety and Monitoring Board** help in quality assurance and uniformity across sites. Complex regimens that require intensive training may not be appropriate for multicentric trials.

Despite all the problems just stated, multicentric trials are commonly conducted in view of their positive features. Chen et al. [13] have reported a multicentric trial conducted in the United States on inactivated monovalent influenza virus vaccine. Du Toit et al. [14] have described a multicentric trial in the United Kingdom on different strategies of peanut consumption and avoidance to determine which strategy is most effective in preventing the development of peanut allergy in infants at high risk for the allergy.

Adaptive Trials

Adaptive trials are those that plan to modify one or more aspects of study design (such as sample size) and sometimes even the hypothesis on the basis of the results of interim analysis of data while the trial is progressing. These trials provide flexibility that is not otherwise available in regular trials and can sometimes help in expediting the development process of the regimen when the adaptation plan is correctly executed. There is an opportunity in this design to correct the course of the trial based on the learning from the ongoing trial. However, this plan must be made beforehand at the time of protocol writing and you should be able to anticipate situations where modifications may be needed and also the aspects of design that may possibly need modification. This could be in sample size, participant selection process, allocation process, outcome of interest, or any others.

Despite clear advantages, the adaptive trial is not popular. The first reason for this is that it has to be pre-planned and it is difficult to foresee the modifications needed in future. The second is that changes midway may introduce bias, particularly because the interim data have been reviewed. Control of type I errors to the specified level and maintaining statistical power are difficult in this setup. The third reason is that the statistical analysis of data from such trials is intricate and requires considerable expertise.

A variant of adaptive design is a **two-stage design** under which response rate is assessed in the first stage and only in the case of minimum acceptable response rate is further accrual of cases done for stage 2. Otherwise the trial is stopped. A formal test of hypothesis is done at each stage. Methods are available to optimally determine the sample size n_1 and n_2 for the respective stages that could minimize the total expected sample size. For details, see Evans and Ting [15].

4.2 Basics of Clinical Trials

Certain aspects are basic to almost every trial, such as the arms of a trial, various phases in which a trial is conducted, and randomization. A fair knowledge of these is essential to plan a good trial.

4.2.1 Arms of a Trial

A clinical trial generally will have two arms – the test arm and the control arm – as mentioned earlier, but the test also can have more than one arm if two or more regimens or doses are under investigation. In this case this becomes a **multi-arms trial**. The test arm can also be called the treatment arm if the regimen is for the treatment of a disease, or an experimental arm if it is an experiment.

A clinical trial necessarily contains a group on whom the regimen is tried to find its efficacy and side effects. This group may provide an estimate of the efficacy by itself but would not provide any comparison. Many researchers use the pre-intervention status of the subjects for comparison. This could provide an estimate of the change brought about by the intervention if nothing else has changed between the initial and final measurements. However, part of this effect could be due to placebo and **Hawthorne effect**. You cannot say how much of it is due to pure psychological effect and how much is due to the regimen. Thus, a parallel **control group** is also investigated in most trials and receives a placebo. A group receiving the existing regimen can also serve as control. The purpose of the control arm is to serve as a comparator so that the effect can be meaningfully interpreted.

4.2.2 Phases of a Clinical Trial

A clinical trial is done in three primary phases as follows. Sometimes post-marketing surveillance is also added as the fourth phase.

Phase I Trials

Phase I of a clinical trial is done for the first time on human volunteers to study the pharmacokinetic properties of the regimen, to investigate toxicity, food interactions, and major side effects, and to delineate the maximum tolerated dose. Thus, it is also sometimes called a dose escalation trial. This phase seeks to establish that the regimen is safe in humans and can be pursued further.

It may not be easy to find volunteers for this kind of trial, except possibly hopeless cases who find a ray of hope in the new regimen, or courageous, often healthy people, who agree to participate for some inducement. The inducement should be proportional to the expected discomfort and not excessive, as it could be frowned upon as coercive. Note that healthy subjects can be used in this phase because therapeutic efficacy is not an issue at this stage. In fact, some researchers advocate that phase I should be done on healthy volunteers only except for diseases that compromise tolerance, such as in cancer and other such diseases. For example, Nguyen et al. [16] conducted a phase I trial of an intravenously administered vascular endothelial growth factor trap on patients with choroidal neovascularization due to age-related muscular degeneration. Generally speaking, though, comorbidities in participants should be ruled out so that the side effects are not unnecessarily attributed to the treatment. Symptomatic conditions in any case are part of exclusion criteria, but asymptomatic conditions such as anemia and abnormal lipid profile can also affect the outcome. These also should be excluded. This phase generally needs 20–40 participants.

Because a slow intrapatient dose escalation is either not possible or not practical, investigators often use 5 to 7 doses selected from "safe enough" to "effective enough." The starting dose selection of a phase I trial depends heavily on pharmacology and toxicology from preclinical studies. Although the translation from animal to human is not always a perfect correlation, toxicology studies offer an estimation range of a drug's dose–toxicity profile and the organ sites that are most likely to be affected in humans. Once the starting dose is selected, a reasonable dose escalation scheme needs to be defined. There is no single optimal or efficient escalation scheme for all drugs. Generally, dose levels are selected such that the percentage increments between successive doses diminish as the dose is increased.

Phase II Trials

Phase II of a trial is done on patients for whom the test regimen may be eventually indicated. The objectives of this phase are to investigate potential efficacy in a clinical setup and short-term incidence of side effects, identify a dose schedule for various kinds of cases (such as for mild, moderate, severe conditions; or for children and adults), and to collect further pharmacologic data. A phase II trial could also compare drug-induced effects in individuals with and without comorbidities or taking other drugs (in this phase there is no need to exclude such patients) that will help define exclusion criteria for a phase III trial. However, beware that comorbidities can skew and confound the drug effect. Do not restrict too much because generalizability could suffer.

Phase II also establishes or refutes that the new regimen is likely to meet at least the minimum level of efficacy. If this level is not met, there is no use pursuing the regimen any further. Thus, this is also called the **proof of concept** phase. This is a crucial phase that really establishes whether the regimen is going to be useful or not. The number of participants in this phase is generally 100–150. Sometimes it is a randomized trial with a control group on the pattern of a phase III trial. Failure of phase II helps to identify problems with the regimen and to go back to basics to improve it.

Sometimes phase II is divided into phase IIA and phase IIB. This is more relevant to vaccine trials, which were discussed earlier in a brief summary of these divisions on vaccine trials.

Phase III Trials

Phase III is a large-scale trial to confirm the efficacy and safety meeting the regulatory standard of license. There must be a control group in this phase, and subjects are randomly allocated to the test arm and the control arm. For this reason, this is called a **randomized controlled trial (RCT)**. Generally, 300 or more subjects are recruited for each arm of this trial. The exact number depends on the statistical considerations described in Chapter 8. The number can go up to several thousands. The follow-up must be sufficiently long in phase III for efficacy and side effects to emerge, and to rule out that any relief to the patients is transient. It may take up to 10 years from the start of phase I to the end of phase III.

Phase IV Trials

Very important research these days emanates from monitoring side effects of a drug after it is marketed. Patient preference due to cost, ease of ingestion, ready availability, and other such considerations is also evaluated. This is called **post-marketing surveillance** and is often considered as phase IV of a clinical trial. All adverse reactions or any such events attributable to long-term use of the regimen are monitored. This may be based on several thousands or millions of users. Effectiveness is also evaluated. Recent findings about tamoxifen carrying a risk of endometrial cancer, and arthroscopic surgery not beneficial for osteoarthritis of knee, are results partially attributable to such surveillance. Adverse drug reactions have started to gain prominence among causes of deaths in the United States and this makes phase IV even more important.

4.2.3 Randomization and Matching

The difference in outcome can be legitimately ascribed to the intervention when the participants with and without intervention are equivalent to begin with. Randomization is the process by which participants are allocated to receive one or other treatment. It generates an unpredictable allocation sequence and is a very potent tool to achieve equivalence and to minimize selection bias. Randomization insulates against biased allocation that can occur when participants choose to be in a particular group. This works well for trials on a large number of participants, but occasionally fails for small samples. If sample size is small, the best strategy is to identify pairs of participants matched for baseline characteristics, and randomly allocate one of each pair to the test arm and the other to the control arm.

Randomization should be done with the help of random numbers (Box 4.1) so that there is no pattern. Some trials use nonrandom allocation for which the appropriate term is **controlled trial** after dropping the term "randomized," but it remains controlled because a control group is still present. Nonrandomized controlled trials are valid only when the test and the control groups match for baseline characteristics.

Whether random or nonrandom, the effectiveness of allocation in achieving equivalence can be checked by post-hoc comparison of the participants in the test and the control groups, although some researchers consider it unnecessary as it amounts to doubting the randomization. If there is appreciable difference, appropriate adjustments are made at the time of statistical analysis. A less-realized importance of randomization is that it provides a valid base for using statistical methods because these methods require random samples. Randomization is not random sampling, yet it helps to provide a base to use statistical methods.

Random Allocation of Consecutive Patients Coming to a Clinic

The general practice is to do a trial on consecutive patients reporting in a clinic after excluding those who are not eligible or do not provide consent. If the patients indeed come

BOX 4.1   RANDOM ALLOCATION IN CLINICAL TRIALS

In the wake of unaccounted variations and uncertainties, the best insurance of initial equivalence among groups by far is randomization, though this is not a guarantee. By giving equal opportunity to the subjects to be assigned to one group or the other, it is fair to expect that unaccounted factors such as age, gender, and grade of disease will be distributed nearly equally, thereby helping to achieve baseline homogeneity across groups. No group is likely to have participants of a particular type that can favor or go against the test regimen. Beware, though, that random allocation is not random sampling. The former is a strategy to achieve initial equivalence of the groups so that the difference emerging after the intervention can be legitimately ascribed to the intervention (internal validity), while the latter is for representativeness of the target population so that the results can be generalized (external validity). The objective of random selection is that the participants mirror the target population.

If the number of available eligible subjects is large (say 4000) and a few (say 30, 40, and 45, in three groups) are to be randomly assigned to the three groups, respectively, select 30 + 40 + 45 = 115 distinct random numbers after assigning a serial number to each of the 4000 subjects. All these numbers should be less than or equal to 4000. Decide beforehand that, for example, the first 40 will go to group II, the next 45 to group III, and the last 30 to group I. If the first random number is 2187, the subject with this number goes to group II under this scheme, and if the second is 141, this subject goes to group III, and so on. The website *www.randomization.com* can do all this easily in a more adequate manner. In this example, the number of subjects in the groups is unequal, but generally these numbers would be equal.

If the patients are consecutively attending a clinic, a **systematic allocation** beginning with assigning the first patient to a random group is easiest to implement. This works well when the arrival of patients does not follow any specific pattern. Another method is to include all consecutive eligible patients arriving in a clinic beginning at a pre-specified date. In addition, there are methods such as block and stratified randomization, as presented in this section.

in random order and the consent does not introduce any bias, then the even-numbered patients can be assigned to one group and the odd-numbered patients to the other group. For three or more groups, the first patient can be randomly allocated to any group by, say, drawing lots and the remainder allocated in a systematic way. If there are four groups and the first patient is randomly allocated to group 3, then the allocation for the incoming patients will be group 4, 1, 2, 3, 4, 1, etc., respectively.

This sequential scheme will fail in achieving unbiased allocation if the subjects follow a known or unknown design in the sequence of their arrival. Also, it is difficult to enforce blinding (see next section) with this kind of allocation. A more acceptable method is to draw or generate a random number between 1 and K (both inclusive), where K is the number of groups. When an eligible subject arrives, assign him or her to the group bearing this number. If the random number drawn is 3, then the subject is allocated to group 3. If the random number is 1, then the subject goes to group 1, and so on. This is called **simple randomization**. This requires the number of subjects in each group to be the same.

A difficulty in simple randomization is that one particular group may have its full quota of subjects much before the other groups. This is called imbalance because the subjects appearing late will not have the chance to be allocated to the group that is already completed. In that case, the process of allocation can continue as follows, although this also is not free from flaws. The subjects for whom the allocated group turns out to be the already completed group are excluded from the trial. Suppose there are three groups, and each is planned to have 30 subjects. It is possible in simple randomization that the full 30 are allocated to group 2 when group 1 has only 22 and group 3 has 26 after the allocation of 78 subjects. In this case, ignore the 79th subject if the random number for this subject is 2. This subject is not included in any group. If the random number for the 80th subject is 3, then the subject is assigned to group 3. This process continues until each group has its full quota of 30 subjects. This procedure may mean wastage of some eligible subjects. Because it is not fair to assign the last few subjects to only one or two groups and deny them the chance to be theoretically in the other groups, this scheme of randomization is not considered adequate.

If there are only two groups, the allocation can also be made by tossing a coin, but this should be done before the patient physically appears. Otherwise, the patient's confidence may be shaken. It is sometimes considered convenient to include patients who report to a clinic on alternate days or during a specified time of the day. This may introduce bias because some patients may choose a time and day according to the availability of a particular physician, and the management of cases by this particular physician may have prognostic implications. Similarly, allocation of subjects on the basis of even and odd date of birth may apparently look random but can be misused. All such methods are called **quasi-random allocation**. The biggest problem is that such allocations cannot be kept blind and the chances of bias in assessment remain.

Block, Cluster, and Stratified Randomization

Another popular method is block randomization. This requires that subjects are divided into M blocks of size $2n/M$ each, where n is the stipulated size of each of the two groups. The sample size in each group is not necessarily equal, but we are giving the details for the simple case of equal groups. The block size must be a multiple of the number of groups. For two groups, the block size can be 4 or 6 or 8 but not 5 or 7. If you have enrolled a total of 80 subjects, you can make 20 blocks of four subjects each. Within each block, allocate two subjects at random to group 1 and the other two to group 2. Thus, you can have one of the following allocations:

(1,1,2,2), (1,2,1,2), (1,2,2,1), (2,2,1,1), (2,1,1,2), (2,1,2,1)

While allocating randomly, one of these six is randomly chosen. This method is called block randomization and can be implemented with the help of websites such as *www.randomization.com*.

An advantage of block randomization is that the possibility of one group becoming full before the other is ruled out. But the difficulty is that you know that the fourth subject after the first three going to groups 1,1,2 must go to group 2. Thus, blinding is also difficult in this scheme. To remedy this, several random block sizes are advocated that are concealed from the investigators.

For a large trial, particularly in a community, such as for evaluating the impact of special education on sexual behavior in adolescents at school, you can randomly allocate five schools out of the 10 participating to receive the education and the other five to serve as controls. This is called cluster randomization. Schools serve as a cluster in this case because all students in the selected schools will be included.

Another method, though rarely used, is stratified randomization. This ensures that the subjects with important covariates at baseline, such as severity of disease, are equally distributed to the groups. If the study is on an anticipated wonder dose that controls blood sugar level for one month, and if it is known that the effect could be different in males of age <50 years than females of age ≥50 years, you may want to divide the enrolled subjects as <50 M, ≥50 M, <50 F, and ≥50 F so that each of these strata is adequately represented, and then allocate them equally to group 1 and group 2. The reasons why this kind of randomization is not popular are that it requires information on stratifying characteristics before starting the trial, it requires independent randomization in each stratum, and the method of analysis of data becomes complex because it needs to take account of the stratifying factors. However, multicentric trials commonly use stratified randomization with each center as a stratum.

Matching

As already stated, randomization works well in the long run and is advocated for a setup in which an adequate number of eligible subjects who are willing to be randomized are available. If the number of cases is not as large, examine if **matched pairs** are available and if the two persons forming a pair can be randomized to receive the test and the control regimen. Matched pair design may be suitable for acute rather than chronic conditions. If the number of eligible subjects is even less, controls may have to come from elsewhere. In this situation, matching becomes even more important.

Experiments using matching instead of randomization are called **quasi-experiments**. This term is used for all those experiments and trials where the element of randomization is missing. This may happen because randomization was not feasible or for any other reason. Evidence from such experiments is not considered as strong as from randomized trials.

In the case of matching, ideally all relevant characteristics that might influence the outcome, except those under study, should be matched on a one-to-one basis. This does not stop at age and sex as is sometimes done. Nonetheless, comprehensive matching for all prognostic factors may not be feasible in all situations and some constraints on conclusions may become necessary. For example, in a trial of a new oral antidiabetic drug, the subjects in the test and the control group could be matched for age, sex, and, perhaps, obesity, but it may be difficult to match for genetic factors and stress conditions. These two factors can also influence the outcome. The other important prognostic factors in this case are severity of disease and any coexisting disease. They may have to be adjusted at the time of analysis.

In addition, matching can be tried only for known factors. There may be other factors in the epistemic domain about which nobody knows yet – an uncertainty that still remains. Note that *randomization has the advantage of giving chance to the known as well as the unknown factors to be equally distributed.* Matching lacks this feature.

It is possible in some situations to simultaneously give a different treatment to known pairs such as two eyes or two limbs of the same person. Twin studies also come under this category. Randomization can be done within each pair to determine which one will receive the test regimen and which the control regimen. Thus, randomization and matching can go on simultaneously – they are not mutually exclusive. If the trial is on a comparison of methods such as pulse oximeter and sphygmomanometer blood pressure readings at the same time in both arms, many pairs would be easily available. In some other situations, it could be extremely difficult to find matched pairs, such as the same severity of glaucoma in the two eyes or both limbs with the same degree of paralysis.

It may not be possible to find a control aged 62 years for matching with a case of the same age. In most situations, matching within ±2 years for adults is considered adequate.

Such relaxation can be possibly allowed for other factors as well. In tough situations, **group matching** is done instead of one-to-one matching. This means that if 30% of cases are females, 30% of controls are also females; if 60% of cases have body mass index ≤ 25 kg/ m^2, a similar percentage is in the controls. This is also called **frequency matching**.

You can see that matching may mean incurring extra cost due to baseline investigation on a large number of subjects, many of whom may be discarded as unmatchable. Generalizability suffers as the control group is somewhat distorted and interactions cannot be properly assessed. Special statistical methods are required to analyze such paired data, particularly when one-to-one matched.

4.2.4 Control Groups in a Clinical Trial

Controls are needed for fair comparison – like with like. Two broad kinds of controls can be identified. One is in the case of a before-and-after trial or in a repeated measures study where the baseline status of the subjects is used as control. In the case of crossover trials also, the same subject is used as the control. The other is a separate group of subjects on a control regimen. This is called **parallel control**, although the term "parallel" is often dropped.

Controls are needed to realistically assess the difference brought about by intervention. They provide a yardstick against which gains are measured. Parallel controls might match for baseline because of randomization, but it is also necessary for them to be exposed to the same procedure and maneuvers as the cases, except for the regimen under trial.

In the case of disease, ethics requires that the controls be given an existing proven therapy. There is always a question about using a placebo on patients who are known to have the disease because they need an active ingredient to treat their ailment. However, **placebos** can be used in the following situations:

1. No standard treatment is available, i.e., the existing treatment modality has very doubtful results – perhaps no better than placebo.
2. New evidence has emerged regarding the doubtful efficacy of the standard therapy.
3. The existing regimen is too costly or is rarely available to the population at large.
4. Patients have already been given standard treatment and not benefited, and no second line of treatment is available for them.
5. The test regimen is an add-on to the existing regimen. This means that all patients in the trial, including those in the control group, would receive the normally prescribed therapy anyway.
6. Patients refuse to accept existing therapy and are willing to be part of a trial where they know that they can receive placebo.
7. Where for compelling, scientifically sound and methodological reasons, a placebo-controlled group is necessary to determine the efficacy and safety of a regimen.
8. Where a regimen is being investigated for a minor condition and the patients who receive placebo will not be subject to any additional risk of serious or irreversible harm.

In situations where these conditions are not met, a group on existing therapy can serve as the control. In any case, other provisions such as appropriate ethical and scientific review by a third party must be adhered to so that the validity of placebo can be examined in addition to the other aspects.

Sometimes randomization is blamed for exposing some patients to an inferior regimen. In fact, this is no fault of the method of randomization, but is due to wrong choice of intervention. Including a known inferior or a potentially harmful treatment in a trial is unethical. Placebo can be used only in restricted conditions as just enumerated, otherwise the control group receives the existing therapy. As mentioned earlier, the motto "Do no harm" must be scrupulously followed in all medical research, including clinical trials.

An apparently simple approach could be a comparison of the group on a new regimen with a group previously treated with an alternative regimen. The latter are called **historical controls**. They must be similar subjects but the flaw in this approach is that some factors may have changed over time, such as diagnostic technology and profile of cases. Thus, use this approach only after ensuring that no such change has occurred. If a change has occurred, it should be properly accounted for in the interpretation of the results.

The associated concepts of blinding, concealment of allocation, and masking are explained later in this chapter.

4.3 Validity of a Clinical Trial

As discussed in Chapter 3, validity is the ability to provide correct answers to the questions under investigation. In the context of clinical trials, besides randomization and other features of design as already discussed, the main tools to achieve validity include the proper selection of subjects, blinding, and adequate compliance. Details of these are as follows.

4.3.1 Selection of Participants

The validity of results of a clinical trial depends heavily on proper selection of participants. They should really represent the target group. When an inordinately large number of eligible subjects are available that pass the inclusion and exclusion criteria, the participants must be randomly selected for inclusion in the trial. This allows generalizability. One method could be systematic (e.g., every fifth), and the second method is to include consecutive eligible patients arriving in a clinic/hospital within a specified period. In addition, random numbers can be used for selection as per the procedure mentioned earlier.

Ethical considerations such as informed consent can preselect a biased group. Some patients or clinicians may have a strong preference for a particular therapy and they can refuse randomization. Some eligible patients may refuse to participate when they are told that they could be randomized for placebo or the existing therapy. Some may refuse because it is a trial and not a treatment per se. Considerable efforts may be needed to keep such refusals to a minimum.

Size of the Trial

The number of subjects should be reasonably large in each group so that the full clinical spectrum is represented and a trend, if present, can clearly emerge. This also ensures the reliability of results. It should have adequate power (Chapter 8) to detect a minimum medically relevant difference when present.

The discovery of completely new treatment strategies that are clearly effective, such as Viagra, is rare. Most trials are on a variation of the existing modalities in the hope that some improvement in a specific type of case can be achieved. Additional benefits from such minor different modalities are also likely to be small because the comparison is with the existing modality and not with placebo. Statistical power considerations tell that detection of small difference requires a large-sized trial. For this reason, trials involving thousands of patients are increasingly becoming the norm. For example, for comparing alteplase and streptokinase with and without heparin in suspected acute myocardial infarction, a trial on more than 20,000 patients was done [17] to reach a reliable conclusion.

However, the size of the trials cannot continue to increase forever. Large trials are expensive, difficult to manage, and run the risk of lacking uniformity. Insufficient availability of patients in one center may force you to conduct a multicentric trial. This is even more difficult to manage as centers may like to retain their freedom to adopt modifications as per their wisdom. Thus, a balance is required. In addition, basic characteristics of cases such as food habits and nutrition level in different centers may differ that may confound the results. This can happen even when uniform eligibility criteria are followed.

For a graduate thesis, time and expenses (such as for kits) tend to limit the size of the trial. Rarely would a thesis-based trial involve more than 100 patients per arm. In many cases, only 30 cases and 30 controls are included. Less than these would not be adequate even for training purposes.

4.3.2 Blinding, Concealment of Allocation, and Masking

Blinding, concealment of allocation, and masking are now considered highly desirable ingredients for a successful trial, though not essential. These three terms seem to convey the same meaning, but that is not actually so.

Blinding

An important method to minimize bias is blinding. When patients do not know that they are receiving placebo or therapy then this is called **single-blinding**. This eliminates the possibility of patients psychologically changing their response when they know that they are in the placebo group. They may feel discriminated against. Also, patients who know that they are receiving a new regimen may either exhibit increased anxiety or may have favorable expectations. The objective of the trial is to assess the effect of the treatment and not the expectation of participants. Bias resulting from all these is called the **Hawthorne effect**, as mentioned earlier.

If the assessing physician also does not know that the patient belongs to the test group or the control group, this is called **double-blinding**. This removes the possible bias of the physician in patient assessment – at least it mitigates against any subconscious influence of the assessor on the outcome. Such blinding is an important criterion for validity of the results of a trial. A double-blind RCT is considered a "gold standard" to assess the efficacy of a new regimen. Sometimes the results are statistically evaluated without breaking the code for case and control group to eliminate statistician's bias. Then the trial is called **triple-blind**. The codes are broken after the analysis is over.

Although morality issues are attached to blinding because some information is withheld from participants, it has distinct scientific advantages. It not only reduces possible bias in responses and assessments but in fact can improve compliance and retention of subjects by clearly demonstrating that all are being treated alike. Merely stating in a protocol that blinding would be done is not enough. Give full details of how the blinding is to be implemented, including how the two groups would be assessed and handled similarly for medical maneuvers. The difference between the two should only be the active regimen under test, and nothing else that can possibly alter the outcome.

BOX 4.2   METHODS OF BLINDING AND MASKING

Blindness is the term used for patients and assessors. To implement blinding faithfully, it is necessary to have a referee who keeps the code and assigns subjects to the test or control group according to a pre-devised plan such as random allocation. See the text for the meaning of single-blinding, double-blinding, and triple-blinding. Many times, the term blinding is used to include masking.

Masking is the term used for apparent similarity of the regimens under trial and of the procedures followed during the trial. The top ingredient of masking is that the placebo or control should have exactly the same physical properties – packaging, labeling, handling, color, size, shape, smell, and possibly taste – so that patients and nurses are not able to distinguish between them, nor the physician who is assessing the outcome. This provides insurance against a prejudiced response by patients and biased assessment by investigators. The control subjects must pass through the same medical maneuvers in terms of physical and laboratory assessments, diet, change of wards or beds so that there is no scope: (i) for deciphering the group to which the patient belongs; and (ii) for a biased response due to differential procedures. Masking is making arrangements that the identity of the groups does not break till the trial is over.

Blinding is easier said than done. Some features of blinding are given in Box 4.2. There are situations where blinding is not possible. For assessing outcomes such as quality of life, readmissions, and falls after hip surgery, blinding is just not possible if one maneuver is keeping patients in hospital for a specified number of days, and the other is early discharge and home rehabilitation. In most surgical interventions, the control has to be another kind of surgery, and not a "placebo." Sham surgery may be unethical because it exposes a patient to surgical risks. In either case, it is extremely difficult to enforce blinding in a surgical trial. The patient can be kept blind after proper consent, but the surgeon definitely knows. However, mechanisms can be developed that all assessments subsequent to the operation are done by another surgeon who does not know whether the patient belongs to the test surgery or the control surgery.

Concealment of Allocation

Rigid coding systems such as code A for the treatment and code B for the placebo should be avoided because breaking the code for one patient breaks it for the rest of trial. Allocation concealment is the procedure to ensure that the person allocating the treatment in a clinical trial is not able to guess what treatment the next person is going to get. The allocation of the subject to the treatments under trial is generally done with the help of opaque sealed envelopes that contain the allocation. They are opened only after the subject's name and other identification have been written on the envelope so that the treatment cannot be changed. Concealment means that the envelopes are in random sequence and the serial on the envelope is not able to reveal what treatment it contains. A third party keeps all the records of the random sequence. This prevents bias of the allocating person in choosing which subject gets which treatment. Using a pharmacy as the third party is common for concealment of allocation in the case of drug trials. Concealment operationalizes the blinding and states how this was implemented. The details of this should be given in the protocol itself.

Do not confuse concealment of allocation with blinding. Concealment seeks to protect the sequence of the assignment whereas blindness is not knowing who is getting what. The question of sequence before actual allocation does not come in the case of blinding, but it comes in the case of concealment of allocation. Concealment is always feasible, but blinding is not always feasible. Blinding protects the secrecy after allocation and is a safeguard for response and ascertainment bias that occurs after the treatment is administered. When the allocation is not concealed, even random assignment can be subverted. This could lead to selective withdrawals before the treatment starts. An example of how all this was implemented in a trial on antibiotic prophylaxis is given by Sheth et al. [18].

Masking

Many times, the term blinding is used to include masking, although masking is different. Masking is the collection of steps that make the test and the control regimen difficult to distinguish by subjects and assessors alike. There is a natural curiosity in participants and assessors to decipher the treatment. Thus, continuous vigilance is required. Masking ensures that the allocation remains concealed throughout the trial.

The top ingredient of masking is that the placebo or the control regimen has exactly the same physical properties – packaging, labeling, handling, color, size, shape, smell, and possibly taste. They must be administered in an undifferentiated fashion. If one regimen is once-a-day (OD) and the other twice-a-day (BD), the OD group should be given a placebo as a second dose to give it an identical look.

The next ingredient of masking is that the control subjects must pass through the same medical rituals in terms of physical and laboratory assessments, diet, change of wards or beds, duration and frequency of examination, and attention paid to the complaints, so that there is no scope for deciphering the group to which the patient belongs and of altered response due to differential procedures. Once blinding is done, this kind of masking will naturally follow. Yet, masking is the arrangements made to ensure that the identity of groups is not revealed till the trial is over. In fact, this can improve compliance and retention of subjects by clearly demonstrating that groups are being treated equally. While trying to implement a perfect masking, beware of regimen-specific complaints such as bradycardia in those receiving beta-blockers. Such complaints can still unmask the code. A very careful strategy may have to be devised in some situations so that bias is minimized, if not eliminated.

A protocol should provide complete details of how masking would be done, otherwise the audience remains skeptical. They must be convinced that masking would remain in effect until all opportunities of bias have passed.

Example 4.5: A Double-Blind RCT on Probiotic Supplements for Gestational Diabetes Mellitus

Kijmanawat et al. [19] conducted a randomized double-blind placebo-controlled trial on pregnant women with diet-controlled gestational diabetes at 24–28 weeks of gestation and randomized to receive either probiotic supplements or placebo daily for 4 consecutive weeks. Primary outcomes were mean differences in insulin resistance, fasting insulin, and fasting plasma glucose between the two groups. Data from 28 patients in the probiotic group and 29 in the placebo group were analyzed. The researchers observed that this supplement significantly lowered fasting glucose and increased insulin sensitivity, and the authors suggested that probiotic supplements may be considered as an adjunct treatment for glycemic control in these subjects.

4.3.3 Compliance

Bias can still occur in subtle or unknown ways in an RCT despite random allocation and blinding. A major source of bias is loss to follow-up. If the follow-up requires recalling or revisiting patients, some may not turn up or refuse to cooperate, some may be untraceable, and some may die from unrelated causes. Even if the outcome assessment is within the hospital stay, some can leave against medical advice. Another factor that could affect a clinical trial is the need to change the treatment modality midway if a patient develops a serious illness. Thus, there may be patients who did not follow the full regimen. This is called partial compliance. The best strategy is to anticipate and take pre-emptive steps to minimize such losses. Also, plan to adjust the results if needed.

Another important aspect of compliance is participants intentionally flushing the drug (or placebo) down the toilet. If this is done because of side effects, it certainly adds to the bias. The patient will hardly ever confess having done so and this bias may never surface. Another instance of bias can arise if a patient occasionally takes a double dose after having missed the previous one. A side effect may occur that otherwise would not if the prescription is adhered to, and the efficacy may also alter due to such aberrations. If there are few such patients, examine if these can be excluded as dropouts without affecting the validity of the trial.

Suppose 2 patients out of 500 randomized to receive placebo exhibited liver failure and it is subsequently discovered that these patients received the test drug due to an administrative error. Extra care is needed in a clinical trial that such errors do not occur, and one has to remain on guard while monitoring the administration process. If a lapse is found, the analysis will have to be geared to the new realities.

Another form of lack of compliance is when patients are switched from one group to the other as per their wishes.

4.3.4 Uncertainties in Clinical Trials

In Chapter 1, we mentioned the large number of sources of uncertainties in medical research. These sources are particularly prominent in clinical trials. In addition, there are considerations such as equipoise that are typical to clinical trials. All these have to be properly managed in a clinical trial setup so that valid results are obtained.

Equipoise

Uncertainty about the outcome is considered a moral prerequisite for a valid trial. **Equipoise** is espoused as the essence of this **uncertainty principle**. Among various equipoises, the most important is **clinical equipoise**. This is collective uncertainty among clinicians about the efficacy of the regimens under trial. (Published definitions of equipoise vary and are often conflicting.) Ricotta and Piazza [20] cite the example of carotid endarterectomy and carotid artery stenting for clinical equipoise, although in their opinion these are complementary therapies. Clinical equipoise is the condition under which doctors would rationally accept randomization for their patients. This also provides insurance against prejudiced assessment of patients by the investigators. In addition, the groups should be such that there is a priori uncertainty about the efficacy of the test therapy in them. This is called **patient equipoise** and helps to ensure that the patients are homogeneous material. The third is the **personal equipoise** of clinicians so that they do not feel uncomfortable about their own views regarding the patients to be included in the trial. A particular clinician may have a strongly positive or a very bitter feeling about a regimen even though clinical equipoise in terms of collective uncertainty exists. A clinician who is convinced that one treatment is better than another for a particular patient cannot ethically agree to randomization. Personal equipoise may be difficult to achieve, but efforts can be made by discussing evidence regarding the underlying uncertainties and trying to be certain that equipoise does indeed exist. Cheng et al. [21] have discussed these three types of equipoise in the context of a trial for melioidosis, and the concepts are explained very well.

Statistical Uncertainties

It is generally believed that statistically significant (see Chapter 11) better performance of a new regimen under trial compared with the existing regimen is the gold standard for accepting the new regimen. However, such "significance" is under intense debate for its utility in reaching a valid conclusion. Also, this "statistical significance" controls the type I error of wrongly accepting a result only under strict statistical conditions. It requires that the sample is random – at least, representative of the target population – and the distribution of values is the same as required for the statistical test used for evaluating significance, and there are no errors in the data. Many researchers do not worry about the distributional aspect unless it is dramatically different. In addition, in clinical trials, the inclusion and exclusion criteria can be too strict, showing a benefit to the restricted class of patients but having little benefit for the general class of patients. Also, subgroup analyses are sometimes done to identify a beneficial segment and the results are rarely adjusted for testing multiple hypotheses. All these substantially increase uncertainty in the results and limit the applicability.

Sometimes a regimen is approved on the basis of a single-arm trial. Remember that such a trial does not establish superiority or equivalence. Belinostat was approved for relapsed peripheral T-cell lymphoma on the basis of such an uncontrolled trial [22]. Even in RCTs, the effect size may be statistically significant due to a large sample but actually too small to have clinical significance. Some trials look at surrogates such as progression-free survival where quality of life is possibly more relevant. Just beware of such fallacies and take steps to avoid them.

4.4 Choosing a Design for an Efficacy Trial

After describing so many types of trials, it could be expedient to provide a guideline on choosing an appropriate design. The choice depends on a host of factors such as the phase of the trial, research question, and resources available. It also depends on whether the new treatment is for a condition for which an effective treatment already exists, whether the disease is life-threatening, how great the risk is to the participants, availability of cases, and other such considerations [23]. This section is restricted to efficacy trials that are generally phase III trials.

Box 4.3 gives choices for experimental strategy in order of preference for efficacy trials. Use the first type of design wherever feasible. If not feasible, use the second, and so on. The validity of the trial is best when the first strategy is used and declines as we go down the list in this box.

**BOX 4.3   CHOOSING A DESIGN OF A TRIAL FOR
EFFICACY IN ORDER OF PREFERENCE**

- Whenever feasible, choose a random sample of subjects from the target population. Divide eligible subjects randomly into the test and control groups. Blind the subjects and the observers about allocation and make arrangements for this to remain concealed until the results are available.
- If random selection is not possible, choose the available subjects who meet the inclusion and exclusion criteria and allocate them randomly to the test and control groups. Blinding is desirable wherever feasible.
- If random allocation is not feasible, match the cases and controls for their baseline characteristics. Use this strategy for small samples even if randomization is feasible.
- If matching is not feasible, use a before–after strategy, i.e., assess the subjects before the intervention and after the intervention.
- If baseline information is difficult to assess, use existing information on the baseline of another group of similar subjects.

References

1. ICH. International Conference on Harmonisation Guidelines for Good Clinical Practice (E6). 1996. www.ich.org/fileadmin/Public_Web_Site/ICH_Products/Guidelines/Efficacy/E6/E6_R1_Guideline.pdf – last accessed 15 May 2019
2. Friedman LM, Furberg CD, De Mets DL, et al. Fundamentals of Clinical Trials, Fifth Edition. Springer, 2015.
3. Chow S-C, Liu J-P. Design and Analysis of Clinical Trials: Concepts and Methodologies, Third Edition. John Wiley, 2013.
4. Korting HC, Schafer-Korting M (Eds.). The Benefit/Risk Ratio: A Handbook for the Rational Use of Potentially Hazardous Drugs. CRC Press, 1998.
5. Fazaa A, Souabni L, Ben Abdelghani K, et al. Comparison of the clinical effectiveness of thermal cure and rehabilitation in knee osteoarthritis: A randomized therapeutic trial. Ann Phys Rehabil Med 2014 Dec;57(9–10):561–569. www.ncbi.nlm.nih.gov/pubmed/25447748
6. Hartenbach M, Hartenbach S, Bechtloff W, et al. Combined PET/MRI improves diagnostic accuracy in patients with prostate cancer: A prospective diagnostic trial. Clin Cancer Res 2014 Jun 15;20(12):3244–3253. http://clincancerres.aacrjournals.org/content/20/12/3244.long
7. Oken MM, Marcus PM, Hu P, et al. Baseline chest radiograph for lung cancer detection in the randomized Prostate, Lung, Colorectal and Ovarian Cancer Screening Trial. J Natl Cancer Inst 2005;97:1832–1839. http://jnci.oxfordjournals.org/content/97/24/1832.full.pdf+html
8. Lindholt JS, Juul S, Fasting H, et al. Preliminary ten-year results from a randomised single-centre mass screening trial for abdominal aortic aneurysm. Eur J Vasc Endovasc Surg 2006;32:608–614. www.sciencedirect.com/science/article/pii/S1078588406003364
9. Sankaranarayanan R, Mathew B, Jacob BJ, et al. Early findings from a community based, cluster-randomized, controlled oral cancer screening trial in Kerala, India: The Trivandrum Oral Cancer Screening Study Group. Cancer 2000;88:664–673. www.ncbi.nlm.nih.gov/pubmed/10649262
10. Vik I, Bollestad M, Grude N, et al. Ibuprofen versus pivmecillinam for uncomplicated urinary tract infection in women – A double-blind, randomized non-inferiority trial. PLoS Medicine 2018;15(5):e1002569. www.ncbi.nlm.nih.gov/pmc/articles/PMC5953442/.

11. Roland M, Torgerson DJ. Understanding controlled trials: What are pragmatic trials? BMJ 1998;316:285. www.bmj.com/content/316/7127/285.short

12. Kim A, Kim YE, Yun JY, et al. Amantadine and the risk of dyskinesia in patients with early Parkinson's disease: An open-label, pragmatic trial. J Mov Disord 2018;11(2):65–71. www.ncbi.nlm.nih.gov/pmc/articles/PMC5990909/

13. Chen WH, Jackson LA, Edwards KM, et al. Safety, reactogenicity, and immunogenicity of inactivated monovalent influenza A (H5N1) virus vaccine administered with or without AS03 adjuvant. Open Forum Infect Dis 2014 Oct 8;1(3):ofu091. www.ncbi.nlm.nih.gov/pmc/articles/PMC4324222/

14. Du Toit G, Roberts G, Sayre PH, et al. Randomized trial of peanut consumption in infants at risk for peanut allergy. N Engl J Med 2015 Feb 26;372(9):803–813. www.nejm.org/doi/full/10.1056/NEJMoa1414850

15. Evans S, Ting N. Fundamental Concepts for New Clinical Trialists. CRC Press, 2015.

16. Nguyen QD, Shah SM, Hafiz G, et al. A phase I trial of an IV-administered vascular endothelial growth factor trap for treatment in patients with choroidal neovascularization due to age-related macular degeneration. Ophthamol 2006;113:1522e1–1522e14. www.ncbi.nlm.nih.gov/pubmed/16876249

17. The International Study Group. In-hospital mortality and clinical course of 20 891 patients with suspected acute myocardial infarction randomised between alteplase and streptokinase with or without heparin. Lancet 1990;336:71–75. https://doi.org/10.1016/0140-6736(90)91590-7

18. Sheth J, Rath S, Tripathy D. Oral versus single intravenous bolus dose antibiotic prophylaxis against postoperative surgical site infection in external dacryocystorhinostomy for primary acquired nasolacrimal duct obstruction – A randomized study. Indian J Ophthalmol 2019 Mar;67(3):382–385. www.ncbi.nlm.nih.gov/pubmed/30777957

19. Kijmanawat A, Panburana P, Reutrakul S, et al. Effects of probiotic supplements on insulin resistance in gestational diabetes mellitus: A double-blind randomized controlled trial. J Diabetes Investig 2019 Jan;10(1):163–170. www.ncbi.nlm.nih.gov/pmc/articles/PMC6319478/

20. Ricotta JJ 2nd, Piazza M. Carotid endarterectomy or carotid artery stenting? Matching the patient to the intervention. Perspect Vasc Surg Endovasc Ther 2010;22:124–136. www.ncbi.nlm.nih.gov/pubmed/20858617

21. Cheng AC, Lowe M, Stephens DP, et al. Ethical problems of evaluating a new treatment for melioidosis. BMJ 2003;327:1280–1282. www.ncbi.nlm.nih.gov/pmc/articles/PMC286254/

22. Lee HZ, Kwitkowski VE, Del Valle PL, et al. FDA approval: Belinostat for the treatment of patients with relapsed or refractory peripheral T-cell lymphoma. Clin Cancer Res 2015 Jun 15;21(12):2666–2670. http://clincancerres.aacrjournals.org/content/21/12/2666.long

23. Evans CH Jr., Ildstad ST (Eds.). Small Clinical Trials: Issues and Challenges. National Academies Press (US), 2001.

5

Observational Studies

Observational studies were briefly discussed in Chapter 3. This chapter contains details.

Some 'interventions' occur naturally with no human intervention. Some people exposed to iodine deficiency in water and some women naturally have a high body mass index. The study of such naturally occurring events can provide invaluable help in studying cause–effect relationships with conviction. Such a study can be based on records or on actual observations, or a combination of both. This is generally categorized as an observational study because it requires recording of observations only – sometimes also referred to as an **epidemiological study**. Whereas both beneficial and harmful "natural interventions" can be studied by observational studies, such studies are particularly helpful in studying the effect of harmful processes and conditions because, for them, human intervention is ruled out. For example, you cannot ask any group of people to live with polluted air for 10 years to see the health consequences.

Because there is no deliberate human intervention (such as a drug) in this setup, such studies carry little risk of harm to subjects or society. However, such a study is generally conducted for specific groups such as those with high disease prevalence – thus, extrapolation to the general population is not immediate. Many observational studies are done in a hospital setup rather than in a community.

As mentioned earlier, there are three basic formats in which an observational study can be carried out – prospective, retrospective, and cross-sectional. A summary of these is given in Box 5.1. This chapter describes these formats and discusses their merits and demerits so that a judicious choice can be made depending on the problem at hand.

5.1 Prospective Studies

Let us pursue an example similar to the one we gave in Chapter 3. Suppose our interest is in finding out how much maternal anemia affects gestational age of the newborn. Anemia is the antecedent and gestational age is the outcome in this study. The natural format for studying this relationship is that antenatal women with different levels of Hb are selected and followed for gestational age of their babies. Antecedents are assessed prior to the outcome in this format in the sequence in which they naturally occur. A study following such a design is called a prospective study. As some follow-up is essential in this format, this is also called a **follow-up study**.

**BOX 5.1   BASICS OF PROSPECTIVE, RETROSPECTIVE,
AND CROSS-SECTIONAL STUDIES**

Prospective Study: Investigates outcome for known antecedents. Requires follow-up of subjects with the antecedents under investigation to elicit the outcome and sometimes also those without those antecedents.

Retrospective Study: Investigates antecedents for known outcome. Mostly includes subjects with the outcome under investigation, called cases, and controls without that outcome. Antecedents are elicited.

Cross-Sectional Study: Simultaneously elicits the outcomes and the antecedents in a relevant group of subjects.

Statistically, a study is called prospective when it investigates the outcome for a given set of antecedents. Antecedents could be the exposure of interest, natural intervention under study, or a set of risk factors to be studied. The follow-up could be in minutes, hours, days, or years depending on whether the outcome is quick or slow to appear. Some researchers do not consider studies with a short follow-up as prospective, and for them the study assessing the effect of anesthesia in surgical cases is not prospective. However, these studies also use a prospective format. The follow-up can be just at one time point or at multiple time points. Examples are cited later of rare prospective studies that do not require actual follow-up in a time frame. The defining feature remains that prospective studies are those that move from antecedent to outcome. Recruitment of subjects in future as they come to a clinic or otherwise does not make it a prospective study, because this refers to the recruitment process and not to the design.

Prospective studies can be contrasted with retrospective studies that move from outcome to the antecedent, and cross-sectional studies that elicit both antecedent and outcome together, as explained later in this chapter.

Prospective is an umbrella term that includes various types of studies based on the follow-up of the subjects: a cohort study with concurrent or historical cohort; longitudinal study; and repeated measures study. All of these are prospective studies, but note that prospective, cohort, longitudinal, and repeated measures are not mutually exclusive terms. The studies where the subjects are measured before and after an intervention are also technically prospective, although such an opportunity is rare in the case of observational studies.

Prospective studies can also be based on past cases. For example, Sokal et al. [1] reported a cancer risk study in 1995 on the basis of the records of women sterilized with transcervical quinacrine hydrochloride pellets in Chile between 1977 and 1991. Traceable women were also interviewed. Despite being based on past records, it is not a retrospective study because the direction of investigation is from antecedent to outcome. Terms such as **retrospective follow-up** and **historical prospective** are also used for this kind of design. This requires that past records are complete and accessible.

Exceptional prospective studies can be cited that do not require any follow-up in an actual time frame. In a study on the effect of profession on smoking habits, a cohort of people joining different professions in one particular year can be followed up for a 10-year period. This would be a standard prospective study. But the effect can also be studied by selecting people who have been in different professions for nearly 10 years and noting their present smoking status at the end of the 10-year period in the profession and their

---

BOX 5.2   SALIENT FEATURES OF PROSPECTIVE STUDIES

- Moves in the right direction, from predetermined antecedent to unknown outcomes – several outcomes can be investigated
- Not a good format if the outcome is rare because the yield of the cases could be low even with a large sample
- Heavy on time and resources as it requires a follow-up for as much time as required for the outcome to develop in at least a sizeable number of subjects
- The only format that gives an estimate of the incidence of the outcome, and the relative risk when "controls" are also included

---

smoking in the past 10 years. This also is a prospective study because the direction of the study is from antecedent (in this case, profession) to outcome (in this case, smoking), but there is no follow-up of the subjects in a conventional sense.

For those interested in the analysis aspects of prospective studies, the analysis of data from such studies is mostly done in terms of **relative risk (RR)** and **attributable risk (AR)**. These refer to the occurrence or nonoccurrence of an event of interest, such as recovery, a medical parameter reaching a threshold, and death. The outcome must be qualitative for these measures to be applicable. If the outcome of interest is quantitative, such as actual creatinine level, and when average over subjects at different time points is sensible, think of **regression** with time as a factor of interest for analyzing such data. You can also have other covariates in this model.

When the data at different time points are required to be considered together, **generalized estimating equations** may be a better method, particularly when the objective is to study the contribution of various factors to the outcome. This method allows correlated values (if values at differ time points are correlated) that most other regression methods prohibit. When the duration of appearance or occurrence of an event at different points in time is the variable of interest, including occurrence of the event within the follow-up period, the data are analyzed by **survival analysis** methods. This considers survival rate (or event occurrence rate) at different points in time.

A brief explanation of prospective studies is given in Box 5.2.

5.1.1 Subjects in a Prospective Study

The validity of the results of a prospective study substantially depends on the proper selection of subjects and an appropriate comparison group.

Selection of Subjects for a Prospective Study

An important consideration in the selection of subjects for any study is the feasibility of obtaining data on them. This means that the subjects must be approachable and cooperative. For a prospective study, especially, accurate and complete information must be available on them at baseline so that they can be correctly classified into exposed and nonexposed groups, and the effect of other characteristics on the outcome can be properly assessed. It is natural to expect that the subjects included in the study truly represent the target population. Thus, the target population must be clearly defined. It could be, for example, patients attending a particular group of diabetes clinics who are observed for development of retinopathy, or those exposed to a carcinogen in a particular district for development of cancer. Note the geographic limitation associated with the definition of a population.

In a prospective study, generally only one risk factor will be of primary interest, but other risk factors to be concurrently studied also need to be properly identified. For example, in a study of maternal complications due to poor nutrition, the concurrent factors could be parity, Hb level, and the nature of natal care. Decide in this case whether the study is to be restricted to women who are currently pregnant or will include all women who gave birth during the last year. Such specification is important for any study.

Comparison Group in a Prospective Study

A basic feature of a prospective study is that the incidence of outcome such as disease or relief is evaluated in those subjects who are exposed. It is often helpful to study a parallel group, also called a **control**, which is not exposed, so that a proper comparison can be made. Thus, case–control nomenclature is sometimes applied to such prospective studies which otherwise is restricted to retrospective studies. However, in this case, they are exposed and unexposed groups, and not diseased and nondiseased groups.

Proper selection of the comparison group enhances the validity of conclusions from a prospective study. Quite often the control group comes from within the cohort, in which some subjects are naturally exposed and some are not. For valid comparison, the exposed and unexposed groups must be similar at baseline, particularly with regard to the factors that can influence the outcome not under study. If the objective is to study the effect of recently acquired central obesity on electrocardiogram changes over time, factors such as age, gender, personality traits, stress conditions, and smoking need to be matched between the study group (with central obesity) and the control group (without central obesity). If complete matching is not possible, as would generally happen in practice, statistical methods are used to do the required **adjustment** at the time of analysis. Such an adjustment can become incomprehensible if done for a large number of factors and should be done for a few factors that are more relevant than others.

An external group can be used for comparison in some situations. An adequate number of nondiabetics may not be available in a diabetes clinic to assess the development of coronary events. External controls can be included in such a situation; however, they should come from the same milieu and should preferably be matched for all factors except the exposure. In a rare situation, when an appropriate external group is also not available, comparison can be done with outcome rates in the general population. For example, the incidence of birth defects in babies born to women aged 45 years or more can be compared with that in births to women of child-bearing age in the general population. The actual control group in this setup should be births to women aged less than 45 years, but a separate incidence of birth defects in them may not be easily available. The incidence in births to women aged less than 45 years may not be much different from that in all women of child-bearing age because births after that age are rare. However, in many situations, the rate in the general population is not comparable with the rate in the unexposed group and a great degree of precaution is required in using such a general group as the control.

In some prospective studies, it is useful to have multiple groups for comparison. For example, the effect of profession on smoking habits can be investigated by including several categories of profession in the same study where none would be the control group in the conventional sense. Subjects with different exposure levels can also be chosen for follow-up that would also provide multiple groups for comparison of the outcome.

It is sometimes impossible to find a group that is completely nonexposed. An example is exposure to dichlorodiphenyltrichloroethane (DDT). Even people in remote locations, such as Canada's Baffin Island, harbor traces of DDT. In such cases, the comparison effectively would be between the less exposed and the more exposed.

5.1.2 Potential Biases in Prospective Studies and Their Merits and Demerits

A large number of biases are listed in Chapter 3 and all those should be considered in a prospective study. Biases typically occurring in a prospective study setup are the following. Merits and demerits are described later in this section.

Biases

Selection Bias: A prospective study group is rarely a random sample from the target population of subjects, although this is desirable. Selection bias is said to have occurred when the study group has a different composition with regard to etiologic factors such as comorbidity, heredity, age, gender, nutrition status, and addictions compared with the composition in the target population. Studies on volunteers or on clinic subjects almost invariably suffer from such a bias. A method of selection that has a random component is considered insulation against this kind of bias, but such random selection fails to take cognizance of special bias that can result from extraneous sources such as improper definition of the population. In a study on causes of psychiatric illness in the elderly, if the subjects are those who are single and age 70 years or above at the time of enrollment, the bias occurs because some with severe illness may have already expired before attaining the age of 70 years. Only those who remain are robust or have minor illness.

Bias Due to Loss in Follow-Up: A major task in prospective studies is to accomplish successful follow-up of all subjects. Loss occurs due to change in residence to an unknown or remote address, unrelated death, severe illness other than the one under study so that the required investigations cannot be done, loss of motivation of the patient to cooperate, fault developing in machines such as a treadmill whose rectification takes time, absence of a trained technician, and other such reasons. In a clinic-based follow-up, when the patients are advised to report at periodic intervals, some may not come on the required day, and one or two follow-ups may be missed. Such loss constitutes a threat: first because the size of the group shrinks, and second because those lost are seldom a random subgroup. They are generally typical, for example, subjects who are seriously ill and not hopeful of living long, or those who are mildly affected and who consider continuation in the study not worth the risk. If the rate of disease and the rate of severity are different in the subjects who have discontinued, it would affect the validity of the results. Where possible, a random subsample of the discontinued subjects should be investigated intensively to evaluate their characteristics versus the characteristics of those who have not discontinued. If they are really different either with respect to outcome or even with respect to the baseline information collected at the time of first contact, an adjustment may be required at the time of analysis to remove the effect of such bias. When nonrespondents cannot be contacted despite best efforts, the baseline information can still be used for adjustment.

Assessment Bias and Errors: Human error can occur in assessing the condition of the patient. This can be due to either carelessness or lack of expertise of the observer. The physician may lack competence and the recording clerk may lack training or motivation. Assessment during the later part of a longitudinal study may be less accurate as fatigue sets in or can become more accurate due to learning effect.

Bias Due to Change in Status: In a prospective study on central obesity and coronary artery disease, it is possible that some subjects of the nonobese group become obese while the follow-up is still in progress. In a study on the effects of smoking, a nonsmoker at the initial stage may start smoking in the middle of the study, or a smoker may quit smoking. Exclusion of cases whose status has changed is one option, but is feasible only when their number is small. A long-term cohort is also affected by environmental changes such as introduction of a new drug to the market that can influence the incidence of the disease under study.

Validity Bias: Some prospective studies try to develop criteria to distinguish subjects with greater risk of disease from those with less risk. If sufficient distinguishing features are detected, these criteria can indeed be developed. Such criteria may work wonderfully well on the group from which they have been derived, but they need to be externally validated on another group of similar subjects. Although statistical principles say that criteria based on a representative sample should work nearly equally well on another sample from the same population, evidence of external validation is considered essential before such criteria are accepted. This validation could be done on another sample from the same population or even on a sample from a different population. The latter, of course, provides evidence that the results could be valid for the other populations as well.

All such biases and errors in assessment can be reduced simply by being more careful and by using precise instruments, measurements, and classification criteria that have been pretested for their validity. The identification and resolution of bias are primarily matters of epidemiological judgment. The success of a prospective study often depends on the care taken by the investigator in recognizing and correcting these biases. Although some bias can be handled at the time of data analysis by using appropriate statistical techniques, the applicability of these techniques depends on validity considerations, particularly on the adequate number of cases with the outcome of interest in groups and subgroups. This cannot be ensured beforehand in this situation. Thus, precautionary steps are preferable wherever feasible.

Merits and Demerits of Prospective Studies

The advantages of prospective studies will be clearer if you are aware of other designs of observational studies – namely, retrospective and cross-sectional studies. These designs have been briefly described earlier and are discussed in detail later in this chapter. Nevertheless, it is evident that the temporal sequence between exposure and disease can be more easily established by prospective studies than by any other format. The risk of outcome such as disease, or the chance of being cured, can be directly measured in a prospective study. Also, the **incidence** of an outcome cannot be assessed by any other method. Prospective studies are particularly well suited for assessing the effect of rare exposure such as of a specific chemical or of a new therapeutic modality because the cohort is expected to start with an adequate number of exposed subjects. These studies allow for examination of multiple effects of a single exposure. If the outcome of interest is death and the records are not adequate, a prospective design is the only choice.

There are also several demerits. Sometimes an outcome, such as carcinoma, may take years to appear after exposure. It may occur only in a small percentage of subjects, which could mean recruiting a very large cohort to obtain an adequate number of subjects developing the disease. Thus, prospective studies tend to be heavy on time and resources. In some situations, the natural course of the disease or the characteristics of the subjects may change during the follow-up period. As already stated, obesity, dietary pattern, and smoking all can change in a long-term follow-up. In a prospective study, subjects know that they are being observed and this awareness may change their behavior and outcome, called the **Hawthorne effect**. If the study spans several years, it is difficult to maintain motivation and retain trained staff. Supervision may also lose sharpness. *Notwithstanding these difficulties, prospective studies are technically the most correct designs because they move in the natural direction from antecedent to outcome.*

5.1.3 Cohort Studies

A **cohort** is a group of subjects who share a common base, and is observed forward in time. In the case of a usual prospective study, the subjects can be enrolled continuously and leave the study abruptly, whereas in the case of a cohort, enrollment or joining in the middle, is not optional. In a study on use-effectiveness of oral contraceptive pills [2], the users joined the group when they started using the pills and left when they stopped using them. They could not join 2 or 3 months after starting the pill. All subjects of a cohort do not have to start from the same calendar time, but they all start from the time of occurrence of the same event. There could be a cohort of children born in a particular year (see Example 5.1) who are followed for level of cognition, or a cohort of adults residing in an area at a particular time who are followed for diet and exercise and occurrence of coronary events. There could be a cohort of smokers and a matched cohort of nonsmokers followed for 20 years for the development of chronic obstructive pulmonary disease. Such cohorts are called **concurrent cohorts** when exposed and unexposed groups are followed up in the future. If the group identified for the study is the one that was recently exposed to a risk factor, it is called an **inception cohort**. For example, an inception cohort of early rheumatoid arthritis can be studied to assess predictive factors of orthopedic surgery. Some studies are based on past cases, called **retrospective cohorts** (see Example 5.2) or **historical cohorts**. For example, Kendzerska et al. [3] did a record-based follow-up of cases of obstructive sleep apnea that were earlier investigated between 1994 and 2010. The outcome was the development of diabetes by the year 2011. The data for this study were already available because of the earlier investigation.

Example 5.1: Birth Cohort Followed Up for Level of Cognition

Richards et al. [4] report the findings of a 53-year follow-up of a 1946 birth cohort, initially consisting of 5362 children of nonmanual and agricultural workers, and a random sample of one-in-four manual workers selected from all single and legitimate births that occurred in England, Scotland, and Wales during one week in March 1946. (Note the rigorousness with which the specifications are stated.) The cohort was studied on 21 occasions between birth and age 53 years. Information about socio-demographic factors and medical, cognitive, and psychological function was obtained by interview and examination at each point of contact. The authors concluded that birthweight and postnatal growth are independently associated with level of cognition at different ages. In this case, the main outcome of interest was level of cognition and the antecedents were birthweight and postnatal growth. The outcome was repeatedly measured over the period so that the cognition achieved at different ages could be studied.

Side note: Postnatal growth may be a function of birthweight but as far as cognition was concerned, this study found that the two act independently.

Example 5.2: Retrospective Cohort Studies of Orthopedic Cases for Risk of Death

Neary et al. [5] carried out a retrospective cohort study of all nonelective general and orthopedic surgical procedures performed on a total of 1869 patients in a hospital in the UK during the calendar year 2000. Outcomes were identified from various hospital databases related to this surgery, and the case notes of those who died were reviewed. Note that the study was from antecedent to outcome but the subjects belonged to a past period. The study found that increasing age, size of operation, and American Society of Anesthesiologists grade were significantly associated with higher risk of death by 1 year. The authors concluded that a simple scoring system could be used to identify high-risk patients for death among those who required nonelective surgery. Such patients could be targeted for interventions to reduce the risk of death. The conclusion reached is the same as anticipated by common sense, yet the study has value, first for documenting the evidence and second for linking it to the scoring system.

Side note: The study would hold greater value if the relative risk had been quantified and if the confidence interval had been provided.

Some researchers use the term prospective study as a synonym for cohort study, but this is not entirely correct. A study of antenatal women for birth outcome, coming to a clinic staggered over a period of time at different gestations, is a prospective study but would not be called a cohort study. A cohort is a predefined group of subjects followed up for one or more outcomes. All cohort studies are prospective, but not all prospective studies not cohort studies.

5.1.4 Longitudinal Studies

Another version of prospective study is longitudinal, when observations or measurements are repeatedly made at several points of time, particularly over a long period. When a cohort of low-birthweight children born in the year 2008 is followed up every year for growth, development, anthropometry, biochemical profile, pathological conditions, and so on, it is a longitudinal study. The Framingham Heart Study is among the most popular longitudinal studies, now going on for more than 60 years. In a longitudinal study, different subjects can be observed at different points of time. When each subject is observed at the same fixed time, it is generally called a repeated measures study, as explained next.

As just stated, in most longitudinal studies, measurements are taken at different points in time such as one patient is investigated before surgery, during surgery, and 1 hour, 2 hours, and 3 hours after surgery, and another patient is measured before, immediately after, and 90 minutes after surgery. The same characteristics, such as extent of pain, can be measured at these points in time. The objective is to assess change over time, and often the outcome of interest is the time taken to reach a particular endpoint, such as the time when the pain score is 1 or less on a scale of 0–10. In some situations, the interest may be in the pattern of change, such as whether pain is high initially and then declines either rapidly or slowly, or declines initially and increases thereafter. In this case, the interest may also be in the time at which the pain is the most severe or the least severe.

The primary objective of a longitudinal study is to track the trend over time, generally of a quantitative measurement. This means that the time points are an important consideration. For example, a **pharmacokinetic study** that evaluates peak concentration of a drug and time to reach peak would require a longitudinal study because observations at several time points are needed for this kind of study. Similarly, a study on growth of children would need a longitudinal study to track their trajectory. In both these setups the outcome is quantitative, but that is not a prerequisite for a study to be longitudinal. Time-invariant risk factors such as gender and family history may be measured only at baseline and other associated risk factors may be measured repeatedly over time in a longitudinal study.

Many of the statements made in the next section on repeated measures studies apply to all longitudinal studies. These should also be considered when conducting any longitudinal study.

5.1.5 Repeated Measures Studies

In many medical situations, as in the case of administering an anesthetic agent, it is necessary to monitor a subject by repeatedly observing vital signs such as heart rate and blood pressure at *specified intervals*. The key feature is that all subjects are measured at the same time points, as opposed to a general longitudinal study where different subjects can be measured at different time points.

The basic feature of a repeated measures study is the longitudinal follow-up, although it can be short, as in the case of trials on anesthetic agents, or can last for years as for quality of life after surgical interventions. The purpose is to measure the change with respect to the previous values, to assess the trend, and sometimes to identify the time point when the changes are significant. This is valid only if there is no natural or man-made change in values over time; that is, when any change can be assigned purely to the intervention. Guard against subjects showing improvement because of self-regulating mechanisms in the body without intervention because that may contaminate the effect of the intervention. Repeated measures help to study the short-term outcome separately from that emerging in the long term and the trend can be studied.

A repeated measures study may have two or more experimental groups such as different dose groups or subjects with different forms of a disease. Each subject in each group can be measured at several time points to study the trend of quantitative outcomes such as various enzyme levels. The objective in this case is to find if the average time trend in one group is the same as in the other groups. This is the same as assessing absence of **interaction** of a group with time. For studying such interactions, the size of each group must be sufficiently large so that the study has the power to detect this kind of interaction.

Repeated measures have the potential to provide unnecessary satisfaction of having a large volume of data. If blood pressure of 10 subjects is measured hourly 12 times during the day for diurnal variation for a week, this will have a total of 840 data points for systolic and 840 for diastolic level. This can mislead you to believe that a large sample of values is available. Actually there are only $n = 10$ subjects. The reliability of the conclusions will not be high in this case despite a large number of data points because of the small sample size.

Analysis of such repeated measures requires special methods because the outcome at different time points is not independent. Subsequent values depend on previous values and this violates the validity of most statistical methods such as analysis of variance (ANOVA). Special methods such as **repeated measures ANOVA** that may require a Huynh–Feldt correction to the degrees of freedom are used for this setup.

Example 5.3: A Repeated Measures Study on Blood Ammonia after an Oral Protein Challenge

Spacek et al. [6] evaluated the dynamic range of ammonia in response to an oral protein challenge in healthy participants, and measured blood and breath ammonia at baseline and every hour for 5 hours. They observed that the change in blood ammonia over time varied by dose. Change in breath ammonia over time also varied by dose. According to the authors, these pilot data may contribute to understanding normal ammonia metabolism.

5.2 Retrospective Studies

The second format for examining gestational age in relation to maternal anemia is that babies with different gestational ages are chosen and the records are used to find anemia status during the antenatal period. The first assessment in this format is the outcome and the antecedents are subsequently assessed for each type of known outcome. This is called a retrospective study because it moves from outcome to antecedent. This format is considered more efficient because of the speed with which a study can be completed. Evidently, only the subjects for whom the outcome is already known can be studied with a retrospective design. The cases can arise or can be recruited in future such as of breast cancer coming to a clinic from now on, yet the study is technically retrospective so long as it investigates the antecedents for a known outcome. The retrospective method is especially suitable for rare outcomes because the study can start after enough numbers of cases become available.

Many studies do not proceed from the outcome to the antecedent yet are termed as retrospective in the medical literature. This usage indicates the time frame and not the etiological sequence. For example, Hilska et al. [7] in 2001 reported an analysis of 150 patients with primary proximal colon cancer in Finland who were operated upon from 1981 to 1990, but the outcome measure was a 5-year survival rate. The study still is from the antecedent (colon cancer) to the outcome (survival). It is a prospective study going by the terminology we use, and could be called a retrospective cohort, but technically is not a retrospective study.

A retrospective study can also be conducted in the current time frame in special situations. Women with pre-eclampsia can be assessed for their present nutrition level and parity as risk factors in the hope that the level of such risk factors was the same before the occurrence of pre-eclampsia and contributed to the condition. The direction of investigation in this study is also from the outcome to the antecedent – thus, it is technically retrospective. For salient features of retrospective studies, see Box 5.3.

Sampling in Retrospective Studies

Because a retrospective study is based on cases with the selected condition to begin with, the sample size must be adequate to represent the entire spectrum of such subjects and provide reliable results suitable for generalization. Cases included should ideally be representative of all persons with the specified outcome, but many retrospective studies are carried out on a nonrandom sample. Random selection is especially important for **descriptive studies**, but probably not as important for **analytical studies**, including retrospective studies. Experience

BOX 5.3   SALIENT FEATURES OF A RETROSPECTIVE STUDY

- Moves in the reverse direction from outcome back to the investigation of the antecedents
- Requires fewer subjects and drastically less time to complete the study as there is no need to wait for the outcome to develop
- May suffer from recall lapse
- Generally requires an equivalent control group without the outcome as a comparator for valid conclusion

suggests that the relationship between antecedent and outcome can be adequately assessed despite a nonrandom sample in many situations as long as the bias is under check, the requirement for which is the baseline equivalence of the cases and the controls.

At the same time, these studies also involve estimation of a parameter such as odds ratio (OR), finding the confidence interval (CI), and testing of hypothesis. These statistical procedures require a random sample of the subjects. Indeed, a random sample should be taken whenever feasible. In addition, many of these statistical methods require a large sample in order to draw reliable conclusions.

Sampling of subjects in a retrospective study is based on the outcome – thus, the first step is to identify and define the outcome of interest. This could be negative, such as disease or death, or positive, such as relief or a specified minimum reduction in cholesterol level. The criteria for diagnosis of a disease and its severity must be fully specified. For example, in cancer cases, the stage of the disease must be specified and, of course, the affected site. Depending on the amount of information available, it is sometimes useful to keep track of definite cases separately from suspected cases. Obtaining information on possible risk factors that could have given rise to this outcome is the next step. The most common approach for eliciting such a history is the interview with the respondent. Because of **recall lapse** and intentional misreporting in some cases, it is better to depend on records if they are relatively complete.

5.2.1 Case–Control Design

The dominant format of a retrospective study is case–control, in which subjects with and without disease are investigated for past exposure. Those suffering from the disease or who have the health condition of interest are called **cases**, and those without that particular health condition are called **controls**. All case–control studies are retrospective, but not all retrospective studies are all case–control studies. Investigating the past history of cases of myocardial infarction is a retrospective study, but there may not be any control. Then it is not a case–control study. Obtaining the history of cervical cancer patients regarding infections, diet, and use of oral contraceptives is retrospective but not a case–control study if noncancer subjects are not part of the study. However, a control group provides a legitimate base for attributing differences in the two groups to the antecedents, such as high cholesterol level and obesity in patients with myocardial infarction – thus, the case–control setup is considered a natural format for retrospective studies.

The term control is used generically for any reference group against which the case group is compared. In comparing patients of myocardial infarction with those of stroke for risk factors, the group of primary interest is the case group, and the other is the control group, although this also is a group with disease. In a study on the efficacy of diagnostic tools, if the interest is in comparing ultrasound images with computed tomography images, the former could be the control group and the latter the case group. Note that cases are their own controls in this situation. As the control group is not necessarily "without disease," it is sometimes prudent to call this a **case-referent study**.

In a case–control design, the frequencies of antecedent in these two groups are compared, and analysis is mostly by **logistic regression**, where the **odds ratio** of each antecedent are obtained to assess its contribution to the outcome.

Example 5.4: A Case–Control Study on Leucopenia Associated with Metamizole Use

Blaser et al. [8] studied patients who took metamizole. Those who developed complications (leucopenia) were considered as cases and those without complications were the controls. The antecedents under study were history of allergies, previous leucopenic episodes, concomitant cytostatic agents, and prevalence of hepatitis C infection. The study of 57 cases and 139 controls revealed that these antecedents are possible risk factors for leucopenia associated with metamizole use.

Nested Case–Control Design

An extension of retrospective studies is nested case–control studies. In this setup, a cohort of subjects is followed up, and the cases who develop the outcome of interest and controls who do not develop the outcome are chosen from this cohort. Thus this combines cohort and case–control features. Consider a cohort of persons aged 40–44 years who are followed up for 15 years for the development of cataracts. Now the persons who develop cataracts become cases for investigation of those risk factors that could not be studied in the cohort setup. This would require matched controls. They can come either from the same cohort amongst those who did not develop cataract, or from outside. Note that cohort studies start with one or two specific antecedents but the case–control format allows for the investigation of a large number of antecedents. Thus, new hypotheses can be examined. The baseline data are already available from the cohort study, and these data may be free of recall bias. This type of design is called nested case–control design since the case–control setup is nested within a cohort. See Example 5.5 for a nested case–control study to assess the effect of body mass index (BMI) on ovarian cancer.

Example 5.5: A Nested Case–Control Study on the Inverse Association between BMI and Ovarian Cancer

A prospective study was conducted in France to investigate any association between BMI and ovarian cancer [9]. Information on anthropometry, demographic characteristics, medical history, and life style was obtained at the time of recruitment of subjects. (Note the advantage of the availability of a lot of information in this setup.) Women diagnosed with primary invasive epithelial ovarian cancer ($n = 122$) diagnosed 12 months or later after recruitment served as cases. (Note that n was still large.) Two controls for each case matched for menopausal status, age, and date of recruitment were randomly chosen from the same cohort. This is an example of a situation where nested case–control design can be useful. The advantages of a case–control design were derived from within the cohort that was being followed any way.

Side note: Appropriate logistic regression showed an inverse association between BMI and ovarian cancer risk, i.e., for increasing quartiles of BMI, the odds ratio exhibited a decreasing trend. Such dose–response type of relationship is one of the many indicators that the relationship could be causal.

5.2.2 Selection of Cases and Controls

The source of cases with the disease or any other outcome of interest can be hospital inpatients, or patients seen as outpatients, cases identified in a survey, available in the records of a health facility, or any other source. Control subjects should preferably come from the same setting as the cases. They may be patients with other diseases or relatives of the cases if that does not hinder the objectives. In some situations, controls can come from the population at large.

Case–control studies look simple, but can produce severely biased results if not done with proper care. The case definition should be sharp so that there is no room for doubt for a third person. For example, if cancer cases are being studied, specify their exact site and stage. An unbiased sample survey, such as random, of the target population is preferable, although that is not a prerequisite for analytical studies. The sample size must be adequate in order to represent the entire spectrum of subjects and provide reliable results. Only then the results are generalizable. Bias can appear in several other forms, as discussed earlier. For example, the use of incident cases rather than prevalent cases can remove some biases such as longer survival of those with a mild form of the disease, or of those who are physically strong. Cases surviving for long are more likely to have recall lapse.

Controls should be matched with cases for confounding factors. The results are much more valid if it is one-to-one matching. That is, each case should have one matched corresponding control. These are also called **matched pairs**. The attempt should be to simulate the situation of identical twins. The purpose is to be able to conclude that any difference between the cases and controls is attributable to the antecedent under study and nothing else. When controls are available in abundance and easy to elicit, two or three controls can be taken for each case. This helps to increase the reliability of the results without commensurate cost.

It is an uphill task to match more than two or three antecedents. Generally, matching stops at age and gender that are confounders in almost every medical setup. If so, an acceptable but less valid procedure is **group matching** (also called **frequency matching**). Under this scheme, as described earlier, average controls are matched with average cases or with regard to the pattern of the presence of the confounding factors. If obesity is a confounding factor, and if 35% of cases are obese, then almost the same percentage of controls should also be obese for group matching.

In addition to selection, matching should be in ascertainment. The controls must be assessed with the same keenness and with the same methodology as the cases. Cases may be more motivated, but try to extract the same cooperation from the controls as well. Controls should be able to provide a correct estimate of the rate of occurrence of antecedents in subjects without the disease. Wherever possible, get assistance from the records because they are likely to be far less biased than verbal responses, but the records should be complete.

5.2.3 Merits and Demerits of Retrospective Studies

Retrospective studies have many inverse properties to prospective studies. They can be accomplished with a relatively small number of subjects with less time and resources.

A retrospective study is efficient for rare outcomes because it can begin with a sufficient number of cases. It can simultaneously evaluate many causal hypotheses and is efficient also in the evaluation of interactions between different risk factors. A case–control study also allows easy control of confounders. All such advantages accrue mostly because a large number of affected cases are generally studied in this format.

On the downside, **recall lapse** is common in a case–control study that can bias the results. Differentials such as the ability of cases to recall events more easily than controls can cause additional bias. It can also be biased because only those who already have had the required outcome can be included. Many severe cases may have already died and cannot be a part of this type of study. A case–control format will not be able to establish the sequence of events.

5.3 Cross-Sectional Studies

The third format for the gestational age–anemia study is that a group of deliveries is chosen irrespective of maternal anemia and gestational age, and both of these are elicited. This is a cross-sectional study because the presence or absence of either antecedent or outcome is not a consideration at the time of the selection of subjects in this kind of design. Although this kind of format is more appropriate for descriptive studies, such as for estimating the prevalence of a health outcome, it is also appropriate to generate a hypothesis regarding etiology. Cross-sectional descriptive studies are better understood as surveys while cross-sectional (analytical) studies are not surveys because of cause–effect overtones.

The validity of conclusions from a cross-sectional study depends on the proportional representation of various levels of responses. Thus, it is important that a cross-sectional study is done on a randomly selected sample of adequate size from the target population without recourse to any consideration of the presence or absence of antecedent or outcome. If adequate representation is compromised, the conclusions based on a cross-sectional study could be biased.

Cross-sectional studies are also done in situations where the distinction between antecedent and outcome is blurred. Consider cleft lip and thalassemia in children: neither is a known cause of the other, yet the dependence of one on the other can be investigated to generate a hypothesis. For studying the association between blood group and gender, if male and female subjects are selected and tested for their blood group, it could be difficult to categorize this as either a prospective or retrospective study, though it might merit being called a case–control study if one gender is regarded as the case and the other the control. When the antecedent and the outcome are not identifiable, some would prefer to call the study descriptive rather than analytical. In our example, such a study would only indicate the blood group profile in the two genders without aspersions on the exposure–outcome type of relationship. Such a study would continue to be of a descriptive type until at least one factor is identified as an antecedent, or at least a suspected antecedent for the purpose of the investigation. A study on evaluation of concordance between two or more methods is also cross-sectional and not descriptive as it is concerned with the relationship.

Consider the following example. A study was conducted on 137 extremely obese subjects (mean BMI = 46.9 kg/m^2) and their diabetes status and obstructive sleep apnea were elicited [10]. Thus, this is a cross-sectional study. Among subjects with normal glucose tolerance, 33% had obstructive sleep apnea. This was 67% in pre-diabetic subjects and 78% in type 2 diabetes patients. Thus, the association between obstructive sleep apnea and diabetes status in extremely obese subjects was clear. This continued to be so after age, gender, BMI, and other such factors, were adjusted for. This cross-sectional study excluded the role of various confounders yet the conclusion rightly is of association and not cause–effect. Also see Example 5.6.

Example 5.6: A Cross-Sectional Study on HbA1c Level and Decayed Teeth

Suzuki et al. [11] investigated the relationship between blood HbA1c level and decayed teeth in patients with type 2 diabetes by conducting a cross-sectional study of 1897 patients in Japan. The study suggests that a poorly controlled blood HbA1c level is a risk factor for dental caries and concluded that more thorough oral hygiene instruction and education on preventive treatment for dental caries are needed in patients with poorly controlled diabetes.

The first step for sampling for a cross-sectional study is, as usual, to identify the target population for which the results would generalize. Then decide which sampling method would be appropriate. For age- and gender-related disease such as hypertension and diabetes, stratification by age and gender might be useful. For a community-based study in a large population, a **multistage sampling** involving selection of counties and households can be adopted, or a **cluster sampling** might be more convenient. In a clinical setup where subjects come in queue, **systematic sampling** could be adopted.

For analysis of data from a cross-sectional study, any one of the characteristics that can plausibly be considered as the outcome can be considered to be dependent on the others. **Logistic regression** or usual **multiple regression** can be used to find the joint or net effect of each of the independent factors in the model. In the case of cross-sectional studies, the assessment is generally made in terms of **odds ratios** for qualitative-dependent, but sometimes the **prevalence rate ratio** (PRR) is preferred.

5.3.1 Merits and Demerits of Cross-Sectional Studies

The following paragraphs describe the demerits of cross-sectional designs before describing the merits, because for such studies demerits should be considered first when investigating antecedent–outcome relationships.

Cross-sectional studies give a snapshot view and cannot measure risk. They may turn out to be a poor choice in situations where either the antecedent or the outcome or both are rare. If the outcome of interest is testicular cancer or the antecedent under investigation is exposure to synthetic estrogen, a cross-sectional study is not appropriate. An extremely inadequate number of subjects with the characteristics of interest may render the entire exercise futile.

There are other demerits too. The analysis can certainly be extrapolated to evaluate the net relationship between any two characteristics, keeping the others constant, but it should be clear that a cross-sectional design investigates the presence and not the appearance of the condition. Transient cases or rapidly fatal cases may inevitably remain under-represented in this kind of design. The causes that determine the appearance are confounded with those influencing the duration of the disease, and it may be difficult to draw a clear inference about either set of causes on the basis of the existing cases. Dropouts or migrants tend to be excluded in a cross-sectional study.

The other serious difficulty in a cross-sectional study is that it cannot be ensured that the antecedent has actually preceded the outcome. This might have important implications for a causal inference. A firm conclusion on cause–effect can rarely be drawn from cross-sectional studies, and this is a major limitation for such studies to be truly analytical. The concept of a control group is not relevant to cross-sectional studies. The biases seen in other observational studies are largely applicable to cross-sectional studies as well. However, information bias or memory lapse may be practically absent in this setup.

Caution is required in interpreting the results of a cross-sectional study. Such a study might reveal, for example, that the prevalence of hypercholesterolemia increases with age, but the fact could be that it is not age-induced but due to changes in the diet pattern of younger subjects resulting from increased awareness of the harmful effects of a high-cholesterol diet. Such awareness was less common 30 years ago and practically absent 50 years ago. A high-cholesterol diet consumed by older subjects for a long time when they were young because of lack of awareness may still have a carryover effect that persists despite a change to a low-cholesterol diet. Cross-sectional studies fail to take account of such confounders.

It follows from the preceding discussion that the cross-sectional design is particularly well suited for acute conditions with a short latent period or for chronic diseases that are stable and nonfatal. As already stated, this design can be recommended for situations in which the distinction between antecedent and outcome is blurred. In disease–anxiety syndrome, disease can cause anxiety and anxiety can cause disease – thus either could be an antecedent. Also, a cross-sectional study is generally considered a rapid and inexpensive way to provide clues for further and more valid investigations.

Cross-sectional studies are more appropriate for assessing the relationship between fairly stable entities, such as gender and hypertension, which do not change during the course of the study. Note that a cross-sectional study provides a one-time snapshot of the status of the characteristics, and not a long-term perspective.

In a cross-sectional study, **confounding factors** can also be investigated at the same time. For example, in a study on determinants of the increase in triglyceride level with age in adults, a group of subjects could be elicited for gender, diet, BMI, and other such factors, in addition to age and triglyceride level. All measurements would be considered valid for the date of investigation, although assessment of diet in this case could be based on food intake during the previous 3 days. The investigation might have the objective of determining the role of age in increasing the triglyceride level, but the design is such that the role of gender, obesity, and diet can also be investigated with the same validity. Statistically, any characteristics in a cross-sectional study can be considered dependent on the rest; the only restriction is the plausibility or justifiability of the relationship obtained.

5.4 Comparative Performance of Prospective, Retrospective, and Cross-Sectional Studies

Caution is the bottom line for results obtained from any observational study. Because of a large number of confounding factors in this setup, some of which may be obscure and beyond redemption, firm conclusions may be difficult. Results from such studies are often considered suggestive and not conclusive. The confidence level increases when the same result is obtained in a variety of settings in different studies. A single inconsistent observation can disprove the result.

Although three formats of observational studies and their merits and demerits have already been discussed, it would be helpful to provide another view. See Tables 5.1 and 5.2 for a comparison of the features and performance of prospective, retrospective, and cross-sectional studies. A brief evaluation is given next, some of which is repetition to reinforce what has been stated earlier.

TABLE 5.1

Comparative Features of Case–Control, Cohort, and Cross-Sectional Designs

Item	Prospective	Retrospective	Cross-Sectional
Main antecedent	Mostly known at the time of recruitment, but in a cohort of the general population may be assessed as a baseline after recruitment	Elicited	Elicited (the distinction between antecedent and outcome may be blurred)
Outcome	Elicited after the assessment of antecedents	Already present and known	Elicited
Recruitment of subjects	On the basis of the antecedent	On the basis of the outcome	Neither outcome nor antecedent is considered
Definition of a case	Subject with the specified antecedent	Subject with the specified outcome	Any subject in the defined population
Definition of a control	Subject without the specified antecedent	Subject with outcome other than specified	No control is required
Measure of disease frequency	Incidence	None	Prevalence
Samples required	One cohort of exposed and sometimes one cohort of unexposed	One group of cases and one group of controls	One sample from the population
Direction of investigation	Forward – into the outcome	Backward – into the antecedent	Cross-sectional situation as it exists

TABLE 5.2

Comparison of Performance Parameters of Prospective, Retrospective, and Cross-Sectional Designs

Criteria	Prospective	Retrospective	Cross-Sectional
Cost and time	High	Low	Low
Number of subjects required	Large	Small	Large
Suitability for rare exposures	Good	Poor	Poor
Suitability for rare outcomes	Poor	Good	Poor
Spectrum of etiologic factors that can be investigated	Small	Large	Large
Spectrum of outcome factors that can be investigated	Large	Small	Large
Recall lapse and other biases	Not likely	Very likely	Not likely
Completeness of information	High	Low	Full, but only cross-sectional
Dropouts	More	Less	None
Changes in characteristics of the subjects over time	More likely	Less likely	None
Assessment of temporal relationship	Good	Difficult	Not possible
Suitability for assessment of sensitivity and specificity	No	Yes	Yes, if the sample is representative
Suitability for assessment of predictivities	Yes	No	Yes, if the sample is representative
Evaluation and control of confounders	Poor	Good	Fair
Assessment of risk	Direct by relative risk	Indirect by odds ratio	Approximate by prevalence rate ratio
Assessment of cause–effect relationship	Good	Fair	Poor

5.4.1 Performance of a Prospective Study

More than one outcome such as absence of side effects, recovery, and duration of survival can be simultaneously investigated in a prospective study. The greatest strength of a prospective study is that it gives more accurate results because the events as they occur are observed. The time sequence of events can be studied. A prospective study is the only methodology by which true incidence can be estimated.

Among the demerits, a prospective study is time-consuming and expensive, yet it is suitable for rarely seen antecedents. Generally, a large number of subjects with particular antecedents are required so that a reasonable number of cases with the desired outcome are available at the end for reliable conclusions, but it can have dropouts during follow-up that may introduce bias, as explained earlier. If the dropouts are random (unconnected with exposure or outcome) then the only loss is statistical power – otherwise bias could be severe. During the course of the follow-up period, characteristics of the subjects can change, such as the person stops smoking and an obese person becomes thin.

5.4.2 Performance of a Retrospective Study

A retrospective study, generally a case–control study, has inverse properties. It can be accomplished with a relatively small number of subjects in less time and using fewer resources.

A retrospective study is efficient for rare outcomes because it can begin with a sufficient number of cases. It can simultaneously evaluate many causal hypotheses. It is efficient also in the evaluation of interactions between different risk factors. **Interaction** is the extent and manner in which the presence or absence of two or more factors together modifies the outcome. A case–control study allows easy control of confounders. All these advantages accrue because a large number of affected cases are available in this format.

Among the demerits, recall lapse is common in a case–control study. Differentials such as cases being more easily able to recall events than controls can cause additional bias. It may be biased also because only those who have already had the required outcome can be included. Many severe cases may have already died and cannot be a part of this type of study. The case–control format is not able to establish the sequence of events. The assessment of risks of adverse outcomes (or any outcome) is done in terms of OR in this case instead of the actual RR, although the OR may be a good approximation of RR in most practical situations (OR and RR are explained in Chapter 10).

5.4.3 Performance of a Cross-Sectional Study

The cross-sectional format is rarely used for an analytical study because it fails to provide a good assessment of cause–effect types of relationships. However, it is suitable when it is not clear what the antecedent and what the outcome is. In the case of peptic ulcer and milk consumption, either could be a cause of the other.

A cross-sectional study is a good tool to generate a hypothesis, which can be subsequently tested by a case–control or a prospective study. A cross-sectional study is certainly good as a descriptive study. It is quick and easy to complete. It starts with a reference population, so generalization is immediate when based on a genuine random sample. Repeated cross-sectional studies are good for detecting changes in known risk factors besides, of course, the time trend of the disease.

As explained later in Chapter 7, it is often helpful to obtain sensitivity–specificity or predictivities of a test procedure as indicators of its validity. The former requires a case–control study and the latter a prospective study. Sometimes a cross-sectional study is used to calculate both types of indices. When the subjects are representative of the target population, the percentage of subjects with disease and without disease would be nearly the same as in the target population. The test positives and test negatives would also be in the representative proportion, but they will be prevalent cases and not incident cases, nor "incidence" of antecedents. As explained in a later chapter, prevalence may be in proportion to incidence under stable conditions. In such a situation, cross-sectional results can be used to obtain both types of indices. Besides the restrictive conditions just mentioned, also note that a cross-sectional study fails to reach severe cases that tend to be rapidly fatal.

References

1. Sokal DC, Zipper J, Guzman-Serani R, et al. Cancer risk among women sterilized with transcervical quinacrine hydrochloride pellets, 1977 to 1991. Fertil Steril 1995;64:325–334. http://citeseerx.ist.psu.edu/viewdoc/download?doi=10.1.1.305.826&rep=rep1&type=pdf
2. Indrayan A, Bagchi SC, Verma V. Medico-social factors contributory to dropouts in a rural cohort of oral contraceptors. J Fam Welf 1972;18:65–75. www.popline.org/node/480324
3. Kendzerska T, Gershon AS, Hawker G, et al. Obstructive sleep apnea and incident diabetes: A historical cohort study. Am J Respir Crit Care Med 2014 15;190(2):218–225. https://doi.org/10.1164/rccm.201312-2209OC
4. Richards M, Hardy R, Kuh D, Wadsworth MEJ. Birthweight, postnatal growth and cognitive function in a national UK birth cohort. Int J Epidemiol 2002;31:342–348. http://ije.oxfordjournals.org/content/31/2/342.full.pdf+html
5. Neary WD, Foy C, Heather BP, et al. Identifying high-risk patients undergoing urgent and emergency surgery. Ann R Coll Surg Engl 2006;88:151–156. www.ncbi.nlm.nih.gov/pmc/articles/PMC1964060/
6. Spacek LA, Strzepka A, Saha S, et al. Repeated measures of blood and breath ammonia in response to control, moderate and high protein dose in healthy men. Sci Rep 2018;8(1):2554. www.nature.com/articles/s41598-018-20503-0
7. Hilska M, Gronroos J, Collan Y, et al. Surgically treated adenocarcinomas of the right side of the colon during a ten-year period: A retrospective study. Ann Chir Gynaecol 2001;90 (Suppl 215):45–49. www.ncbi.nlm.nih.gov/pubmed/12016748
8. Blaser L, Hassna H, Hofmann S, et al. Leucopenia associated with metamizole: A case-control study. Swiss Med Wkly 2017;147:w14438. https://smw.ch/article/doi/smw.2017.14438
9. Lukanova A, Toniolo P, Lundin E, et al. Body mass index in relation to ovarian cancer: A multi-centre nested case-control study. Int J Cancer 2002;99:603–608. https://onlinelibrary.wiley.com/doi/full/10.1002/ijc.10374?sid=nlm%3Apubmed
10. Fredheim JM, Rollheim J, Omland T, et al. Type 2 diabetes and pre-diabetes are associated with obstructive sleep apnea in extremely obese subjects: A cross-sectional study. Cardiovasc Diabetol 2011;10:84. www.ncbi.nlm.nih.gov/pmc/articles/PMC3206416/
11. Suzuki S, Yoshino K, Takayanagi A, et al. Relationship between blood HbA1c level and decayed teeth in patients with type 2 diabetes: A cross-sectional study. Bull Tokyo Dent Coll 2019 Apr 10;60(2):89–96. www.jstage.jst.go.jp/article/tdcpublication/advpub/0/advpub_2018-0039/_article

6

Assessment of Medical Factors

Medical factors can be broadly classified into: (i) etiological factors that give rise to risk factors; (ii) risk factors that promote or inhibit a health condition; (iii) diagnostic factors that help to identify the presence or absence of a disease; (iv) treatment modalities that aim to alleviate suffering and bring the patient back to health; and (v) prognostic factors that determine the outcome (outcome can be complete relief, dissatisfaction, discomfort, disability, disease, or death). In a research setting, all or a subset of these may require assessment. These should be clearly identified and properly assessed by suitable indicators.

To clarify the semantics, a "factor" in our terminology is a characteristic of the subjects, and "indicator" is its measurement. Obesity is a factor and body mass index (BMI), waist–hip ratio (WHR), and skinfold thickness are its indicators. Condom use is a factor and its regularity can be measured, for example, as always/regular/irregular/never, or more specifically as number of times used in the last four experiences of sexual intercourse. These are the indicators. Nutrition status is a factor and serum albumin level, retinol level, and hemoglobin level its indicators. The indicator converts a factor into its operational definition. This distinction is important for the implementation of research and enough thought must be given at the time of protocol writing to identify the relevant indicators for the factors under investigation. For example, depending upon what aspect of obesity is most relevant for research, decide that BMI is the more appropriate indicator or WHR or skinfold thickness. These will have to be clearly stated in the protocol.

Section 6.1 discusses the intricacies of assessment such as univariate and multivariate assessments, and assessment in the implementation and results phase of the study. Section 6.2 is on the types of medical factors and choice of indicators, and Section 6.3 provides details of the assessment of mortality, various durations, and quality of life that require special handling.

6.1 Intricacies of Assessment

Some aspects of data quality that include correct assessment are discussed later in Chapter 7, but there are other aspects of assessment that need attention. The timing and circumstances of all assessments should be standardized to minimize irrelevant variations. For example, decide for blood pressure (BP) measurement that the patient would be supine or sitting, how much time is to be given for rest before BP reading, what would be the gap between two measurements, what instrument would be used, what time of day it will be measured, whether rounding off would be to an even number or to the nearest integer, and such other aspects.

Decide also that the research interest is in the exact quantity or occurrence of an "event." Iron deficiency in a group can be measured either by mean hemoglobin level or by finding how many have level <11 g/dL. The two indicators may give different results. The incidence of a disease may give different results from prevalence, and efficacy is different from effectiveness. Similarly, decide that the appropriate indicator to meet the objective is relative risk or attributable risk (see Chapter 10 for an explanation of these terms). The interest may be in duration of disease in some situations and in, say, 5-year survival in others. Sensitivity and specificity have different implications than positive and negative predictivities. The choice is dictated by the objectives of the study and by the specific hypotheses under research. All these issues need to be considered while drafting a protocol.

When using two or more indicators for the same factor, beware of the threats posed by possibly different results. For example, findings for total cholesterol levels may disagree with those on triglyceride levels – which one would you believe? The advantage is that the correspondence between two or more such indicators increases the level of confidence in the findings, but contradictions may be challenging to resolve.

6.1.1 Univariate and Multifactorial Assessments

The occurrence of hypertension depends on heredity, diet, exercise, obesity, stress, and other such factors. Generally, the presence of several factors together is required to trigger the disease. Thus, hypertension has multifactorial etiology. Compare this with the occurrence of malaria, the diagnosis of which solely depends on the presence of the malaria parasite in the blood. Thus, malaria is a univariate disease with single-factor etiology. When the parasite is not detected, malaria diagnosis is multivariate because then it depends on the presence of fever with rigors, splenomegaly, and other such signs. Hypertension by itself is a univariate disease because diagnosis is based on BP level alone, but it has multifactorial etiology, as mentioned earlier. Thus, exercise caution when using terms such as univariate and multifactorial disease.

A further implication of univariate and multifactorial terms is in risk assessment. Lung cancer can occur from smoking, exposure to radiation, asbestos dust, and other such toxicities. Any one of these factors can cause cancer. Also, one risk factor such as smoking can cause many diseases (lung cancer, asthma, coronary disease, etc.). An assessment of medical factors in research should give due consideration to such distinctions. In the case of noninfectious diseases, the latent period from exposure to onset can be long and the presence of other factors during this period can complicate the assessment.

6.1.2 Assessment in the Implementation Phase and the Results Phase

Any research has to be monitored in the implementation phase before the results are assessed. The first component of the implementation phase is providing inputs such as diagnostic and treatment facilities in clinic-based research. Then the process that includes activities such as blinding and actual adherence to the regimen in a clinical trial setting is followed. This process also needs monitoring from time to time. The third assessment during the implementation phase is of outputs such as relief of signs and symptoms. For research in a community, inputs in the implementation phase may be in terms of providing health education and screening facilities, process in terms of their timeliness and adequacy, and output in terms of improvement in specific aspects of health.

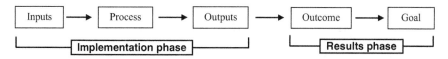

FIGURE 6.1

Components of the implementation and results phases of a research project.

FIGURE 6.2

Types of medical factors and their flow.

After the implementation phase is assessment of the results phase (Figure 6.1). The first part of the results phase is the outcome and the second part is the achievement of the ultimate goal. Note the difference between output and outcome. Outcome is in terms of the efficacy of the regimen that could be assessed by a combination of outputs such as relief in signs and symptoms, improvement in biochemical markers, and ability to lead a normal life. The goal could be to provide better treatment, of which efficacy is just one component. The others could be the cost and convenience. An analogy can be drawn for community-based studies.

While assessing medical factors, ensure that the three aspects of implementation and two aspects of the results phase (Figure 6.1) are properly assessed.

6.2 Types of Medical Factors

It is important in research to make a distinction between the factors that can be modified and the factors that cannot be modified. Age and gender may be important risk factors for many chronic diseases but nothing can be done to change them: only precaution can be advised. Most genetic factors too are unmodifiable, although counseling and perhaps engineering can manage some of them. The primary target of research should be factors such as diet, lifestyle, biochemical, and pathological parameters that can be modified either through advice, such as for diet and exercise, or by physical intervention such as medication and surgery.

A convenient division of medical factors is distal, proximal, physiological, pathophysiological, pathological, morbidity, and mortality (Figure 6.2). Some examples of these factors are given in Box 6.1. Note that distal factors can seldom be outcome and mortality can never be the antecedent for the same person. All others could be antecedent in one setup and outcome in the other. Lipid profile is an outcome for dietary changes but antecedent for coronary disease.

The list in Box 6.1 may help to identify factors that are relevant for your research and also possibly not to miss any out, or to demarcate factors for future research. A categorization and flow (Figure 6.2) may help in assessing the role of various factors and in assessing their modifiability that may have deep implications in arriving at implementable conclusions.

Some methods of assessment of various types of factors, and the problems in their assessment, are discussed in the following paragraphs. The discussion is restricted to

---

BOX 6.1   EXAMPLES OF VARIOUS TYPES OF MEDICAL FACTORS

Distal Factors: Demographic structure; socio-economic status and inequities; cultural practices; environment; health infrastructure; laws and their enforcement; and such other macro-level factors

Proximal Factors: Diet and nutrition; obesity, exercise, and physical activity; quality of life, stress, and strain; smoking and other addictions; health and hygiene practices; personality traits, attitudes, etc.; family history and such other factors that directly affect health

Physiological and Pathophysiological Factors: Levels of blood pressure, heart rate, etc.; blood and urine chemistry; liver, kidney, and lung function; cognitive and psychomotor function; electromagnetic status; gestation, childbirth, growth; menarche, reproductive history, and menopause; anthropometry; immunity level and tolerance to toxicity

Pathological Factors: Blood constituents; urine, blood tests for pathogens; histology and cytology of cells and tissues; images; serology

Morbidity: Type and severity of disease, infirmity, injury, etc.; signs and symptoms; onset and remissions; previous history; prevalence, duration, and severity; parts affected; medical treatment and surgery; duration of hospitalization; side effects and complications

Mortality: Crude, standardized, age- and cause-specific death rates; standardized mortality ratio; live birth–based mortality (stillbirths, perinatal, neonatal, and infant mortality, under-5 mortality, maternal mortality); proportional deaths; case-fatality

Duration of Survival: Expectation of life; event-free survival and survival with residual disability; quality of life; healthy life expectancy; years of life lost

---

commonly studied factors, perhaps representative of their category. Mortality and duration of survival require special methods that are discussed separately in the next section.

6.2.1 Distal and Proximal Factors

These are those factors that either work in the background or those that directly determine the health outcome. They define the vulnerability for some conditions and the cause in others.

Distal Factors

Distal factors work from behind and give the opportunity to proximal factors to emerge when other favorable conditions are present. The most prominent distal factors are the socio-economic status of patients, their cultural practices, and environment. Socio-economic status is measured as social class I (highest) to class V (lowest) depending upon level of education, income, and occupation. Indrayan [1] has devised one such classification that can be used internationally.

Cultural practices include vegetarianism that affects nutrition, gender preference for birth that could mean feticides and neglect of a girl child, belief in supernatural powers (such as *tantrik*) that could affect the utilization of health facilities, and family bonds that provide social security, particularly at the time of serious illness. No widely acceptable scoring system is available to convert these factors into measurable indicators. The only way to assess them is as present/absent, or in some situations in full/partial/nil types of categories. Because of the difficulty in their assessment, cultural factors tend to be ignored in most medical research. Do not do so if the disease under investigation is significantly affected by varying cultural practices in your target population and try to devise a scoring system.

The age and gender structure of subjects is always an important feature of any disease profile. This can point to the etiology of the disease and can help to create workable strategies to resolve problems in controlling or alleviating the disease.

The infrastructure in the hospital comprising the availability and sincerity of the doctors, nurses, technicians, and housekeeping staff is also a distal factor that partly determines the outcome in inpatients and to some extent in outpatients as well. The functionality of gadgets, instruments, machines, and the computer network can be important contributory factors.

In public health research, distal factors could be the demographic and socio-economic structure of the population, per-capita availability of hospital beds and specialists, health inequities, and other such macro-level considerations. The environment can be studied in terms of climate and the resulting flora and fauna, such as thriving pathogens and vectors, by pollution inside and outside the home and workplace, by the kind of housing, traffic, and roads, and other such factors. In a hospital setting, nosocomial infections and sanitation can be important environmental factors.

Proximal Factors

Factors directly affecting health are called proximal. They are also called risk factors in the classical sense. Prominent among them are nutrition, obesity, addictions, health practices including hygiene, stress, and occupational hazards, and sexual practices.

Problems in assessing proximal factors can be very aptly illustrated by the example of smoking. Often it is assessed in individuals only as never smoker, past smoker, and current smoker. But smoking has many dimensions. One is the type of smoking: cigarette, *bidi*, *hukka*, cigar, pipe, and so on. Further dimensions of cigarette smoking are number smoked per day that can vary from year to year, years of smoking, filter or nonfilter cigarette, age at start, and time elapsed since quitting by ex-smokers. In addition are finer aspects such as depth of inhalation, early-morning smoking, and the size of the butt left. The most commonly used indicator of smoking is the cigarette-years smoked. This obviously ignores other dimensions of smoking. It also assumes that the "burden" on health of smoking 10 cigarettes a day for 20 years is the same as smoking 40 cigarettes a day for 5 years. Many would not agree with this equivalence, but no correction is available for this discrepancy. However, Indrayan and Malhotra [2] have developed a comprehensive index on the premise that the burden of smoking on health is rapid in the beginning but increases slowly later as the cigarette-years increase. It also takes into account age at start, filter/nonfilter cigarette, variation in smoking from year to year, and time elapsed since cessation.

Indicators for assessing a factor such as health practices are neither available nor easy to develop. Health practices include personal hygiene; awareness and adoption of good health practices such as balanced diet, exercise, and good sleep; utilization of health care facilities such as when a doctor is consulted, and where; and child feeding such as mother's milk and supplements. Separate information on each relevant item may have to be obtained.

Height and weight are used as indicators of stature as well as for assessing obesity. A large number of indicators are available for different age groups, such as ponderal index and birthweight ratio for neonates; weight-for-age, weight as percent of median, Z-score for children; and BMI, WHR, waist–height ratio, Broca index, and conicity index for adults.

> **BOX 6.2   GUIDELINES FOR CHOOSING AN INDICATOR**
>
> An indicator should have documented validity and reliability for the specific objective of the research.
>
> - It must be precise, unambiguous, and measurable.
> - It must also have biological relevance and should be appropriate for the topic of research.
> - It should be sensitive so that it reflects changes over time or across groups and specific in the sense that it reflects changes only in the situation concerned.
> - It should be simple, feasible, and inexpensive, and should require the minimum of effort and time. Thus, a univariate indicator is preferable over a multivariate index.
> - It should not require repeat measurements at the same time.
> - It should be least inconvenient to the subject and easy to implement for the assessor.
>
> For an outcome indicator, the convention is to talk about clarity, relevance, economic, adequacy, and monitorability, with the acronym **CREAM**. All other features are the same as mentioned above, but an additional requirement for an outcome indicator is that it should be amenable to independent validation.

Such complexity can arise for many factors. A judicious choice is not always easy. Some guidelines for this choice are given in Box 6.2.

In a clinical setting, the emphasis is generally on physiological and pathological assessments as discussed next.

6.2.2 Physiological and Pathophysiological Factors

BP and pulse rate; blood and urine chemistry; evoked potential; lung, kidney, and liver function are examples of physiological factors. All these are directly measurable. However, cutoffs for normal, marginally abnormal, and abnormal levels are frequently not clear. A level of 50 mg/dL serum urea may be considered normal by one physician and abnormal by another. Peak expiratory flow rate of 4 L/s and intraocular pressure of 22 mmHg are also borderline values. Thus, there is always the risk of misdiagnosis and missed diagnosis in such cases. The normality or otherwise of a measurement should be assessed after considering the values seen in healthy and sick subjects taking sufficient precautions with overlapping values (see Section 10.4 in Chapter 10).

Pathophysiology refers to functional changes that accompany a disease. For example, kidney and liver functions change in diseases affecting these organs. These are generally measured in terms of indicators such as urinary creatinine and blood urea nitrogen levels for kidney function, and albumin and serum bilirubin levels for liver function. Similar indicators are used for other diseases. Problems in their assessment are the same as mentioned in the preceding paragraph.

6.2.3 Pathological Factors and Disease

Problems in assessing pathological factors are similar to physiological factors. For example, pain assessment can be done in several ways: visual analog scale (VAS), verbal rating scale, McGill score, and global perceived effect. Some make a distinction between intensity of pain and quality of pain. It is preferable to use a scale for which reliability and validity are documented for your target population. Once a choice is made, implement it as faithfully as possible. For example, for assessing pain by VAS, ensure that the patient has understood the scoring and that they are providing a correct response.

Precautions are required not only for subjective assessments such as pain and other symptoms but also for relatively objective signs. Judging the size of the prostate per rectum could be difficult, particularly if the enlargement is marginal. The spleen may be palpable for one physician and not for the other. Rashes can be interpreted differently. Even an electrocardiogram is sometimes interpreted differently by different physicians.

Whereas objective criteria are generally available for laboratory-based quantitative investigations such as platelet count, erythrocyte sedimentation rate, and serum ferritin, this is not so for histology, cytology, and images. Different physicians can interpret the same X-ray differently. All such assessments should be based on a standard set of criteria and followed uniformly throughout the research, preferably by one observer who is fully trained for this purpose.

Medical tests can be false-positive or false-negative. A urine culture may show exotic pathogens because of contamination or may not be able to grow the microbe. Fine-needle aspiration cytology may not agree with a mammogram for a lump in the breast. Plan in advance to take care of such anomalies.

Disease assessment also has several dimensions. It can be based exclusively on clinical picture, on laboratory investigations, on images, on scoring system, response to therapy, or any other such consideration. Generally, a combination is used, but acceptable criteria can be difficult to devise. Assessment of severity of a disease on which prognosis depends is even more difficult. If the interest in research is to find whether or not a particular intervention is able to inhibit severe sequalae, or the interest is in delaying the onset of disease or its consequences, take care that the assessment is appropriate for these objectives.

Duration of follow-up of cases depends on the kind of disease and the type of response of interest. For research on an anesthetic block, a few minutes of follow-up may be enough in some situations. To assess a response to a drug, the cardiovascular system may reveal changes within a week, the respiratory system may take a month, and the central nervous system would need perhaps 6 months.

For a serious disease such as cancer, the concern may be the duration of survival and quality of life. For less serious diseases, the focus may be on progression of disease, such as blood count. In the latter case, the pre-existing level is important.

Example 6.1: Various Types of Medical Factors in Research on Antidepressant Medication Use and Breast Cancer Risk

Steingart et al. [3] report a case–control study on antidepressant medication use and breast cancer risk among women in Ontario, Canada. Cases were 3077 women with primary breast cancer, and controls were randomly sampled from the female population of Ontario. Various medical factors studied can be grouped as follows:

Distal: Education, income, and marital status

Proximal: Smoking, alcohol, physical activity, breast cancer in first-degree relatives, and oral contraceptive use

Physiological: Age at menarche, age at first live birth, parity, history of breast feeding, age at menopause, height, and weight

Pathophysiological: None

Morbidity: Ever diagnosed with depression, traumatic stress, anorexia, history of benign breast cysts, hormone treatment, use of antidepressants (regularity, duration, time since last use, time since first use, and class of depressant)

Note the classification of factors.

Side note: The study found a modest association between ever use of antidepressants and breast cancer, which evaporated when known factors for breast cancer risk were adjusted for.

6.3 Assessment of Mortality, Duration, and Quality of Life

Death is inevitable, yet it agitates. One of the basic aims of medical science is to reduce levels of mortality. Realize, however, that death cannot be avoided: it can only be postponed, and the level of mortality is reduced through postponement. We will discuss duration of survival and quality of life later in this section, but the initial concern is with the level of mortality – either in the general population or in specific groups such as among infants and in cases of cardiovascular disease. Different indicators for various types of outcomes are listed in Box 6.3.

6.3.1 Assessment of Mortality

Mortality is assessed in conjunction with the population, with live births, or with cases of a particular type. Different denominators may give different results. Mortality is just about the most important consideration for many chronic diseases and end-stage conditions.

BOX 6.3   INDICATORS OF MORTALITY, DURATION OF SURVIVAL, AND QUALITY OF LIFE

Population-Based Death Rates: Crude death rate, age-specific death rate, standardized death rate (direct and indirect), standardized mortality ratio, cause-specific death rate

Live Birth–Based Mortality Rates: Stillbirth ratio, perinatal mortality, neonatal mortality (early and late), infant mortality, child mortality, maternal mortality ratio

Proportional Mortality: Percentage deaths in specific age groups, percentage deaths due to specific causes or groups of causes

Disease-Specific Mortality: Case-fatality within a specific period

Survival: Probability of survival (or death) for a specific period, median survival time, expectation of life at birth and at other ages, healthy life expectancy

Quality of Life: Physical quality of life index for communities, activities of daily living index, quality-of-life score based on various questionnaires, duration of disability, severity of disability (disability weights)

Global Measures: Equivalent years of life lost due to disability and premature deaths, i.e., disability-adjusted life-years (DALYs) lost

Perhaps the most important consideration in a hospital setting is **case-fatality**. This is the percentage of admitted cases who died during their hospital stay. Because the duration of hospital stay could be long, say, 35 days, for some patients or short, such as 3 days, for others, case-fatality is sometimes qualified as 7-day mortality. Case-fatality could be high for critical conditions such as peritonitis and low for mild cases such as enteric fever. Often, case-fatality in patients on one regimen is compared with patients on another regimen to decide which one is better at reducing mortality.

Case-fatality must be assessed in relation to the age of patients, as old patients are prone to death anyway, whether treated or not. If there are two or more groups in a trial, their age structure should be nearly the same so that age is ruled out as a contributory factor. Age-specific death rates may be more appropriate if the number of patients is large. If there are substantial age differences, use a standardized death rate or standardized mortality ratio. For details of these methods, see Elandt-Johnson and Johnson [4].

Additional care is required for the assessment of mortality in a research setting. In a follow-up study on a critical disease, the care may be substantially better toward the end because the number of surviving patients declines and those surviving may be resilient – patients developing complications but not dying.

In public health research, population-based death rates such as crude death rate, age-specific death rate, and cause-specific death rate, or live birth–based mortality rates such as perinatal and neonatal mortality, infant and child mortality, and maternal mortality may be more appropriate. All these indicators are listed in Box 6.3, but if you want to know the method of calculation, see the book by Indrayan and Malhotra [2].

6.3.2 Quality of Life and Duration

Measurement of quality of life requires special instruments, and duration, such as of survival, require special care.

Quality of Life

The following is restricted to assessment of quality of life of individuals rather than of communities. The focus here is on patients, particularly those suffering from chronic conditions and unable to lead a normal life.

Myocardial infarction, breast cancer, multiple fractures, and peritoneal surgery are examples of conditions that have many survivors, but quite a few of them are not able to lead the normal life of a healthy person. The disability may be apparent, such as in walking and talking, or more subtle, as in doing heavy work for long hours. Quality-of-life assessment is gaining importance as more and more people are able to live longer due to medical interventions but retain residual disability of one kind or the other. It is being increasingly assessed for the general population as well, or for patients of various other types with no disability. It is also commonly used as an outcome measure in research on the relative benefits of different treatment modalities.

Several instruments are available for measuring quality of life in different kinds of subjects, particularly for patients of chronic disease. For coronary heart diseases, Thompson and Yu [5] have reviewed many questionnaires. The one considered appropriate for your patients can be chosen. For cancer, there is an EORTC QLQ-C30 questionnaire containing 30 items of enquiry [6]. Its modules for different types of cancers are also available. For the general population, there is a WHO-QOL questionnaire with 100 items [7] and a short form with 36 items called SF-36. There are several others. Choose the one that is most appropriate for your subjects.

Duration

The duration of hospitalization and duration of survival are the most prominent examples of duration used in medical research. They require that a beginning point and an endpoint are sharply defined. For example, the duration of a disease can be measured from the time of detection, the time when the first symptoms were noted, the time when the laboratory test was positive, or any other point in time, and the endpoint could be when the test is negative, when the patient reported relief, when the patient is discharged, and such other events.

Durations have special statistical significance because they generally follow a highly **skewed distribution** – meaning that whereas most subjects will have a typical duration, some will have a long and a few a very long duration. Also, sometimes duration cannot be fully observed in cases where the subject is lost to follow-up for some reason. These are called **censored values**. For these two reasons, special statistical methods of **survival analysis** such as **Kaplan–Meier curves** are used to study duration.

References

1. Indrayan A. Medical Biostatistics, Third Edition. Chapman & Hall/CRC Press, 2012.
2. Indrayan A, Malhotra RK. Medical Biostatistics, Fourth Edition. Chapman & Hall/CRC Press, 2018.
3. Steingart A, Cotterchio M, Kreiger N, et al. Antidepressant medication use and breast cancer risk: A case-control study. Int J Epidemiol 2003 Dec;32(6):961–966. www.ncbi.nlm.nih.gov/pubmed/14681256
4. Elandt-Johnson RC, Johnson NL. Survival Models and Data Analysis. John Wiley, 2014.
5. Thompson DR, Yu CM. Quality of life in patients with coronary heart disease-I: Assessment tools. Health Qual Life Outcomes 2003 Sep 10;1:42. www.ncbi.nlm.nih.gov/pmc/articles/PMC201013/
6. EORTC Quality of Life Questionnaires. https://qol.eortc.org/questionnaires/ – last accessed 7 January 2019.
7. World Health Organization. World Health Organization Quality of Life (WHOQOL). www.who.int/mental_health/publications/whoqol/en/ – last accessed 7 January 2019.

7

Methodology of Data Collection

All empirical research that we are focusing on in this text is based on data. The word **data** is the plural of *datum*, and stands for a collection of measurements. These are not necessarily quantitative: they can also be qualitative. Signs and symptoms are qualities yet are "measurements" in the statistical sense. Blood pressure (BP), creatinine level, peak expiratory flow rate, and so forth, are quantitative measurements anyway. Qualitative data also convert to numerics when summarized for a group. For example, if the measurement is the presence or absence of ascites for a group of 50 patients with complaints of pain in the abdomen, one can say that ascites was present in 18 of them. Thus, qualitative data also become quantitative when related to a group. This would invariably happen in a primary medical research setting.

Where should we get the data for medical research? In a clinical setting, they come from patients' interviews and examinations, and their laboratory and radiological investigations. Sometimes, only the observations of the subjects such as their behavior and personality traits are recorded. These are called **primary data** and are recorded in a questionnaire, schedule, or proforma such as an Excel sheet. **Secondary data** are existing records of previous patients and other subjects that can also be used for meaningful research. These may be your own or may belong to someone else, such as databases available on the websites of various organizations.

All measurements are easily understood statistically as **variables** because they vary from person to person. Thus, there are qualitative variables and there are quantitative variables. These could be on a nominal, ordinal, or metric scale. This distinction is important, because the method of inference is different for different types of variables. The merits and demerits of various types of measurement will help to decide which ones to use for different kinds of assessment in research. All these issues are discussed in this chapter.

Types of measurements such as different scales and qualitative–quantitative, discrete–continuous, and other types are discussed in Section 7.1. Tools of data collection such as questionnaire, schedule, record, interview, and examination are described in Section 7.2. Quality of data such as reliability and validity is discussed in Section 7.3, and assessment of validity of medical tools such as pilot study and pretesting, sensitivity–specificity and receiver operating characteristic (ROC) curves are presented in Section 7.4.

BOX 7.1 TYPES OF MEASUREMENTS

Quantitative: Measured for each individual in numerics, such as body temperature, hemoglobin level, and creatinine level. The other name for the same is metric.

Qualitative Ordinal: Assessed for each individual as a quality that can be graded, such as disease severity into mild, moderate, serious, and critical categories. The number of categories is three or more—thus, it is generally polytomous (see next).

Qualitative Nominal: Assessed for each individual as a quality that cannot be ordered, such as site of injury as head, chest, limbs, etc. This can be of two types – dichotomous, when the number of categories is two, and polytomous, when the number of categories is more than two.

Intensity of pain when measured by a visual analog scale as 7 out of 10 is quantitative; when measured by verbal rating scale as mild, moderate, or severe is ordinal; when measured as present or absent is nominal as well as dichotomous. Most scientists prefer quantitative measurements to qualitative measurements because quantities are more exact.

7.1 Types of Measurements

Loading this text with statistical terminology will defeat the purpose of keeping it intelligible to medical research workers. At the same time, it is necessary to be conscious of the types of measurements and their consequences. We try to explain all this in simple terms in this section.

A blood group is a quality and blood glucose level is a quantity. The former is assessed in terms of words or attributes whereas the latter is assessed in terms of numerics. As already mentioned, both are "measurements" in the technical sense. See Box 7.1 for a summary of the various types of measurements.

7.1.1 Nominal, Metric, and Ordinal Measurements

A scale is an instrument on which a characteristic is measured. It can be quantitatively calibrated in the usual sense or can be qualitative. Blood glucose level and urea clearance are measured in terms of quantities whereas the stage of cancer is a quality although expressed as I, II, III, etc. Age can be measured in days and hours but is often categorized in years as (0–4), (5–14), (15–49), etc., for a population. Disease severity and extent of malnutrition are actually quantities but are generally measured as none, mild, moderate, and serious. Site of malignancy is also a measurement in a statistical sense, but is recorded as oral, lung, abdomen, breast, etc. Thus, there are a large variety of measurements. Statistical methods and thus inferences from research depend on the scale of measurements, and can be grouped in a variety of ways. The important ones are described here.

Nominal Scale

As already mentioned, not all measurements are necessarily in terms of quantities. Complaints and site of cancer are only names and the scale of such a measurement is called nominal. All space-related measurements such as the organ affected, the site of a lesion, and the place of occurrence of a disease are nominal, as are attributes such as race and blood group. These names do not have any specific order. Thus, there is no notion of less than or more than in this kind of scale, and the only valid comparison is of equality or inequality. Gender is either male or female, and none is higher or more than the other. Diagnosis of liver disease as hepatitis, cirrhosis, or malignancy is nominal, and so is the nature of a handicap such as visual, speech, orthopedic, and mental. These variables are genuinely categorical, and the only way to associate numbers with them is by way of assigning a **code** to each category. Note, however, that *codes for nominal categories are not metric scores* – a category receiving code 4 is not twice the category receiving code 2. These codes cannot be treated as quantities and cannot be added, subtracted, multiplied, or divided. Codes are not the same as scores.

When the assessment of a characteristic is in terms of only two categories such as yes/ no, present/absent, or favorable/unfavorable, these are called **dichotomous categories**. The corresponding variable is called a **binary**. Recording gender as male or female is the most glaring example of such a variable. If the number of categories is more than two, such as cirrhosis, hepatitis, and malignancy for liver disorders, these are called **polytomous categories**. Statistical methods are simpler for dichotomous than for polytomous categories. If a statistician advises you to collapse three or more categories into two for the sake of convenience during calculations, you should agree only if this does not reduce relevance and the operational value of the conclusion is not compromised. Clinical relevance should not be sacrificed for statistical expediency. Computers have largely obviated the need to compromise on this aspect.

Metric Scale

At the other end of the spectrum are characteristics that can be exactly measured in terms of a quantity. Duration of a disease, hemoglobin level, heart rate, and parity are examples of such characteristics. These are said to be measured on a metric scale. Often these are recorded in categories such as years of age in (0–4), (5–14), (15–49), (50–69), and (70+) groups. Such categorization tends to convert the metric scale into ordinal and results in loss of information, yet it is preferred in some situations, as discussed in a short while.

There is a tendency in health and medicine to develop a **scoring system** for the **soft data** such as the degree of severity of disease. Soft data are those that arise from hard-to-measure characteristics and are recorded as text instead of a numeric. A scoring system introduces a metric scale for soft data and definitely helps in achieving better exactitude. Such scores are statistically satisfying but sometimes lose clinical relevance. If you are using a scoring system, ensure that it adequately represents the varying grades of the observations. Assigning a number should not be at the cost of an unjustified air of accuracy.

Sometimes a metric scale is divided further into interval and ratio scales. In an **interval scale**, there is no absolute zero, for example, body temperature. A temperature of 105°F cannot.be interpreted as only 5% higher than 100°F. Similarly, it is incorrect to say that a person with an intelligence quotient (IQ) of 160 is twice as intelligent as a person with an IQ of 80. Differences matter, but ratios are irrelevant in this kind of scale. This is so for those measurements in medicine which do not start from zero. Plasma glucose levels, BP, and heart rate are all examples of this kind of measurement. On the other hand, in a **ratio scale**, a zero point can be meaningfully designated. It is correct to say that the duration of survival of 6 years is twice as much as 3 years, and parity 3 is thrice as much as parity 1. However, in this case also, their medical interpretation may not be based entirely on a proportional factor. The fine distinction between interval and ratio scales in most cases is not required for managing uncertainties through statistical methods and for arriving at correct results.

The disadvantages of measurements on the metric scale are that, in many cases, such measurements are relatively more difficult, more time-consuming, and more expensive. A large number of parameters may have to be considered together to say that the extent of burns is 78% while it is easy to say on visual inspection alone that the burns are "extensive." However, such shortcuts invariably lack objectivity. Whenever feasible, prefer the metric scale to the ordinal scale. It is always wise to ensure that the metric measurements you are using are indeed valid and reliable.

Ordinal Scale

There are certain characteristics that should be measured in terms of quantity, but the nonavailability of a good instrument compels measurement in terms of what is called an ordinal scale. Disease severity when measured as none, mild, moderate, serious, or critical; likelihood of the presence of a particular disease when measured as ruled out, unlikely, doubtful, likely, and confirmed; and self-perception of health from very bad to very good on, say, a 7-point scale are examples of such characteristics. These are inherently metric, but an ordinal scale is more convenient in such measurements. The main reason for non-availability of a metric scale is that many of these characteristics are **multifactorial**; for example, disease severity depends on signs and symptoms, measurements such as BP and plasma glucose levels, and radiological assessment, which makes assigning a single quantity extremely difficult.

Sometimes a device to measure a characteristic is easily available but is not adopted because such a level of accuracy is not needed. Smoking can be measured as the number of cigarettes smoked, but categories such as none, light, moderate, and heavy seem to serve the purpose sufficiently well in many clinical situations. Age can be measured in terms of years, but categorization into child, adult, and old may be adequate in situations where disease structure is the same within each of these categories.

The basic advantage of using an ordinal scale rather than a metric scale is convenience in eliciting, recording, and reporting, and nondependence on any sophisticated device for measurement. Ordinal categories are often easier to comprehend than metric categories although valuable and accurate information is lost in the process, and the analysis of data is rendered less efficient. Metric measurements are amenable to a host of mathematical manipulations that are not possible with ordinal measurements. Thus, prefer hard measurements such as BP level instead of grade of hypertension, and prostate volume instead of grade of enlargement. If the efforts required for hard measurements are enormous, such as in measuring the size of the brain, or when no metric scale is available, use an ordinal scale. However, beware of anomalies in some ordinal categories because such categories are rarely strictly defined. What is mild for one may be moderate for another.

Between nominal and ordinal, there may be measurements that are **semiordered**. Classification of malignancy as definitely absent, probably absent, uncertain, probably present, and definitely present is an example of a semiordered scale. These categories are partly nominal and partly ordinal.

Quite often, numerals are associated with ordinal categories, such as 0 for none, 1 for mild, 2 for moderate, and 3 for serious. These numbers are then subjected to all sorts of algebraic calculations. Such calculations are valid only when the moderate degree is considered twice the mild degree and the serious degree is considered three times the mild. These numerals also assume that the difference between mild and no disease is the same as that between serious and moderate disease. In practice, this may not be so, and sufficient caution is required in assigning numerals to ordinal categories, and in drawing conclusions when based on calculations involving such numbers. Note that these numerals are not codes but are used as scores.

7.1.2 Other Types of Scales for Measurement

Several other types of scales are used in medical research. Among these, commonly used are Likert scale and Guttman scale – both are used for items in a questionnaire.

Likert Scale

This is a specific kind of tool for psychometric assessment of opinion, belief, and attitude. For a particular construct such as satisfaction from hospital services, a set of items is developed so that all aspects of that construct can be assessed. For hospital services, these items could be on the competence of doctors, humanitarian nursing services, proper diagnostic facilities, and other such services. A declarative statement such as "I am happy with the nursing services in this hospital" is made in each item and respondents are asked to specify their level of agreement on generally a 5-point scale, such as strongly disagree, disagree, indifferent (neutral), agree, and strongly agree. This is called the Likert scale.

The response for each item is graded on the same scale – not necessarily 5-point – it could be 7-point, 9-point, or any other scale. An attempt is made so that the options from strongly disagree to strongly agree are equally spaced so that they can be legitimately assigned scores of 0–4, 0–6, or 0–8 depending upon the number of options. Instead, these scores can be –2 to +2, –3 to +3, –4 to +4, etc. You may prefer 1–5, 1–7, 1–9, etc. Various scoring patterns can give different results and the choice is yours as long as it can be justified.

Options for some items are reversed so that "strongly agree" is the first option and "strongly disagree" the last option. Or, some items are negatively framed. This helps to elicit a well-thought-out response instead of consistently selecting the same response, like "agree," for most items. At the time of analysis, such reversed items and corresponding scores are rearranged in the proper order.

Add the scores of all the items to get the total score for each respondent. This total is called the **Likert score** of that respondent for the construct under study. For a 10-item questionnaire where each item is on a 5-point scale (0–4), the total score for each respondent will range from 0 to 40, and can be analyzed just as any other numerical measurement. Second, the analysis can be focused on each item. If item 3 is on satisfaction with diagnostic facilities, and there are $n = 50$ responses on a 0–4 scale for this item, you can calculate the median score to get an assessment of satisfaction with diagnostic facilities, or to compare it with, say, nursing services. Thus, an assessment can be made regarding which component of the construct is adequate in the hospital and which needs strengthening.

Rodriguez et al. [1] used a 1–5 Likert scale to assess the satisfaction of patients, primary care providers, and specialty physicians with electronic consultation in a veteran setting in the United States Wong et al. [2] used the same scale for patients' beliefs about generic medicines in Malaysia. These examples may give you an idea of how the Likert scale is used in practice.

Guttman Scale

A binary (yes/no) set of questions or items is said to be on the Guttman scale when they follow a hierarchy so that yes to any item implies that the answer is yes to all subsequent (or all preceding) items. The characteristic to be measured is arranged in a continuum from minimum to maximum (or vice versa). For example, visual acuity (VA) is assessed in stages and if a person with a cataractous eye can read a font size of 24 from a distance of 14 inches, this implies that they can read a font size of 48. Thus, a threshold can also be obtained and one response can predict all other responses in a lower hierarchy. Gothwal et al. [3] conducted such a study on subjects with cataracts using the Guttman scale. This scale is mostly used to develop a short questionnaire that can still discriminate, such as for assessing disease severity and the level of satisfaction from hospital services.

The scale cited in the preceding example on VA is fully scalable in the sense that there will be hardly any case who is able to read font size 16 but not font size 24. In many practical situations, this hierarchy is not as nice. Efforts are sometimes made to frame items from least to most difficult in the hope that more able persons will be able to correctly answer more difficult items. However, in this case, the correct answer to item 3 does not necessarily imply the correct answer to items 2 and 1. Such "errors" make the scale really probabilistic.

For further details of the Guttman scale, see Indrayan and Holt [4].

7.1.3 Continuous and Discrete Variables

It is important in research to distinguish between two types of quantitative measurements. First are those that can take, at least theoretically, any value in a specified range. They can be measured arbitrarily to many decimal places. Albumin levels can be 3.4 g/dL or even 3.432 g/dL. It is a different matter that it does not help to measure it that accurately, nor do we have instruments to give that kind of accuracy. Such measurements are called continuous. The second type of quantity is parity, that can be only 2 or 3 or any other integer but cannot be 2.7 or 3.2. Such measurements are called discrete. Statistically, characteristics with continuous measurements are treated as continuous variables and characteristics with discrete measurements as discrete variables for analysis.

Any count is always discrete, but if the number of subjects has a large range, such as the number of hypertensive individuals in various cities, it is treated as continuous for the purpose of statistical analysis because the methods for continuous data are generally simpler and well known. It is seen that treating them as discrete gives nearly the same results as treating them as continuous. Categories are always discrete. They are assigned values so that they can be analyzed as discrete variables.

The distinction between discrete and continuous variables is important if you plan to analyze the data yourself; otherwise the statistician would take care. Statistical inferential methods are different for discrete variables than for continuous variables. This is analogous to different methods of assessment of cardiovascular disease than for gastrointestinal tract disease.

The methods for discrete variables are generally based on **binomial distribution** for dichotomous categories and on **multinomial distribution** for polytomous categories. For large samples, chi-square test is used for such data. Remember, though, that dichotomous categories, where a quantitative measurement is divided into two groups, are a class apart from the nominal dichotomous categories. Examples of nominal dichotomous are male–female, case–control, and cancer of prostate or cancer of esophagus. These have no order – no one category is better than or superior to the other. These are the situations where binomial distribution can be legitimately applied with full authenticity when the categories are **mutually exclusive and exhaustive**. Quantitative dichotomy is when, for example, fasting plasma glucose level is divided into <120 mg/dL and ≥120 mg/dL. In this case, there is an order as one is less than the other. Quantitative dichotomous variables can also be handled with binomials, but sometimes the underlying distribution can also be used to provide additional information. For example, if you know that fasting blood glucose level follows a Gaussian (normal) distribution, the threshold 120 mg/dL is not simply of yes/no type but has additional information, such as how far this is from the mean or mode in absolute value or in standard deviation units. For counts, **Poisson distribution** is mostly used. For details of these distributions, see any biostatistics book.

For continuous variables, the statistical methods are generally based on Gaussian distribution, in some cases after necessary transformation. In rare cases, other distributions such as gamma or Weibull are invoked for a continuous variable.

7.2 Tools of Data Collection

Data for medical research can be collected with the help of a variety of tools. Questionnaires, schedules, and proformas help to collect the data on a uniform pattern without missing any item for any particular subject. These are completed by interview of the subjects, their physical examination, and/or by laboratory and radiological investigations. The details of these tools are as follows.

7.2.1 Questionnaires, Schedules, and Proforma

It is always desirable in empirical research to follow a predefined pattern for collecting data and to record them in a standardized format. A standardized form is a big help in retaining the focus on the objectives and in ensuring uniformity, and also serves as a repository of information for later reference. In view of such important functions, sufficient time and thought should be invested in designing the forms. The format could be a questionnaire or a schedule or a proforma for a master chart. There is considerable confusion among the medical community about these terms. This section explains these terms. The contents, however, of all three formats are basically the same as outlined in Box 7.2. These include information on variables that characterize the subjects, the interventions, and the outcomes.

**BOX 7.2   BROAD CONTENTS OF A FORM OF DATA
COLLECTION FOR MEDICAL RESEARCH**

- Identification data (name, address, ward, patient ID, date, name of the observer, etc.)
- Demographic characteristics (age, gender, area, ethnicity, education, income, etc.)
- Basic measurements (height, weight, addictions, sexual practices, blood pressure, pulse rate, etc.)
- Disease measurements (signs and symptoms, duration, severity, biochemical measurements, pathological and radiological assessments, etc.)
- Intervention received (treatment, prescriptions, actual intake, surgery, etc.)
- Health outcome (mortality, residual disability, quality of life, duration of survival, side effects, duration of hospital stay, change in physiological and biochemical parameters, etc.)
- Follow-up in case needed

Questionnaires

As the name implies, a questionnaire contains a series of questions that are required to be put to a subject verbatim at the time of interview. Thus, the phrasing of questions and their sequence are important. Such features have the potential to change the response. For side effects, for example, asking generally about any problems caused by the treatment may elicit much less response than asking separately for each possible side effect, but in the latter case, all possible side effects should be known at the time of framing of the questionnaire. Also the last asked side effect is likely to be reported much less than the first asked.

Avoid questions such as "Don't you use painkillers for acute pain?" They suggest the answer and are called leading questions. Such questions are not recommended. Also, do not seek two pieces of information in one question. The wording must not be ambiguous. Minimize hypothetical questions on the future or regarding attitudes because the response to such questions depends on the mental frame of the subject at the time of the interview and the response may change when asked a second time. In place of asking what patients would do in a particular situation, ask what they did last time in that situation.

A questionnaire could be self-administered also, where the subject fills responses without interfacing with an interviewer. For this to be successful, the respondent must be fully literate to understand and interpret the questions properly and the questionnaire must contain all the explanations and instructions for its completion. Use simple language for this purpose. If the language of the questionnaire is different from the language of the respondent, the translation should be appropriate. Despite all these precautions, portions of a self-administered questionnaire are likely to be left blank, but more accurate information can be obtained by this method on sensitive issues such as sexual behavior. Face-to-face interviews may not yield the same quality of response on such sensitive issues.

In postal questionnaires, chances of response can be increased by offering incentives, advance contact, personalized letter, stamped return envelope, follow-up contact, and other such steps.

The language used in framing the questions should be simple and easy to understand for the target population, should avoid unrelated questions and should be focused on the research topic. The questions should not be too long, and no question should have dual answers. The sequence of questions should be logical to sustain interest and the questionnaire should be short. This may contain an explanation of the objectives of the research so that the respondent feels involved.

Structured Questionnaire

A questionnaire is called structured when the language and the order of questions are fixed. When the list of possible answers is also given and the respondent has to just tick one or more as applicable, this becomes **closed-ended**. One possible answer in this can be "Any other (specify)" to cover the possibility of the list not being exhaustive. A question can be framed as closed-ended only when enough is known about the types of responses so that the responses under "Any other" category are minimum, say, not exceeding 10%. If they are more, this reflects that the questionnaire was not prepared with sufficient thought. If the responses cannot be anticipated, perform a **pilot study** to find out what responses are common that need to be separately listed in a closed-ended fashion. If substantial responses occur under "Any other" category despite best efforts, invoke the "specify" component and identify which responses are common that can be separated. Remember that a large number of responses for "Any other," without identifying what, can throw research out of gear. Also, at the time of statistical analysis and conclusions, this category can cause problems because it contains the assorted left-over that generally defies interpretation.

Schedules and Proforma

A schedule contains only the items on which the information is to be elicited. Framing a question to get that information is left to the interviewer in this case. A schedule will have an item such as age, whereas a questionnaire will have "What is your age?" A bed-head ticket or a case sheet is a schedule because it contains only the items of information.

A proforma is the prototype or a sample providing the items of information on which the information is to be collected. It is neither a questionnaire nor a schedule. Perhaps this can be used to prepare columns in an Excel sheet where information for each patient can be recorded in one line, as done in a database or a master chart. Table 7.1 clarifies the difference between a questionnaire, schedule, and proforma.

TABLE 7.1

Illustration of Differences between a Questionnaire, Schedule, and Proforma
(The following assumes that there will not be more than four complaints in any person and not more than three family members will be affected.)

Questionnaire	Schedule
Unique ID	Unique ID
1. What is your name? _____	1. Name _____
2. What is your age (in completed years)? ___Years	2. Age (completed years) _____Years
3. What is your gender (tick one)? M/F	3. Gender (tick one) M/F
4. What are your complaints?	4. Complaints
(i) _____	(i) _____
(ii) _____	(ii) _____
(iii) _____	(iii) _____
(iv) _____	(iv) _____
5. Does any other member of your family suffer from the same complaints?	5. Family history, if any, and relationship
Yes/No	(i) _____
If yes, what is your relationship with each of them?	(ii) _____
(i) _____	(iii) _____
(ii) _____	
(iii) _____	

Proforma

Complaint codes: 0. None, 1. Abdominal pain, 2. Vomiting, 3. Acidity, 4. ————, etc.

Family history codes: 0. None, 1. Mother, 2. Father, 3. Brother, 4. Sister

Sl. no.	Name	Age (Years)	Gender (M/F)	Complaints (Code)				Family History (Code)		
				1	2	3	4	1	2	3
1.										
2.										
3.										
:										
:										

7.2.2 Interview, Examination, and Investigation

Primary data on subjects of your choice can be obtained by interview, examination, and investigation. In most situations, all three methods are deployed to supplement each other, but the data obtained by different methods are not equally reliable.

Interview

History-taking by personal interview is an integral part of a medical maneuver. This is the most direct method of obtaining the data, but the interviewer has to go down or come up to the level of the respondent to elicit correct responses. Make sure that the person is not casual or evasive, and not giving misleading information as on commercial sex in the case of sexually transmitted disease, or on knife injury that may have legal implications. Guard against recall lapse. Elderly people may not report on cataracts or coughs, perceiving them as a natural consequence of old age. For such reasons, assess if the interviewer requires training to be able to elicit full and correct responses.

In community-based research, interviews can be done by mailed questionnaire, telephone conversation, or personal interface. The response of a mailed questionnaire could be low and highly selective. Telephone interviews can be done only with those who have a telephone, and thus could make the sample biased in some countries. Also, the refusal rate can be high. Face-to-face interviews are the most common and most valid form of eliciting information. The types of information that can be obtained by interview are: (i) facts such as age and sex; (ii) complaints or symptoms; (iii) behavior such as smoking, feeding practices, and hygienic practices; (iv) knowledge about health practices and services; and (v) opinion such as on contraception, or preference for system of treatment.

Resist the temptation to collect too much information from a person lest the focus is lost and the person loses interest: they may evade the questions and start giving casual answers if the interview is too long. Only necessary information as required under the protocol should be collected.

Physical Examination

Examination is considered to be the most important source of getting the medical data on a subject. This includes measurements such as weight, body temperature, and BP, besides the signs. There could be some hiccups, though. You may find the spleen palpable in a case where the other physician cannot. You may observe and note pallor in a suspected case of leukemia whereas another physician may consider it inconsequential. In a research setting, take steps to achieve standardization so that the same examination is done on all subjects. Perhaps the same physician should examine all the patients, and with uniform dexterity.

Sometimes the subject is just observed and not examined. This is predominant in behavioral research where the observation is regarding how the person is walking, talking, and carrying out other such activities. Features such as inconsistency or incoherence are noted. This is part of the process of examination, although it is not physical examination per se.

Investigation

Radiological and laboratory investigations are gradually gaining centrality in establishing a diagnosis, and in monitoring the progress of a patient. Although there are many physicians who believe that nothing can replace clinical acumen, their number is dwindling. Because of relatively higher objectivity, investigation results carry much more weight in research than clinical observations. Ensure, though, that the laboratory is reliable and the investigation results are believable. The same investigation should be done on all subjects and the same method should be used.

Decide beforehand what specific information is to be obtained by the respective methods. They should corroborate or supplement each other. If a male patient age 65 years or more complains of increased frequency of micturition, poor stream, large prostate on rectal examination, but has normal prostate-specific antigen on laboratory examination, then this provides corroborative evidence of an enlarged prostate, namely, benign prostatic hyperplasia. If corroboration is lacking, the patient may not have enlarged prostate, and possibly may not be suitable for inclusion among cases for research if that is on benign prostatic hyperplasia.

7.3 Quality of Data

"Garbage in, garbage out" is a very appropriate phrase for medical research. If correct information is not elicited about the patient at a personal level, do not hope that prescriptions or surgery will still bear fruit. If sufficient care is not adopted about the information collected during research, the results will be equally sloppy. Much of the medical research in some countries fails to attract attention because of a general feeling that some research workers in those countries are not sufficiently careful. Such "researchers" also tend to undermine the work of others in the same country who use immaculate care. It is not so much about using expensive instruments or procedures but about being careful about whatever is being done. If BP is being measured by a sphygmomanometer, attention to the Korotkoff sounds, their proper correspondence with the mercury reading, the subject in a comfortable position without any stress, and three readings if required – all this makes up the quality of measurement. Whatever tools are used, be it mercury sphygmomanometer or magnetic resonance imaging, they must be valid and reliable. A large part of modern medical research is devoted to searching methods and instruments that are inexpensive and fast, yet valid and reliable. Accuracy, completeness, relevance, and other such characteristics, are the other dimensions of quality.

Remember that anecdotal evidence lacks scientific basis and the plural of anecdote is not data. Second, as Tukey once remarked, the availability of data and the aching desire for an answer do not ensure that a reasonable answer can be extracted.

7.3.1 Errors in Medical Data

Medical data are prone to errors because they involve intricate interactions among persons, instruments, and environment. We have been talking about them from time to time. The following list may help you to be alert about these errors and obtain the right data.

Medical Errors

Medicine is a highly complex science with the enormous risk of committing error. The following list may help in being careful.

1. A medical decision depends on the history a patient provides and on the records available with the patient. These may not be of perfect quality.
2. It depends on the competence of a physician to elicit a correct history, to do a complete examination as required, and to order appropriate laboratory investigations. Some expensive investigations may not be immediately available, although highly desirable.
3. It depends on the accuracy and timeliness of the investigation reports.
4. It depends on the validity and reliability of tools used such as BP instrument and ophthalmoscope.
5. It depends on the correctness of the diagnosis, and the choices and preferences for treatment strategies. For example, for borderline hypertension, you may prefer exercise and diet control whereas another physician may start an antihypertensive drug.
6. It depends on proper use of the tools and the expertise to handle them.
7. It depends on the nursing care and right instructions.
8. It depends on what drugs are available locally or within the means of the patient.
9. It depends on proper compliance – whether the patient is really following the regimen.

The list is still not exhaustive. In the wake of so many variations and uncertainties, errors do occur. For example, injury to an organ can occur during surgery. The key is that such errors should be rare and under control. Statistical methods are available that help to assess whether such errors are under control. The data available for research should be free of such errors as much as possible.

Errors in Measurements

Errors in measurement can arise due to several factors, as listed below.

Lack of Standardization in Definitions: If it is not decided beforehand that an eye will be called practically blind when VA < 3/60, VA < 1/60, or any other, then different observers may use different definitions. When such inconsistent data are merged, an otherwise clear signal from the data may fail to emerge, leading to a compromised conclusion. A similar example is of the variable definition of hypertension used by different workers; for example, Chambless et al. [5] use BP $\geq$ 140/90 mmHg for hypertension, and Wei et al. [6] use BP > 140/90 mmHg: one considers BP = 140/90 mmHg to be hypertensive and the other normotensive. Another such example is age, which can be recorded in completed years (age at last birthday) or as on the nearest birthday. These two are not necessarily the same. A difficulty might arise in classifying an individual as anemic when the patient's hemoglobin level is low but hematocrit is normal. Guidelines on such definitions should be very clear, and all observers involved in a particular study should follow the same definition.

Lack of Care in Obtaining or Recording Information: This occurs when, for example, sufficient attention is not paid to the appearance of Korotkoff sounds while measuring BP by sphygmomanometer or to the waves appearing on a monitor for a patient in a critical condition. This can also happen when responses from patients are accepted without probing and some of them may not be consistent with the response obtained on other items. If reported gravidity in a woman does not equal the sum of parity, abortions, and stillbirths, then obviously some information is wrong. A person who may say that they do not know anything about AIDS in the early part of an interview but states sexual intercourse as the mode of transmission in the latter part of the interview is an example of inconsistent response that requires further probing. The observer or the interviewer has to exercise sufficient care so that such inconsistencies do not arise.

Inability of the Observer to Gain the Confidence of the Respondent: This inability can be due to language or intellectual barriers if the subject and observer come from widely different backgrounds. They may then not understand each other and generate wrong data. In addition, in some cases such as in sexually transmitted diseases, part of the information may be intentionally distorted because of the stigma or inhibition attached to such diseases. An injury in a physical fight may be ascribed to something else to avoid legal wrangles. Some women hesitate in divulging their correct age, and some refuse physical examination, forcing one to depend on less-valid information. Correct information can be obtained only when the observer enjoys the full confidence of the respondent.

Bias of the Observer: Observer bias is the systematic discrepancy between the truth and the observed values. According to Mahtani et al. [7], evidence shows that estimates of the effect size can be exaggerated by at least one-third due to observer bias. Hadjistavropoulos et al. [8] discuss observer bias in pain assessment in elderly patients with dementia because these patients are not able to communicate properly. These examples illustrate situations where observer bias can be serious but minor observer bias is common in medical data because of individual preferences.

Variable Competence of the Observers: Quite often an investigation is a collaborative effort involving several observers. Not all observers have the same competence or the same skill. Assuming that all observers work to their fullest capability and faithfully follow the definitions and protocol, variation can still occur in measurement and assessment of diagnosis and prognosis because one observer may have different acumen in collating the spectrum of available evidence than the others.

Many inadvertent errors can be avoided by imparting adequate training to the observers in the methodology proposed to be followed for collection of data, and by adhering to the protocol as outlined in the instruction sheet. Many investigations do not even prepare an instruction sheet, let alone address adherence. Intentional errors are, however, nearly impossible to handle and can remain unknown until they expose themselves. One approach is to be vigilant regarding the possibility of such errors and deal sternly with them when they come to notice.

It is sometimes believed that bad data are better than none at all. This can be true if sufficient care is exercised in ensuring that the effect on the conclusion of bias in bad data has been minimized, if not eliminated. This is rarely possible if the sources of bias are too many. Also, care can be exercised only when the sources of bias are known or can be reasonably conjectured. Even the most meticulous statistical treatment of inherently bad data cannot lead to correct conclusions.

7.3.2 Reliability, Validity, and Accuracy of Data

Medical research gives correct results when the data are not just free of errors but also reliable, valid, and accurate. These terms have been explained earlier in Chapter 3. In this section, we are concerned with these features of the data. Validity of tools is separately discussed in the next section in detail.

Reliability and Validity of Data

The concepts of reliability and validity are the two most important components of quality. Reliability is also called consistency, reproducibility, repeatability, and precision. A question to sex workers about the number of sex partners in one week has no reliable answer; first because it may vary widely from week to week, and second because of failure to recall correctly. Memory-based questions are always less reliable. At the macro-level, reliability of results of research increases as the sample size increases.

Validity has several dimensions – face, content, concurrent, construct, criterion, and internal and external validities, as discussed by Indrayan and Holt [4]. The indicators of validity of medical tests are sensitivity, specificity, and predictivities. These indicators are discussed later in this chapter.

A telling example illustrating the difference between reliability and validity is assessment of age by asking how old the subject is, asking what the subject's date of birth is, and inspecting the birth record that may be the ultimate truth. Agreement between the first two is reliability, and agreement with the third is validity. Thus, an assessment could be reliable without being valid and the reverse can also happen.

No medical measurement is fully valid in an absolute sense. Errors in classification such as misdiagnosis and missed diagnosis do occur no matter what test is used. Misdiagnosis occurs when the person does not have the disease but is diagnosed as having it. Obviously this is a serious error. Missed diagnosis occurs when the patient has the disease but the disease escapes detection. This could lead to deterioration of the patient. A measurement or test is more valid than another when such errors are relatively fewer.

Various biases discussed in Chapter 3 are threats to validity. Assuring confidentiality helps in some cases to get correct information. Implement it faithfully by deleting all the items of information that could identify the respondent. Also take precautions in case the presence of other people at the time of interview can affect the response.

Accuracy of Measurements and Recording

Accuracy is neither validity nor reliability. It is the correctness of the measurement. The measurement should be devoid of error and recorded to the last digit for it to be accurate – it is nearness to its true value. Age 30 years 5 months and 2 days is more accurate than just 30 years. In a conventional sphygmomanometer, calibrations are at an interval of 2 mmHg: thus, BP measurements also have only that kind of accuracy, although actual BP can be in decimals. However, in many situations, such high accuracy is not required for clinical assessment.

The data, whether obtained in terms of quantities or in terms of verbatim text, should be clearly and correctly recorded. Before grinding it through a computer for statistical analysis, scrutinize the data for their internal consistency. For example, make sure that systolic BP = 126 mmHg is not inadvertently written as 162 mmHg, or the presence of a disease is not recorded with its contradictory features. Scrutiny of forms should be done immediately after they are filled in when memory is fresh. Incomplete forms, unclear information, and illegible writing can be easily corrected at that time without revisiting the subject. If any information is suspicious, repeat contact should be made for verification. The information should look just about right. All forms must be signed and dated so that the responsibility can be fixed.

There may be errors in keying the data into the computer. It is not unlikely that an adjacent key is pressed, such as 8 for 9. Also guard against misreading visually similar digits such as 1 for 7, and 5 for 3 when they are handwritten. A decimal might be missed. Check also for internal consistencies. A systolic BP level of 152 mmHg can rarely rise to 160 mmHg after taking a proven antihypertensive therapy. Similarly, a woman of 22 years can rarely have a child of age 10 years. Double check such records for accuracy. Investigators who have been a part of the data collection or data-recording process may not be able to detect their own errors. Whenever feasible, all checking should be done by an independent person.

Errors sometimes occur in reversing the codes for males and females, and calculating severity score of patients based on wrong columns such as columns 10, 11, 12, 25, and 26 where 10, 11, 12, 24, and 25 should have been used. The scores may incidentally turn out as expected and not arouse suspicion. They are detected on second scrutiny. In another instance, one set of values could be unwittingly exchanged with another set of values or one row may have been copied to another at the time of data entry. In another case, while computing change from pre- to post-, a minus sign could be missed. Such errors may be inadvertent but substantially compromise the credibility of the research.

7.3.3 Other Aspects of Data Quality

Quality is adhering to the defined standards. This innocuous-looking concept is difficult to implement. It encompasses validity and reliability for sure, as discussed earlier, but also completeness, timeliness, and relevance, and such other features.

Completeness

Completeness of data can hardly be overemphasized. Incomplete data introduce bias and can lead to erroneous conclusions. Simple rules for completing a form are outlined in Box 7.3.

To ensure completeness, check all the filled-in forms for errors, omissions, and discrepancies. These lapses can easily occur with self-administered questionnaires and will not be uncommon in interviewer-filled questionnaires. Call back to respondents is in any case needed for those who were not available at the first contact, but it may also be needed for those whose information was incomplete or inconsistent.

BOX 7.3   RULES FOR COMPLETING A FORM

- Give respondents enough time in an interview to think or recall and to give correct answers.
- Write the responses faithfully without imputing your own views or interpretation.
- Ensure that the responses are consistent across various items. If a patient says he is diabetic, his plasma glucose level without drug can rarely be 100 mg/dL.
- Do not leave any item blank. Write "Not applicable," "Not available," "Refused to cooperate," "Died," or any other, as applicable. All missing data should have a sufficient reason and none should be due to carelessness or a casual attitude.
- All writing must be legible. Remember that scrutiny of the form may be done by a third person and data entry into a computer by yet another. They should be able to read the writing properly.

Training and Supervision

Correct implementation of a protocol in a large research project may require a full manual of instructions on how to approach the subjects, strategies needed to elicit the correct data, when to substitute the subject, if at all, by another subject, how to get the cooperation of various agencies, an explanation of the terms and concepts, where to go for help if needed, and other such issues. However, the best bet for quality assurance is training and supervision. The data collectors and health assessors should be trained to follow uniform procedures in as identical a fashion as possible. These are also required on a mini-scale for a graduate thesis. In a long-term study, periodic refresher training may be needed after feedback is received. The staff may behave in a responsible manner yet supervision is needed from time to time. This is to ensure that no digression occurs from the predefined protocol. Supervisors should be equipped to tackle any problems that interviewers or assessors face.

The other aspects of training are improved techniques of questioning and quality interviews that help to elicit correct information with minimal nonresponse. These aspects are sometimes overlooked in medical research, but they can have a bearing on conclusions where history and other enquiries are important components. The interviewer should reassure the respondent about the confidentiality of the information and should scrupulously maintain this assurance. They should have perseverance and patience.

7.4 Validity of the Tools

As mentioned in an earlier chapter, validity is the ability to measure what is intended to be measured. Validity of research data is discussed in the previous section under quality of data, but that depends substantially also on the validity of the tools used to collect and record the data. For this, steps such as a pilot study and pretesting, and assessing sensitivity, specificity, and predictivities of medical tests are undertaken. These are important for large-scale research and also relevant for a graduate thesis.

7.4.1 Pilot Study and Pretesting

While framing the items for collecting the information — either as questionnaire or as schedule — it is necessary to assess that those items provide adequate information on each objective of the research. Also, it should be clear as to how various medical parameters are going to be measured. If the outcome of interest is recovery of the patient, clarify whether this would be in terms of physiological parameters, or ability to do certain activities, or based on imaging evaluations. The endpoints should be clear and relevant for the research in hand. Whether these would be assessed every day, or once in 2 or 3 days, and so on, should also be specified. Who would assess them, with the help of exactly what tools, if any, should be a part of the protocol. In this context, pilot study and pretesting are valuable steps.

Pilot Study

Protocol writing (see Chapter 9) can be a frustrating experience when baseline information regarding the subjects or the disease is missing. In such a case, it is advisable to carry out a small-scale preliminary investigation on the same type of subjects that are proposed

---

BOX 7.4   UTILITY OF A PILOT STUDY

- Assesses feasibility of the study as a whole and of various measurements proposed to be taken
- Confirms that the collected information is enough to fulfill the objectives
- Helps in standardizing tools
- Evaluates the reliability and validity of tools
- Gives an idea of expected variations among subjects that helps to determine the size of the sample
- Anticipates the problems that might come up during implementation
- Assesses the time frame within which various phases of the study would be complete
- Gives feedback that the instructions are not confusing or incomplete
- Assesses the requirements of staff and reveals training and supervision needs, including for data management
- Assesses the adequacy of logistical support

---

to be studied. Such a forerunner, which is done to get a feeling of the subjects and of the conditions, is called a pilot study. Such a study helps in several ways, as described in Box 7.4.

Pilot studies have extremely important functions yet get little attention in research methodology training. A pilot study helps to refine data collection procedures and tools, and to prepare a better protocol. For a large-scale study, a pilot study is considered an essential step. For a small-scale investigation such as for a master's thesis, this may not be needed, although in this case a preliminary investigation may also be needed to finalize the protocol. It is possible to conduct a pilot study on a subsample of subjects from the main study, but it is often difficult to include these observations in the final analysis because they could be incomplete or inconsistent with the main phase of the study.

Pretesting of Tools

It is generally considered highly desirable that all questionnaires, laboratory procedures, imaging modalities, and so forth, are tested for their efficacy before they are finally used in the main study. This is called pretesting. Many unforeseen problems or gaps can be detected by such an exercise, and the tools can be accordingly adjusted and improved. Pretesting can reveal whether the items of information are adequate, whether the sequence is logical, the wordings are clear, the list of possible answers is exhaustive, respondents are able to answer correctly, the space for open-ended questions is adequate, the length of the interview is within limits, the instructions are adequate, and other such aspects. This also serves as a rehearsal of the actual data collection process and helps to train the investigators. Sometimes pretesting is repeated to standardize the methodology for eliciting correct and valid information.

In the case of measurement tools such as pulse oximeter, testing may have to be done at regular intervals to check their validity. Standardization of laboratory procedures can also be tested. Modifications as needed are made. Some features of this exercise such as standardization of tools may overlap with those of the pilot study.

Despite pilot study and pretesting, it will not be uncommon that the data collection form or the procedure requires further changes while the study is in progress. If this change is done, ensure that the corresponding changes are also made in the data that have already been collected.

7.4.2 Sensitivity and Specificity of Medical Tests

Medical tests are commonly used in research to identify cases and to monitor progress. For example, an electrocardiogram (ECG) is a test for myocardial infarction (MI), a chest X-ray tests for tuberculosis of lungs, enzyme levels test for liver disease, and lung function tests for chronic bronchitis. These are not limited to the conventional laboratory-based tests but can also be clinical signs and symptoms. For example, the initial diagnosis of abdominal tuberculosis is based on complaints such as long-standing pain in the abdomen, constipation, and vomiting. For correct results, these tests must have high validity. The validity of a medical test is its ability to correctly identify cases with the particular condition under investigation, called positive predictivity, and correctly exclude subjects without that condition, called negative predictivity. However, these are better appreciated when explained in light of the other two commonly used concepts – sensitivity and specificity. Sensitivity–specificity and positive and negative predictivities are the indicators that assess this validity. See Box 7.5 for details. Before you use a test in your research, assess its validity using the following methods.

The sensitivity of a medical test is the chance that it is positive in established cases of the disease and specificity is the chance that it is negative in subjects without the condition. If an ECG is positive in 80% of known cases of MI, the sensitivity of this test is said to be

---

BOX 7.5   WHAT IS A VALID TEST?

A valid test should be able to give the required information correctly. Postprandial blood glucose level is not as valid a measurement for glucose intolerance as fasting level. Thyroid-stimulating hormone level by itself is not a valid measure of thyroidism. For validity, a test or measurement is compared against an established gold standard. Ideally, the gold standard should give correct results in all cases, but there is hardly any such gold standard in medicine. Thus, the best available test is considered the gold standard. This may be very expensive or difficult to perform. Other tests, which are less expensive and convenient, are judged against this gold standard.

For the purpose of evaluating the inherent validity of a test, sensitivity and specificity are used as indicators. A test is inherently valid if it is positive in most people with the disease (high sensitivity) and negative in those without the disease (high specificity). Subjectively, a test can be considered inherently valid if sensitivity and specificity each exceed 90%. It is excellent if these exceed 95%. Combined **inherent validity** of the test is obtained by adding true positives and true negatives out of the total subjects. In a representative cross-sectional study, combined inherent validity is the same as predictive validity, as explained below. This may not be so in a case–control study and a prospective study.

From the diagnostic point of view, acceptable measures of validity are positive predictivity and negative predictivity. These are the performance of the test in correctly predicting the presence or absence of disease, respectively. The combination of these two is called the **predictive validity**. Generally speaking, a test or measurement with predictive validity of 90% or above can be considered excellent. Some researchers use the term accuracy for the combination of the two predictivities but, in our opinion, accuracy signifies correctness to the last digit of measurement.

BOX 7.6   SIMPLE FORMULAS FOR SENSITIVITY, SPECIFICITY, POSITIVE PREDICTIVITY, AND NEGATIVE PREDICTIVITY

Consider the following 2×2 table that gives the number of subjects with positive and negative tests, and with and without disease in a cross-sectional random sample from a target population. It is only for such a sample that all four indices can be calculated from the same data.

	Disease		
Test	Present	Absent	Total
Positive	a	b	$a+b$
Negative	c	d	$c+d$
Total	$a+c$	$b+d$	n

In this table, positives are in the first row and first column, and the disease confirmation is in two columns (and not rows). To use the formulas given below, ensure that the table is structured in this manner. Also note in this table that:

True positives	=	a	Persons with disease with positive test
True negatives	=	d	Persons without disease with negative test
False positives	=	b	Persons without disease with positive test
False negatives	=	c	Persons with disease with negative test
Sensitivity of the test	$= a/(a+c)$		Ability of the test to be correctly positive among those who are known to have the disease
Specificity of the test	$= d/(b+d)$		Ability of the test to be correctly negative among those who are known to be without disease
Inherent validity of the test	$= (a+d)/n$		Ability of the test to be correctly positive or correctly negative
Positive predictivity of the test	$= a/(a+b)$		Ability of the test to correctly predict the presence of disease
Negative predictivity of the test	$= d/(c+d)$		Ability of the test to correctly predict the absence of disease
Predictive validity of the test	$= (a+d)/n$		Combined ability to predict presence or absence of disease

80%. A test is 90% specific if it is negative in 90% of subjects not suffering from the disease in question. Without disease in this case are those who were otherwise suspected to have disease but were finally confirmed to be negative because it is only in suspected cases that the test is done. Note that sensitivity and specificity can be evaluated only when the disease status of the patients is known. A "gold standard" is required to confirm or rule out the diagnosis before sensitivity and specificity are evaluated. This is more easily said than done. No test is infallible. Nevertheless, a combination of criteria could be developed that could provide a near gold standard. In a clinical setting, response of the patient after treatment can fairly well establish that the suspected disease was indeed present. For malignancy, histological evidence is often considered the gold standard.

Sensitivity and specificity are inherent properties of a test. They should be invariant in different situations, but they severely depend on how a case is defined. If coronary artery disease is restricted to include MIs only, then an ECG would be a highly sensitive test. If cases of angina are also included, then the sensitivity of an ECG would be low.

A case–control study is needed to evaluate sensitivity and specificity of a test, where cases are those confirmed with disease, and controls are confirmed without disease but previously disease had been suspected. For example, for polymerase chain reaction (PCR) test of tuberculosis, the test should be used on a group of confirmed cases and another group of confirmed nontuberculous subjects that clinically fake as tuberculosis. Then only sensitivity and specificity of PCR can be calculated. Realize that a diagnostic test is used only on suspected cases.

For formulas of sensitivity and specificity, see Box 7.6.

Example 7.1 explains the calculation from another perspective.

Example 7.1: Sensitivity and Specificity of X-Rays for Lesions

Consider the following data on X-rays and presence of lesions. The table is based on X-ray results in 60 cases known to have the lesion and 200 cases without lesions. These 200 may have some other condition that has a similar presentation; otherwise the question of X-ray would not arise. Note that the design of this study is case control.

X-ray (Criterion)	Lesion (Actual)		
Result	Present (+)	Absent (–)	Total
Positive (+)	48 (TP)	52 (FP)	100
Negative (–)	12 (FN)	148 (TN)	160
Total	60 (TP + FN)	200 (FP + TN)	260

TP= true-positive; FP = false-positive; FN = false-negative; TN = true-negative.

$$\text{Sensitivity} = \frac{\text{Number of test-postive out of persons with disease}}{\text{Number of persons with disease who underwent the test}}$$

$$= \frac{TP}{TP + FN}$$

$$= \frac{48}{60} = 0.80 \text{ or } 80\%$$

$$\text{Specificity} = \frac{\text{Number of test-negative out of persons without disease}}{\text{Number of persons without disease who underwent the test}}$$

$$= \frac{TN}{FP + TN}$$

$$= \frac{148}{200} = 0.74 \text{ or } 74\%$$

7.4.3 ROC Curves and Youden Index

In the context of thyroid disease, a legitimate question is whether thyroxine (T_4) or thyroid-stimulating hormone (TSH) is better at discriminating between hyperthyroid and euthyroid cases. Comparison of the performance of two quantitative tests over a range of values can be obtained by the area under the ROC curve. This area can also be used to assess the validity of a test without comparison. Conventionally, an ROC curve is obtained by plotting sensitivity (i.e., true-positive rate) vs. (1 – specificity) (i.e., false-positive rate) for different values of measurements, as illustrated in Example 7.2.

Example 7.2: ROC Curve for T4 Level T_4 level is a routine investigation in thyroid cases. Suppose there are 50 confirmed hyperthyroid cases and 100 euthyroid cases. The results are as given in the following table.

T_4 level (µg/dL)	Hyperthyroid cases In the interval	Cumu-lative	Euthyroid cases In the interval	Cumula-tive	Sensitivity*	Specificity*	1 – Speci-ficity
<5.0	12	12	3	3	12/50=24%	(100−3)/100=97%	3%
5.0–9.9	27	39	28	31	39/50=78%	(100−31)/100=69%	31%
10.0–14.9	6	45	39	70	45/50=90%	(100−70)/100=30%	70%
15.0–19.9	3	48	20	90	48/50=96%	(100−90)/100=10%	90%
≥20.0	2	50	10	100	50/50=100%	(100100)/100=0%	100%
Total	50		100				

*Computed for the upper limit of each interval.

The ROC curve for T_4 level for this example is shown in Figure 7.1. The area under the curve (AUC) in this case is 0.76, which is adequate but not good enough to inspire confidence.

The closer the ROC curve to the left and top border (Figure 7.1), the more valid the test is in terms of sensitivity and specificity. The maximum possible AUC is 1.0, and the actual AUC measures the test validity in the sense of its ability to correctly identify those known with and without the disease. The curve and the area (called *C*-statistic) can be easily obtained through any standard statistical software. Because of inherent variations and uncertainties in all biological phenomena, no test can be perfect. It is considered excellent if the AUC is 0.90 or more, and good if the AUC is between 0.80 and 0.89. The area 0.50 corresponds to the diagonal and indicates that the test is absolutely not helpful. In a rare case if this area is less than 0.50, conclude that the test is misleading. In this case, reverse the definition of presence and absence of disease.

The ROC curve can also help in identifying the threshold that gives the highest sum of sensitivity and specificity. This corresponds to the Youden index given by

$$\text{Youden index} = \text{maximum of (sensitivity + specificity} - 1)$$

Appropriate software will tell you where this point is. This point will give the sensitivity and specificity that could be used to get the threshold of the value of the quantitative test where (sensitivity + specificity) is maximum. Youden index measures the performance of the test on a (0,1) scale at the best threshold. You may have to interpolate between plotted values to obtain this threshold. In this example (Figure 7.1), such a threshold corresponds to sensitivity = 77% and specificity = 71% (1 – specificity = 29%). From the table

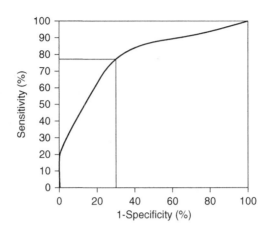

FIGURE 7.1
Receiver operating characteristic (ROC) curve for thyroxine (T_4) level in Example 7.2.

in Example 7.2, the threshold corresponding to these values of sensitivity and specificity is approximately 9 µg/dL. This is where the sum of sensitivity and specificity is the highest. This procedure of finding the optimal threshold is applicable when both sensitivity and specificity are equally important. If they are not, a more complex method is required to find an appropriate cutoff.

The real utility of the ROC curve is in comparing the performance of two or more tests. For example, to compare triiodothyronine (T_3), T_4, and TSH for discriminating between euthyroidism and hyperthyroidism, draw an ROC for T_3, T_4, and TSH. The one with the highest AUC is better. For more details of ROC curves, see Indrayan and Malhotra [9].

7.4.4 Predictivities and Prevalence

Scientific prediction is not the prophecy of Nostradamus. It has to be rational and based on solid evidence. Subjectivity has very little role in such predictions. How to find the likelihood of a test to correctly predict the presence or absence of disease?

Two Types of Predictivity

The actual utility of a diagnostic or screening test is in its ability to correctly identify or correctly exclude the disease in suspected cases. The right question is: If a subject has a positive test, what is the probability that they actually have the disease? In terms of notations,

$$\text{Positive predictivity} = P(D+\,|\,T+)$$

$$\text{Opposed to sensitivity} = P(T+\,|\,D+)$$

where P is for probability, D+ is for presence of disease and T+ is for test positivity. After the vertical slash ($|$) sign is the known status, which is D+ in the case of sensitivity and T+ in the case of positive predictivity. Note the reversal of the notation within parentheses. Thus, they are kind of inverse probabilities. Positive predictivity (in fact, short for predictivity of a positive value) is the chance that a patient who has a positive test (say, with ECG changes) really has or had the disease (say, MI). Positive predictivity can also be understood to measure how good the test is as a marker of the disease. For exclusion of a disease,

$$\text{Negative predictivity} = P(D- \,|\, T-)$$

$$\text{Opposed to specificity} = P(T- \,|\, D-)$$

Again, one is the inverse of the other in a directional sense. See Example 7.3 for a calculation of the two types of predictivity, as well as for sensitivity and specificity, based on the formulas given in Box 7.6.

Example 7.3: Calculation of Sensitivity–Specificity and the Two Predictivities from Cross-Sectional Data

Joyee et al. [10] isolated *Chlamydia trachomatis* by culture and also detected it by direct fluorescent antibody (DFA) testing in 143 sexually transmitted disease cases. The results obtained are as follows.

	DFA		
Culture	+	−	Total
Positive	26	1	27
Negative	9	107	116
Total	35	108	143

Although culture negativity is not a confirmed indication of the absence of the organism, it is still considered a gold standard because of the unavailability of a better criterion. Following this convention in this example,

Sensitivity of DFA = 26/27 = 97.3%
Specificity of DFA = 107/116 = 92.2%
Positive predictivity of DFA = 26/35 = 74.3%
Negative predictivity of DFA = 107/108 = 99.1%

The two tests have high agreement: (26 + 107)/143 = 0.93; but this is mostly for negative results. DFA can replace culture to exclude the organism because negative predictivity is so high. But the situation for detecting the presence of the organism is not as satisfactory. Nine cases are culture-negative but DFA-positive and positive predictivity of DFA is low, at 74.3%.

Bayes' Rule

Sensitivity and specificity are easy to evaluate by a case–control study, but predictivity requires that the subjects are followed up until such time that their disease status is confirmed as present or absent. This could be very time-consuming and expensive. Thus, predictivities are difficult to evaluate. Luckily, there is a statistical procedure, called Bayes' rule, which helps to get one from the other, provided some ancillary information is available. This is illustrated in Example 7.4, where the formulas are also given.

Example 7.4: Predictivity from Sensitivity/Specificity and Bayes' Rule

Consider hypothetical data of Pap smears of 4000 apparently healthy women aged 40 years and above for cervical cancer, where each was also independently evaluated for histology through biopsy as a gold test. This is a representative cross-sectional study as it starts from healthy women and they are subsequently categorized for histology and Pap smear results. The following results are obtained in this study.

Pap smear	Cervical cancer by histology		Total
	Present	Absent	
Positive	190	210	400
Negative	10	3590	3600
Total	200	3800	4000

The results of the gold test (histology) are in two columns in the above table, whereas they are in two rows in the table in Example 7.3. Using the definitions given earlier,

Sensitivity of Pap smear = 190/200 = 95.0%
Specificity of Pap smear = 3590/3800 = 94.5%
Positive predictivity of Pap smear = 190/400 = 47.5%
Negative predictivity of Pap smear = 3590/3600 = 99.7%

Despite extremely high sensitivity and specificity (both nearly 95%), the positive predictivity of the Pap smear is still low (less than 50%). Therefore, this is not a good diagnostic tool for cervical cancer in this population, although it is extremely good at ruling out the disease (negative predictivity 99.7%). This is what makes it a good screening test. Thus, good sensitivity and specificity do not necessarily make a good diagnostic test. The prevalence of cervical cancer in this group of subjects is $P(D+) = 200/4000 = 0.05$. Bayes' rule says that

$$\text{Positive predictivity} = \frac{\text{Sensitivity} \times \text{Prevalence}}{\text{Sensitivity} \times \text{Prevalence} + (1 - \text{Specificity}) \times (1 - \text{Prevalence})}$$

$$= \frac{0.95 \times 0.05}{0.95 \times 0.05 + (1 - 0.945) \times (1 - 0.05)} = 0.476 \text{ or } 47.6\%$$

This is nearly the same as obtained earlier directly from the data also. A minor difference is due to decimal approximation in the calculation of specificity, which more accurately is 94.4737% but we used 94.5% as an approximation. Similar equivalence can also be shown for negative predictivity. For this,

$$\text{Negative predictivity} = \frac{\text{Specificity} \times (1 - \text{Prevalence})}{(1 - \text{Sensitivity}) \times \text{Prevalence} + \text{Specificity} \times (1 - \text{Prevalence})}$$

$$= \frac{0.945 \times (1 - 0.05)}{0.945 \times (1 - 0.05) + (1 - 0.945) \times 0.05} = 0.997 \text{ or } 99.7\%$$

If prevalence is known, predictivity can be obtained by using sensitivity and specificity. Bayes' rule converts $P(T+|D+)$ to $P(D+|T+)$ and $P(T-|D-)$ to $P(D-|T-)$ using the prevalence rate. Herein lies the importance of the concepts of sensitivity and specificity. Based on confirmed cases, they are easy to obtain, and these then help to calculate diagnostically important predictivities with the help of Bayes' rule. This obviates the need to carry out expensive follow-up studies. Sensitivity and specificity of a test remain the same across populations, but predictivity changes depending upon the prevalence of the disease in the target population. However, both can be calculated on the basis of a representative cross-sectional study.

The dependence of predictivity on prevalence arises from putting the information in its proper context. A patient with a high temperature and who is shivering might be diagnosed as having influenza in Europe, but malaria in West Africa [11].

Where to Use Which Test

As already mentioned, a test with good positive predictivity is required to confirm the presence of disease, and a test with good negative predictivity is required to exclude the disease. Screening tests, which are used in the initial stages, or in a community setting, should be able to correctly exclude all negative cases. Cervical cytology (Pap smear) is used for screening of cervical cancer, and mammography for breast cancer. Fasting blood glucose level is used for screening of diabetes, and Mantoux test for tuberculosis infection. These are tests with high negative predictivity. When the test is negative it is safe to assume in these cases that the disease is absent.

The goal of diagnosis is to ferret out cases with disease while keeping false-positives to a negligible level. False-positivity can create an unmanageable backlog of cases that actually do not require medical attention. This can lead to organizational fatigue and staff may become worn out, causing loss of alertness. Thus, a diagnostic test is good if it has high positive predictivity. Histology is good to confirm malignancy, as is X-ray for bone fracture. Try to use such tests in your research.

References

1. Rodriguez KL, Burkitt KH, Bayliss NK, et al. Veteran, primary care provider, and specialist satisfaction with electronic consultation. JMIR Med Inform 2015 Jan 14;3(1):e5. http://medinform.jmir.org/2015/1/e5/
2. Wong ZY, Hassali MA, Alrasheedy AA, et al. Patients' beliefs about generic medicines in Malaysia. Pharm Pract (Granada) 2014 Oct;12(4):474. www.ncbi.nlm.nih.gov/pmc/articles/PMC4282766/
3. Gothwal VK, Wright TA, Lamoureux EL, et al. Guttman scale analysis of the distance vision scale. Investig Ophthal Visual Sci 2009;50(9):4496–4501. https://iovs.arvojournals.org/article.aspx?articleid=2185952
4. Indrayan A, Holt MP. Concise Encyclopedia of Biostatistics for Medical Professionals. CRC Press. 2017.
5. Chambless LE, Shahar E, Sharrett AR, et al. Association of transient ischemic attack/stroke symptoms assessed by standardized questionnaire and algorithm with cerebrovascular risk factors and carotid artery wall thickness. The ARIC study, 1987–1989. Am J Epidemiol 1996;144:857–867. https://academic.oup.com/aje/article/144/9/857/95185

6. Wei M, Mitchell BD, Haffner SM, et al. Effects of cigarette smoking, diabetes, high cholesterol, and hypertension on all-cause mortality and cardiovascular disease mortality in Mexican Americans: The San Antonio Heart Study. Am J Epidemiol 1996;144:1058–1065. https://academic.oup.com/aje/article/144/11/1058/102937

7. Mahtani K, Spencer EA, Brassey J, et al. Catalogue of bias: Observer bias. BMJ Evid Based Med 2018;23 (1):23–24. https://ebm.bmj.com/content/23/1/23

8. Hadjistavropoulos T, Herr K, Prkachin KM, et al. Pain assessment in elderly adults with dementia. Lancet Neurol 2014 Dec;13 (12):1216–1227. www.thelancet.com/journals/laneur/article/PIIS1474-4422(14)70103–6/fulltext

9. Indrayan A, Malhotra RK. Medical Biostatistics, Fourth Edition. CRC Press, 2018.

10. Joyee AG, Thyagrajan SP, Sowmya B, et al. Need for specific and routine strategy for the diagnosis of genital chlamydial infection among patients with sexually transmitted diseases in India. Indian J Med Res 2003;118:152–157. www.ncbi.nlm.nih.gov/pubmed/14700349

11. Chatfield C. Confession of a pragmatic statistician. Statistician 2002;51(Part-I);1–20. www.jstor.org/stable/3650386.

8

Sampling and Sample Size

Medical decisions are almost invariably based on samples. Samples of blood, urine, sputum, stool, and biopsies are everyday occurrences. Sampling is the only feasible method in this situation because the complete material of these biological substances for anybody cannot be studied. A sample of blood from anywhere in the body gives nearly the same picture as from anywhere else because it is so thoroughly mixed inside the body. Yet, repeat investigations are not uncommon. Biopsy results in many cases are not reliable, and some other form of confirmation becomes necessary. Sampling results are always interpreted with caution.

The thrust in this chapter is on samples from individuals. Whether the research is descriptive or analytical, it is conducted on a sample of subjects. **Sample** is the statistical term for the group of subjects included in the study, which almost invariably would be a fraction of the target population. Sample studies are not only cost effective and quick but often are more reliable also because more accurate methods and better care can be exercised for a small group. Even if resources can be garnered to study all the existing cases of, say, glaucoma in the world, it would still be incomplete because cases arising in the future cannot be studied. Medical research requires that the findings on existing cases be used on future cases! Sampling is a prerequisite for this paradigm. However, if the objective is to find the prevalence of diabetes mellitus in the year 2020 among females of age 40 years and above residing in a particular city, complete enumeration is possible. If a complete registry of cancer cases in a defined population is available, perhaps sampling is not needed to assess the *existing* situation. However, sampling is needed for most medical research.

Not that sampling has no disadvantages. It can create a feeling of discrimination when sample subjects get different attention than others. Sometimes an explanation is necessary to dispel the feeling of discrimination. Samples can fail to provide valid results when they are not representative, and can fail to provide reliable results if the size is small.

There are two dimensions of adequacy of a sample. First, it should represent the full spectrum of subjects in the target population. Various methods of sampling are adopted in different situations to meet this objective. These methods are discussed in Section 8.1 for descriptive studies and in Section 8.2 for analytical studies. A list of these methods was given in Figure 3.1 in Chapter 3 and a preview is given in Box 8.1. Some of these methods may not provide a representative sample if not correctly implemented. Second, the sample size must be reasonably large to give reliable results, without being excessively large. Size also has a role in its ability to represent a cross-section of the population. Sample size is discussed in Section 8.4. In between in Section 8.3 is a discussion on nonsampling errors in contrast to sampling errors. Controlling nonsampling errors frequently assumes

BOX 8.1   A PREVIEW OF THE METHODS OF SAMPLING

Purposive (Nonrandom)

- Volunteers, who agree to participate
- Snowball, where one case identifies other similar cases (e.g., intravenous drug users)
- Convenient cases, such as captive medical students or other readily available groups
- Quota, with at-will selection of a fixed number from each group
- Referred cases, who may be under pressure to participate
- Haphazard, with a combination of two or more of the above methods

Random

- Simple, which gives equal chance to all individuals (as in a lottery): consecutive cases arriving in a clinic can also be considered random when there is no bias in their arrival
- Systematic, where consecutively every kth (such as, every fifth) person is selected or any such scheme is followed
- Stratified, which requires separate random samples from relevant subgroups (strata) to give adequate representation of all the subgroups
- Multistage, wherein nested samples are successively selected within the larger units selected earlier
- Cluster, where a group is selected instead of individual subjects
- Probability proportional to size, where larger units have more chance of selection – this gives a self-weighting scheme for statistical purposes

more importance because these have the potential to vitiate the results beyond redemption, whereas sampling errors can be handled by choosing a representative sample of adequate size.

8.1 Sampling Methods and Sampling for Descriptive Studies

Figure 3.1 in Chapter 3 listed sample survey, case series, and census as the three strategies of descriptive studies. Census is a complete enumeration of all individuals without leaving anyone out, and case series is done on available subjects without recourse to sampling. These two do not involve any sampling, and are rarely used in graduate work.

The dominant format of descriptive studies is a **sample survey**. This term is generally used for a population-based study, but technically descriptive studies done on clinic subjects are also surveys. The main feature of a survey is that a selected section of the target population is investigated instead of the whole population with the objective of understanding and describing the characteristics of the population such as the prevalence rate of a health condition, its distribution in different segments of the population, and what is more common or what is less common, and where. A study of the profile of cases of a particular disease also comes under the descriptive category. A cause–effect type of relationship or even an association between an antecedent and outcome is not the objective of a survey. In fact, no characteristic is identified as antecedent or outcome in a survey. Sometimes surveys are done at periodic intervals in the same target population to assess a trend. These are called **serial surveys**.

The term "population" is used differently in different contexts. Statistically, the term **population** is used for the whole group of units of interest to which the findings would extrapolate. More specifically this is called the **target population** or the target group. This could be healthy children in an area, pregnant women who register in an antenatal clinic, patients of renal disease reporting in a group of hospitals, blood units received as donation in an area, or any other such group. This chapter is focused on individuals, although other types of units such as biopsy specimens and antigens, when available for a large number of patients, can also be studied for profiling, using the same methods.

Sample studies do need to make a distinction between a **unit of sampling** and a **unit of enquiry**. The latter is also called a **unit of study**. In a population-based study on diarrhea, it is possible that the ultimate unit of sampling is a family, but the unit of study could be all the children in the family, or the most recent episode of diarrhea in the family. One unit of sampling can have two or more units of study, although generally there will only be one. A list of all sampling units in the target population is called the **sampling frame**.

Because of profound variations in a medical setting, as mentioned in Chapter 1, it is important for the validity of the results of a survey that the sample of subjects included in the study is truly representative of the target population. This is especially important for descriptive studies. As mentioned earlier, representativeness depends both on the method of selection and the size of the sample. Among the methods of selection, the following are more commonly used in descriptive studies.

8.1.1 Purposive Sampling (Nonrandom Methods)

When not enough eligible subjects are willing to cooperate in research, **volunteers** are used. This is a purposive sample. The other possibility is to use those subjects who are easily and captively available. Many studies are done on medical students or medical professionals. This is a **convenience sample**. Another method is **snowball sampling**. This is used for an obscure group of people. In this case, one eligible person such as an intravenous drug user (IVDU) is identified, and their help is taken to identify others they know. Then those are asked to identify others known to them. Otherwise, IVDUs are so obscure that their detection and sampling are difficult. Patients referred to a clinic also are a nonrandom sampling. In **quota sampling**, a pre-specified number of subjects is selected from various segments of the population without recourse to random selection. Sometimes a mix of these procedures is followed. This is called **haphazard sampling**.

Nonrandom samples have two basic problems. The first is that the larger group they represent is difficult to identify, and may not match the intended target group. This is not a limitation when generalization of results is not required. The results would be valid for the sample itself, and they can provide useful clues for further studies that can be based on random samples. Phase I trials use subjects selected by nonrandom methods. The second problem is that statistical inferences such as confidence interval (CI) and test of significance require a random sample and cannot be applied on nonrandom samples. Researchers sometimes pretend that a clearly nonrandom sample is random and statistical inferences for a larger group are made. This is statistically inadmissible and can be dangerous in some situations. Yet, the more important question should be whether the sample is representative of the target population or not. Random selection is the means but representativeness is the goal [1]. When nonrandom samples are representative, generalization could be possible, but practical experience suggests that nonrandom samples are seldom representative of the target population.

8.1.2 Random Sampling

When the sample size is adequate, a basic feature that provides reasonable assurance of representativeness is random selection. This essentially means that each individual is given some chance of being included. These chances across subjects may or may not be equal.

Simple Random Sampling

When the list of sampling units (called the **sampling frame**) in the target population is available or can be prepared such that each unit is assigned a number, the best statistical strategy is to use random numbers to select the sample that provides equal chance for all the units (Example 8.1). This is called simple random sampling (SRS), or just random sampling in short, and tends to give an unbiased sample.

Example 8.1: Simple Random Sampling

For the purpose of illustration, consider a random selection of five individuals from a total of 60 attending a Nowhere clinic. Assign them numbers from 01 to 60. The highest is 60, which is a two-digit number. Thus, two-digit random numbers are required for selection. A computer can easily generate such numbers. Suppose these are as given in the box. Start from any random point: in this case, say, number 38. Go in any predetermined direction and select the first five distinct random numbers less than or equal to 60. In the usual sequence, these are 38, 09, 17, 41, and 25 in this example. Individuals bearing these numbers constitute an SRS of size 5 out of 60. Alternatively, computer programs (e.g., *www.randomization.com*) are available that would select five random numbers out of 60, or as many as needed.

Two-digit random numbers				
77	03	56	41	47
89	60	77	74	38 ← random start
09	17	41	78	68
25	97	32	76	69
28	01	35	67	90
83	95	55	42	24

SRS is easy when the total population is fixed and not large. In a field study, such as on hypertension in young adults in a community, the target population could be large and it may be difficult to prepare a sampling frame. A large sample may be required in this study and drawing a large SRS can be a tedious process. Also, in a field study, SRS may yield a sample of subjects that are located in far-flung areas, causing inconvenience in field work, and increasing the cost and time requirements. This is not the case with a clinic-based study. SRS also ignores considerations such as age and gender that might be important factors influencing the parameter under study. It is possible that SRS under-represents or over-represents a particular group. To ensure adequate representation of such groups, the best option is stratified sampling, as described next.

Stratified Random Sampling

If factors such as age, gender, and obesity are important, divide (stratify) the population by these factors where feasible, and draw separate independent samples of desired size from each group using the SRS method. This is called stratified random sampling (StRS) and ensures all relevant groups are adequately represented. Example 8.2 illustrates the application of this method to a study of blood pressure in different age groups.

> **Example 8.2: Stratified Random Sampling to Study Blood Pressure (BP) in Relation to Age**
>
> Normal BP levels are severely affected by age, besides other factors. In a study to delineate BP levels in kidney patients, it is helpful to divide them into age groups such as 40–49, 50–59, 60–69 years, etc., and draw independent simple random samples from each age group. Such StRS would ensure that all relevant age groups are adequately represented in the sample.
>
> If a central representative value such as mean is needed for all age groups combined in an StRS, the age-specific mean is multiplied by the population of that age, added across age groups, and then divided by the total population.

StRS is feasible only when the sampling frame for each stratum is available or can be constructed. This requirement can be a severe constraint in many practical situations. In addition, information on the stratifying characteristic is needed for each unit.

Strata size may or may not be equal. In case of unequal strata, a **proportionate sample** from different strata is preferable. For example, if a stratum is size 30, a sample of 3 units is taken and if the size is 60 a sample of 6 units is taken. However, proportionate sampling is not mandatory. When not proportionate, the chance of different units being in the sample is not the same, although the method is still random.

Systematic Random Sampling

An easy alternative to SRS is the systematic method. If there are N subjects in the target population out of which n are to be included in the study, the **sampling fraction** is $k = N/n$. If this is not an integer, take the integer part of this number. If $N = 350$ subjects of liver cirrhosis are expected in a clinic in a year's time, and $n = 40$ are to be selected, then $k =$ integer part of $350/40 = 8$. Select one randomly out of the first 8, and the others are automatically selected, adding 8 every time. If the first randomly selected subject is 7, the others are 15, 23, 31, etc., in this example.

Systematic random sampling (SyRS) is easy to implement in a clinic-based study where the patients come in a sequence. This method does not require a full sampling frame as needed for SRS but requires information about the total number of subjects in the target population. If the total number of subjects is not known, it is still possible to systematically select, say, a 5% sample, by continuing to select one in 20 until the end of the frame is reached. However, in this case the sample size cannot be fixed in advance. If you want a fixed sample size, say 30, select one in five from the first 150. An application of a systematic sample with fixed size in a clinical setting is given in Example 8.3.

Example 8.3: Systematic Random Sampling for Biopsies

Systematic sampling can have a useful application in biopsies. Chon et al. [2] describe how biopsies at 10 systematically selected sites from the prostate yielded 36% detection of cancer in those who otherwise had negative biopsies. The researchers performed 10 core biopsies in these patients in place of the usual six. Extended systematic sampling in such cases removes possible bias in picking the exact biopsy site and can reveal positivity that otherwise was concealed in the conventional scheme.

One difficulty with SyRS is that some subjects at the end of the list may never get selected. In the example of selecting 40 out of 350, the last number in the selection would be 320. The subjects at numbers 321–350 would never be selected. If these numbers were included, the total number of subjects in the sample would be 43 and not 40. To overcome this problem, a method called **circular sampling** is adopted. A random number is selected between 1 and N, and every kth beginning that number is selected in a cyclical fashion, that is, $(N + 1)$th becomes the first subject. This is done until n subjects are selected. Such a circular method gives the same chance to all units for inclusion in the sample.

Cluster Random Sampling

In large-scale surveys in a community, availability of subjects in close proximity is a big operational convenience. These are called **clusters**. To assess prevalence of cataracts in the elderly, you may like to visit one residential colony and find how many people have cataracts, then move to the next area. Thus, the full colony is in the sample as one cluster. In the case of cluster sampling, as the name implies, clusters are selected. This method is rarely used in medical graduate theses and we omit the details. If needed, see Indrayan and Holt [3].

Multistage Random Sampling

For extremely large-scale surveys covering a full state or a full country, it is desirable that the sampling is done in stages. Select a few counties randomly and then a few census block areas within each selected county, and a few families or target individuals within each selected census block. In this way a relatively small sample can represent the entire population. An application to a clinical setting is given in Example 8.4. Instead of the entire sampling frame, this strategy requires only the frame of nested units that are to be selected in successive stages. Some sections of literature describe it as multistage cluster sampling, but that is an erroneous label. This method is another example of sampling that does not give equal chance to the units but is still random.

Example 8.4: Multistage Random Sampling for Assessing Dietary Calcium Intake and Physical Activity Levels in Orthopedic Patients and Their Relatives

Raj et al. [4] used multistage random sampling to assess dietary calcium intake, physical activity, and their predictors in a hospital-based study in India. They randomly selected a maximum of 5 patients from the inpatient register of an orthopedic ward on 2 randomly selected days in a week for as many weeks as needed to complete the predetermined sample size.

Probability Proportional to Size Sampling

Although the details are not provided in this text, the method of estimation of a summary measure such as prevalence rate of a disease in a population depends heavily on the sampling method. Bigger strata and bigger units at different stages in a multistage method have to be given proportionate weight at the time of estimation. A self-weighting mechanism is to select units with probability proportional to size. Under this scheme, bigger units are given a better chance of selection and called probability proportional to size (PPS) sampling.

> **Example 8.5: PPS Sampling for a Study on Hepatitis B Seroprevalence among Children**
>
> Lopez et al. [5] used what they called a three-stage cluster design to select a sample to estimate hepatitis seroprevalence among 5 to 6-year-old children in the Philippines. They selected 25 provinces using the PPS method and then, in the second stage, selected 12 *barangays* (villages) per province, again using the PPS method. All children of the selected *barangays* were included in the sample.

Other Methods of Random Sampling

The methods described in the preceding paragraphs are standard textbook methods. The situation where each is appropriate is given in Box 8.2. In practice, it may be convenient to include all eligible subjects who come to a clinic beginning on a specific date and terminate the sampling when a predetermined size is reached. This is called **consecutive sampling**. This would provide a random sample so long as all subjects meeting the preset inclusion and exclusion criteria are considered and special conditions such as an epidemic do not exist that can alter the basic character. This is a form of **inverse sampling** that is randomly done in sequence one by one till such time that the requisite number of subjects meeting the preset criteria is available. If you are looking for 30 males with esophagus cancer in a cancer clinic, you continue until such time that this many are included. This method does not require knowledge of the sampling frame.

For further details on the types of popular sample designs and most of the methods described in the preceding paragraphs, see Indrayan and Malhotra [6].

> **BOX 8.2   WHERE TO USE WHICH SAMPLING METHOD?**
>
> The method of choice is always SRS unless it is difficult to adopt. The estimate provided by SRS is generally the most precise. Some problems it can create are:
>
> * Nonavailability of the sampling frame
> * Too dispersed subjects in the sample, making the approach difficult
> * Less representation of specific groups that are important and must be adequately represented
> * Obtaining so many distinct random numbers
>
> The first two problems can be handled by either cluster or multistage sampling. The answer to the third is stratified, and the remedy for the fourth is systematic sampling because it requires only one random number. Also, a systematic method does not require the full frame. In any case, with wide availability of computers, generating distinct random numbers is not a problem.

8.2 Sampling for Analytical Studies

The primary objective of an analytical study is to assess the relationship between pre-specified antecedents and outcomes. This can be either an observational study (prospective, retrospective, or cross-sectional) or an experimental study (laboratory experiment or clinical trial). Sampling methods for such studies can be explained as follows.

8.2.1 Sampling Methods in Observational Studies

Because observational studies do not involve any man-made interventions, it is relatively easy to adopt a random sampling scheme. This can be any of the six schemes discussed in the previous sections, or a new one can be generated in the context of the study. The essentials in a specific context are as follows.

Sampling Methods for Cross-Sectional Studies

The validity of conclusions regarding the association of two or more factors depends on their proper representation in the sample in proportion to their presence in the target population. Random sampling serves as a great facilitator to achieve such representation. Assessments such as sensitivity–specificity and predictivities, which we discussed in Chapter 7, is adversely affected if these proportions are biased in any manner. Thus, random sampling is especially important for cross-sectional studies.

The first step for sampling for a cross-sectional study is, as usual, to identify the target population to which the results would generalize, and then decide which sampling method would be appropriate. For age- and gender-related diseases such as hypertension and diabetes, stratification by age and gender might be useful. For a community-based study in a large population, a multistage sampling involving selection of counties, villages/municipalities, and households can be adopted, or a cluster sampling might be more convenient. In a clinic setting, where subjects come in a queue one after the other, systematic sampling could be appropriate.

Sampling Methods for Prospective and Retrospective Studies

As explained later, random sampling is not as important for prospective and retrospective studies as for cross-sectional studies and descriptive surveys. At the same time, these studies too involve estimation of parameters such as incidence rate, relative risk (RR), and odds ratio (OR), finding the CI, and testing the hypothesis on them. These statistical procedures do require a random sample of subjects. Whenever feasible, a random sample should be taken. See Example 8.6 for a nested case–control study that uses stratified sampling to assess the effect of serum selenium levels on cancer mortality.

Example 8.6: Stratified Sample for a Nested Case–Control Study

Serum selenium level is widely suspected to affect cancer mortality, but the results across studies are not coherent. Belgium has a system to follow each patient till death. A stratified (for gender – male and female) random sample of 201 cancer deaths of age 25–74 years out of a total of 343 during a 10-year period was studied for their selenium level as well as some other factors [7].

Side note: Three controls were selected for each case and these were matched for age and gender. Thus, a total of 603 controls were also studied. Serum selenium level was found to be a significant predictor of cancer mortality in males but not in females.

In Example 8.6, gender stratification of the subjects helped to develop a conclusion that is different for males than for females. Thus, the stratification strategy paid off well in this case. Also note that the investigations are from outcomes (cancer deaths) to antecedent (serum selenium levels) and thus the study is retrospective in nature. Because controls were also investigated, it is a case–control study. It is **nested** because follow-up of each person is routinely done in Belgium and cases are chosen from this follow-up. Controls were easily available and choosing three controls per case helped to increase the reliability of results without corresponding cost.

On the flip side is the sample of 201 cancer deaths out of 343 in this example and the claim that it is a random sample. This type of 60% sample is not a norm: one can legitimately wonder why all 343 could not be included in the study. Had all these been investigated, it would still be a sample in the sense that they occurred in a specific 10-year period. Previous deaths and future deaths would still not be incorporated.

Many good prospective and retrospective studies are done on nonrandom samples and they provide valid results if the cases and controls happen to be equivalent at baseline. At the same time, we reemphasize that random samples should be taken wherever feasible so that the external validity remains firm.

Sometimes consecutive cases attending a particular clinic within a specified period are included in prospective or retrospective studies. As mentioned earlier, this procedure simulates random selection when the subjects come without preference for the study period. However, cases coming to a clinic on particular days such as on Tuesdays and Fridays may not be random because only specific types of cases may be seen in special clinics on those days, or because a particular specialist is available on those days. This causes self-selection.

8.2.2 Sampling Methods in Clinical Trials

An essential feature of experiments and trials is human intervention. This raises ethical issues and thus random sampling may not be feasible in some situations.

As mentioned in Chapter 4, the first phase of a clinical trial is generally done on volunteers that by nature are nonrandom. The second phase is also frequently done on a nonrandom sample of subjects. If it is on a random sample, the following comments for the third phase also apply to the second phase.

The third phase, as much as possible, should be done on randomly selected patients such as every tenth (SyRS) reporting in a clinic, but the requirement for consent can make it difficult to adopt such sampling. Patients agreeing to participate generally form a biased sample. If many patients with consent are available, a random sample can be taken that will minimize further bias. If not, a reasonably valid trial can still be carried out by random division of subjects into two or more groups and allocating them to the control and treatment groups. This process is called **randomization**, as already explained. Though not fully, such random allocation largely takes care of the statistical requirement and helps to achieve baseline equivalence across groups. When other sources of bias, as mentioned in Section 3.6 of Chapter 3, are under control, the results are considered valid for those among the target group who give consent. This validity again is due to baseline equivalence of groups that allows any emerging difference to be ascribed to the intervention or the treatment. However, the results are always interpreted with caution. They are obtained in "ideal" clinical trial conditions and not in usual clinical practice conditions under which treatments are carried out. Thus, efficacy is correctly evaluated but the effectiveness in practical conditions remains unanswered.

Example 8.7: Random Sample of Control Subjects But Not of the Cases in a Trial

Abnormal mammograms can cause anxiety in some women who possibly need help. Barton et al. [8] performed a trial in the United States to evaluate the effect of an educational intervention that taught the skills to cope with anxiety. The subjects were women of age 39 years or older in seven mammography sites who came for screening. Of 8543 such women, 1439 had an abnormal mammogram. These were included in the trial. A random sample of 1405 women was also taken from the remaining 7104 women with normal mammogram. Thus, these control subjects may not be matched for baseline characteristics such as age. The authors possibly expected that the age might not affect the response or that the age structure of the controls would not be much different from that of cases.

Side note: Subsequent investigations in subjects with abnormal mammograms showed that many of these were false-positive. The authors concluded that immediate reading of mammograms was associated with less anxiety than educational intervention targeting coping skills because many were in fact false-positives.

8.3 Sampling and Nonsampling Errors

A so-called sampling error actually is not an error. This term is used for variation across samples when repeated samples are taken. The result obtained on the basis of one sample, in all likelihood, will not be the same as on the basis of another sample from the same population. This variation is better understood as **sampling fluctuation**, although statistically called sampling error. Note that this is endogenous to the investigation. On the other hand, nonsampling error is indeed an error that arises from misreporting, misjudgment, mis-recording, nonresponse, and other such deficiencies. This is exogenous in nature. This section explains some methods that can be used to manage these two types of errors.

8.3.1 Sampling Errors

Samples by themselves are a great source of uncertainty. Yet, sampling is considered a preferred strategy in most situations because of the advantages enumerated earlier. Statistical methods help in reaching a conclusion regarding a population parameter on the basis of just one sample. Sampling error is managed as follows.

Point Estimate

In descriptive studies, sample mean and sample proportion do provide a reasonable idea of the mean and proportion in the corresponding target population. As usual, this "reasonability" is assessed in terms of validity and reliability. When the sample subjects represent the full spectrum of a population, which is likely if one of the random methods described earlier is followed and if the sample size is reasonably large, sample mean and sample proportion are indeed valid point estimates. That is, they are unbiased in the sense of being able to reach the corresponding population value when the sample size is increased, and fairly stable across samples. This statement has two underlying assumptions. First, the mean or proportion is calculated after due consideration of varying group size, as can happen in the case of stratified sampling. Second, the data obtained from the sample subjects are correct, that is, no wrong data are reported or recorded.

In analytical studies, the RR and OR type of summary measures based on samples are also considered a fair reflection of the true status in the population, provided again that the samples are truly representative. This also holds for experiments and trials.

Standard Error of an Estimate

The reliability of sample summary measures such as mean, proportion, RR, and OR is assessed by what is called their standard error (SE). SEs are also used to obtain CIs, as described later in Chapter 11. To understand SE, realize that samples too differ from one another – thus, a mean or proportion based on one sample would be different from the ones based on another sample. This variability in summaries across samples is assessed by their SE. The size of the sample, n, in one form or the other is in the denominator of all SEs. The implication is that larger samples have smaller SEs. Intuition also says that large samples would not differ from one another as much as small samples would. The other situation giving small SE for not so small a sample is when the subjects themselves are homogeneous so that the variation (measured by the standard deviation) among them is small.

A large SE implies unreliable results. This could render all the efforts and time a waste. There is no way to retrieve this unfortunate situation, except by increasing the sample size. It is unethical too to expose subjects to such small-sized investigations that are not likely to produce reliable results. Thus, exercise care and conduct a study on an appropriate sample size. Determine the size by using the methods given in the next section. However, a pilot study is done on a small sample because reliability is not a consideration in this kind of study.

8.3.2 Nonsampling Errors

Samples will differ from one another no matter what you do, but the nonsampling errors can be controlled – and perhaps eliminated. They may arise due to faulty design, biased sample, inaccurate tools, nonresponse, sloppy measurement, inappropriate method of interview or examination, wrong reporting by the patient, inadequate method of analysis of data, misreporting of findings, and other such lapses. Most researchers do not assess or report nonsampling errors, although these errors can have a major influence on the validity of the results. Whereas sampling errors can be directly quantified and calculated using a statistical formula, nonsampling errors have to be only empirically guessed using techniques such as reassessment, comparison with an otherwise expected response, internal consistency checks, and replication. An ingenious method may have to be devised to measure them.

Biases

The main source of nonsampling error is bias. There is a long list of biases in Section 3.6 of Chapter 3. Any of them has the potential to distort the results, but the more common ones are design bias, confounding bias, ascertainment or assessment bias, response bias, and bias due to lack of power. Take care with these and other biases so that the results are not suspicious.

Nonresponse

Although nonresponse is also included in our list of sources of biases in Section 3.6, this needs special mention in the context of nonsampling errors. As stated earlier, nonresponse has two types of adverse impacts on the results. The first is that the ultimate sample size available to draw conclusions reduces, and this adversely affects the reliability of the results. This deficiency can be remedied by increasing the sample size corresponding to the anticipated nonresponse. The second, more serious, adverse impact is that the nonresponding subjects are not a random component but are of a specific type, such as seriously ill cases who do not want to be a part of the study, or very mild cases who opt out after feeling better, or some such segment. Their exclusion can severely bias the results. An alternative is to take a subsample of the nonrespondents, and make intensive efforts for their full participation. Assess how these subsample subjects are different from regular respondents and adjust the results accordingly. Provisions for such extra efforts to elicit a response from some nonrespondents should be made at the time of planning of the study.

Experience suggests that some researchers fail to distinguish between nonresponse and zero value or characteristics that are absent. Take care that this does not happen in your data.

Wrong Assessment

A large part of nonsampling errors inadvertently occurs due to unknown or unanticipated biases in the assessment of the factors under study. This can occur due to various reasons, such as unstandardized instrument (e.g., questionnaire) that partially fails to give the required information in the correct format, and a machine that is not correctly calibrated. Sometimes such inadequacies are ignored and suspicious results are obtained.

8.4 Sample Size

"How large should the sample be?" is among the most commonly asked questions in empirical research. It is a crucial element in the design of a study. The sample size should be neither too small nor too large. Conducting a study on an inadequate number of subjects may be unethical because the persons are unnecessarily subjected to an investigation that is not likely to produce results either way due to limitation of its size. All the efforts and time go to waste. A small sample is rarely able to represent the full cross-section of the population. Thus, small n is luxurious in most situations and even the best-executed study may fail to answer the research questions if the sample size is too small. At the same time, an exceedingly large sample is also a waste of resources when reliable conclusions can be drawn on the basis of a smaller sample. Besides resources, it is unethical to expose an unnecessarily large number of people with compromised health to an investigation when a smaller sample can provide conclusive results. If a trial on a few patients can tell you that a new chemotherapy regimen is ineffective, why try it on a large number of patients?

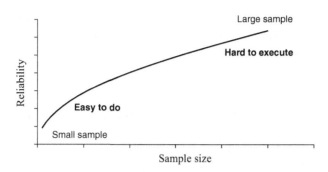

FIGURE 8.1
Sample size and reliability of results.

A very big study is hard to execute and should be avoided as much as possible (Figure 8.1) unless it is multicentric. What is the right size of sample?

The right number of subjects in different groups depends on a variety of considerations, such as interindividual variability, chances of error in conclusions that can be tolerated (no conclusion in empirical research can be completely free of error), the size of effect aimed to be detected, confidence level desired in the results, anticipated nonresponse, and other such considerations. For example, it is easy to imagine that a small effect is difficult to detect and a large sample is required for a small effect to show up. Also, if values have high variability from person to person, detection is difficult unless a large sample is available. See Box 8.3 for the advantages of a large sample.

The formulas given later in Appendix 1 of this chapter require an understanding of the concepts of level of confidence (denoted by $1 - \alpha$), level of significance (maximum type I error denoted by α), and power ($1 - $ type II error, denoted by $1 - \beta$). These concepts are explained in later chapters. We are taking the liberty of using them in this chapter on sampling in the hope that reference will be made to later chapters by those who need to understand these concepts. The sample size obtained by these formulas is the minimum and is

---

BOX 8.3   ADVANTAGES OF A LARGE SAMPLE

A large sample is a waste of resources when a reliable conclusion can be drawn by studying a small sample. Sometimes a large sample aggravates bias and cost also increases. However, there are several advantages of a study on a large sample.

- *Power*: A large number of subjects substantially raises the chance of detecting a medically relevant difference if present.
- *Reliability*: Results based on a large number of subjects are more reliable.
- *No Wasted Effort*: As a consequence of the previous two advantages, the efforts do not go to waste – some conclusion one way or the other is drawn.
- *Less Effect of Missing Data*: When the sample size is large, few missing observations are not able to influence the conclusion that much.
- *Distribution Advantage*: There is no need to worry about the underlying distribution of the measurement when the sample size is large – Gaussian methods can be applied with confidence in practically all situations.
- *Easy Computation*: Exact statistical methods for small samples are complicated and the computer packages for these are rare – large samples are easy to handle.

valid for SRS or StRS from each stratum. For other methods of sampling, an adjustment, called the **design effect**, is made. Also, the sample size is adjusted for nonresponse so that the required sample size is finally available for analysis.

8.4.1 Sample Size for Descriptive Studies

The primary objective of a descriptive study is to estimate a particular population parameter with specified precision. This characteristic could be the mean of a quantitative measurement such as average homocysteine level among cardiac cases, or a proportion such as the percentage of postmenopausal women who happen to have breast cancer. Sometimes a descriptive study is done to test a hypothesis that a mean or a proportion has some specified anticipated value or not. Intuitively, a larger sample implies a smaller margin of error in conclusions. The statistical formulas for determining the sample size for descriptive studies in different setups are given in Appendix 1 at the end of this chapter. The sample size is adjusted for expected nonresponse, if any.

Determination of sample size requires some knowledge of the expected variability from person to person. It is legitimate to ask how we are to know this variation even before the study is done. This paradox is resolved by using a previous similar study that has reported this variation. This will give an approximate size of sample and seems to work well in most practical situations.

Sample size calculation for estimating a proportion requires some explanation. This could be the proportion of subjects of a particular type or a chance of occurrence of a particular event. Two kinds of formulas are available for this parameter. One uses **absolute precision** and the other **relative precision**. When absolute precision is used, the sample size is maximum for anticipated $\pi = 0.50$, where π is the proportion in the target population. Absolute precision is specified, for example, as ±5% or ±0.05, which for $\pi = 0.50$ implies that the sample providing an estimate between 0.45 and 0.55 is acceptable. If $\pi = 0.06$, absolute precision ±0.05 gives a range of 0.01–0.11. Relative to the small value of π, this range is too large. If the prevalence of tuberculosis in diabetes patients is 6% and the sample estimate is anywhere between 1% and 11%, practically nothing is achieved. Such low precision can be a result of a small sample. Thus precision for a proportion should be stated in terms of relative value, such as 10% of π. Ten percent of $\pi = 0.50$ is 0.05 and of $\pi = 0.06$ is 0.006. A much larger sample size is required for such precision if the anticipated π is small.

8.4.2 Sample Size for Analytical Studies and Clinical Trials

Analytical studies can have two purposes. One is to estimate the RR or the OR depending upon whether the study is prospective or retrospective, and the second could be to test the hypothesis that two groups have the same mean or the same proportion. The calculation of sample size is different in these two setups. In some clinical trials, the objective is just to estimate the efficacy of a regimen without any comparison group.

Sample Size for Estimation of Efficacy

As just stated, in some situations, the objective of a trial is only the estimation of the efficacy of a regimen, without any comparison group. This is particularly so in phase II trials. Efficacy is generally measured by the response rate, which is a proportion. For this, the usual formula for estimation of proportion within a specified margin of error with high probability as given in Appendix 1 can be used.

Sample Size for Estimation of Relative Risk or Odds Ratio

The basic issues in this situation are the same as already stated for descriptive studies, although the formulas change. These formulas are also given in Appendix 1. The formulas require specification of the relative precision. This delimits the acceptable error in the estimate. If actual OR is 2.5 and the acceptable relative precision is 10% of OR, an estimate within 0.25, that is, between 2.25 and 2.75, would be acceptable. The wider the range, the less the requirement for sample size.

Sample Size for Testing of a Hypothesis

The other problem under investigation in analytical studies is test of a hypothesis. This generally takes the form of whether or not two or more groups have the same mean or the same proportion. This can also transform to same OR or same RR. For comparison of two groups also, the formulas are given in Appendix 1. The sample size calculation for studies involving three or more groups becomes complex. For this refer to Ryan [9]. As an approximation for multiple groups, two-group formulas can be used with α-level adjusted according to the Bonferroni principle. This is also explained later.

In place of precision of the estimate, the sample size calculation in the case of testing of hypothesis requires specification of the statistical **power** corresponding to the least difference that would be considered medically relevant. Power is denoted by $(1 - \beta)$. This is the chance that the study is able to detect a specified medically relevant least difference. Power calculations have become important these days and have pushed sample size in research studies to at least 10-fold of what they were 40 years ago. Another consideration in the case of testing is whether a one-tailed test would be used or a two-tailed test. This concept is also explained later in Chapter 11.

Other principles regarding inflating the sample size for nonresponse and using prior values of standard deviation (SD) and RR or OR are the same as stated for descriptive studies.

Example 8.8: Sample Size for a Prospective Study on Disability in Work-Related Musculoskeletal Disorders

Turner et al. [10] report a prospective study of workers in the United States who filed claims for work-related musculoskeletal disorders. The primary outcome of interest was duration of work disability in 1 year after filing the claim. The purpose was to develop statistical models that could predict the duration of chronic work disability after the initial suffering from the disorder. The required sample size was calculated as 1800 workers for low-back injuries and 1200 for workers with carpal tunnel syndrome. Statistical powers used for these calculations were 0.96 for low-back injuries and 0.85 for carpal tunnel syndrome, and the significance level chosen was α = 0.05 (two-tailed) for both.

Side note: The example illustrates that the sample size could be quite large for prospective studies when statistical considerations such as power and significance level are considered. The concept of power is related to the minimum medically relevant difference, but the abstract of this article does not specify this difference. A large sample size was feasible in this case because the study is mostly based on an administrative database and the follow-up interviews were done by telephone.

Additional Considerations for Determining the Sample Size

Sample size determination procedure as discussed so far assumes that the interest is in only one outcome parameter – the mean if it is quantitative and the proportion if it is qualitative. Note that RR and OR are ratios of the same proportion in two groups, and are univariate in this sense. The difference between means or proportions in two groups in any case is also univariate. In practice, the interest might be in more than one parameter. For example, in a case–control study on risk factors for breast cancer, the interest could be in age at menarche, age at first live birth, total duration of breast feeding of all children put together, and the number of first-order blood relatives who have a positive history. If there are many parameters such as in this example, which one should be used to determine the sample size? If the focus is on only one outcome, say, age at menarche, and others are just concomitants to remove their confounding effect, use the cancer prevalence rate in different categories of this variable only. If there are two groups such as case and control, use OR or RR. If two or more variables have nearly the same importance, calculate the sample size for each of them separately and take the largest. In any case, SD, proportion, OR, or RR, required for calculation of sample size, would have to be based on a previous study in a similar setting, and the precision in the case of estimation or the medically relevant least difference in the case of testing of hypothesis must be specified.

An additional consideration not accounted for in the formulas in Appendix 1 is the number of concomitant variables or covariates that are proposed to be studied together. The higher this number, the greater the requirement for sample size. Another consideration, many times overlooked, is the inflation of α-level in the case of multiple comparisons. Almost all studies give several P-values as though they are independent. The fact is that in most cases a joint conclusion is obtained. This increases the probability of a type I error. For this, a **Bonferroni adjustment** is the most commonly used method whereby the level of significance for each is kept at α/K, if the number of P-values is K. This will accordingly increase the sample size.

The sample size quickly multiplies and can become an enormous number if cross-classifications of a number of factors are under consideration. For only two factors, namely, age at menarche as <12 years and $\geq$12 years, and age at first live birth as <23 years and $\geq$23 years, the four cross-classifications are: (i) menarche at <12 years and first live birth at <23 years; (ii) menarche at <12 years and first live birth at $\geq$23 years; (iii) menarche at $\geq$12 years and first live birth at <23 years; and (iv) menarche at $\geq$ 12 years and first live birth at $\geq$ 23 years. If there are four factors and all are dichotomized, the number of cross-classifications is $4^2 = 16$. The results would be reliable if each of these classifications has an adequate number of subjects. No guidelines are available about the sample size that would be adequate to take care of, say, five risk factors as opposed to two risk factors, but a rule of thumb is that each cross-classification should have a sample of at least 30 subjects. This is applicable when the disease prevalence is large, say at least 20%. In our breast cancer example, the study might include only the suspected cases where the prevalence would be high. A size of at least 30 implies for four dichotomous factors that there must be at least a total of $16 \times 30 = 480$ subjects, evenly distributed to the 16 categories. All these considerations, including the ones mentioned earlier, are summarized in Table 8.1.

The sample size frequently depends on the resources and the time available for a project. For a graduate thesis, only 1–2 years is generally available with practically no funding. Thus, the sample size would be small regardless of what the formulas say. The advice

TABLE 8.1

Considerations Requiring a Larger Sample

Consideration	Sample size
Smaller type I error	Larger
Smaller type II error (higher statistical power)	Larger
Smaller difference to be detected	Larger
Higher interindividual variability or smaller proportion	Larger
Higher anticipated nonresponse	Larger
Higher number of subgroups	Larger
Higher number of variables to be considered together	Larger

in such situations is to choose a topic for which an adequate number of subjects is available within the allotted time, and restrict it to the investigations that are feasible. Perhaps a graduate thesis should not be done on rare diseases. Otherwise, be clear that it would be a pilot study in nature and the results will not have much reliability but can provide important clues to plan a major study.

Even for large studies, resources and time constraints sometimes dictate the sample size. Vickers [11] gives this interesting example: a colleague points out that the drug under trial is safe and inexpensive, and could be advocated if it is able to reduce average pain score by even half a point. A recent paper shows an SD = 2 for the change in pain score. For these values, the formula gives $n = 774$ for 95% level of confidence. Funding limitation do not allow for such a large trial. What if SD = 1.5? The sample size reduces to 380 but it is still high. Lower the bar and aim at detecting a pain score reduction by 0.75 instead of half a point. Now $n = 170$. This is doable. If this is chosen, the size of the study is dictating the research objective whereas actually the research objective should dictate the sample size. In practice, this happens and is acceptable for a graduate thesis.

Having said all this, there are some statistical "tricks" that can reduce the requirement for a large sample. These are: (i) for continuous data, use an optimal cutoff for binary classification wherever this is done; (ii) do not stratify the population unless necessary because each stratum must have sufficiently large n; (iii) use an appropriate design such as crossover, factorial, and adaptive; (iv) use a balanced design that is most efficient in detecting the differences; (v) use homogeneous subjects that will focus on specific groups of subjects; and (vi) target a population that is likely to have a higher response rate so that you have an adequate number of responses even with a small sample.

Rules of Thumb

Rules of thumb lack scientific basis and many scientists dislike them. When no baseline information for computation of sample size is available and the constraints do not permit a pilot study either, the following rules of thumb can be used.

A large-sized medical trial should include nearly 300 subjects in each group, a midsized trial nearly 100 in each group, and a small-sized trial at least 30 in each group. The last can be used for graduate theses where time and resources are limited. A larger study is multicentric with these numbers in each center. The same norms can be used for retrospective or case–control studies. However, in the case of a prospective study, the number to be followed up should be such that at least 30 persons are finally available with the outcome of interest in each group. In this case, an extremely large group may be needed to yield an outcome such as developing HIV infection in at least 30 subjects after

administration of a protective vaccine even when high-risk subjects are included. To calculate exact numbers, use the formulas given in Appendix 1.

For a descriptive study that seeks to find normal levels in healthy subjects, the rule of
thumb is to include at least 120 [12] subjects in each group for which norms are required,
although in this case also exact numbers can be calculated using an appropriate formula.
For pathological levels in patients, the group size could be smaller. However, all these
may have to be modified because of feasibility considerations when resources and time are
limited. Such limitations obviously compromise reliability.

Appendix 1: Some Sample Size Formulas

Note: All the following formulas provide a sample size per group in the case of two groups
and assume a large sample for Gaussian conditions to hold. Also the sampling assumed
here is SRS. In practice, replace the population parameter by the values seen in previous
similar studies.

1. Sample Size Formulas for Descriptive Studies

Estimation

1. Estimation of mean with specified precision:

   $n = z_{1-\alpha/2}^2 \sigma^2 / d^2$, where d is the specified precision on either side of the mean.

2. Estimation of proportion with specified absolute precision:

   $n = z_{1-\alpha/2}^2 \pi(1-\pi)/d^2$, where d is the specified absolute precision on either side of the
   proportion.

3. Estimation of proportion with specified relative precision:

   $n = z_{1-\alpha/2}^2 \pi(1-\pi)/(\varepsilon\pi)^2$, where ε is the specified relative precision in terms of fraction
   of π.

Test of Hypothesis

4. Test of hypothesis for a mean:

   $n = \dfrac{(\sigma_1 z_{1-\alpha/2} + \sigma_2 z_{1-\beta})^2}{\delta^2}$, where the medically relevant difference to be detected between

   means in the two groups is at least δ. σ_1 and σ_2 are the SD in the two populations.

5. Test of hypothesis for a proportion:

   $n = \dfrac{[z_{1-\alpha/2}\sqrt{\pi_0(1-\pi_0)} + z_{1-\beta}\sqrt{\pi_a(1-\pi_a)}]^2}{\delta^2}$, where π_0 is the value under null hypothesis

   and π_a under the alternative hypothesis and the medically relevant least difference to be
   detected is δ.

2. Sample Size Formulas for Analytical Studies

The following formulas are applicable when there are only two groups and both have the same sample size. The formulas give sample size per group. One formula is for retrospective studies with multiple controls.

Prospective Study – Estimation of RR

1. Estimation of an incidence rate with specified relative precision:

   $n = (z_{1-\alpha/2}/\varepsilon)^2$, where ε is the specified relative precision as fraction of the anticipated incidence rate on either side.

2. Estimation of RR with specified relative precision:

   $n = \dfrac{z_{1-\alpha/2}^2[(1-\pi_1)/\pi_1 + (1-\pi_0)/\pi_0]}{[\ln(1-\varepsilon)]^2}$, where ε is the relative precision in terms of fraction

   of RR ($RR = \pi_1/\pi_0$, and π_1, π_0 are the anticipated incidence rates in the exposed and unexposed group, respectively).

Prospective Study – Test of Hypothesis

3. Test of hypothesis for an incidence rate:

   $n = \dfrac{(z_{1-\alpha/2}\lambda_0 + z_{1-\beta}\lambda_a)^2}{\delta^2}$, where λ_0 and λ_a are the incidence rates under the null and the alternative hypothesis respectively, i.e., the least difference considered medically relevant for detection is δ.

4. Test of hypothesis for difference in incidence rates (attributable risk):

   $n = \dfrac{[z_{1-\alpha/2}\sqrt{2f(\lambda)} + z_{1-\beta}\sqrt{f(\lambda_1)+f(\lambda_2)}]^2}{(\lambda_1 - \lambda_2)^2}$, where $f(\lambda) = \lambda^3\,T/(\lambda\,T - 1 + e^{\lambda T})$ if the duration of

   study is fixed as T (censored observations), and $2f(\lambda)$ is to be calculated at $\lambda = (\lambda_1 + \lambda_2)/2$. (When T is not fixed, replace $f(\lambda)$ by λ^2, $f(\lambda_1)$ by λ_1^2 and $f(\lambda_2)$ by λ_2^2; λ_1 and λ_2 are the anticipated incidence rates in the two groups.)

5. Test of hypothesis for RR:

   $n = \dfrac{[z_{1-\alpha/2}\sqrt{2\pi(1-\pi)} + z_{1-\beta}\sqrt{\pi_1(1-\pi_1)+\pi_0(1-\pi_0)}]^2}{(\pi_1 - \pi_0)^2}$, where $\pi = (\pi_1 + \pi_0)/2$, and medically

   relevant least RR is π_1/π_0.

Retrospective Study – Estimation of OR

6. Estimation of OR with specified relative precision (for small disease prevalence):

   $n = \dfrac{z_{1-\alpha/2}^2[1/\{\pi_1(1-\pi_1)\}+1/\{\pi_0(1-\pi_0)\}]}{[\ln(1-\varepsilon)]^2}$, where ε is the relative precision in terms of

   fraction of OR. ($OR = \dfrac{\pi_1/(1-\pi_1)}{\pi_0/(1-\pi_0)}$, and π_1, π_0 are the anticipated exposure rates in the case and control groups, respectively. (These are not the same as the incidence rates of the disease.)

Retrospective Study – Test of Hypothesis

8. Test of hypothesis for OR:

(a) 1 control per case:

$$n = \frac{[z_{1-\alpha/2}\sqrt{2\pi_0(1-\pi_0)} + z_{1-\beta}\sqrt{\pi_1(1-\pi_1) + \pi_0(1-\pi_0)}]^2}{(\pi_1 - \pi_0)^2},$$ where the medically relevant least

OR is π_1/π_0 (when exposure rate among the controls, π_0, is known with high precision; otherwise replace $2\pi_0(1-\pi_0)$ by $2\pi(1-\pi)$ where $\pi = (\pi_1 + \pi_0)/2$).

(b) C controls per case:

$$n_1 = \frac{[z_{1-\alpha/2}\sqrt{\left(1+\dfrac{1}{C}\right)\pi(1-\pi)} + z_{1-\beta}\sqrt{\pi_1(1-\pi_1) + \pi_0(1-\pi_0)}]^2}{(\pi_1 - \pi_0)^2}, \quad \pi = \frac{\pi_1 + C\pi_0}{C+1}$$

and $n_2 = Cn_1$ (number of controls)
with conditions as stated in 7 (a).

Any Type of Study – Estimation

8. Estimation of difference in two means with specified precision:

$n = z_{1-\alpha/2}^2(\sigma_1^2 + \sigma_2^2)/d^2$, where d is specified precision on either side of the mean difference.

9. Estimation of difference in two proportions with specified absolute precision:

$n = z_{1-\alpha/2}^2[\pi_1(1-\pi_1) + \pi_0(1-\pi_0)]/d^2$, where d is the specified absolute precision on either side of the difference.

Any Type of Study – Test of Hypothesis

10. Test of hypothesis on difference in two means:

$(\sigma_1 z_{1-\alpha/2} + \sigma_2 z_{1-\beta})^2/\delta^2$, where δ is the least difference considered medically relevant for detection.

11. Test of hypothesis on difference in two proportions

$$n = \frac{[z_{1-\alpha/2}\sqrt{2\pi(1-\pi)} + z_{1-\beta}\sqrt{\pi_1(1-\pi_1) + \pi_0(1-\pi_0)}]^2}{\delta^2},$$ where $\pi = (\pi_1 + \pi_0)/2$, and the least

difference considered medically relevant for detection is δ.

(This formula is nearly the same as for test of hypothesis on RR.)

Note: For one-sided estimations and one-sided tests replace $z_{1-\alpha/2}$ by z_α. This is the value from the Gaussian table corresponding to the $100(1 - \alpha)\%$ level of confidence or $100\alpha\%$ level of significance. Similarly, $z_{1-\beta}$ is the Gaussian value corresponding to the power $100(1 - \beta)\%$.

(Adapted from Lwanga and Lemeshow [13] and Indrayan and Malhotra [6].)

References

1. Chatfield C. Confession of a pragmatic statistician. Statistician 2002;51(Part-1):1–20. http://citeseerx.ist.psu.edu/viewdoc/download?doi=10.1.1.93.3273&rep=rep1&type=pdf
2. Chon CH, Lai FC, McNeal JE, et al. Use of extended systematic sampling in patients with a prior negative prostate needle biopsy. J Urol 2002;167:2457–2460. www.ncbi.nlm.nih.gov/pubmed/11992057
3. Indrayan A, Holt MP. Concise Encyclopedia of Biostatistics for Medical Professionals. CRC Press, 2016.
4. Raj JP, Venkatachalam S, Shekoba M, et al. Dietary calcium intake and physical activity levels among people living in Karnataka, India – An observational hospital-based study. J Family Med Prim Care 2018;7(6):1411–1416. www.ncbi.nlm.nih.gov/pmc/articles/PMC6293932/
5. Lopez AL, Ylade M, Daag JV, et al. Hepatitis B seroprevalence among 5 to 6 years old children in the Philippines born prior to routine hepatitis B vaccination at birth. Hum Vaccin Immunother 2018;14(10):2491–2496. www.ncbi.nlm.nih.gov/pmc/articles/PMC6284498/
6. Indrayan A, Malhotra RK. Medical Biostatistics, Fourth Edition. CRC Press, 2018.
7. Kornitzer M, Valente F, de Bacquer D, et al. Serum selenium and cancer mortality: A nested case–control study within an age- and sex-stratified sample of Belgian adult population. Eur J Clin Nutr 2004;58:98–104. www.ncbi.nlm.nih.gov/pubmed/14679373
8. Barton MB, Morley DS, Moore S, et al. Decreasing women's anxieties after abnormal mammograms: A controlled trial. J Natl Cancer Inst 2004;96:529–538. www.ncbi.nlm.nih.gov/pubmed/15069115
9. Ryan TP. Sample Size Determination and Power. John Wiley, 2013.
10. Turner JA, Franklin G, Fulton-Kehoe D, et al. Prediction of chronic disability in work-related musculoskeletal disorders: A prospective population-based study. BMC Musculoskelet Disor 2004;5:14. www.ncbi.nlm.nih.gov/pmc/articles/PMC428578/
11. Vickers AJ. Let's dance! The sample size samba. www.medscape.com/viewarticle/584026 (posted 2008) – last accessed 3 January 2019.
12. Clinical and Laboratory Standard Institute. EP28-A3c. Defining, Establishing and Verifying Reference Interval in the Clinical Laboratory: Approved Guidelines, Third Edition. CLSI, 2010. https://clsi.org/media/1421/ep28a3c_sample.pdf
13. Lwanga SK, Lemeshow S. Sample Size Determination in Health Studies: A Practical Manual. World Health Organization, 1991.

9

Research Protocol

Once the steps mentioned in the preceding chapters have been completed, you are ready to develop a protocol for your research project. The protocol is the document that outlines the proposed research, its full rationale, including the objectives and the hypotheses, and the complete methodology, including the system for reaching an unbiased and credible conclusion. This is the final step in planning research and is the backbone that supports it in all steps of its execution. It serves as a reference for the members of the research team whenever needed. Thus, sufficient thought must be given to its preparation. Sometimes it gradually evolves as more information becomes available and is progressively examined for its adequacy.

The contents of a thesis protocol are such that its development or preparation by the candidate helps him or her to understand the ongoing research activities on the topic and helps in creating exposure to the nuances of medical research. This exposure helps in the problem-solving capacity of the candidate and implementing this to improve clinical practice.

A protocol should consist of full details with no shortcuts, yet should be concise. It should be to the point, and coherent. The reader, who may not be fully familiar with the topic, should be made absolutely clear about the why, what, and how of the proposed research. To the extent possible, it should embody the interest of the sponsor, the investigator, the patients, and society. It should be complete and easy to implement.

The protocol is also a great help at the time of writing of the thesis or a paper. The introduction and methods sections remain much the same as in the protocol although in an elaborate format. The objectives as stated in the protocol help to retain the focus in the report. Much of the literature review done at the time of protocol writing also proves handy at the time of writing a report such as a graduate thesis.

A research protocol is generally approved by a competent authority such as the scientific committee and the ethics committee of the department or the institution. The researcher is generally required to present this to the concerned audience and satisfactorily answer the questions raised by them. Quite often, the protocol is revised on the basis of the suggestions received. Patient-based medical research can be undertaken only after such approvals have been granted.

This chapter describes the structure and contents of a medical research protocol, and is divided into two sections. Section 9.1 is on the structure of the protocol such as title, collaborators, and supervisors, executive summary, and logistics. Section 9.2 is on the contents of the main body of the protocol such as background, review of the literature, objectives and hypothesis, target population, sampling and sample size, method of eliciting the information, data collection and analysis, and the system of reaching a valid conclusion. For an alternative view of how to prepare a protocol, see DeRenzo and Moss [1].

9.1 Structure of the Protocol

A research protocol generally comprises the title, the details of the researcher, the supervisors in the case of a graduate thesis, the collaborators, an executive summary, the main body of the protocol, and the logistic details for carrying out the project. The main body of the protocol is discussed in Section 9.2. A summary of this structure is given in Box 9.1 and the details are as follows.

BOX 9.1   SUMMARY OF THE STRUCTURE OF A PROTOCOL

The structure of an empirical-based medical research protocol:

1. *Title*
   What is actually intended to be studied? The title should be sufficiently informative yet specific and brief
2. *The Researcher*
   The name of the researcher, affiliation, study site, and the degree/diploma for which the work is being done, if any, and the year of starting the work
3. *Supervisors and Collaborators*
   Name, position, and affiliation of the advisors/supervisors and co-supervisors. Also include the details of collaborative departments and/or persons
4. *Executive Summary*
   Contains the salient features of the protocol, including the rationale of the problem and the planned process for its successful execution
5. *Main Body of the Protocol*
   Background (introduction), review of literature, objectives and hypotheses, target population, sampling and sample size, recruitment of subjects, method of eliciting the information, data collection and analysis, the system intended to be followed to reach a valid conclusion, and the references
6. *Logistics*
   The source of funding to carry out the project, any conflict of interest, training to ensure data quality, details of how various steps of research will be carried out, including informed consent and other aspects of ethics, and compliance with the regulations. This may also include data archiving if that is a requirement of your institution
7. *Appendices*

   Include a consent form and the data-recording sheets with instructions

9.1.1 Title, Researchers, Supervisors, and Collaborators

The first page of a medical research protocol contains the title and the details of the researcher, including the supervisor or advisor in the case of a graduate thesis, and the name of the collaborators, if any, as per the following details.

Title

The choice of the research topic was discussed in Chapter 2. The title is the topic in brief, but provides full information on what the study is all about and what basic methodology (such as randomized controlled trial or case–control study) is proposed to be followed. It should clearly indicate what is aimed to be achieved by the proposed research, and should arouse interest in the reader. Sometimes the title is finalized after the first draft of the protocol has been completed.

The first part of the title could be in the form of a question, such as "Is regimen A better than regimen B in managing the cases of disease X?" it could be in terms of a statement, such as "Regimen A is better than regimen B for managing the cases of disease X," or it could be neutral, such as "Comparison of regimen A with regimen B for managing the cases of disease X." It depends on the personal choice of the researcher. The second part may be on the basic methodology as mentioned earlier. For studies focused on specific groups of subjects such as those residing in a particular area or those suffering from a severe form of the disease only, the same also should be specified so that the reader knows what to expect from this research.

Having said all this, it also needs to be emphasized that the title should be brief and not detailed. You may like to try different forms of the title for your research and judge what is precise yet gives sufficient details of the investigation. Remember that the full details of the project are going to appear in the main body of the protocol.

The Researcher

In the case of a graduate thesis, the student is the researcher. His or her qualifications and affiliation with a unit/department/institution should be mentioned along with the address. In the case of research work other than a thesis, such details are mentioned for the principal investigator. Also mention the year when the study will begin and possibly its full duration.

Supervisors and Collaborators

Various designations are used in different universities for graduate thesis supervisors. They may be called advisors, guides, mentors, or by any other such name. The role of the supervisor is to guide the student in all phases of research from the conceptualization of a problem to the submission of the thesis. Generally, only one faculty member serves as the chief supervisor and any others are called co-supervisors. The latter are generally from other departments or units when their help is needed to efficiently complete the work. For example, for a thesis on a particular cancer, the help of a radiotherapist may be needed. These supervisors are identified before the start of a project and the choice is based on their interest and possible contribution.

Collaborators may not be required for a graduate thesis but may be important for other research. These are those who provide significant help in the execution of the project.

Whereas in a multicentric study they are the people who will look after the execution for their respective centers, in a unicentric study also, they might be from other departments which have significant stakes.

9.1.2 Executive Summary

For the convenience of readers on the go, a summary of the entire research process is provided in one or two pages in a self-contained manner. This is known by several names, such as executive summary, project summary, and **synopsis**. This is slightly more than a conventional abstract of a paper but is much less than the details of the project. It is important that the summary provides the gist of the *essential* aspects of the project such that it is complete and independent without reference to any external material. Thus, it should contain a brief description of the background, justification of the problem, the methodology including statistical analysis, and the expected conclusion. Also state how this research will help medical science in particular and humanity in general.

It is generally considered a good idea to provide a short summary of the research in the first paragraph and support each statement of this paragraph briefly in subsequent paragraphs. A good executive summary will successfully omit nonessential details and will incorporate only those that have a direct bearing on the conceptualization and execution of the project. This should be a factual statement without imputing opinions or comments. There is no scope for repetition in an executive summary.

9.1.3 Main Body of the Protocol

See Section 9.2.

9.1.4 Logistics and Appendices

Logistics is the process of organizing and implementing the research that is proposed to be followed from the beginning to the end. It is mostly concerned with mobilization of resources for successfully completing the project and their effective utilization. In the context of medical research, the resources include not just financial but also staff, regulatory agencies, and data-recording forms.

Funding and Training

Almost all empirical research needs financial resources. For medical research, these are needed for buying kits, for carrying out laboratory and radiological investigations, for institutional fees to compensate investigators and respondents for their time, for developing and possibly printing forms on which the elicited information will be recorded, and for statistical help in the analysis of the data.

Mention how these resources are proposed to be arranged. In the case of a graduate thesis, these resources may come from the institution or the department funds, or may be fully or partially borne by the student. It is sometimes possible to enlist the help of an organization or a company that might be interested in that research. For relatively large-scale research, a sponsor is almost invariably required. Ensure that there is no **conflict of interest** and the findings remain independent of the sponsor. Also mention how the responsibilities are to be shared between investigators, supporting units (e.g., pathology, radiology, biostatistics), hospital and administration, funding agency, and other collaborators.

Training of the investigators is an integral part of the research process and helps in procuring good-quality data. No research will succeed unless the data obtained are correct. As mentioned in Chapter 7, a pilot study and pretesting might be enough to provide adequate training to the student in the case of a graduate thesis. For most other research, some investigators are hired to elicit and record the information. These investigators need training on what to elicit and how, and how to record it correctly.

Compliance with Regulations

Medical research needs to be fully sensitive to human needs. Thus, most countries have strict regulations for research involving humans. The researcher is expected to be thoroughly aware and follow these regulations. Most institutions have offices or committees to help students in framing a research protocol that meets regulatory requirements. Consult these or websites of the regulatory agencies and clearly state in the protocol how all these regulations will be complied with.

In addition to national and state regulations, institutions also sometimes have their own regulations. Review boards, scientific committees, and ethics committees function in most institutions to keep a tab on medical research. They authorize the research and give waivers where needed.

If a research is a clinical trial, it needs to be registered with an agency such as *clinicaltrials.gov*. Their website will tell you what is needed to be submitted for registration. By the time you reach the protocol stage, you will generally have all the required information. The registration may require setting up a **Data Monitoring and Safety Board** to oversee the research and to ensure that the research is carried out as per the protocol, and also that no harm is done to participants.

Development of Data Collection Forms and Ethics

See Chapter 7 for structured and unstructured questionnaires and schedules and the questions/items being closed-ended or open-ended. All the questions must be inoffensive and neutral so that the right answer can be elicited. For most graduate theses, developing a form is not an intricate exercise so long as there is clarity about what is to be obtained from respondents through interview and examination, what from the records, and what from the laboratory and the radiological investigations. Nonetheless, pretesting may be required that might indicate some modification. For other large-scale research, developing an appropriate form may require a detailed examination of the items to be included and the format in which all the information is to be recorded. Some institutions have a dedicated facility to help develop an appropriate form.

Ethics of medical research has several components, but the bottom line is that no harm is done to individual participants during the course of the research. The individual person or patient must be made fully aware of the pros and cons of the proposed research. For this purpose, an **informed consent form** is designed specifically for this particular research, wherein an explanation is given to the patient or close relatives of the benefits and especially the harms that can occur, and the safeguards and remedies available at cost or without cost to the patient. Signing the form should not be merely a legal consent but one the participant actually feels comfortable with. Some institutions may require a witness. The consent form is generally accompanied by a patient information sheet that explains the purpose of the study, what the participant is expected to do, how the new information from the research will be used, how the personal identity of the participant will be masked, who should be contacted for help if needed, and other such aspects. For details on all these, see Comstock [2].

Appendices

The consent form and the data collection forms, sometimes called the **case report forms**, are placed in the appendix of a protocol to apprise the reviewer that the researcher is aware of the importance of these tools and that the tools are adequately drawn up. The format and content of questionnaires and schedules have already been discussed in Chapter 7 of this book. A set of instructions for participants and investigators is also included in the appendix.

9.2 Main Body of the Protocol

The main body of the protocol is also generally prepared on a structured format with headings such as introduction, containing background that exposes the gaps needing research, review of literature with details of various views and findings of others on the issue, including those that are in conflict, a clearly worded set of objectives and the hypotheses under test, the methodology for collection of valid and reliable observations, a statement about the methods of data analysis, and the process of drawing conclusions. These components are listed more systematically in Box 9.2. The details are given in this section.

9.2.1 Specifics of the Content of the Main Body of the Protocol

Introduction

1. How did the problem arise? In what context?
2. What is the need for the study? What new information is expected that is not known so far? Is it worth investigating? Is the study exploratory in nature, or are definitive conclusions expected?
3. To what segment of population or to what types of cases will the solution be applicable?

Review of Literature

4. What is the status of the present knowledge on this topic? What are the gaps and how does this work relate to these gaps? Are there any conflicting reports? How has the problem been approached so far? With what results?

Objectives and Hypotheses

5. What is the broad objective and what are the specific objectives? What hypotheses will be addressed by the study? Are these clearly defined, realistic, and evaluable?

Methodology

6. What are the subjects, what is the target population, what is the source of subjects, how are they going to be selected, how many in each group, and what is the justification?

**BOX 9.2   ELEMENTS OF THE MAIN BODY OF
A MEDICAL RESEARCH PROTOCOL**

Introduction: Identification of the problem area, background information including gaps in the knowledge, and why it is important to fill this gap

Review of Literature: Critical appraisal of the findings of others that could have a bearing on this research; this may have global overtones, but must be focused on the local environment so that the relevance is clearly established; confine it to the topic and include the latest developments

Objectives and Hypotheses: A clearly worded short statement of what exactly is intended to be achieved by this research, and for what segments of population or patients it would apply; statement of what hypotheses are under test

Methodology: Inclusion and exclusion criteria for subjects (Box 9.3), specification of various groups, number of subjects to be included in each group with justification, method of selection of subjects, type of control group if any, method of allocation of subjects to different groups, blinding and other strategies to reduce bias, matching criteria with justification, specification of intervention if any and treatment schedule, definition of variables to be assessed, assessment of compliance, identification of confounders and their control, method of eliciting information, validity and reliability of devices, and time sequence for collecting data and their frequency

Ethics: List of ethical problems and how they are proposed to be resolved, including protocol deviations, safeguards for participants, and data safety

Statistical Evaluation: Methods to be used for various estimations, and to test various hypotheses, to detect trends, etc., as dictated by the objectives; comment on likely internal validity and external generalizability of the results, including strategies for handling missing data, confounding, and biases

Limitations: Conditions or groups to which the results would not apply along with the reasons thereof

Inference: Training of the investigators, resolution of conflicting findings; feasibility of the study within the time frame and resources; various possible contingencies and how they would be handled

References: Those cited in the text of the protocol and possibly a bibliography of other literature on the topic that could be of interest to the reader

Appendix: Forms such as questionnaires, schedules, or proforma to be used: structured or open, pre-coded or not, and pretested or not; consent form; letter of support; and other such ancillaries

What will be the statistical power of your study to detect a clinically relevant difference? What are the inclusion and exclusion criteria (Box 9.3)? Is there any possibility of selection bias, and how is this to be handled?

7. What exactly is the intervention, if any – its duration, dosage, frequency, and so on? In what way, if any, is this intervention different from what is routinely prescribed? What instructions and material are to be given to subjects at what time to avoid any mishaps?

8. Is there any comparison group? Why is it needed and how will it be chosen? How will it provide a valid comparison?

9. What is the exact design of the study? Is it descriptive or analytical? If analytical, is it observational (prospective, retrospective, or cross-sectional), experimental, or a human trial? If it is a trial, is it without parallel control (before–after, crossover, repeated measures, etc.) or with a parallel control group? Is it a superiority trial, equivalence trial, or a noninferiority trial? Is the experimental design one-way, two-way, or what?

10. What are the possible confounders? How are these and other possible sources of bias to be handled? What is the method of allocation of subjects to different groups? If there is any blinding, how will it be implemented? Is there any matching?

11. On what characteristics would subjects be assessed? What are the antecedents and outcomes of interest? When will these assessments be made? (Consider the format of the design to decide what will be assessed in the beginning and what will be assessed later.) Who will assess them? Are these assessments necessary and sufficient to answer the proposed questions?

12. What is the operational definition of various assessments? What methods of assessment are to be used? Are they sufficiently valid and reliable? What information will be obtained by inspecting records, what by interview, what by laboratory and radiological investigations, and what by physical examination? Is there any system of continuous monitoring in place? What is the schedule? What mechanism is to be adopted for quality control of measurements?

13. What form is to be used for eliciting and recording the data? (Attach it as an appendix.) Who will record the data? Will it contain the instructions?

14. What system is to be followed to obtain and record data, or to ensure their accuracy? What mechanism would be in place to check for internal consistency and for errors in recording?

15. What is to be done in the case of contingencies such as dropout of subjects or non-availability of the kit or the regimen, or development of complications in some subjects? Or, when protocol violations occur? Also, when will the study be stopped if a conclusion emerges before the full course of the sample? Under what conditions will a subject be withdrawn from the study?

16. What is the period of the study and the timeline (Figure 9.1)?

Data Analysis

17. What is the plan to check the correctness of entries in your worksheet for mistyping, unintentional copying, errors in calculating scores based on entered data, and other such errors?

18. What estimations, comparisons, and trend assessments are to be done at the time of data analysis? Will the quality and quantity of available data be adequate for these estimations, comparisons, and trend assessments?

19. What statistical indices are to be used to summarize the data? Where would you use percentages, where mean, where odds ratio, etc.? Are these indices sufficiently valid and reliable under the conditions of the study?

20. How is the data analysis to be done? What statistical methods are to be used and are these methods really appropriate for the type of data, and to provide correct answer to the questions? What level of significance or of confidence is to be used? How are the missing data, noncompliance, and nonresponse to be handled?

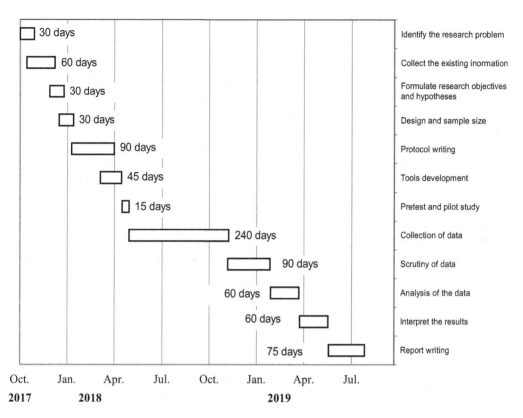

FIGURE 9.1
An example of a timeline (Gantt chart) for a medical research project.

21. What is the expected reliability of the conclusions? What are the limitations of the study, if any, with regard to generalizability or applicability?

System for Conclusion

22. How will the internal inconsistency in the results, if any, and the conflict with the results described in the literature be resolved? How will the results be coordinated with the setting and the environment in which the study was carried out, and how will the generalization be achieved?

In short, the protocol should be able to convince the reader that the topic is important, the data collected would be reliable and valid for that topic, and that contradictions, if any, would be satisfactorily resolved. Present it before a critical but positive audience and get their feedback. You may be creative and may be in a position to argue with conviction, but skepticism in science is regularly practiced – in fact, it is welcome. The method and results should be continuously scrutinized for possible errors. The protocol is the most important document to evaluate the scientific merit of the research proposal by the funding agencies as well as by the accepting agencies (the teaching faculty in the case of graduate research). Peer validation is a rule rather than an exception in scientific pursuits. A good research study is one that is robust to such reviews.

BOX 9.3   INCLUSION AND EXCLUSION CRITERIA

Inclusion Criteria: These are the characteristics such as age group, type of disease, severity of disease, and comorbidity that are necessary for a subject to be considered eligible for inclusion in the study. Whether or not such a subject is actually included will depend on the selection procedure. Some subjects may become ineligible when exclusion criteria are imposed.

Exclusion Criteria: These are the conditions the presence of which will exclude an otherwise eligible subject from the study. Generally, these conditions are indicative of a severe form of disease or complications that render a subject unsuitable for that research or are confounders that complicate the interpretation.

Inclusion and exclusion criteria are part of the case definition that delineates the target population. The purpose is that only appropriate subjects participate and they remain safe. Sometimes the research requires that only very specific types of cases are included so that unadulterated results are obtained, but then generalizability suffers. Nonetheless, investigations on such a restricted class prove a point about, say, the efficacy of a regimen in those specific types of cases.

9.2.2 Further Details of the Contents of the Main Body of the Protocol

Different institutions require protocols in their specific format, but the general pattern as stated earlier is title, introduction, review of literature, objectives and hypotheses, material and methods, data analysis, system of conclusions, and references. The protocol does not have a discussion section, which is important for any thesis or research paper. Many of these have already been discussed in the previous section and stated in Box 9.2. However, some need more elaboration.

Background or Introduction

The introduction in a protocol should be short, say not exceeding one page, and give details of how the problem crossed your mind. Begin the introduction by clearly identifying the subject area of investigation and the specific problem to be investigated, and state why this is being done. Identify the gaps in the existing knowledge. Elaborate the important words in the title. The purpose is not to lose focus and to avoid a general discussion. Briefly state the broad plan to approach the problem without discussing the actual technique. The details of these techniques will follow in the Material and Methods section. Finish the Introduction section by clearly stating the purpose and/or hypothesis proposed to be investigated, such as "The purpose of this study is to determine the effect of enzyme concentration on reaction rate in the cases of benign prostatic hyperplasia." The question intended to be answered should not be vague because no methods are available to transform a vague question into a methodologically rigorous study.

Review of Literature

Restrict the review to the literature directly pertinent to the topic of research. The review must support your contention about the gaps in knowledge that the proposed research is expected to plug. Most efficient in this respect are review articles because they tend to highlight the lacunas. The latest articles are more helpful as they provide a recent picture.

The review of the literature should be balanced and impartial. It should include all recent literature and not be selective. Include those papers also that are inconsistent with or opposed to the hypothesis. Justify the rationale of research with reasons that effectively counter the opposite or indifferent view. Remember that research is a step in the relentless search for truth, and it must pass the litmus test put forward by conflicting and competing facts.

Objectives and Hypotheses

These were discussed in detail in Section 2.3 of Chapter 2. There is nothing new to add.

Materials and Methods

Consider this as the most important constituent of the protocol, particularly for a graduate thesis.

Specify the geographical area of recruitment of subjects. Besides the area, also mention whether the subjects are outpatients, inpatients, or those undergoing a health checkup. They may also come from the records. As much as possible, choose subjects by a random method from the target population. If a large pool is not available for random sampling, include subjects who consecutively attend participating clinics. They will, of course, be filtered by inclusion and exclusion criteria, and by informed consent, but this could still provide valid results.

The most important statistical consideration will be the number of subjects you plan to investigate. This depends on a host of specifications, as mentioned in Chapter 8, including reliability required and statistical power to be able to detect a medically relevant effect.

Make no compromises and adopt the most suitable methodology that can directly achieve the stated objectives. If the most suitable is not feasible (such as a long-term follow-up) due to resource constraints, specifically say so and justify why the most appropriate methodology can't be used. In this case, choose an alternative methodology but explain why this not so optimal methodology can still provide valid results.

Besides explaining the methods for collecting and collating the evidence, comment also on their validity and reliability. Identify the variables that would provide information on each specific objective. Do not collect more data than you need because that will divide the attention, deviate the focus, increase your load, and unnecessarily load the patients under the study.

Data Analysis

This is discussed in detail in Chapter 10. The task at the protocol stage would be to visualize the data and identify the statistical methods. If needed, consult a biostatistician for this part.

System for Conclusion

It is important to realize the distinction between a result and a conclusion. The result is what your data tell after they have passed through the rigmarole of analysis. This is restricted to the aspect specifically studied and pertains to the subjects included in the sample. This result is interpreted in light of the knowledge on peripheral issues, previous results, and the environment in which the study was carried out. When such extraneous factors are given due consideration, a conclusion is arrived at. For example, the result might tell you that practicing yoga for 30 minutes a day, 5 days a week for 4 weeks reduces diastolic blood pressure on average by 7 mmHg in those who are borderline hypertensive. When this is juxtaposed with the physiological and metabolic changes that yoga can make and supported by evidence from literature, a conclusion that yoga tends to reduce diastolic blood pressure in borderline hypertension is reached.

At the protocol stage, see if you can anticipate and state the other knowledge and evidence that would be considered to draw a conclusion. Also state the plan to resolve the conflict if the results contradict present knowledge, or if the results do not meet expectations.

Citing the References

The last wrinkle is about the system followed in the protocol for citations in the text and for listing these citations at the end. Two systems are available. The first is to cite the reference in the text by the last name of the first author and the year of publication, such as Mehta et al. (2009). Et al. stands for "and others" and is used if there are three or more authors. For two authors, the last name of both is cited. In this system, the listing at the end is done in alphabetical order of the last name of the first author.

The second system, followed in most medical journals, is to cite references in the text by a number either in parentheses or as superscript in the sequence of their appearance, and to list them at the end in the order of these numbers. The last name of the first author can also be cited in the text. Thus you can either say, for example, that "risk of miscarriage is partly dependent on previous induced abortions,[x]" or that "Sun et al.[x] observed an association between risk of miscarriage and previous induced abortions," but follow the same system uniformly throughout the protocol. The method of listing of references based on the **Vancouver format** is discussed in Chapter 12. This book follows this system.

Do not confuse the list of references with a bibliography. All references in the list must be cited in the text. A **bibliography** is a list of all related literature – cited or not.

References

1.   DeRenzo E, Moss J. Writing Clinical Research Protocols. Elsevier Science, 2006.
2.   Comstock G. Research Ethics: A Philosophical Guide to the Responsible Conduct of Research. Cambridge University Press, 2013.

10

Processing of Data

After a research protocol has been prepared and approved by a competent authority comes the stage of actual collection of information from the subjects selected for this purpose on the lines proposed in the protocol. The methodology of data collection is discussed in Chapter 7 and we assume that all those steps have been taken. All precautions stated in the protocol must be taken to ensure data quality and completeness. For example, ensure that the medication is given correctly within the shelf life and proper randomization has been done after faithfully following the inclusion and exclusion criteria. However, lapses may occur, and it is important to scrutinize the data after they have been collected. Suspicious data may have to be validated by rechecking or by record linkage. There may be some weird values, called outliers, that do not fit into the pattern of other data, and there may be missing values, which may require a revisit to the record or to the subjects.

When you are satisfied with the information collected for each subject, the data are generally entered into a spreadsheet, called the **master chart**. This would be automatically obtained in the case of electronic collection of data. The data entered into a master chart are sometimes converted to a more useful quantity such as body mass index (BMI) from height and weight. Some studies require calculation of scores to assess the severity of the disease. These calculations are done separately for each subject and are discussed in Section 10.1.

The next step is to use the entire data set and prepare summaries. Some researchers consider this as a part of statistical analysis, but they are better understood as data-processing activities. Epidemiological indices such as rates and ratios, including relative risk (RR) and odds ratio (OR), are discussed in Section 10.2 and data summary measures such as mean and standard deviation (SD) are presented in Section 10.3. Section 10.4 is on tabular and graphical representation of data, including a brief outline of Gaussian and non-Gaussian distributions. Medical research often requires that the quantitative measurements obtained for individual subjects be classified as normal or abnormal. This is discussed at the end of Section 10.4 as it requires an understanding of the shape of the distribution of the values.

The discussion in this chapter is focused and brief and would serve the purpose of most graduate research, but some endeavors may require a deep understanding of other methods such as standardization. For these, consult a comprehensive book on biostatistics such as by Indrayan and Malhotra [1].

10.1 Collation of Data and Scrutiny

Collection and recording of data for research are done in an established systematic manner so that the answers to the questions proposed in the protocol can be easily extracted. The tools required for data collection are discussed in Chapter 7, wherein the precautions required are also mentioned. In this section, we describe some additional considerations to enhance data quality.

10.1.1 Uniformity of the Process of Data Collection

In most research, including for a graduate thesis, more than one person is involved in the process of data collection. Whereas patient interviews and examination can be uniformly done by one investigator, particularly for a graduate thesis, there would most likely be laboratory and radiological investigations by another department. Despite automation, subjective elements do creep into these investigations, particularly at the time of interpretation. Thus, the collected data should be carefully scrutinized and affected values should be modified as needed to remove any discrepancy.

Record Linkage

Another method of improving data quality after collection is record linkage. This exploits the premise that some patients have the tendency to take advice from more than one physician in different institutions, particularly for long-term illnesses. A record is generated at each point of contact. Linkage is the process of pooling of disparate data to make a comprehensive single record for each individual. This process in a way is routinely followed for admitted patients in a hospital when the results of laboratory and imaging investigations are sent to the main folder of the patient. But linkage of records in different hospitals pertaining to the same patient, or with private practitioners, is a difficult process.

Separate data are generated on patients under research if they receive some treatment outside the protocol. This treatment can influence the results. Thus, linkage to that extent is necessary. Asking the subjects, probing them, and maintaining a vigil seem the only answer to make a comprehensive record.

Record linkage may find some inconsistencies between the sources. Whereas some of these may be due to differential emphasis by the health care facility depending on their perception or may be due to the psychology of the patient at the time of contact, some may be factual. Factual inconsistencies may be due to a real change in the health condition of the patient or due to different technology used in different facilities. An expert may be able to resolve these differences and generate a factual record. Sometimes, the patient may need to be contacted again to resolve such discrepancies.

10.1.2 Data Validation

Validity, as explained earlier, is the ability to provide correct information. Data validation is the process of cleansing the data so that they can be used with confidence to draw conclusions. Grossly inconsistent values such as a male giving birth to a child or duration of active smoking 15 years for a child of 15 years need to be located and corrected. In addition, suspicious values such as age at menarche of a girl more than the age at first conception should also be re-examined. However, most data-cleaning activities are for missing values and outliers.

Missing Values

Missing values are those for which data should be available but for some reason could not be collected or recorded. Collation of data starts with scrutiny for missing values. In empirical research such as in medicine, there is always the possibility of some incomplete records. They should be treated according to the procedure outlined in the protocol. This may require revisiting the record or recontacting the patient. Subjects with incomplete records can be removed altogether if they are few and do not have the potential to cause bias. If they are moderate in number, the records can be artificially completed by **imputing missing values** using the pattern of available values. If the missing values are too many, use the data to draw lessons and plan another study.

Some genuine missing values can be nonserious. If a patient missed taking a drug for 1 or 2 days in a 4-week trial this is generally not serious. If required for statistical purposes, perhaps such missing values can be imputed using the trend on other days. Such imputation helps to retain in the analysis the data for that patient that otherwise will have to be excluded. If many patients are dropped like this, the final available sample could be substantially reduced. Thus, imputation does help in certain situations (see, e.g., Carpenter and Kenward [2] for imputation methods). Imputation is advisable when the missing data are neither too few nor too many. A patient absenting for 2 weeks in a 4-week trial is a serious breach of protocol, and taking a prohibited concomitant drug for a considerable period is also a serious violation. Such patients may have to be excluded from the analysis. If the pattern of such exclusion is similar in the two groups under comparison, this may not affect the tenor of results except for reducing the sample size. This would not occur in most occasions.

Treatment-related dropouts should be counted as not cured by the treatment. An unrelated dropout such as due to accidental death can be excluded, or impute the values for the unobserved follow-up period by following one of the standard procedures [2].

Outliers

Outliers are those exceptional values that do not fit into the pattern of a large majority of values. They are difficult to identify and manage. Although statistical methods are available to identify outliers, it is advisable to depend more on common sense. If in doubt, give the benefit of the doubt and leave it in the data set. If you are convinced that a particular value is an outlier, the first step is to assess if it is due to an error in recording, coding, or data entry. If so, restore the correct value. A genuine outlier will have a biological explanation and can alert us to new findings. However, outliers have the potential to distort all statistical analysis and the usual practice therefore is to exclude such values. It is safe to analyze the data with and without outliers and see what difference they make in the results. Retain the one that can be reasonably explained.

10.1.3 Master Chart and Data Entries

After dealing with missing values and outliers, it is time to prepare a master chart that collates information on each subject in one row. As many rows are needed as the number of subjects. A master chart is an excellent tool to provide an overview of the data and to begin further collation. Prepare this after coding wherever needed if not already incorporated in the form. Identify baseline and repeated measures, such as heart rate before, during, and 1, 5, 10, and 30 minutes after surgery so that they can be properly analyzed as repeated measures. Before preparing tables and graphs, do calculations such as albumin–globulin ratio and disease score from the signs and symptoms, as explained next.

Although a master chart should be prepared only after thorough scrutiny of individual case records, it is generally at the stage of the master chart that many errors are detected. In place of doing these corrections in the original record, the changes are sometimes done in the master chart – wrong values are replaced with correct values, missing values are inserted from the case record, and so on. If so, make a note of these changes in the master chart itself in a separately defined comments column. In all probability, you will forget about such changes if the comments are not properly noted. These comments help in re-examining the data in case a doubt arises later.

10.1.4 Indexes and Scores for Individual Subjects

As mentioned in Chapter 6, factor is a characteristic and indicator is its measurement. A lipid profile is a characteristic and levels of various lipids are the indicators. There may be many indicators for the same factor. Sometimes one indicator is not enough by itself and it has to be seen in combination with one or more of the others. A combination of two or more indicators is called an index. For example, a smoking index may incorporate indicators such as the number of cigarettes smoked per day, duration of smoking, age at initiation, duration elapsed since quitting, and other such measurements. Another problem in measurement is converting qualities such as signs and symptoms into quantities. This is done by scoring. Both these can be explained as follows when calculated for individual values.

Indexes

An index is a combination of two or more indicators that provides a relatively more comprehensive picture of the status. When properly constructed, an index can enhance the utility of indicators and can sometimes even generate new information.

As already mentioned, the most popular example of an index in medicine is BMI that combines height and weight. Among other popular indexes is the shock index, used for patients with ST elevation in myocardial infarction, and ankle–brachial (pressure) index, bispectral index, glycemic index, and craniofacial index used in other contexts. At the community level, human development index, physical quality-of-life index, and disability-adjusted life-years are used. All these are a combination of two or more measurements.

An index is quantitative and therefore involves calculation that could be a nemesis for some clinicians. Some indexing instruments come ready with software to perform the calculations and directly provide the results. A bispectral index is automatically calculated by software. A high-pressure liquid chromatography automatically calculates the peak area of intensity of signals corresponding to concentrates of drug-evoked potentials. Thus, for some indexes, calculations are not much of a problem. Perhaps a greater problem is their **validity** and **reliability**. These two concepts are briefly explained in Chapter 7. A large number of indexes is available and many are being devised every year, but studies that provide evidence of their reliability and validity for different segments of population are rare. For example, the utility of BMI is sometimes questioned in comparison with the waist–hip ratio, which can be seen as a better correlate of coronary events. Thus, the choice of an index can be an issue in situations where two or more indexes are available to assess the same aspect of health, and you need to be judicious in making the choice.

Scores

A score is a quantity attached to a grade of an ordinal characteristic when it is not directly measured. Systolic blood pressure (BP) when measured as 132 mmHg is not a score in its conventional form, but when it is divided into categories such as below normal, normal, high, and very high, it can be assigned scores such as –1, 0, 1, and 2, respectively. These are *linear* scores because the difference between two adjacent categories is always the same. This is the most common form of scoring as it is the easiest way to assign scores. Another way, however, is to choose scores of +2, 0, 3, 6 that would, in this case, imply that "very high BP" (with a score of 6) is twice as important for, say, patient management as "high BP" (with a score of 3). It also implies that "below normal BP" (with a score of +2) prognostically sits between "normal BP" and "high BP" with scores of 0 and 3, respectively.

This BP example illustrates that the choice of scores is not always easy. Arbitrary scores can jeopardize the validity of conclusions. A common and acceptable method of scoring is based on standardized coefficients in ordinary or logistic regression. This method can be used to assign scores to nominal characteristics as well, and for a particular outcome of interest that could be quantitative or qualitative. For example, APACHE-II score assigns a score of 2 for previous history of elective surgery and 5 points to emergency surgery in the past [3]. These are nominal characteristics. Thus, scoring also provides an opportunity to quantify the qualities.

Z-Score and T-Score

Comparison of a value of a measurement with the other is difficult because of different units. For example, serum creatinine level cannot be compared with glomerular filtration rate (GFR) as the former is measured in mg/dL and the latter in mL/min/m^2. However, both can be converted to a Z-score that gives an assessment of how far a value is from its mean in sd units.

$$Z\text{-score} = \frac{\text{Value-Its population mean}}{\text{Its population sd}}$$

If the serum creatinine level for a person is 1.2 mg/dL where the population mean is 0.8 mg/dL and the sd is 0.03 mg/dL, the Z-score is $\frac{1.2-0.8}{0.03} = 1.33$. If the GFR in this patient is 108 where the population mean is 140 and the sd is 12, the Z-score for GFR is $\frac{108-140}{12} = -2.67$. Thus, GFR is much further away from the mean in this patient than the serum creatinine level and it is on the lower side, whereas creatinine is on the positive side.

A useful property of Z-scores is that they have mean 0 and sd = 1. Because of this, they are also called **standardized deviates** or **standardized variates**. The process of subtracting the mean and dividing by the sd is called the **standardization of values**.

The primary difficulty with Z-scores is that the population mean and population sd are rarely known. In many such cases, the sample mean and sample sd are used to provide an estimated Z-score. For highly skewed distributions, median is used in place of mean because, in this case, the mean is not an appropriate representative value.

T-score uses an ideal value in place of the mean. This is particularly used for bone mineral density where the ideal is the peak average density such as at age 30 years in a healthy male. *T*-score measures how far a value in a person is from the ideal value in SD units.

10.2 Epidemiological Indices

The research may or may not be epidemiological, but there is a high likelihood that it would use the epidemiological indices discussed in this section. These are calculated for the group and not for the individuals. Rate, risk, hazard, incidence, and prevalence are everyday indices of disease occurrence that are used in a large number of medical research endeavors. Although these indices apparently look simple, many researchers are not fully comfortable with their usage. The following description should be helpful in that case.

10.2.1 Rates and Ratios

Rates and ratios are special kinds of indexes at macro-levels that require a comparator. For example, birth rate is the number of births in 1 year per 1000 population in an area and sex ratio is number of females per 1000 males. Just as an index requires some calculations, rate and ratio are also derived from the collected data. The details of these two "indexes" are as follows. Some clinical indicators such as heart rate and HDL-LDL cholesterol ratio are measured at individual level.

Rate

Rate is a measure of the frequency of occurrence of a phenomenon. It counts the number of events occurring in a specific period per unit of time. Time is an essential element of this concept – per day, per month, per year, or any other duration. If 18 deaths occurred per 1000 patients of a specific type in a particular year, this becomes the mortality rate for that year for that disease. When the variation from time to time is not large, the reference to the point in time can be omitted, but new discoveries and advances in technology can alter any rate even when the ground situation remains the same. Thus, exercise caution in comparing rates over time.

Essential components of a rate are: (i) a numerator; (ii) a denominator; (iii) a specification of duration; and (iv) a multiplier such as percent or per thousand. The multiplier helps to convert an awkward-looking fraction to a convenient and nice number. The denominator is generally the number of subjects in the group *at risk* for the events counted in the numerator.

Ratio

Generally speaking, a ratio is one quantity relative to another. It can be expressed as *a:b* or as *a/b*. In a broad sense, all rates are also ratios because there is a numerator and there is a denominator, but in practice the usage of the term ratio is restricted to a situation in which the numerator is not a part of the denominator; nor is the denominator part of the numerator. Both are separate and distinct entities. The ratio of white blood cells to red blood cells is 1:600. Waist–hip ratio, acid output basal to maximal ratio, and albumin–globulin ratio are other examples although these are computed at individual level. Odds ratio and relative risk are the examples of ratios at macro level. In public health research, the interest may be in doctor–population ratio or dependence ratio. All these ratios have biological meaning – they convey the state of health or disease in some sense.

10.2.2 Prevalence and Incidence

Prevalence and incidence are the measures of frequency of occurrence of an event. Prevalence is the extent to which a condition is present in a defined group of subjects, whereas incidence measures the rate of the new occurrences. Prevalence is expressed as a percentage or per million (for a rare disease) at a point of time and incidence is related to a duration such as in one year. Both are generally used to measure morbidity in a segment of population, but can be used for other conditions, such as prevalence of self-care. Incidence is the inflow and prevalence is the stock. This stock depletes by recovery or by death. Incidence is affected by the physiological and environmental conditions such as malnutrition and mosquito density. Further details are as follows.

Prevalence

Cross-sectional surveys or descriptive studies give prevalence that measures the magnitude of presence of disease. If peptic ulcers are found in 5% of adults of upper socioeconomic status in a survey in Timbuktu in 2019, this is the prevalence rate. *Actually it is not a rate, but is only a proportion.* It does not measure speed of occurrence. Prevalence is an appropriate measure for chronic conditions and not for acute disorders. Note that prevalence counts all existing cases at a point in time. It is easy to imagine that the longer the duration of disease, the higher is the backlog and the greater the prevalence if outflow in terms of remissions and deaths is not equally rapid.

Incidence

Incidence is the development of new cases in a specified period of time. Follow a group of persons without the outcome for a certain period and see in how many the outcome of interest develops over a period of time. Incidence is factual – based on empirical evidence.

Incidence is difficult to obtain because it requires a prospective study, but it can be easily obtained from prevalence and duration of disease in certain conditions. Prevalence can be easily obtained by a cross-sectional study and average duration of disease is generally known to clinicians by experience, or can be obtained from records. When these two are available, incidence can be obtained under stable conditions by the following formula, thus saving the cost of a prospective study.

$$\text{Incidence} = \frac{\text{Prevalence}}{\text{Average duration of disease}}$$

However, the relation is not as simple in many situations due to changing rates and other intervening factors.

The concept of incidence is based on the premise that the event of interest can occur only once in the lifetime of one person, or at least during the defined time period under review.

But events such as asthma, otitis media, and angina can recur within a short period. The term then used is **incidence density**. This is comparable to hazard, discussed in the next section.

Person-Years

In many prospective studies, it is extremely difficult to follow each subject for the same length of time. For a study on breast cancer to be completed in 5 years, 2–3 years may be required for just enrolling the desired number of women with a lump in the breast. Once enrolled, some may quit the study and some could become untraceable after some time. Thus, the duration of follow-up will vary from woman to woman. In such instances, one epidemiological tool is person-years. Just add years of follow-up for different women to get person-years. Use this to calculate incidence per 100 person-years. This concept assumes that the risk in, say, the fourth year of follow-up is the same as in the second year of follow-up. That is, the risk should be time-invariant. In most practical situations this condition is satisfied, but watch out if this is indeed so in your research setting. An example where time invariance does not hold is risk of kidney failure after transplantation. This risk is much greater in the beginning than 2 years after receiving the kidney.

The concept of person-years is useful also in the case of recurrent episodes in the same person. Time of follow-up after each episode can be added to calculate person-time. If the first child is followed up for 12 months, the second for 15 months, and the third for 10 months, and a total of 7 episodes of diarrhea occurred, the incidence density is $7 \times 100/(12 + 15 + 10)$ or 18.9 per 100 child-months.

> **Example 10.1: Prevalence from Incidence of Breast Cancer**
>
> Suppose an average of 3 new cases of breast cancer are detected each year per 1000 population of women of aged 45–54 years in the hypothetical city of Nomanstown. If the average duration of survival is 5 years, the prevalence of breast cancer at any point of time would be nearly $(3 \times 5 =)$ 15 cases per 1000 population of such women. If the population of such women is 30,000 in that city, expect to see 450 cases. Hospitals should be geared to meet the demand of services for 450 cases of breast cancer in that city.

10.2.3 Risk, Hazard, and Odds

Risk, hazard, and odds measure the chance that an outcome or antecedent will occur in a group of subjects. In general conversation, risk and odds are used interchangeably, but they do not have the same meaning and are used differently in different contexts, as explained below.

Risk

Risk is the chance that a person without the disease will develop the disease in a defined period. It can be any other event or outcome such as accidental injury and vision becoming $<6/60$. The term is generic and not restricted to adverse outcomes. It could be the "risk" of survival or a risk of reduction in side effects, or a risk of conception. Risk could be 1 in 1000 or 0.05 or 0.20, but cannot exceed 1. It is a decimal number calculated per person although it is often expressed as a percentage. The implication of risk is for future events, but the calculation is based on previous experience. The denominator is the number of persons exposed to the risk and the numerator is that part of the denominator that develops the outcome in the specified period. For example, 10-year risk of coronary heart disease may be 9% in a population of age 40–79 years. Such an estimate can be obtained only after follow-up of subjects for a 10-year period. The population at risk for this calculation is not what was in the middle of the period but what was in the beginning of the period because all those are exposed to that risk. A measure of risk is the incidence rate, as discussed in the preceding section.

Risk perception can be different in different contexts: if a celebrity is affected, the risk is highlighted manifold even if it is one in a million. Also, stating it as 0.001 is perceived differently than one in a thousand, although both are the same.

Hazard

Risk cannot exceed 1, but hazard has no such restriction, although this also is generally a small quantity. If hundreds die within a few hours after a plane crash, obviously the hazard of death is exceedingly high at that time compared to at a normal time. Hazard can be understood as the instantaneous rate of death – for that matter, of any event of interest. It is sometimes called the **force of mortality** for deaths, force of morbidity for ill health, and force of event occurrence in general. It can also be understood as the intensity with which events occur at a point of time. It is time specific. Hazard can increase steeply in specific situations such as calamity and epidemic. If constant over a period of time, hazard can be obtained by dividing the number of events in the target population by the exposure period.

In many research settings, hazard in the exposed group is compared with the hazard in the unexposed group, such as comparing the rate of adverse reactions in the test and the control group. In such setups, the interest generally is in the **hazard ratio** instead of the hazard itself. Hazard of death due to local anesthesia may be 1 in 100,000, but it could be 1 in 1000 for general anesthesia. Thus, the latter is 100 times the former. Hazard itself may continuously vary over the follow-up period, but in many situations the hazard ratio remains constant throughout that period.

Relative Risk

The ratio of risk of an outcome such as disease in one group (say, the exposed group) to that in any other group (generally the control group – the unexposed group) is called the relative risk (or **risk ratio**). If RR of HIV infection in persons with sexually transmitted disease (STD) versus those without STD is 6.5, it says that the persons with STD are 6.5 times as likely to contract HIV infection than persons without STD – other factors remaining the same. A prospective study is required to calculate RR, and that could be very expensive, but it has future overtones. Assessment of RR is considered important to discuss the consequences with the patient and to prepare a management strategy. Methods are available to check whether an RR is statistically significant. RR = 1 implies that the two groups have the same risk. Thus, significance here implies that RR is different from 1. RR > 1 has the usual meaning of increased risk, but RR < 1 could mean that there is a protective effect of the factor under consideration.

If the risk in an unexposed group is low, the RR can be a high value. If risk in the unexposed group is 2% and in the exposed group is 70%, the RR is 35. If the risk in the unexposed group is 60%, RR cannot exceed 100/60 = 1.67. Thus, use caution to interpret an RR.

Odds Ratio

Now reverse gears and consider the chance of the presence of an antecedent in a group of subjects. If 67% of all hypertensive patients are obese, the odds are said to be 67:33 or 2 to 1. A hypertensive person is twice as likely to be obese as nonobese. This quirky measure is generally calculated for an antecedent rather than an outcome.

Because case–control studies move from disease to antecedent, they are relatively easy to conduct. For example, cases with pancreatitis and matched controls can be asked whether or not they smoke or smoked. Such a design gives the prevalence of smoking and of no smoking in cases with pancreatitis and in the controls. If the prevalence in the cases is 80% and 20%, respectively, the odds of smoking in cases of pancreatitis is 4:1. Similar odds can be calculated for controls, which in this setup are persons without the disease. Suppose the odds of smoking in them are 3:1. Thus, the OR is 4/3.

When the prevalence of the disease is low among the patients under consideration, OR can be interpreted in the same way as RR. Our example is on pancreatitis whose prevalence is generally small in patients coming to a clinic. Therefore, it can be safely concluded on the basis of the OR, without worrying about calculating RR, that the risk of pancreatitis in smokers is 4/3 times that in nonsmokers. OR = 1 indicates that the concerned factor is not a risk.

Odds Ratio vs. Relative Risk

As just mentioned, it can be mathematically shown that OR is approximately the same as RR when the prevalence of disease is low, say less than 5%. This equivalence property is extremely useful because most diseases have a low prevalence, and there is no need to conduct expensive prospective studies to obtain RR for such diseases. A retrospective study is much easier and requires fewer inputs, and would give an OR that fairly approximates RR. However, be careful. Not all diseases or health conditions are rare. Anemia in women in developing countries is widespread, and nearly one-third of all births may have low birthweight in some areas. Hypertension in Nigeria may be present in 20% or more of adults in some segments of the population. Many postmenopausal women around the world are obese. In conditions with a high prevalence such as these, OR cannot be used as an approximation to RR.

Neither RR nor OR can be calculated if no event of interest occurs in the control group. If there is no person with exposure in the control group of a case–control study, the denominator for OR would be zero, and that would make the OR an impossible infinity. This underscores the need to have a reasonably big sample so that at least a few persons are found with exposure in both cases as well as controls. The minimum required is 5 persons for valid conclusions.

If the focus shifts from the occurrence of event to its nonoccurrence (e.g., survival instead of death), the only effect on OR is that it becomes inverse, but RR can substantially change. This happens because the calculation of RR markedly differs from OR. For this reason, decide beforehand whether the interest is in occurrence or nonoccurrence.

Rate Ratio

Another index, called the rate ratio, is also used in some situations. If 22 episodes of myocardial infarction (MI) occur in 480 person-years of follow-up of people aged 60 years and above with positive family history, the rate (incidence density) is $22 \times 100/$

480 = 4.6 MIs per 100 person-years. If this rate in those without family history is 2.7 MIs per 100 person-years, the rate ratio is 4.6/2.7 = 1.7. A similar ratio can also be obtained for prevalence rates.

Example 10.2: Odds Ratio in Rheumatoid Arthritis

Rodríguez-Lozano et al. [4] reported a significant OR of 20.57 between periodontitis and rheumatoid arthritis in a case–control study in Spain. This was adjusted for other confounders. Such a high OR indicates a definite association between periodontitis and rheumatoid arthritis.

Example 10.3: Prevalence Ratios as a Surrogate for Risk Ratios

Pantoja-Torres et al. [5] analyzed data on 118 healthy adults and observed high triglyceride/high-density lipoprotein (HDL)-C ratio in 17.8% and prevalence of insulin resistance (IR) in 24.6%. When adjusted for other factors, the prevalence ratio is 3.16, which was statistically significant. They concluded on the basis of this and other such prevalence rates that a high triglyceride/HDL-C ratio was associated with IR markers and appears to be a clinically useful tool to assess IR in normal healthy adults.

Attributable Risk

The difference between the risk in exposed subjects and unexposed subjects is called the attributable risk (AR). If the 10-year risk of lung cancer among smokers is 16.5% and in nonsmokers of the same age and gender is 1.7%, the risk attributable to smoking is (16.5 − 1.7 =) 14.8%. This can also be understood as **risk difference**. For this to be valid, it is necessary that the groups are similar with respect to all factors except the antecedent under review. That is, there is no other factor that can alter the risk.

Frequently, AR gives more valid information to health managers, particularly when the disease is rare that occurs several times more frequently if a particular antecedent is present. Suppose cancer throat has a risk of 0.0003 in nontobacco-chewing persons but is 0.019 in those who chewed tobacco for 10 years or more. Thus, the RR = 0.019/0.0003 = 63, but the AR is only 0.019 − 0.0003 = 0.0187 (less than 1.9%). Changing habits of tobacco chewing will not make much of a difference to the overall incidence of throat cancer: RR = 63 notwithstanding. It can be shown that this is all the more true if only a small percentage, such as 3%, of the population chews tobacco. AR is a better index of the public health importance of the risk factor in terms of the impact its reduction can make on overall incidence of disease.

Why then is RR such a popular measure with researchers around the world? One reason is that it can be easily estimated even by case–control studies for rare diseases. AR cannot. The second is that RR often comes close to multiplying individual RRs when two independent factors act jointly in concert. This does not happen with AR. The third is that the same risk difference, such as 5% between 70% and 75%, has entirely different implications than between 3% and 8%. A large RR is a definite indicator of a strong association between an antecedent and outcome. Thus, it is a better index of the etiological role of a factor in disease.

For further details of risk-related indicators and OR, see Indrayan and Malhotra [1].

10.3 Representative Summary Measures

Primarily, there are two types of summary measures that are used in medical research for quantitative data: one that represents location such as the central value and the value is seen in, say, more than 75% subjects, and the other that describes how different values are from one another. For qualitative data, proportions or percentages are commonly used. Almost all empirical research endeavors to use these measures to describe their results. All such researchers are expected to be familiar with the nuances of such measures.

10.3.1 Summary Measures for Quantitative Data

As explained earlier, quantitative data arise from metric measurements of individual subjects. However, if a measurement is done on 300 subjects in a research study, how can these 300 values be summarized without losing much information? The following summary measures are commonly used for this purpose.

Mean, Median, and Mode

Levels in a group can be represented either by a single value, or by a range of values. The representative single value is called the **central value**. It is computed in terms of mean, median, or mode. Mean is the usual average and need not be explained any further. Statistically inclined researchers understand that the usual mean is the **arithmetic mean**. The other types of mean are geometric and harmonic. **Geometric mean** has application in multiplicative measurements such as antibody titer and gamma radiation count (where log values are used), and **harmonic mean** is sometimes used for averaging rates. Such special applications are avoided in this text because the emphasis is on the basics.

Median is the most middle value obtained after arranging the data in ascending (or descending) order. It is an intermediary value that divides a group into two equal halves. Median is a good representative of central values when extremely high or extremely low values (outliers) are present. If the duration of hospitalization after surgery is mostly 3–5 days but one or two patients have to be in the ward for 30 or 40 days because of complications or any other reason, the mean will be highly vitiated. Use the median in this situation because such outliers do not affect the median. The median is also used for highly skewed distribution, described in Section 10.4.

The mode is the most commonly occurring value. If the most commonly seen incubation period from exposure to appearance of a rash for measles is 10 days, this is the mode. Mode can also be used for ordinal data. For example, one can say that the most common response to the occurrence of nosocomial infection in a long hospital stay is "strongly possible" when this possibility is graded as none, slight, moderate, or strong. Similarly, mode can be used for nominal variables also. Mean and median do not have this flexibility. Also, for quantitative measurements, more than one mode can exist. This would happen when the distribution has two or more peaks, although one peak can be smaller than the other. Age distribution of Hodgkin's disease and leukemia is **bimodal** with one (smaller) peak around 20 years and the other (bigger) peak at age around 60 years.

Example 10.4: Mean, Median, and Mode

Imagine survival duration (in years) after detection of cervical cancer in a group of 12 patients with radical hysterectomy:

7   4   7   5   2   29   8   6   24   3   5   2

The mean survival duration is 92/12 = 7.6 years. This obviously is not representative of these values because 9 out of 12 patients have survival less than this average. The mean is vitiated in this example due to extreme values 29 and 24 years for patients who probably lived their normal life. In such situations, the appropriate measure is the median. For $n = 12$, this is the average of the sixth and seventh values after arranging them in increasing order. These values are 5 and 6 years. Thus, the median is 5.5 years. This looks like a good representative value in this example. Apparently there are three modes in this example – 2 years, 5 years, and 7 years – each occurring twice. Multiple modes are rarely acceptable. No mode can be obtained in this example until data for more patients are available.

Calculating mean, median, and mode is simple, but their usage requires caution. Saying that *a person with a head in an oven and feet in a freezer is comfortable on average* epitomizes the caution required. It must always be accompanied by a measure of dispersion such as SD that we describe in a short while. The number of observations should also be mentioned. Mean of values in three subjects has little meaning. The mean value in 300 subjects may be the same but has very different reliability. Outliers have tremendous impact on mean. Can a person drown in a channel with an average depth of 12 inches? Yes, if there is an 8-foot deep pit somewhere!

Conclusions based on mean alone without considering other correlates could be misleading. If an antihypertensive drug is able to reduce diastolic BP by 10 mmHg on average after 1 week of use by hypertensives, the other considerations such as side effects, cost, and convenience of intake cannot be ignored altogether while evaluating the usefulness of the drug. Mean, median, and mode are much more meaningful when they are based on a homogeneous group. For example, mean survival period of assorted patients admitted in a hospital could be an inappropriate measure of efficiency because there would be cases of hernia with minimal risk of death and cases of advanced malignancy with grave prognosis: their survival periods could be widely different.

Percentiles

Sometimes the interest is not in the central value but a threshold seen in a certain percentage of the subjects. These are called percentiles. In child growth, it is common to say, for example, that 14 kg is the 90th percentile of weight for 2-year-old girls. This implies that 90% of girls aged 2 years weigh 14 kg or less. The method to obtain kth percentiles is to pick up $(k \times n/100)$th value after arranging the values in ascending order. For survival duration in Example 10.4, the 70th percentile is the $70 \times 12/100 = 8$th value (approximately) in ascending order, which is 7 years.

Example 10.5: A Good Use of Percentiles for Assessing the Risk of Heart Disease

Evidence is growing that children with low birthweight but with rapid gain in weight and increase in BMI after the age of 1 year are at greater risk of coronary heart disease later in life, particularly males [6]. Rapid gain implies that a child who was at a lower percentile for birthweight reaches a higher percentile at, say, age 8 years. A boy with birthweight in the bottom 10% (10th percentile) who rapidly gains weight to reach the top 25% (beyond the 75th percentile) at age 5 or 10 years is at much greater risk of coronary heart disease. This is called crossing the centiles, and illustrates a very apt application of the concept of percentiles.

Quartiles, tertiles, and deciles are special percentiles. Twenty-fifth, 50th, and 75th percentiles are called first, second, and third **quartiles**, respectively, because they divide total subjects into four groups of equal size. Tenth, 20th, etc., percentiles are called **deciles** because they divide the subjects in 10 equal groups. If a man's height is 188 cm, he may be in the top decile; that is, less than 10% of men will be as tall as that or taller. **Tertiles** are the points that divide the group into three equal parts. Choose the one that is most appropriate for your research.

Standard Deviation and Variance

Some measurements, such as body temperature in healthy subjects, do not vary much across healthy individuals whereas others, such as cholesterol level, are highly variable. Thus, dispersion (scatter) is important. A universally accepted measure of dispersion is SD.

Dispersion is the difference one value has from another. Instead of calculating so many differences, it is convenient to find the difference each value has with the group mean, called the **deviation**. Some of these deviations would be negative and some positive. To get rid of negative values, a standard statistical practice is to square them. Accordingly, all deviations are squared. The average of these squared deviations is called the variance. To retrieve the original units (i.e., μg in place of μg^2 in variance), the square root is taken. The value so obtained is the SD. Thus, SD actually is the root mean square deviation and measures dispersion around the mean. If SD of systolic BP in males of age 40–49 years is 8 mmHg and in females 10 mmHg, it shows that the systolic level varies more in females of age 40–49 years than in males of this age. SDs are extensively used to delineate normal reference ranges also, as discussed later in this chapter.

SD must be interpreted with caution when comparing variability of one measurement with the other. A small-looking SD such as 0.2 mEq/L for serum magnesium is in fact high compared to SD = 10 mg/dL for cholesterol because the mean is only 2.0 mEq/L for serum magnesium while it is 150 mg/dL for cholesterol. A unit-free measure of variability for comparison of dispersion in different measurements is the **coefficient of variation** (CV). This is calculated as:

$$CV = SD \times 100/mean$$

In the above example, CV is $0.2 \times 100/2.0 = 10\%$ for serum magnesium and $10 \times 100/150 = 6.67\%$ for cholesterol level. Thus, variability in magnesium is relatively higher. A higher CV indicates that the measurement is less reliable and its research utility is less. The CV cannot be calculated when the mean is zero, and should not be calculated when the mean could be very small. This can happen when negative values are also present. For example, average gain after treatment over the baseline level could be very small in some situations.

Variance, although in square units, is a more popular term particularly in the context of attributing part of variation to a certain set of risk factors. For example, 60% of variance in P3 amplitude (a measure of cognitive functioning) explained by genetic factors implies that 60% of the differences among individuals in P3 amplitudes is attributable to the differences in their genetic factors. Such apportionment of variance is briefly discussed in analysis of variance in Chapter 11.

Example 10.6: Use of CV for Changes in Cardiac Structure

In a follow-up of nearly 5 years of a cohort of 455 type 2 diabetes mellitus patients, Tang et al. [7] measured fasting plasma glucose (FPG) level on every visit of the patients to the hospital. In a multivariable regression analysis, they found that the annualized changes in left ventricle are independently associated with CV of FPG levels over time. Interventricular septum, left posterior wall thickness, left ventricular mass index, and left ventricular ejection fraction were all significantly affected by CV of FPG levels. The authors opined that visit-to-visit variability in FPG could be a novel risk factor for the long-term adverse changes in left cardiac structure and systolic function in type 2 diabetes patients.

10.3.2 Summary Measures for Qualitative Data

Not many options are available to summarize qualitative data. Either the count itself or the percentage of subjects possessing a particular characteristic or meeting a set criterion is used as a summary measure. The statistical equivalent of percentage is proportion, which is stated in terms of fraction considering the whole group as one. If 27 patients with peritonitis survive out of 48 admitted to a hospital in a 1-year period, the percentage survival is 56.25, and the proportion is 0.5625. This proportion is denoted by p.

In one group of 48 patients, a proportion may be 0.5625 and in another group only 0.3333. When only two categories (dichotomous) are considered, the number of subjects with specific characteristics follows a **binomial distribution**. For multiple categories (polytomous), the corresponding distribution is called **multinomial**. We do not include this in the purview of this book to keep this text simple for our readers. If necessary, consult a biostatistician to analyze polytomous data, particularly for small n.

10.4 Tabulation and Graphics

Most empirical research studies collect a mass of data that need to be summarized for communication into tables and graphs in a manner that the essential features of the data remain preserved. However, the preparation of appropriate tables and graphs requires a judicious mix of thought and action. In this section, we discuss what important points need to be considered and how to choose an appropriate table or graph.

10.4.1 Categorization of Data and the Choice of Class Intervals

Whereas categories for nominal data and ordinal data arise naturally, they are created for metric data mostly for convenience. For example, it is common to use (0–1), (1–4), (5–14), (15–44), (45–59), and 60+ categories for age in years in a population. Sometimes 10-year intervals are formed. Such categories make the communication of the data easier.

When such categories are formed for metric measurements, we get what is called **grouped data**. In this case, the choice of class intervals is important and should be such that the differentials within the intervals are of no consequence. That is, if an interval for systolic BP is 130–139 mmHg, it indirectly conveys that the BP = 130 has the same consequence as the BP = 139 for subjects under study. It also means that BP = 140 is different from BP = 139 as it goes into the next category. There might be a legitimate question regarding 140 having different consequence from 139 but 130 and 139 having the same consequence. Thus, rational categories must be formed that can be justified.

Remember, though, that the statistical analysis as much as possible should be done on original uncategorized data because categories sacrifice some information that might be important for proper conclusions. Use categories for presentation of results and not for analysis. Two mutually exclusive categories such as hemoglobin (Hb) < 11 and Hb ≥ 11 g/dL look simpler, but consider whether other categories such as Hb < 8, 8 ≤ Hb < 11, and Hb ≥ 11 are more appropriate. Also, the conclusion from such categories can be very different from uncategorized data, and thus the choice of categories becomes important. This is so for dichotomous categories as much as for polytomous categories.

10.4.2 Types of Data Tables

Tables are powerful tools to summarize a large data set in an intelligible format. They are extensively used in reporting research findings and help in providing structure to the results. Text adds meat. While preparing tables, the variability in the data must be preserved, but it may be counter-productive to use too many categories in one table. Tables can become a source of confusion also when not properly drawn. They should be self-contained but should not be a horrendous mess. The format of tables for qualitative data is slightly different from that of tables for quantitative data.

Frequency Tables for Quantitative Data

For the purpose of summarizing and collating quantitative measurements, data intervals are necessary. If there are 450 subjects whose cholesterol level was measured, it is not feasible to present all 450 values. The table summarizing this measurement can have data intervals such as 100–149, 150–199, 200–219, 220–239, etc., and the number of subjects in each interval would be stated. As remarked earlier, do not make these intervals at the time of data collection. It is only at the stage of data collation that these are formed. Even at this time, mean and sd can and should be calculated based on exact values rather than data intervals. Nevertheless, the intervals would be necessary at the time of reporting of the results. At that time, the intervals should be so formed that a conventional normal range can be easily marked out, and other intervals are easily labeled as below normal, above normal, serious, critical, and so forth. Such qualitative terms are very helpful in assessing patients as well as in reporting the results of a study. The interval 100–149 mg/dL for cholesterol is useful because the conventional cutoff for normal range starts at 150 mg/dL. A level of 150–199 can be considered borderline without making any distinction that it is 150–159 or 170–179, and so on. After the level goes beyond 200, smaller intervals are proposed because then an increased level may have a different clinical significance. Generally, not more than eight categories are made. Too many categories are confusing and render the table clumsy.

Also note that cholesterol level is never measured to any decimal accuracy. Thus, there is no possibility of anyone with a recorded level between 149 and 150 mg/dL.

The data intervals that we mentioned in the preceding paragraph are a global convention. For example, in the case of age, a person may be 39 years and 8 months, but would still be counted in the age interval 30–39 years because age is conventionally recorded in completed years (or age at last birthday).

Contingency Tables for Qualitative Data

Qualitative data are also collated in the form of tables that contain the count of subjects in different categories of one or more characteristics. When the categories are **mutually exclusive and exhaustive**, that is, each subject belongs to one and only one category, these tables are called **contingency tables**. Contingency arises either because of fixed totals, or because the counts are restricted to specified categories. As described later in this section, you can also have a table with multiple responses which will not be a contingency table.

Example 10.7: A Three-Way Contingency Table

Islamoska et al. [8] analyzed data from the Copenhagen City Heart Study for risk of ischemic heart disease (IHD) in people with various degrees of vital exhaustion. They explain that vital exhaustion is a psychological measure of fatigue and exhaustion. Vital exhaustion score is the number of items present in a person out of a list of 17, such as "feel dejected," "lately have difficulties concentrating," and "sometimes just feel like crying." The authors found that, as the vital exhaustion increased, the hazard ratio of IHD (as well as of all-cause mortality) also increased in both women and men, and suggest that this should begin to be implemented in risk assessment in clinical practice. The following is a three-way table adapted from their results.

Vital exhaustion score*	Women			Men			Both genders together		
	IHD cases	Others	Total	IHD cases	Others	Total	IHD cases	Others	Total
0	43	1307	1350	62	1360	1422	105	2667	2772
1–4	78	2255	2333	122	1670	1792	200	3925	4125
5–9	56	1016	1072	37	488	525	93	1504	1597
10–17	37	449	486	20	202	222	57	651	708
Total	214	5027	5241	241	3720	3961	455	8747	9202

Source: Adapted from Islamoska et al. [8].
*Number of items present out of a list of 17.

A contingency table is called *K*-way when a group of subjects is cross-classified by *K* characteristics. The table in Example 10.7 is a three-way table: the three characteristics are: (i) vital exhaustion scores; (ii) gender; and (iii) occurrence of IHD. A higher-way table is difficult to read and interpret. If there are four or more factors under study, split them and prepare separate tables not containing more than three factors each. Also, the table becomes clumsy when too many categories of any characteristic are used. In this table, score has four categories, gender has two categories, and IHD also has two categories. If gender variation is not of interest, the last three columns of the table that collapse gender for various scores is a two-way table. If the interest is only in distribution of scores and not IHD or gender, the last column provides the one-way table. This incidentally is a frequency table also because the score is quantitative. If vital exhaustion is relabeled as none, mild, moderate, and serious instead of 0, 1–4, 5–9, and 10–17, respectively, the last column would provide a one-way contingency table in its true sense.

When all totals are excluded, the three-way table in Example 10.7 has 16 cells. These cells contain the number of subjects found in various categories, and this is called the **cell frequency**. The total number of cells corresponds to the number of possible categories. Because vital exhaustion score is in four categories, gender in two categories, and IHD also in two categories (IHD and no IHD), the order of this table is 4×2×2, making a total of 16 possible categories.

You will need these basic concepts to collate your data properly and to analyze them later. If collaborating with a statistical department, you will need these concepts to effectively communicate with a statistician.

Features of a Table

Each frequency table or contingency table must contain the total number of subjects – groupwise if groups are present. The first confusion arises at the time of calculating percentages. The base for percentages should be a predetermined number. In a case–control study, the relevant percentage is of those possessing a particular antecedent out of the total cases and total controls separately. If 28 out of 80 breast cancer cases and 21 out of 80 matched controls report age at menarche <12 years, do not calculate the percentage of 28 and 21 out of their total 49. Calculate this out of 80. In a prospective study, the percentage should be based on the exposed and unexposed cohorts that have been followed up. In a cross-sectional study, the percentage should be calculated out of the grand total (and not row totals or column totals) because the grand total is the prefixed number in this case. For the number of decimals in a percentage, use the rules that we describe in Chapter 13. All percentages must add up to 100 except in the case of multiple responses. Example 10.8 illustrates such percentages. The table in this example also illustrates the placing of explanatory matter in footnotes. Use superscripts to link footnotes with the table contents. Codes, abbreviations, symbols, inconsistencies, obscure information, and other such explanations should be explained in the footnotes. If the data are not original, give the source in the footnote without using a connecting symbol.

Example 10.8: Illustration of Features of a Table

Consider the following table containing hypothetical data from Noname Hospital. See if the table is self-explanatory or not. Note that this is not a contingency table because multiple responses are allowed – the complaints are not mutually exclusive: two or more complaints can be simultaneously reported by one patient.

Postnatal complications[1]	Number of women	Percentage
Excessive bleeding	30	7.3
Urinary tract infection	52	12.6
Convulsions	68	16.4
Foul discharge	56	13.5
Others	39	9.4
Total with complications	209	50.5

Postnatal complications[1]	Number of women	Percentage
No complication	205	49.5
Total[2]	414	100.0

1 Multiple responses.
2 Total women are 427 but complication information is not available for 13.

Side note: Calculating the percentage of 30 cases of excessive bleeding out of 209 women with complications would send a wrong message that excessive bleeding occurred in $(30/209) \times 100 = 14.4\%$. Actually, this occurred in only 7.3% of women. Exercise caution in choosing the base for calculating percentages.

Whereas in a graduate thesis you can have one table for one variable, journals prefer **composite tables** to save space in a publication. These tables contain information on many variables and replace many tables with one. For example, you can have number of participants in the case and the control group with age distribution, gender distribution, BMI categories, and smoking status all in one table. Such composite tables may require cut-in headings and indent for subheadings or categories. See Example 10.9 for an illustration, particularly for smokers. Note that text is left-adjusted and numbers are right-adjusted. All percentages have the same number of decimals.

Example 10.9: Features and Layout of a Composite Table

Background Characteristics of the Participants in a Trial

Particulars	Cases (n = 200)		Controls (n = 200)	
	Number	Percent	Number	Percent
Age (Years)				
20–24	32	16.0	40	20.0
25–29	51	25.5	57	28.5
30–34	76	38.0	63	31.5
35–39	41	20.5	40	20.0
Gender				
Male	103	51.5	95	47.5
Female	97	48.6	105	52.5
Smoking status				
Smokers				
Current	45	22.5	36	18.0
Past	23	11.5	24	12.0
Never smokers	129	64.5	140	70.0
Not available	3	1.5	0	0.0

Tables containing statistical results can have mean, SD, OR, confidence intervals, *P*-values, and other such information, but they basically have the same features.

10.4.3 Graphs and Diagrams

Figure is a generic term used for all illustrations, including graphs, diagrams, charts, photographs, and drawings. The purpose of graphs and diagrams is to collate the data and depict the pattern visually. The message borne by these figures is easily grasped and tends to remain in the memory longer than numbers in a table. However, the depiction is approximate rather than exact in the sense that quantities 103.2 and 103.4 can be shown as distinct in a table but rarely in a graph. Diagrams are even more approximate.

A large number of figures feature throughout this text. Figure 3.1 in Chapter 3 on study designs is an example of a chart which is neither a graph nor a diagram. The same is true for Figure 3.4 on prospective and retrospective studies. Graphs in Figure 3.5 on validity and reliability also cannot be classified conventionally. Conventional figures are described in the following paragraphs.

Graphs

A numerical axis is a prerequisite for a figure to be called a graph. Generally, it has a horizontal axis, called the x-axis, and a vertical axis, called the y-axis, but it can have three dimensions or just one dimension depending upon the number of variables shown.

The most appropriate graph for showing the frequency distribution of a quantitative measurement is a **histogram**, and in some situations a **polygon**. These can be drawn for relative frequencies also, which are proportion or percentage of subjects in different categories. See Figure 10.1 for an example of these and other graphs. In a histogram, the categories of the quantitative measurement under collation are generally shown on the horizontal axis and the frequencies on the vertical axis (Figure 10.1a), but they can also be reversed. A polygon (Figure 10.1b) can be smoothened into a **frequency curve**. The shapes of some frequency curves are given later in Figure 10.4.

Use a **line diagram** (Figure 10.1c) to show trends over time, over age, or any such numerical characteristic. Figure 3.2 in Chapter 3 is a line diagram that illustrates interaction. Many lines (or curves) can be shown in one diagram. Visual study of the relationship between two quantitative variables is best done by a **scatter diagram** (Figure 10.1d). Line diagrams and scatter diagrams are in fact graphs, but are conventionally called diagrams.

Log-scale can be used on either or both axes when the range of values to be shown is extremely large, such as gamma radiation counts ranging from 100 to 100,000 per minute. Figures 10.1e and 10.1f are **mixed diagrams** where two diagrams are shown in the same figure. Such combination not only saves space, but also sometimes gives better cognition by putting two pictures together.

Diagrams

In a statistical context, the term diagram is generally used for those figures that show a quantity for different categories of a quality. The most popular of these is the **bar diagram** with categories on the x-axis and quantity on the y-axis. This versatile format can show almost any type of quantity: number of subjects, rate, percentage, OR, and so on. Categories on the x-axis can be nominal, such as site of cancer – lung, breast, ovary, etc. – or can be numerical, such as year 2005, 2010, 2015, etc. Some space between bars is kept to show that the variable is not continuous. The width of the bars is subjective. Figure 10.2a is a 3D version of a bar diagram that shows the number of women with different medical problems in different age groups. Figure 9.1 in Chapter 9, which depicts a timeline, is a variant of a bar diagram. Figure 10.2b is a Venn diagram showing hypertension and diabetes as comorbidities in patients with liver disease in a hospital.

The most appropriate diagram for showing proportion (parts of a whole) is **pie**. This is particularly useful when such proportions are to be shown for two or more groups with unequal numbers of subjects. The size of the pie can be chosen accordingly. See

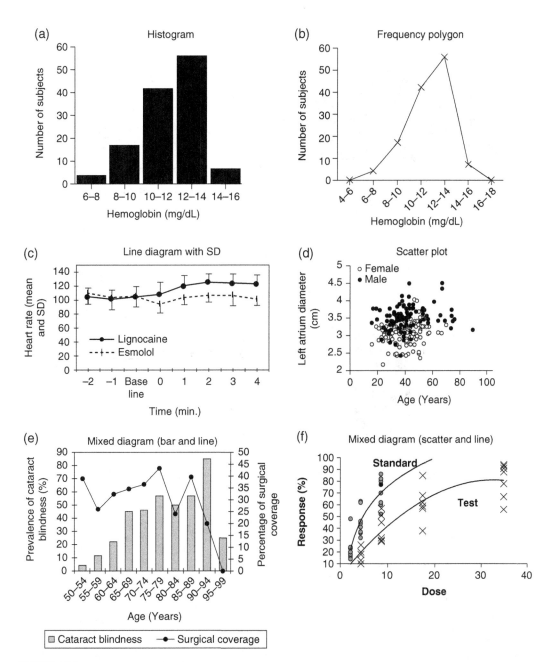

FIGURE 10.1

Common types of graphs. sᴅ, standard deviation.

Figure 10.2c for a variant where the segment of a pie is shown with further subdivisions in a subsequent pie. A pie diagram is not suitable when the number of categories is large or when the proportions in different categories are nearly equal, or when proportions in two or more categories are exceedingly small.

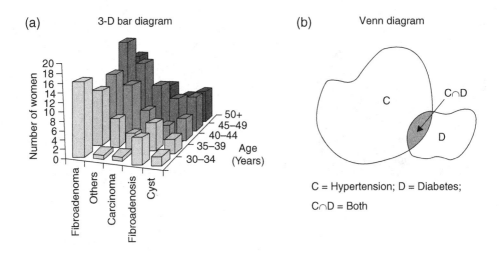

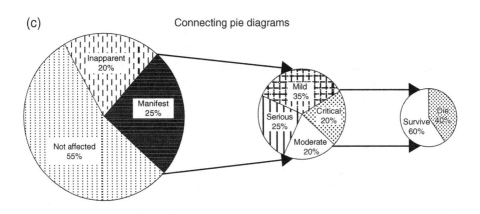

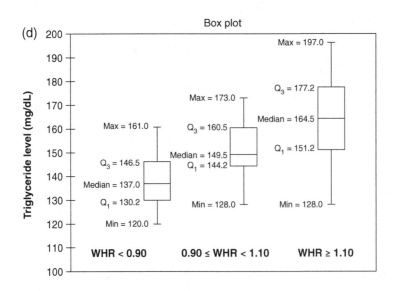

FIGURE 10.2
Examples of some diagrams.

Another diagram is a **box-and-whiskers plot** (Figure 10.2d), which gives a feeling of the variation and skewness in the data. This plot is based on median and quartiles, as discussed earlier. The width of the boxes is subjective.

Guidelines regarding where to use which graph or diagram are given in Box 10.1. All graphs and diagrams must follow certain sets of principles. These are listed in Box 10.2.

BOX 10.1   WHERE TO USE WHICH GRAPH/DIAGRAM?

Except for diagrams such as pie and Venn, at least one of the axes in a graph or diagram must be quantitative. In medical research, the outcome is generally quantitative. It can be the number (or percentage) of subjects surviving in a group, the number of subjects with a particular kind of level, median duration of hospital stay, average level of a measurement in a group, prevalence rate of a condition, or just a level of a particular measurement in individual subjects. It is customary to use the vertical axis to depict the outcome. Broad guidelines for determining an appropriate graph/diagram are as follows.

- If both the measurements under depiction are quantitative levels of individual subjects, use a scatter diagram. This can also be used when one measurement is in categories, or is on the nominal or ordinal scale.
- If the vertical axis is a rate, ratio, or average of a group of subjects:
  - Use a bar diagram when the horizontal axis is nominal or ordinal.
  - Use a line diagram when the horizontal axis is time (chronological year, age, etc.) or a quantity divided into categories. This line would show a trend.
- If the vertical axis is the number or percentage of subjects:
  - Use a histogram (or polygon or curve) when the horizontal axis represents quantitative categories.
  - Use a bar diagram when the horizontal axis represents measurements on an ordinal or nominal scale.

BOX 10.2   CERTAIN PRINCIPLES FOR DRAWING GRAPHS AND DIAGRAMS

- All graphs and diagrams must be self-explanatory containing an informative (what, where, and when) yet concise title, legend to identify various components of a diagram, labels for axes, units of measurement, and other such features.
- The labels and legends must be properly located so that there is no confusion for the reader.
- Lines in a graph should be thicker than the axis lines.
- Do not show more than three variables in one graph/diagram. Use a distinct pattern of line or symbol for each variable.
- The scale of calibrations should be clearly indicated. Choose a scale that is suitable and does not exaggerate or compress the values. When comparing two or more groups, use the same scale.
- Where secondary data are being used to draw a figure, give the source.

10.4.4 Statistical Distribution of Medical Measurements

The fasting blood glucose levels of 100 healthy persons will differ from each other even when the persons are of the same age, gender, obesity, ethnicity, and other such characteristics. However, there is always a pattern amidst variation. This pattern is called the statistical distribution. The term comes from the fact that this delineates how the individuals are distributed over different levels – that is, how many have blood glucose levels (mg/dL) between 60 and 64, 65 and 69, 70 and 74, etc. The best way to depict an observed distribution of a quantitative measurement is with a histogram, as shown in Figure 10.1a.

The most common shape for statistical distribution is Gaussian, but other forms also occur in medicine, particularly in sick subjects. These shapes determine the statistical the method of analyzing the data and help in classifying the subjects with values within normal limits or outside. Such classification may be required for your research or you may like to establish the normal range for a medical parameter for a new group of subjects.

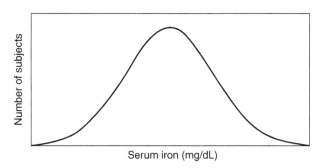

FIGURE 10.3
Distribution of serum iron in healthy females.

Gausssian Shape

Assume for a moment that serum iron level is measured for thousands of females, and the data intervals are very small, such as 90–91, 92–93, etc. The histogram will then tend to smoothen to provide a curve-like picture. It becomes a fully smooth curve if there are an infinite number of intervals and infinite number of persons. The shape of this theoretical curve in the case of serum iron level among healthy subjects could become somewhat like the frequency curve shown in Figure 10.3. Note the following features of this curve.

1. The height of the curve at any interval indicates the number of subjects – called frequency – around that point.
2. There is a peak in the middle and the shape is approximately symmetrical. That is, the number of subjects declines in the same way on either side as the levels are further away from the center.
3. The shape is almost like a bell.

Ignoring mathematical rigorousness, the curve with these general features is called "normal." In view of other meanings of normal in medicine, let us call it Gaussian after the name of the person who first invoked this pattern. Most medical measurements in *healthy* persons follow a Gaussian pattern, but some do not.

Shapes Other Than Gaussian

Some distributions with shapes other than Gaussian are shown in Figure 10.4. The distribution of lipoprotein(a) level among healthy adults is **skewed to the right** as many have levels such as 15, 20, and 25 and the minimum could be 0.1 mg/dL (Figure 10.4a). The most common level may be around 5 mg/dL. This distribution is not symmetric in shape. The distribution of total protein and alkaline phosphatase in healthy subjects is also right-skewed. Hemoglobin level has a **left-skewed distribution** (Figure 10.4b) in females in developing countries because low levels are more common in healthy women in these countries than high levels. Out of total deaths, number of deaths in the neonatal period is large in developing countries, there are very few deaths between 15 and 49 years, and the number is extremely high around the age of 75 years. The number of deaths is low again after this age as not many remain alive to die after this age. This gives the shape of a **smoke-pipe**, as depicted in Figure 10.4c. Fasting insulin level is high in both low-birthweight term neonates as well as in those with high birthweight. Those with normal birthweight (3.0–3.5 kg) have relatively low levels. Thus, this has a **U-shape distribution** (not shown).

Just as healthy individuals have their distribution of the levels of various measurements, so do nonhealthy or diseased subjects. If the fasting plasma glucose level is generally between 75 and 130 mg/dL in healthy people, individuals with symptoms of diabetes may have levels between 120 and 300 mg/dL. Whether discussing fasting plasma glucose or any other level, some overlap in values between healthy and diseased is a rule rather than an exception. The distribution among diseased individuals may or may not be Gaussian.

Knowledge of distribution among healthy and nonhealthy persons is required to understand the **reference values** – generally called the **normal values** – and to understand how they are different from abnormal values. This is especially important if the values in the subjects of your research are to be classified into normal and abnormal.

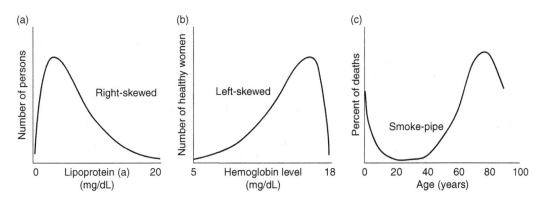

FIGURE 10.4
Some distributions of shapes other than Gaussian.

10.4.5 Normal versus Abnormal Levels

The normal level of thyroid-stimulating hormone is between 0.6 and 5.0 µIU/mL. Most with hypothyroidism will have a level more than 15.0 µIU/mL, but a level such as 7.3 µIU/mL may be found either in a healthy person or in someone with early hypothyroidism. There is no clear cutoff between normal and abnormal in this case.

Normal in medicine has many meanings. For example, it is normal for a 60-year-old to have myopia although this does indicate that the person is not in complete health. Is normal the same as ideal or optimal? If yes, how do we define ideal or optimal levels? How do we know what is our optimal level of body temperature or BP? It is possible that a person with 37.5°C body temperature and 142/92 mmHg BP does exceedingly well when accompanied by other corresponding physiologic changes. Who knows? The normal level of a quantitative measurement can be defined in many ways, as shown in Box 10.3. It is advisable to use disease threshold whenever available, such as fasting plasma glucose level ≥ 126 mg/dL for diabetes and BP $\geq 140/90$ mmHg for hypertension. However, for most medical measurements, such a cutoff is not available and statistical cutoffs based on mean $\pm$ 2 SD or 2.5th to 97.5th percentiles are used. For details, see Indrayan and Holt [9].

BOX 10.3   DIFFERENT TYPES OF THRESHOLDS OF NORMAL LEVELS OF QUANTITATIVE MEASUREMENT

Disease Threshold
A disease threshold of a quantitative medical parameter is the level beyond which most persons would start feeling that a disease has set in – a burden that diminishes work capacity or is a risk factor for adverse outcome later in life. This type of threshold is extremely difficult to obtain. Error of classification can occur.

Clinical Threshold
This is a compromise between the levels seen in healthy persons and nonhealthy persons that carry minimum risk of misclassification. Generally, it is very difficult to obtain. Error of classification remains.

Statistical Threshold
(Mean $\pm$2 SD) limits, where mean and SD are computed on the basis of measurements of fully healthy persons: in some situations, in persons with perfect health. These limits are valid for measurements that have a Gaussian pattern. They are easy to obtain, but always undesirably categorize 5% of healthy persons as unhealthy. Experience suggests that these limits work reasonably well in the long run, but theoretically could begin with nonsensical values such as negative value of serum magnesium level. This has to be set to zero. To obviate the need for a Gaussian pattern, the preferred normal range is from the 2.5th percentile to the 97.5th percentile, which is equally valid for Gaussian distribution also and is the same as obtained by (mean $\pm$2 SD) limits.

References

1. Indrayan A, Malhotra RK. Medical Biostatistics, Fourth Edition. Chapman & Hall/CRC Press, 2018.
2. Carpenter J, Kenward M. Multiple Imputations and Its Applications. John Wiley, 2013.
3. Knaus WA, Draper EA, Wagner DP, et al. APACHE II: A severity of disease classification system. Crit Care Med 1985;13(10):818–829. www.ncbi.nlm.nih.gov/pubmed/3928249
4. Rodríguez-Lozano B, González-Febles J, Garnier-Rodríguez JL, et al. Association between severity of periodontitis and clinical activity in rheumatoid arthritis patients: A case–control study. Arthritis Res Ther 2019;21(1):27. https://arthritis-research.biomedcentral.com/articles/10.1186/s13075-019-1808-z
5. Pantoja-Torres B, Toro-Huamanchumo CJ, Urrunaga-Pastor D, et al. and Insulin Resistance and Metabolic Syndrome Research Group. High triglycerides to HDL-cholesterol ratio is associated with insulin resistance in normal-weight healthy adults. Diabetes Metab Syndr 2019;13(1):382–388. www.ncbi.nlm.nih.gov/pubmed/30641729?report=abstract
6. Eriksson JG, Forsen T, Tuomilehto J, et al. Early growth and coronary health disease in later life: Longitudinal study. BMJ 2001;322(7292):949–953. www.ncbi.nlm.nih.gov/pubmed/11312225
7. Tang X, Zhong J, Zhang H, et al. Visit-to-visit fasting plasma glucose variability is an important risk factor for long-term changes in left cardiac structure and function in patients with type 2 diabetes. Cardiovasc Diabetol 2019;18(1):50. https://cardiab.biomedcentral.com/articles/10.1186/s12933-019-0854-9
8. Islamoska S, Ishtiak-Ahmed K, Hansen ÅM, et al. Vital exhaustion and incidence of dementia: Results from the Copenhagen City Heart Study. J Alzheimers Dis 2019;67(1):369–379. www.ncbi.nlm.nih.gov/pmc/articles/PMC6398840/
9. Indrayan A, Holt MP. Concise Encyclopedia of Biostatistics for Medical Professionals. Chapman & Hall/CRC Press, 2016.

11

Statistical Analysis

After the data are collected, entered, cleaned, and collated, they are ready for the rigors of analysis. This includes procedures such as generating correct estimates of various parameters (e.g., incidence and prevalence), building up confidence intervals (CIs), testing statistical significance, and assessing the strength and type of relationship. The actual methods depend on the nature of data, the type of hypotheses to be examined, and the theoretical conjectures that form the foundation of the study. The basic purpose of this analysis is to come to valid conclusions after minimizing and quantifying the uncertainty level due to sampling. They are minimized by using techniques of adjustment that were discussed in a previous chapter, and quantified using the methods in this chapter. Remember, however, that statistical analysis, howsoever impeccable, is no substitute for a well-planned and carefully executed study. In addition, it is true that statistical analysis is not necessary for great empirical science. Snow's work on identifying cholera as a waterborne disease did not require statistical inference methods.

Statistical analysis of data is done in several ways. For descriptive studies and for some analytical studies, the primary objective is to find the percentage of cases that have a particular outcome, or the average level of a medical measurement. This is called **estimation**. This estimate is accompanied by the CI that delineates the range of values beyond which a sample summary is unlikely to lie in repeated samples. Common methods for finding this are provided in Section 11.1. The other important activity under data analysis is the test of hypothesis whereby we find whether the values obtained in our study can be a presumed value or not. This requires the concept of P-value and power. These also are discussed in Section 11.1. The basic methods for testing significance (this term seems to be on its way out), such as chi-square for qualitative data and Student's t-test for quantitative data, are explained in Section 11.2. Section 11.3 is on regression that gives the methods to study the relationship between two or more characteristics. This includes both the ordinary least square where the dependent is a quantitative measurement and the logistic where the dependent is binary. This section also contains a brief description of correlation coefficients. The methods for assessing the cause–effect relationship and for validation of results are presented in Section 11.4. Statistical fallacies that so commonly arise in medical research are discussed in Section 11.5.

All the discussion in this chapter is brief and limited to common methods as a large number of books, such as by Indrayan and Malhotra [1], provide more in-depth details. Our emphasis in this chapter is on fostering statistical thinking and promoting the responsible use of statistical methods in medical research so that evidence-based results are obtained. Make sure that the data under analysis are right and rightly placed. For example, in the case of clinical trials, decide whether those who drop out or crossover to another regimen are to be excluded or to be considered under adverse outcome or to the other group. A commonly used strategy is **intention-to-treat analysis**, whereby subjects are analyzed in the group to which they were randomly allocated, even if they ended up in another group. Depending on what your choice is, the data should be accordingly arranged.

11.1 Confidence Intervals, *P*-Values, and Power

Suppose a research study finds that the positive predictivity of a new diagnostic procedure is 74%. How confident could we be that a similar study on another group of subjects from the same population would not give predictivity less than 70%? Just as individuals differ from one another, so do groups. It is useful to find how different the results are likely to be in different samples. Statisticians have developed a method that would provide an interval within which the actual value is likely to lie in repeated samples – better understood as the interval beyond which the value is not likely. Loosely speaking, this interval can be obtained by using the data of only one sample when randomly drawn. The likelihood of the interval containing the actual value is called the **confidence level**, and the interval is called the confidence interval or CI.

Because of profound medical uncertainties, particularly the sampling fluctuations about which we have been talking from time to time in this text, it is never possible to work out an interval with 100% confidence. Generally, a confidence level of 95% is used. A 95% CI has probability 0.95 that it will contain the actual value of the parameter. More correctly, the chance is small – 5% – that it will not contain the actual value of the parameter in repeated samples. The parameter of interest is generally a summary measure such as mean, proportion, difference, and correlation.

We mentioned in Chapter 8 about the standard error (SE) of various estimates that measures intersample variability. The Gaussian property for a large sample is invoked to infer that ±2 SE range in 95% of repeated samples is likely to cover the parameter of interest. If the summary measure of interest were mean, mean ± 2*(SE of mean) has 95% chance it would contain the value of the population mean. In general, this is interpreted as saying that 95% of repeated samples will have the parameter within these limits. Because the concern here is with intersample variation and not with variation among individuals, the CI uses SE and not standard deviation (SD). Note that SE would be small for large *n* but large for small *n*. The CI also will be accordingly determined. Under Gaussian conditions (Gaussian distribution or large *n* if the distribution is not Gaussian), the 95% CI is (estimate ± 2*SE of the estimate). There are a large number of SEs, each associated with a specific estimate. For example, SE of mean, SE of proportions, SE of difference in means, SE of difference in proportions, and SE of correlations.

Any standard statistical software is able to obtain CI for any of the popular summary measures. Thus, we are not giving any formula. The emphasis in this text is on the concepts so that situations where a CI would be useful can be identified, and the obtained CI is properly interpreted. A different kind of explanation is in the following paragraphs to convey this concept and its interpretation.

Later in this section is a brief explanation of statistical significance and *P*-values. These are just about the most common statistical concepts used in medical research, although they are being increasingly questioned.

11.1.1 CI for Proportion and Mean

The proportion of subjects with a specified characteristic, such as with a particular sign or symptom, or those responding to a therapy, is just about the most common summary measure used in medical research. For quantitative measurements, the most common summary measure is mean, such as of urinary creatinine in cases of particular kidney disease, and mean forced vital capacity in asthmatic children aged 6–10 years. CIs for these two types of indicators have the following implications.

CI for Proportion and Difference in Proportions

Suppose a new procedure for kidney stones is successful in all 10 cases on which this was tried. Can it be concluded that the failure rate would continue to be zero for all such operations in future? Statisticians have worked out that the failure rate in the long run can still be 25%! If none failed in a string of 50 operations, statistical methods suggest that the failure rate in the long run may not exceed 6%. This underscores the importance of the size of the trial. Such information is obtained by CIs or **confidence bounds** for proportions. The following example explains it further.

> **Example 11.1: CI for Difference in the Rate of Cesarean Delivery in Two Types of Analgesia**
>
> Wong et al. [2] randomly allocated 750 nulliparous U.S. women in spontaneous labor at term to receive intrathecal analgesia at early stage or systemic analgesia at late stage. They report that the rate of Cesarean delivery was 17.8% in the intrathecal analgesia group and 20.7% in the systemic analgesia group. The 95% CI for the difference in these percentages was (–9.0%, +3.0%). The difference in this particular group was 17.8 – 20.7 = –2.9%, but it could be anywhere between –9.0% and +3.0% in repeated studies. A more correct interpretation is that there is an exceedingly small chance that the difference in repeated studies of this type would be either less than –9.0% or more than +3.0%.
>
> Side note: The CI: (–9.0, +3.0) contains zero, and thus the other information obtained from this CI is that the difference in the rate of Cesarean delivery in the two groups could well be zero. We use this feature later for testing of hypothesis purpose.

Additional points regarding CI for a proportion include:

1. Where the study group size is small, use exact methods based on **binomial distribution**. Gaussian approximation is not valid in this situation. Use appropriate software that can give exact CI.
2. When the observed proportion in the study group is extreme – nearly zero or 1 – use the exact method again. If needed, consult a biostatistician.

CI for Mean and Difference in Means

Suppose a new herbal drug is tried on 50 coronary disease patients and it reduced lipoprotein levels by an average of 9 mg/dL over a 3-month period. The mean reduction obtained in this group is just one of many possible values in different samples. For this reason, this is called an estimate. Another group may give an average reduction of 8 mg/dL and a third an average of 11 mg/dL. CI provides the unlikely values.

If the sᴇ of mean reduction is 3 mg/dL, the 95% CI would be $9 \pm 2 \times 3 = (3, 15)$ mg/dL. Chance is small – 5% – that the mean reduction in repeat studies would be either less than 3 mg/dL or more than 15 mg/dL. In individual cases, the reduction could be much larger or much smaller – even increased lipoprotein(a) in some cases. Medical empiricism is about averages rather than individual values.

Both in the case of proportions and in the case of means, the one-sided **confidence bound** can be obtained where needed. For example, for noninferiority trials, the one-sided bound is (mean + 1.645*sᴇ) and for superiority trials is (mean − 1.645*sᴇ). In equivalence trials, two-sided CI is used and the entire CI should fall within the pre-specified equivalence margin.

11.1.2 CI for Relative Risk and Odds Ratio

As explained later in this chapter, a value 1 of correlation coefficient indicates a perfect linear relationship. However, relative risk (RR) and odds ratio (OR) have the annoying feature that a value of 1 indicates no relationship. The value of RR and OR cannot be less than zero, but the maximum value can be 100 or more. Symmetry, which helps in better understanding and in using Gaussian properties, is achieved by taking a natural logarithm (ln). Thus, CI is obtained for lnRR and lnOR, and converted back to RR and OR. Whereas the CI for lnRR and lnOR will be symmetric, it will not be so for RR and OR.

The methods are different for matched pairs, such as one-to-one matching in a case–control setup, than for unmatched groups. Specify this correctly while using statistical software. Generally a logistic regression program, described later in this chapter, is used to obtain the values of RR and OR, and the CIs for them.

> **Example 11.2: CI for OR for Risk Factors of Ischemic Heart Disease among Postmenopausal Women**
>
> A study by Ra et al. [3] used the secondary data on 3636 postmenopausal women from the 2013–2016 Korean National Health and Nutritional Examination Survey to assess the association of ischemic heart disease (IHD) with various risk factors. They report an OR of 1.93 for metabolic syndrome with 95% CI: 1.27–2.95 and 2.56 for depression with 95% CI: 1.66–3.96. Thus, the risk of IHD was apparently higher in these women with depression compared with metabolic syndrome. Several other risk factors were also studied.
>
> Side note: As neither CI contains the null value OR = 1, these ORs were also statistically significant with $P = 0.002$ for metabolic syndrome and $P < 0.001$ for depression. Even if the term "significance" is not used, the P-values show that both these factors are important correlates of IHD in these women.

11.1.3 Statistical Significance, *P*-Value, and Power

Despite recent questions, statistical tests of significance are not just done but also talked about regarding what specific observations caused significance, how they are affected or not affected by confounders, what biological explanation is available, and other such considerations. For this it is necessary to understand the basics of statistical significance.

Philosophical Basis of Statistical Tests

Look at the following example. There are a large number of references of sighting a Yeti, or at least big footprints in the Himalayas. Does that prove that the Yeti exists? The only conclusion you can make is that evidence is not yet sufficient that this exists. The Yeti may be there in hiding – who knows? But where is the conclusive evidence?

Ptolemy in the second century AD propounded that the sun revolves round the earth. It remained "truth" for 14 centuries, until Copernicus came up with evidence against it in the 16th century, and established a new truth that says that the earth revolves round the sun. In medicine, for example, peptic ulcer was believed to be caused by acidity until some time ago when *Helicobacter pylori* was found to be the culprit in many cases. As of today, coronary heart disease is not considered caused by any infection, but this may soon become a topic of research.

The empirical strategy is to find evidence against a hypothesis that is stated in null form. If this evidence is sufficient, the null hypothesis is rejected; otherwise it continues to be considered "truth" by default. Transplanted to the development of a new regimen, it seems reasonable to demand evidence against that there is no effect at all. This process is difficult to conduct without recourse to setting up a null hypothesis [4], which could be rejected in light of the evidence provided by the observations.

Samples by their very nature are uncertain. The conclusion depends on what sort of data are obtained from the selected subjects. One sample differs from the other. Statistical tests are precisely meant to deal with uncertainties arising from sampling fluctuations. They provide the answer to the question: What is the likelihood of the sample values you got when the null is true? If this likelihood is exceedingly small, say less than 5%, the null is considered implausible and rejected. At the same time, it would be wrong to "accept" a hypothesis whose likelihood of giving that sample is, say, only 20%. Thus, the only conclusion drawn is that the sample fails to provide sufficient evidence to reject the null hypothesis. The situation reverses to what it was before as though this study had never been done.

Many would wonder that the sample values are searched for evidence against a null without finding what they are for – what do they support? We will describe an alternative hypothesis soon that would clarify this dilemma, but finding evidence against it is widely followed in empirical settings, as in a court setting described next.

Type I and Type II Errors

It is customary in a court of law that the judge starts with an assumption of innocence – no crime has been committed by the accused. The burden is on the prosecution to provide substantial evidence that can change the judge's initial opinion and pronounce guilt. If the evidence is not enough, the person is acquitted whether or not the offense was committed. The judgment hinges on providing convincing evidence, and the responsibility is on the prosecution.

Statistical methodology is completely analogous. It starts with the assumption that any difference seen is a product of chance, and actually there is no difference between the groups. This is called a **null hypothesis**. This is equivalent to the assumption of innocence in a court setting. Sample observations or measurements obtained in the selected groups of subjects act as evidence. A large difference in samples should be construed as strong evidence and a small difference as weak evidence. This is checked by statistical tests.

It is quite common in court judgments that a real offender is acquitted because of weak evidence. This is not considered a serious error. But the other error also occurs. An innocent person is pronounced guilty because there is strong circumstantial evidence against that person.

If there is no real difference between the groups but the data strongly indicate the presence of a difference, the true null hypothesis has to be undesirably rejected. A false-positive conclusion is reached. This is serious, and is called a type I error or **alpha error**. The seriousness of this error can be understood from the setup of a trial on a new drug where this type of error occurs when an ineffective drug is proclaimed effective, it is unnecessarily marketed, prescribed, and ingested, and side effects tolerated. Imagine the cost and inconvenience caused by this error. Statistical procedure requires that this type of error be kept at a low level, generally within 5%.

A type II error is committed when the drug is really effective but the trial results indicate that it is not. This leads to a false-negative conclusion and this is called **beta error**. Society will be deprived of the benefits of this drug, but the situation will not be worse than what it was before the trial. Also, the deprivation would be short-lived. If the drug is really effective, the manufacturer will not keep quiet and will conduct further trials until such time that convincing evidence emerges in its favor. Then the drug could be rightly placed on the market after the approval. Thus, this error is not serious. The only loss is time. While discussing statistical power a little later, we clarify that a type II error has to be associated with a specified difference between the groups.

The null hypothesis is only one side of the story. When the sample evidence is strong against the null, this hypothesis is discarded. What is adopted is called the **alternative hypothesis**. In a phase III trial for a drug against placebo, the null would be that there is no difference. Although it is not impossible that a drug is worse than placebo, considering this possibility would mean that there was something drastically wrong with the earlier phases of the trial, including laboratory and animal studies on the pharmacological properties of the regimen. Thus, the plausible alternative hypothesis in this case would be that the drug is better than placebo. This is called **one-sided alternative**. When both possibilities (better and worse) are admitted, it would be a **two-sided alternative**. These are also called **one-tailed** and **two-tailed tests**, respectively.

Statistical Significance

Basic statistical procedures for testing a hypothesis use Gaussian properties to find the chance of obtaining observed sample values when the null hypothesis is true. If this chance is small, the conclusion reached is that possibly the null hypothesis is false. This is generally termed statistical significance, although this term is under the scrutiny of scientists. Obviously this conclusion can be wrong and a type I error can occur.

The probability of a type I error is called a **P-value**. (We will soon describe some procedures to obtain this probability.) Thus, the P-value is the probability that a true null hypothesis of no difference is wrongly discarded. This could occur if the patients included in the trial by chance happen to exhibit a difference between groups when actually there is none. Because of interindividual variation, it is not an entirely unlikely scenario. The P-value helps in increasing or decreasing faith in the results.

The seriousness of a type I error requires that a threshold for the P-value is fixed in advance beyond which it would not be tolerated. This threshold is called the **level of significance**. This is denoted by α and also called the **alpha level**. Note the distinction between the alpha error mentioned earlier and the alpha level mentioned now. Also see Box 11.1. Generally, an alpha level of 5% (or $\alpha = 0.05$) is fixed. When this is so, loosely speaking, a difference between the groups is considered statistically significant if the chance of it not

BOX 11.1 *P*-VALUE IS DIFFERENT FROM ALPHA (SIGNIFICANCE) LEVEL

P-Value: This is the probability of the wrong conclusion that an effect is present when actually there is none. The *P*-value could be any value between 0 and 1, such as 0.72, 0.58, 0.37, or 0.02. This is the probability of a type I error, and is obtained on the basis of the actual data set.

Alpha Level: This is the threshold fixed in advance by the researcher for tolerating the maximum *P*-value. The alpha level, also called the significance level, is generally fixed at $\alpha = 0.05$, but could also be fixed at $\alpha = 0.10$ for behavioral research, or $\alpha = 0.01$ or any other level, depending upon tolerance for a type I error for the problem at hand. The alpha level does not depend on the actual data set. Recent developments indicate that the alpha level will be eased out and only the exact *P*-value will remain for making decisions.

being there is less than 5%. Omnipresent variations and uncertainties do not allow this chance to be zero, and it is extremely difficult to reduce this to 1–2%. Five percent was an internationally accepted norm, but is now being questioned.

When the *P*-value for a difference in the samples is less than the predetermined threshold level, such as 5%, the difference is called **statistically significant**, although this term has now fallen out of favor. A statistically significant difference does not mean that it is large or that it is medically relevant – it only means that the chance of the observed values from a population with no difference is smaller than the threshold. The difference could still be small to be of any consequence in medical management. Also, a difference that is not statistically significant is not any assurance that the groups are equivalent. As explained in Box 11.2, a difference of good stead would fail to be statistically significant if the sample size is small.

A researcher almost invariably tries to achieve statistical significance of results, although there is a need to be modest in making claims. In some situations, nonsignificance should be welcome. When a test group is checked post hoc against a control group for matching with regard to baseline characteristics, nonsignificance is considered a valid sign for adequate matching provided the number of subjects is large enough to have sufficient power, as discussed next. When a low-cost test is evaluated against an expensive "gold" test, nonsignificance may imply that it can be equally good. Thus, the general feeling that statistical significance is a good result is not valid in some situations.

Statistical significance is just one aspect of the results, and should not be given undue weightage. It "tells nothing about the quality of thought, planning, or execution in the work; nothing about the biologic or clinical meaning of the difference in numbers (Box 11.2); and nothing about whatever has allegedly caused the difference" [5]. Nevertheless, *P*-values are in epidemiologists' air, and cannot be totally eliminated from the "corpus epidemiologicum" without unacceptable consequences [6]. What is being questioned is not the *P*-value itself but the over-dependence on a threshold such as 0.05.

Medical Significance and Statistical Power

Type II is not a serious error, but that should not be construed to imply that this can be ignored. In scientific pursuits – in fact, anywhere in life – any error is tolerated to a limit

BOX 11.2 STATISTICAL SIGNIFICANCE IS
DIFFERENT FROM MEDICAL SIGNIFICANCE

Some medical professionals consider statistical methods notorious for discovering significance where there is none, and not discovering significance where one really exists. The "difficulty" is that statistical methods give importance to the number of subjects in the sample. If a difference exists in 12 cases of chronic cirrhosis of the liver and 12 cases of hepatitis with respect to average aspartate amino-transferase (AST) levels, it can be considered a fluke because of the small size of the groups. This is like weak evidence before a court of law. But if the same difference is exhibited in a study on 170 cases of each type, it is very likely to be real. The conventional statistical methods of testing a hypothesis only tell whether a difference is likely or not. They do not say by how much. The difference in average AST levels between cirrhosis and hepatitis cases could be only 3 units/mL; this has no clinical relevance, but would turn out to be statistically significant if it occurs in a large group of subjects. Medical significance of such a small difference should be separately evaluated using clinical criteria, and it should not depend exclusively on statistical significance. However, clinical criteria could be very subjective in many situations.

A study on small groups of 12 subjects each may reveal a difference of 10 units/mL in mean AST level, which has great medical relevance, but it would not be statistically significant primarily because the groups are so small. The other important contributory factor in achieving or not achieving statistical significance is the interindividual variability measured by SD. If the variation among patients is large, an unreal big difference can arise due to inclusion of typical cases in the sample.

and not beyond. Thus, there is also a need to control type II errors, and increase the so-called power.

A type II error occurs when a study fails to detect a real difference. Complementary to this is the ability to detect a difference. Measured as probability, this is called **power**. Power relates to a pre-specified clinically relevant difference that needs to be detected. Such a difference may not be easy to specify in some situations. Some subjectivity can creep in, and it is sometimes referred to in a lighter vein as "cynically" important difference. When such minimum clinically relevant difference is specified, the trial should be conducted in a manner that it has adequate power to detect that kind of difference when present. Power measures the degree of assurance that the specified difference will be detected even when clouded by high variability in the measurements.

The most important determinant of power is the number of subjects when all sources of bias and uncertainties such as lack of knowledge and inadequate design are under control. Formulae are available that can give this number for different settings [7]. Most researchers aim to achieve a power of 0.8 or 0.9. For analogy with statistical significance, it is customary to term the existence of a medically relevant difference as the **medical significance** of results.

Statistical methods lack a human face. If, in a trial, 2 out of 400 receiving an oral drug die vs. none out of 400 receiving an injectable, the difference would not be statistically significant, but would you give this oral drug to your family?

In the face of all this, we can still emphasize that the difference must be statistically significant in the sense of small *P*-value for it to be medically relevant. If the *P*-value is not small, no one can be confident that the difference really exists. Thus, the first step is to assess statistical significance by *P*-value. If not significant and the statistical power is adequate, there is no need to worry about its medical relevance. If significant, a further statistical test is used to judge if it reaches a medically relevant threshold. This threshold comes from medical acumen.

The correct strategy is to specify the minimum effect size that would be considered medically relevant and conduct a study on reasonably large groups to be able to detect that size of effect.

Example 11.3: Concern about Statistical Power in "Negative" Trials

There is a growing concern among the medical community regarding the failure of many controlled randomized trials in detecting a medically relevant difference because they do not have sufficient power. The main driving force for power is the size of the trial and interindividual variability. About four decades ago, Freiman [8] observed after studying 71 "negative" randomized control trials on new therapeutic procedures that the sample size was too small in most of them for power 90% to detect a 25% improvement in outcome. In nearly three-fourths of these trials, the sample was inadequate to detect a 50% improvement. In other words, even if there is a 50% improvement in efficacy of the new treatment compared to the old, the trial results were still not statistically significant. It would have most likely become significant had the trial been bigger.

Twenty-three years later, Dimick et al. [9] reported the same for surgical trials. This once again underscores the need to be careful about the size of trial – the number of subjects must be adequate to inspire confidence that a medically relevant difference would not go undetected.

11.2 Some Basic Statistical Tests

This text is on research methods and the discussion is limited to the basic statistical tests that you would most likely need for a graduate thesis. The objective of the present text is not to impart skills for carrying out these tests but only to impart the knowledge of what sort of *basic* methods are available to analyze data and to obtain the *P*-value. Because calculations easily come from computer-based statistical packages, the formulas are being avoided. For details and advanced methods, see any biostatistics text. A summary of the more common statistical tests is given in Box 11.3.

11.2.1 Tests for Qualitative Data

The basic criterion for evaluating statistical significance in the case of qualitative data is chi-square χ^2. This is applicable for large n, no cell frequency zero or 1, and not more than one-fifth of categories containing less than five subjects. However, there is no requirement regarding the shape of the underlying distribution – it could be Gaussian or non-Gaussian. Different forms of chi-square help to find the *P*-value in a variety of situations, such as "goodness of fit," association in contingency tables, and trend in proportions. Some of these are described in brief in this section. Logistic regression is a very powerful tool for

BOX 11.3   BASIC STATISTICAL TESTS

1. For Qualitative or Categorical Data (Small Number of Categories)

When not more than one-fifth of the categories contain less than five subjects, and none has zero or one subject, use chi-square to test:

- Goodness of fit of the observed data to a pre-specified pattern.
- Association between two or more characteristics.
- Trend in proportions when ordinal categories are present.
- Homogeneity of association in different strata (Mantel–Haenszel) – not discussed in this text. For a small number of subjects, use Fisher exact test for 2×2 tables and multinomial test for 2×C tables. Exact tests for bigger tables are also available.

2. For Quantitative Data

When the data are quantitative, the interest generally is in the mean level.

- Use one-sample *t*-test to compare sample mean with a pre-specified value.
- Use paired-*t* for paired data, and use two-sample *t* to compare means in two independent groups.
- For more than two groups or when the effect of two or more factors is to be assessed, use analysis of variance (ANOVA).
- A special ANOVA method is needed when the same subjects are repeatedly measured over a period.

3. For Covariates and Missing Data

- To eliminate the effect of one or more quantitative covariates, use analysis of covariance (ANCOVA).
- When the nonresponse or missing data can affect the conclusion, consider them as a negative outcome in a clinical trial setting. For other settings, examine if missing data can be imputed. Perhaps a small number of missing values can be excluded without affecting the conclusions.

qualitative data and we discuss that in Section 11.3 along with other regressions. Logistic regression is specially used for estimation of OR and RR.

Chi-square is associated with a weird concept called **degrees of freedom (df)**. This depends on the number of categories in which the subjects are divided. Just as people of different age have different levels of lung function, so chi-square is different for different dfs. In most situations the statistical software package will automatically decide df after looking at the number of categories. The package will also give a *P*-value that could decide the statistical significance.

Goodness-of-Fit Test – One-Way Tables

After all, what is "goodness of fit?" Suppose it is believed that Down syndrome in children has a ratio of 2:1 in males and females. This hypothesis can be tested on the basis of actual data that may not exactly follow this pattern. Goodness of fit would indicate whether the fluctuations are within statistical tolerance, or are beyond. If beyond, the ratio 2:1 in all probability does not apply to these cases. Chi-square is used as a criterion to test goodness of fit of the data to a particular hypothesis, such as the one in our example.

Two-Way Tables with at Least One Dichotomous Variable

Now shift attention to a simultaneous consideration of two or more qualitative characteristics. The objective generally in this situation is to investigate if one characteristic has any association with the other – whether one is occurring more commonly with the other than expected by chance.

The simplest of two-way tables is a 2×2 table when the study subjects are simultaneously divided by two binary variables. The most common of these is the division of subjects into case group and control group, and each of these with and without a specific antecedent. A generic 2×2 table is given in Box 7.6 in Chapter 7 in the context of a positive and negative test. Examples 7.1 and 7.3 in that chapter contain data in this format. Presence of association is concluded when the observed pattern of frequencies in various cells is substantially different from the chance-expected pattern under no association. To check whether this difference will persist in repeated samples or not, the **chi-square test** is used. For small n, the **Fisher exact test** is used.

If a new regimen is found to have an efficacy of 78% against 75% of an existing regimen in a study on 40 cases and 40 controls, would you take the risk of using this new treatment on future cases? Two pertinent questions are: (i) whether a rather small sample of 40 each is enough to inspire confidence; and (ii) whether this small difference of 3% in efficacy, even if real, is worth the effort of switching from the existing strategy to the new one. If 3% is too small to take the risk, what minimum gain can be considered medically relevant for adopting the new regimen? For many researchers this is a ticklish question. But the encumbrance of specifying a medically relevant minimum difference is on the researcher. Suppose clinical considerations indicate that the gain must exceed 8% for shifting to a new treatment strategy for future cases. The alternative hypothesis in such a situation is one-sided that says that difference in efficacies is more than 8%. The null hypothesis is that it is 8%. Less than 8% is also part of the null as default. A test to detect such a medically relevant difference in proportions is easy to do with the help of a **z-test** for proportions instead of chi-square, provided that samples are large. We are omitting the details and leave this to statistical texts.

McNemar's Test

Consider the average frequency of micturition per day in 80 cases of enlarged prostate before and after a specific treatment such as finasteride for 6 months. The outcome of interest in this situation is frequency of micturition. This outcome in fact is quantitative but can be categorized as six or fewer times a day and seven or more times a day. If 52 of the cases had higher micturition before treatment and this number came down to 36 after treatment, it is not necessary that all these 36 are out of the previous 52. There is a possibility that some of the other 28, who had less micturition before treatment, experienced increased frequency despite the treatment. Suppose such cases are 8. This gives rise to the data shown in Table 11.1.

The statistical test used in this setup too is also basically chi-square but is calculated in a different manner. This is popularly known as McNemar's test. This test is based on the

TABLE 11.1
Frequency of Micturition per Day in Patients with Enlarged Prostates (Hypothetical Data)

Before Treatment	After Treatment		Total
	6 or less	7 or more	
6 or less	20	8	28
7 or more	24	28	52

number of cases in the disconcordant cells 8 and 24 in Table 11.1 that changed their category. If software for McNemar's test yields $P < 0.05$, the convention is to reject the null and conclude that the treatment is effective. However, in this particular example, significance can also arise if many with less micturition have more micturition after treatment. Check that this anomaly does not occur in your research.

Bigger Tables

Bigger tables could be either two-way that present cross-classification of subjects for two characteristics each with more than two categories, or sometimes three or more characteristics are considered together.

Consider tables where both qualitative characteristics have multiple (three or more) categories each. Peptic ulcer cases can be cross-classified by occupation (as a surrogate for stress level) and the type of milk consumed, such as full-fat, low-fat, and skimmed. Strange as it may sound, the objective could be to explore the relationship between occupation and the type of milk in cases of peptic ulcers. If the occupation is in five categories, this cross-classification will give a 5×3 table because the type of milk is divided into three categories. The analysis of such a table can be done by the usual chi-square using any standard statistical software.

When the number of subjects in the study is really small, you may have to collapse a big table into a 2×2 table and use the Fisher exact test. If such collapsing is found unacceptable in the sense that medically important information is lost, use **exact methods** of analysis of bigger tables. For these, special statistical software may be needed.

11.2.2 Tests for Quantitative Data

Blood pressure (BP), body mass index (BMI), parity, and pain score are examples of quantitative measurement. Some of these are **discrete**, that can take one of only a small number of possible values, whereas others are **continuous** with theoretically an infinite number of possible values.

The summary measure under scrutiny in the case of continuous data is mostly mean. The objective could be to know: (i) whether the mean of the target population from which the sample is drawn has a specified value; (ii) when there are two groups for comparison, such as test and control, whether the respective population means are different, or have some specified medically relevant difference; and (iii) when there are three or more groups, which specific group or groups are really different from others with respect to their means, or whether they follow a particular pattern. For means in one and two groups, the statistical test of choice in most quantitative situations is the Student *t*, and for three or more groups (or subgroups) the *F*-test is used. The latter is based on ANOVA.

Remember that mean is an appropriate summary measure in most situations but is not so in some. For example, when extremely high or extremely low values (relative to the other values) are present, the mean can be a highly distorted value. Another criticism mounted against mean is that an average patient does not exist. Indeed, that is so, but empirical evidence suggests that a large number of patients revolve around the average. Empirical research is about groups of subjects and not about individual patients. The only presumption is that individuals mostly behave as the group suggests. Each individual patient is managed on a personal basis, but that requires guidelines, and these guidelines are obtained by research on groups of subjects.

Student's t-Test

The Student's *t* could be the next most commonly used statistical test after chi-square. It is applicable in a variety of situations, as described below. Again, the formulas are being avoided because the calculations easily come from statistical software.

The fundamental requirement for the Student's *t*-test is that the sample values are independent of each other. In the case of BP measurements, for example, familial aggregation is well known, and if sample subjects include two or more members of the same family, they are not independent. Student's *t*-test cannot be used for mean BP of such a sample unless "family effect" is first removed. In most situations this contingency does not arise and the observations are independent – thus, Student's *t*-test can be safely used.

The second requirement is that the sample mean follows a Gaussian distribution. This is easily met in almost all practical situations for large *n* because of **central limit theorem** that says that the sample mean tends to follow a Gaussian pattern as *n* gets bigger irrespective of the underlying distribution. For small *n*, though, this requirement is met only when the underlying distribution of the measurements themselves is Gaussian. Thus, the only situation when the *t*-test is not applicable is when *n* is small and the underlying distribution is non-Gaussian. Many measurements in diseased persons are non-Gaussian. For such measurements, use a nonparametric test for small samples, as described later in this section.

Other Applications of Student's t-Test

If the average total cholesterol level is 193 mg/dL among a sample of obese persons and 167 mg/dL among a sample of nonobese persons suffering from the same disease, what factors should be considered to decide whether this difference is of some consequence? Foremost is biological plausibility. What postulations are available that can justify this difference? Second is the role of confounding factors. If the persons come from the same social milieu and belong to the same age and gender group, the difference deserves attention. Third is the *P*-value. This in turn depends on the sample sizes and the sDs in the two groups. If the number of subjects is large in each group and/or the sDs are small, and the *P*-value really is small, be quite confident that a difference exists. A two-sample *t*-test would decide one way or the other, but this significance, when tested in the usual manner, would only be able to say that a difference is likely to exist without saying how much. For translating into action, the crucial question is that the difference is enough or not to have medical implications. In this example, if the difference is small, such as 10 or 20 mg/dL, that too on average, perhaps it is not pragmatic to disturb the routine of obese patients. Advising them to exercise or change their diet is unnecessary as such a small difference may not matter in the long run as far as cholesterol level is concerned.

What difference can be considered enough to advise for a change in the routine of the obese patients? Suppose a difference of more than 50 mg/dL in average cholesterol level is considered medically relevant. Although the sample mean difference is 26 mg/dL, it can still be 50 or more in another sample. Thus, the null hypothesis is that the mean difference is 50 mg/dL and the one-sided alternative to be accepted in case of discarding the null is that the mean difference is less than 50 mg/dL. See Example 11.4.

Example 11.4: A Small, Medically Irrelevant, Difference Can become Statistically Significant If the Sample Size Is Large

Taddei et al. [10] observed a statistically significant difference between right femur (4% stronger on average) and left femur in a sample of 198 postmenopausal women. Strength was estimated by a computed tomography (CT)-derived finite element model. The authors comment that the difference was mechanically negligible despite being statistically significant. In this case, the sample was not particularly large.

ANOVA Procedure – F-Test

The ANOVA-based F-test is a versatile procedure used in a variety of situations. The name derives from the fact that the total variance among subjects is broken down to various portions such as between subjects and within subjects, or so much is due to factor A and so much is due to factor B, and so on. For example, ANOVA may reveal that 50% of variation in P3 amplitude in healthy adults is due to genetic differences, 20% due to age differentials, 5% due to gender differentials, and the remaining 25% due to other factors.

The most common application of ANOVA is in testing equality of means of a quantitative measurement in three or more groups, called **one-way ANOVA**. The procedure requires that the variances in different groups are nearly the same – called **homogeneity of variances** – and the means follow a Gaussian pattern. While running an ANOVA procedure on a computer, ask the software to first check that the data meet these requirements.

If the checks show either lack of homogeneity of variances or lack of Gaussianity, or both, consult a biostatistician, if needed. They might advise alternative methods of analysis, such as transformation or nonparametrics, particularly if the group sizes are small. See Box 11.4 for nonparametric tests.

If the group means turn out to be significantly different, the next question is: where exactly is this difference? Each group is compared with each of the others. For this, a **multiple comparison procedure** such as **Tukey**, **Bonferroni**, and **Scheffe** is used. For pairwise comparisons, Tukey is preferred. For comparing each group with control, the **Dunnett procedure** is used.

Statistical procedures are available that would rank groups from minimum mean to maximum mean with an in-between possibility of nearly the same means of two or more groups but different from others. Consult a knowledgeable biostatistician if the interest is in such ranking.

In some situations, subgroups are obtained by further classification of cases and control groups by characteristics such as age, sex, and severity. This would give rise to multiway ANOVA. In this situation, an interaction between, for example, the effect of dose and effect of severity can also be examined. It is possible that dose 2 is effective in serious cases and dose 1 in mild cases. This differential would surface only when the interaction is examined. However, a statistical test may lack the power to detect an interaction if the sample size is based on the size of the factor effects.

BOX 11.4 WHAT IF THE DISTRIBUTION IS NOT GAUSSIAN AND THE SAMPLE SIZE IS SMALL? NONPARAMETRIC METHODS

Statistical methods are sometimes hated for being too centric on a Gaussian form of distribution. The strength lies in the central limit theorem that asserts for large n that any summation type of measure such as mean does follow a Gaussian pattern even if the original values do not. Hemoglobin (Hb) level in women of age 30–39 years may not be Gaussian, but the mean Hb level in samples of size 30 are very likely to follow a Gaussian pattern. The requirement that n be 30 or 100 depends on how severely the underlying distribution is different from a Gaussian pattern. Dichotomous variables that follow a binomial pattern also tend to behave in a Gaussian format when n is large.

A study on a large group of subjects is sometimes very expensive. If the distribution is not Gaussian (e.g., skewed), the conventional statistical methods cannot be used for small n. For such situations, statisticians have developed a class of method that is called nonparametric. Some of these are Wilcoxon (also called Mann–Whitney), Kruskal–Wallis, and Friedman. In addition, there are exact methods that require complicated calculations. Special software is required to perform exact calculations.

ANOVA requires that the values are independent of each other. This is lost when the same subject is repeatedly measured at different points of time. If motor function level is low in cerebral palsy patients before surgery, it probably will not improve as much at 1, 2, 6, and 12 months after surgery as in patients with a good level initially. Thus, subsequent levels depend on the initial level. Because of this dependence, the usual ANOVA cannot be applied and a special procedure called **repeated-measures ANOVA** is used. If your research is giving rise to this kind of data, be careful to use a correct statistical program. Perhaps it would be sensible to ask for the help of a biostatistician who can choose the right procedure after you have explained the entire procedure of conducting the study.

11.3 Relationships and Regressions

Perhaps due to the cumulative effect of salt intake or due to natural hardening of arteries, it is seen in many healthy adult populations that BP naturally rises with age. Suppose that this relationship for systolic BP (sysBP) can be expressed as sysBP (mmHg) = 110 + ½(age in years). Such an equation that expresses one characteristic or measurement in terms of the others is called a **regression model**. It specifies the nature of the relationship, and is applicable to the average of a group and not to the individuals. This particular equation says that average sysBP at age 30 years is 110 + ½×30 = 125 mmHg, and at age 60 years is 110 + ½ × 60 = 140 mmHg. The multiplier ½ is called the **regression coefficient** of age. If this equation is to be believed, change in age by 1 year raises sysBP by ½ mmHg on average in healthy adults. Consider the power of this message in understanding this phenomenon. In some situations, a regression equation can provide deep insight into what is going on, besides providing an effective tool for prediction.

Among the many types of regression, the most common in medical research is logistic. Others are simple and multiple regression. To obtain these for any data, the first step is to understand the concept of dependent and independent variables.

11.3.1 Dependent and Independent Variables

As explained in Chapter 3, analytical studies seek to find how one or more outcome depends on a set of antecedent factors. A regression setup is basically the same but the nomenclature changes. It is customary in regression to call outcome the dependent variable and antecedents the independent variables. The dependent variable is kept on the left side of the regression equation and the independent variables on the right side. Details are as follows.

Dependent Variable

The dependent variable is the actual outcome of interest. It is surmised to be determined fully or partially, directly or indirectly, by one or more of the other variables under consideration. If the primary focus of a research study is to investigate how birthweight is affected by weight of the mother and father, as opposed to the Hb level of the mother, the dependent variable is the birthweight. This is a quantitative measurement denoted by y. In a study of the development of diabetic retinopathy based on duration of diabetes, nutrition level, regularity of treatment, and age, the dependent variable is the development of diabetic retinopathy. This is a dichotomous variable with yes/no categories. If the interest is in the grade of diabetic retinopathy (none/mild/moderate/proliferative), the dependent variable is still qualitative. The statistical method of finding the regression equation is different for qualitative outcomes than for quantitative outcomes.

Independent Variables

Antecedents that can affect the outcome are called independent variables in a regression setup. In the birthweight example described in the previous paragraph, the mother's weight, father's weight, and Hb level are independent variables. They can be manipulated in the sense that you can choose parents of different weights and of different Hb levels in your study to see how these variations affect the birthweight. In the diabetic retinopathy example, independent variables are duration of diabetes, nutrition level, regularity of treatment, and age. They can be quantitative or mixed. (If all of them are qualitative, and the dependent is quantitative, the situation reverses to ANOVA, discussed earlier.) Independent variables are known by several other names depending on the context: regressors, factors, determinants, explanatory variables. Use the term that looks most appropriate for the measurement in hand. This text uses these terms interchangeably depending on the context.

Quite often in research, the objective is to study how an outcome is affected by one particular antecedent x_1, but many other variables $x_2, x_3, ..., x_K$ can also affect the outcome. In this setup, $x_2, x_3, ..., x_K$ are called **concomitant** or **confounding variables**. For example, in a study on change in triglyceride level with age (x_1) in children, the possible concomitants are BMI (x_2), fat intake (x_3), insulin level (x_4), and physical activity (x_5).

Medicine is an intricate science and an outcome is generally affected by a large number of factors. Thus, many candidates would be available as independent variables. A good research study filters out the unimportant ones and concentrates on the few that can really affect the outcome. Regression results intimately depend on the proper choice of the regressors. The guidelines for choosing the right regressors are explained by Indrayan and Malhotra [1].

11.3.2 Basics of Logistic Regression

Statistical literature generally discusses usual simple and multiple regressions before discussing logistic regression. However, in medicine, qualities often take precedence over quantities. And logistic regression is the method of choice for qualitative outcome. A qualitative outcome can be polytomous, but to keep this text simple, we discuss only dichotomous outcomes. Dichotomous in any case is the most common qualitative outcome in medical research. If the interest is in a polytomous outcome, consult a biostatistician before running a logistic regression.

Essential Features of a Logistic Regression

We first describe the general nature of a logistic regression that provides an overview and then discuss a very useful feature of this regression that gives the values of the RR or OR.

Suppose the interest is in studying dependence of survival of critically ill patients on their APACHE score at the time of admission. However, survival also depends, among other factors, on the age of the patients and the quality of care. Quality of care is generally ignored but it can have a profound effect in developing countries where the care can vary widely depending upon factors such as facilities in the hospital and the social status of the patient. An index for quality of care – call it the CareIndex – can be developed. Thus, all three predictors in this setup are quantitative. Age and CareIndex are concomitant variables because the actual interest is in studying the effect of APACHE score. The outcome in this setup is qualitative and dichotomous (survived/died).

The dependent variable in logistic regression should be the probability of positive outcome. This is estimated by the proportion (p) observed in the study group. If 72% of critically ill patients survived in a hospital, $p = 0.72$ for that hospital. However, the number of patients with the positive outcome follows a binomial distribution instead of Gaussian. Thus, a transformation called **logit** is needed. This is given by logit of $p = \ln \dfrac{p}{1-p}$. A logistic regression is the relationship between logit of p and the regressors. This can take the form

$$z = \ln \frac{p}{1-p} = 4.739 - 0.013(\text{Age}) - 0.105(\text{APACHE}) + 0.082(\text{CareIndex})$$

The meaning of logistic coefficients is explained in the next paragraph but mathematically inclined readers can understand that z is zero for $p = \frac{1}{2}$, positive for $p > \frac{1}{2}$, and negative for $p < \frac{1}{2}$. That is, a positive value of z indicates that the chance of survival is more than 50% and negative indicates that it is less. As an exercise, plug in some plausible values of age, APACHE, and CareIndex in this equation and see what value of z you get.

Odds Ratio from Logistic Regression

A very useful property of logistic regression is that the coefficients of independent variables, such as –0.013 for age, –0.105 for APACHE, and +0.082 for CareIndex in the equation in the preceding paragraph, are the estimates of lnORs in retrospective studies. For age in this equation, lnOR = –0.013 and its exponent OR = 0.99. This is close to 1, and indicates that patients with different ages but the same APACHE score and the same care have nearly the same survival rate. In other words, age by itself has no role in survival. This is also true for CareIndex in this example because lnOR = +0.082 gives OR = 1.09, which again is nearly 1. Only the APACHE score has some role. For this, lnOR = –0.105 gives OR = 0.90. A 1-point increase in APACHE score reduces the odds of survival by a factor of 0.90, or by 10%. Thus the equation provides some insight into the prognosis of patients with different APACHE scores.

The most useful application of logistic regression is in case–control studies. When controls are one-to-one matched with cases, a modified method called **conditional logistic** is used, but the interpretation remains the same.

Adjusted and Unadjusted Odds Ratios

In the case of the usual regression discussed later in this chapter, the setup with one regressor is called simple and the setup with two or more regressors is called multiple. The same terminology should prevail for logistic, but conventionally – though wrongly – the setup with one regressor is called univariable and the setup with two or more regressors is called multivariable. If this terminology is followed, the regression discussed in the preceding paragraphs is **multivariable logistic**. The ORs obtained in this setup are rightly called adjusted ORs for the other variables in the equation. For age, OR = 0.99 is adjusted for APACHE and CareIndex. Similarly, OR = 0.90 for APACHE is adjusted for age and CareIndex. Unadjusted ORs are obtained by running separate logistic regressions for each regressor.

Interpretation of a Logistic Regression

Although interpretation of logistic coefficients has already been discussed, there are issues such as overall utility of logistic regression, its external validity, and the choice of regressors.

How to decide that a logistic regression is useful or not? Although a measure in terms of chi-square is available, most researchers find it too complex. Instead, the utility is assessed by the percentage of subjects correctly classified. When the plausible values of the regressors such as age, APACHE, and CareIndex for the patients studied are inserted into the equation, a value of z either more than zero or less than zero is obtained. In our example, if a patient's age is 42 years, APACHE score is 9, and CareIndex is 7, then

$$z = 4.739 - 0.013 \times 42 - 0.105 \times 9 + 0.082 \times 7$$
$$= 3.822$$

Because a positive value of z corresponds to $p > \frac{1}{2}$, the estimated chance of survival of this patient is more than of death (the exact probability can be obtained by using the logit equation). The logistic equation predicts that this patient is more likely to survive than die. If the patient actually died, the equation has misclassified the patient. When such a predicted outcome is compared with the actual outcome for all the patients in the study sample, the percentage correctly classified can be obtained. If correct classification is high – exceeding 80% – the regression can be considered good. Medical uncertainties would almost never allow for 100% correct classification. Ninety percent or more is generally considered excellent.

In this example, the percentage correctly predicted as survived or died by APACHE alone is 93% and continues to remain so even when age and CareIndex are added as predictors. They have almost no role in this particular example.

As explained earlier, statistical significance practically rules out the effect of sampling fluctuations and tells us that the result is likely to be replicated when the study is repeated on another random sample of similar subjects. Statistical significance of each logistic coefficient and hence of corresponding ORs is tested by **Wald test**. Any standard statistical software would do this and give a *P*-value that decides statistical significance. In our example of survival of critical patients, statistical software reveals that ORs for age and CareIndex are not statistically significant, whereas OR for APACHE is. Thus, the conclusion again is that varying age of the patients and various levels of care do not alter the survival rate, although varying APACHE score does.

Validity of a logistic regression depends primarily on: (i) proper choice of regressors; and (ii) external validation. When selecting a few relevant regressors, ensure that no important one is left out. In our example on critical patients, only age, APACHE, and CareIndex have been considered. Survival of such patients may also depend on duration of illness, comorbidities, and previous treatments. The equation ignores these predictors. Thus the choice of regressors is critical for a regression model to be valid. When the list of relevant regressors is long, a few statistically significant ones can be identified by a procedure called **stepwise**. For details, see any regression book, such as that by Vittinghoff et al. [11].

Regression is both an explanatory and a predictive model. A difficulty with any such model is that it tends to work well for the group of subjects that gave rise to that model. Its utility for new groups remains suspect. Validation of the logistic model in different groups requires quite some efforts but should not be left to subsequent users. If the model is able to correctly predict the outcome in at least 75% of subjects in external groups, the logistic regression can be considered good for wider use. If that does not happen, perhaps the choice of regressors is not right – there may be an epistemic gap in knowledge about the regressors. Or else diagnose that the problems exist in correctness of measurements, data entry, or calculations.

Example 11.5: Logistic Regression for the Differentiation of Benign and Malignant Thyroid Nodules

In an analysis of 525 pathological thyroid nodules, Pang et al. [12] picked out diagnostic features by logistic regression. They found that the significant features for malignancy were calcification, suspected cervical lymph node metastasis, and several others. Based on this analysis they established a formula that could predict whether or not thyroid nodules are malignant. The area under the receiver operating characteristic (ROC) curve for this formula was 0.930 and sensitivity–specificity and predictivities each exceeded 80%. With such positive statistical indicators, the formula is likely to be useful in a large percentage of cases.

11.3.3 Ordinary Least Square Regression

Linear regression is used when the dependent variable is quantitative. Although the independents can be qualitative, for simplicity we restrict the explanation in this text to quantitative independents. Another type, called **Cox regression**, is used for hazards. This is complicated and is not discussed in this text.

Regression Among Quantitative Measurements

The setup of one independent variable is discussed first and then generalized to a setup with many independent variables. The dependent variable is only one and it is quantitative in both these setups.

Regression of one quantitative dependent on one quantitative independent is called **simple regression**. The duration of postoperative hospital stay (as an indicator of speed of recovery) of patients with acute cholecystitis depends on several factors but only one factor, such as serum amylase level at admission, can be examined under simple regression. The easiest form of regression is linear, where the increase or decrease in the dependent variable remains proportional to the serum amylase level in different subjects.

The concept of linear regression can be easily illustrated with the help of the hypothetical equation that we started with: sysBP(mmHg) = 110 + ½(age in years) for adults. As an exercise, calculate sysBP from this equation for different ages and plot them on a graph. You will get a line. Hence the name "linear." The constant 110 in front is called the **intercept** and the regression coefficient ½ for age determines the **slope** of the line.

An important criterion to judge reliability of a regression is the coefficient of determination, generally denoted by R^2, and sometimes more correctly by η^2. This is the portion of the total variation explained by the relationship obtained by the regression. In simple linear regression, this portion is the same as the square of the correlation coefficient.

For our sysBP–age equation, if $R^2 = 0.53$, this implies that 53% of the variation in sysBP among subjects is due to the linear effect of age. The remaining 47% is either due to the other forms of effect of age, such as age^2, or due to other factors not included in the equation, such as BMI. One way to improve R^2 is to include other variables as independent variables and run a multiple linear regression.

Multiple Linear Regression

When the number of independent variables is more than one and their joint linear contribution is assessed, the regression is called multiple linear. In the sysBP example, BMI as well as physical exercise (hours per week) can be included as possible predictors. In that case, the equation can take the following form.

$$SysBP = 107 + ¼(age) + ½(BMI) − ⅓(exercise)$$

Note the following for this multiple linear regression.

1. The constant in front (intercept) and the multiplier (the regression coefficient denoted by b) will almost invariably change when other regressors are included. In place of 110 in the previous equation, this now is 107, and the coefficient of age has changed from ½ to ¼.
2. A positive sign of a regression coefficient indicates that the concerned variable has a positive effect and the negative sign indicates that the effect is negative. In this example, exercise hours per week have a negative effect – sysBP decreases as these hours increase – whereas age and BMI have a positive effect.
3. The regression coefficient represents the average effect of that independent variable, duly adjusted for the effect of other independent variables in the equation. In this example, the effect of one unit increase in BMI is increase in sysBP by an average of ½ mmHg (or increase in BMI by 2 units (kg/m^2) increases sysBP by 1 mmHg on average) and it is adjusted in the sense that it is independent of the effect of age and exercise. This has special meaning when BMI decreases with exercise. If BMI is 22 in one group and 28 in the other group, and both groups happen to exercise 8 hours per week, the difference of 6 in BMI changes average sysBP by (6 × ½ =) 3 mmHg.

   Other variables such as smoking are not included in this equation, but they can still confound the relationship. Thus, the coefficient still does not really represent the "net" effect that some researchers erroneously make out of a regression equation that does not incorporate all the factors. **Sensitivity analysis** can be done to assess if inclusion of smoking makes any difference.

4. Any standard statistical software would give the value of R^2 for the best-fitting equation for the variables under consideration. If this is low, such as 0.2 or 0.3, do not place much reliance on the regression. Instead, look for other predictors that are more intimately related, or look for alternative forms of the equation, such as nonlinear. If the situation still does not improve, assume that not enough is known about that outcome, and the research should be directed to remove epistemic uncertainty about the factors responsible for different outcomes in different kinds of subjects.

5. Do not get the impression from the preceding point that small R^2 indicates that regression is useless. The only message in this case is that there are other factors that need to be investigated. A small R^2 may still be statistically significant and may indicate that the independent variables under consideration are likely contributors, although their contribution may be small.

6. Statistical software would easily evaluate the P-value of R^2 and hence of the regression equation. More important is the P-value of the regression coefficient of individual independent variables. Any standard statistical software easily evaluates this individual P-value on the basis of Student's t-test. Variables with high P-values can be dropped without much harm to the utility of the model provided they are not known to be biologically important. A stepwise procedure can also be used to serially find the regressors with low P-value and accordingly restrict the regression to include only the "useful" regressors. This includes statistically useful and biologically useful regressors.

7. The regression coefficients are estimates based on the values obtained in the study group. Another group from the same target population may give different values and different regression coefficients. A minor variation in the value of the coefficient can be tried to assess if the influence on the outcome is minor or major. Such an exercise is part of the **uncertainty analysis**. Note the difference between sensitivity analysis mentioned in point 3 and uncertainty analysis mentioned here.

In many situations, a line is inadequate to represent the relationship and a curve is needed. In this case, terms such as square, cube, and logarithm are included among the independent variables. Another popular regression in medical literature is **Cox regression**, where the dependent variable is the hazard such as hazard of developing a disease or hazard of death. For details on these two regressions, see Vittinghoff et al. [11]. A summary of all the regression tools is given in Box 11.5, which can help you choose the appropriate type of regression for your data.

11.3.4 Correlation and Agreement

The term correlation is used for the strength of the relationship between two or more measurements. We briefly discuss various ways in which a correlation can be assessed. Another kind of relationship arises when the objective is to assess agreement between two or more measurements to decide whether one can be replaced by another. Both these are quite frequently used in a graduate thesis.

BOX 11.5   STATISTICAL TOOLS TO ASSESS VARIOUS ASPECTS OF RELATIONSHIPS

Aspect of Relationship	Preferred Tool
1. *Nature of Relationship*	
Dependent is qualitative	
— Independents are qualitative	Logistic regression
— Independents are quantitative or mixed	Logistic regression
Dependent is quantitative	
— Independents are qualitative	Analysis of variance (ANOVA)
— Independents are quantitative	
• One independent with linear effect	Simple linear regression
• One independent with nonlinear effect	Curvilinear regression
• Many independents with linear effect	Multiple linear regression
• Many independents with nonlinear effect	Nonlinear regression
— Independents are mixed	Analysis of covariance (ANCOVA)
2. *Strength of Relationship*	
Between two qualitative characteristics	
— One is antecedent and the other is outcome	Relative risk or odds ratio depending on the design
— Both have the same status	Contingency coefficient
Between two quantitative measurements	
— Linear relationship	Correlation coefficient
— Nonlinear relationship	Coefficient of determination
3. *Cause–Effect Relationship*	
Any types of factors	Statistical significance after eliminating the effect of all confounders and biases, followed by the other six criteria listed in the text
4. *Agreement (Not Discussed in the Text)*	
Two qualitative characteristics	Cohen's kappa
Two quantitative measurements	Limits of disagreement

Correlation Coefficient

Whereas the regression is for the nature of the relationship, the correlation coefficient is for the strength of the relationship between two quantitative measurements. This ranges from −1 for perfect negative correlation (as one increases, the other decreases) to 0 for no correlation to +1 for perfect positive correlation. The most common is the **Pearson correlation coefficient** that is valid to assess a *linear* relation but not for the relationship expressed by acutely bent curves. This coefficient also gives more valid results for measurements with a Gaussian distribution of at least one of them. For highly skewed distribution, **Spearman correlation coefficient** is used. In addition, there are other types of correlations such as tetrachoric and biserial for other kinds of data. For correlation between more than two variables, multiple and partial correlations are used. For details of various correlations, see Indrayan and Holt [13].

Agreement between Two Quantitative Measurements

When a measurement is taken by two methods, at two times, at two sites, by two observers, on the same set of subjects, the assessment of agreement between these measurements can be useful in many situations. For example, new instruments are invented and new methods are discovered that measure anatomical and physiological parameters with less inconvenience and at a lower cost. A researcher would like to assess how much the new method agrees with the existing method. Acceptance of any new method depends on a convincing demonstration that it is nearly as good as the established method, although the established method may also be in error.

Irrespective of what is being measured, it is highly unlikely that the new method would give exactly the same reading in each case as the old method even if they are equivalent. Some differences would necessarily arise. How do you decide that the new method is inter-changeable with the old? The problem is described as one of agreement. This is different from evaluating which method is better. The assessment of "better" is done with reference to a gold standard. Assessment of agreement does not require any such standard.

The measurement could be qualitative or quantitative. The method of assessing agreement in these two setups is different. For quantitative measurements, the Bland–Altman method is popular and for agreement in qualitative characteristics, Cohen kappa is used. For details, see Doi and Williams [14].

11.4 Cause–Effect Relationships and Validation of Results

Incidence of cardiovascular diseases in India is increasing whereas birth rate is decreasing. They are inversely related. The correlation coefficient between these two entirely unre-lated measurements could be around –0.6. This is an example of a **spurious correlation** that arose because both are related to the process of development. If the interest is in the biological relationship, the process of development is a nuisance variable in this example because it is playing a spoiling game. This example is extreme, but aptly illustrates the diffe-rence between correlation and cause–effect relationship. Another interesting example is the strong correlation between age at onset of disease and survival duration. Older people tend to die quickly anyway and a high negative correlation in these two measurements is trivial.

11.4.1 Evidence of Cause–Effect

Although the term factor is generally used for any characteristic of interest, in an etio-logical context a characteristic becomes a factor for an outcome when it is a contributor or suspected to be a contributor in some respect. It can be either directly responsible or indir-ectly responsible for that outcome; it can be wholly responsible or partially responsible. For example, obesity is a factor in diabetes and coronary disease but not in typhoid.

Cause is a stronger term. Although usage is not uniform, cause is generally used for a factor that is directly responsible for the outcome. Smoking is considered a cause of lung cancer even though its effect is also mediated through nicotine deposits or cotinine level that has the potential to alter cell structure. Smoking causes atherosclerosis that causes hypertension. Thus, smoking has an indirect role in hypertension. Ideally it should not be called a cause of hypertension. It is just a factor. Such a distinction is rarely made in research literature, but there is a gradual realization that not all factors are causes.

It is sometimes argued that a factor is a cause if it is both necessary and sufficient for the effect to appear. This is too strict a condition in the medical context. Smoking is neither necessary nor sufficient to cause lung cancer, yet it is considered a cause. Statistically, if the presence of a factor A raises the chance of the occurrence of B and its absence reduces the chance, A can be considered to be one of the many causes of B.

Criteria of Cause–Effect

Just how much evidence is needed to accept a cause–effect relationship? In medical research, a cause–effect relationship is assessed by evidence regarding the following criteria.

1. *Temporality*: An elementary feature of a cause–effect relationship is that a prospective study should establish a time sequence with the factor preceding the outcome. In most situations this is easily established, but the relationships among concurrent factors such as between blood group and gender are difficult in this respect. Also the relationship must stand the test of time. A cause–effect relationship would be true in the year 1950 as much as in the year 2020.
2. *Experimental evidence*: Because an experiment is conducted in controlled conditions, it is capable of providing convincing evidence for or against the enhanced chance of an outcome in the presence of the purported cause, and reduced chance in its absence. However, experiments on human beings should be conducted only for potentially beneficial factors, and not for potentially harmful factors. Thus, this criterion is not assessed for harmful factors except for specificity, as explained in item 6 in this list.
3. *Dose–response relationship*: For cause–effect, the presence of a cause in greater magnitude should be able to produce a greater effect. BP level and coronary events have a dose–response relationship in the sense that the chance of coronary events is higher if BP is maintained at 160/95 mmHg than if it is 140/90, and still higher for BP 180/100. In some situations, minimum and maximum limits of the magnitude of the causal factor can be specified within which the gradient exists. Salt intake below the minimum physiologic need may give rise to other health problems; thus, there is a minimum beyond which the positive relationship between salt intake and hypertension occurs.
4. *Consistency*: This has two facets. One, the specific magnitude of the cause should always produce nearly the same effect when there are no confounders to subvert the relationship. Two, the relationship must occur across different populations where the cause exists. Several researchers under different settings should report similar relationships. The relationship between homocysteine level and coronary disease, after initial hysteria, has now been observed to lack consistency.
5. *Biological plausibility*: Plausible mechanisms must exist to explain the relationship. Nonarteritic anterior ischemic optic neuropathy may be related to chronic co-morbidities such as diabetes and hypertension, but no mechanism can be conjectured. As remarked earlier, any such explanation depends on the current knowledge. If this is not adequate, the relationship is relegated to mere association.
6. *Specificity*: Absence of the factor must be accompanied by the absence of the outcome, or at least diminish it. Reduced exposure must reduce the chance or magnitude of the outcome. This is just another aspect of a dose–response relationship, but the emphasis now is on negativity.
7. *Statistical significance*: As mentioned earlier, no medical significance can be attached to results that fail statistical significance although statistical significance by itself is not enough to conclude medical significance. The same can be reiterated for a causal relationship. A factor cannot be a cause unless statistical significance is demonstrated that rules out sampling fluctuation as a reason for the relationship.

A weak relationship can be statistically significant if n is sufficiently large. Strength of relationship is not an issue for deciding causality – thus, mere statistical significance is enough to suspect causality. A hereditary role in breast cancer may be small, but it is there as a cause. Much of the medical literature wrongly includes strong association as a requirement for a cause–effect relationship without realizing that a weak association can also be causal, although it would be one of many causes.

The role of the features of a cause–effect relationship just discussed comes after all known sources of bias and confounding have been eliminated. Strictly speaking, all seven criteria must be fulfilled. In practice, though, relaxation is allowed and a cause–effect relationship is concluded even when one or two of these criteria are not fully met.

Assessment of Cause–Effect in Medical Research

Judging a causal relationship is central to human cognition. The procedure to investigate a cause–effect relationship in empirical research is slightly different. The starting point would be to establish that a relationship does exist. This is done by showing statistical significance (call it small P-value if you like) of the association, correlation, regression, or just a difference between two groups. If this significance is lacking, there is no point in proceeding further except to carry out another study, possibly on a bigger sample with proper design, to rule out sampling fluctuation.

After statistical significance, examine if any alternative explanation is available for that relationship. This exercise helps to rule out various sources of bias, such as improper selection of subjects, faulty information or measurement, and inappropriate design, and possible role of confounding factors. When no alternative explanation is available, a causal relationship is strongly indicated.

These steps indicate that a causal relationship is difficult to establish. Caution should be adopted before concluding cause–effect. In most situations, the relationship would be associational and would require additional evidence to qualify as cause–effect.

Example 11.6: Is the Relationship Causal between *Helicobacter pylori* Infection and Atherosclerosis?

It has been generally observed that *H. pylori* infection is seen in disproportionately more patients with atherosclerosis. The relationship of this infection with duodenal ulcer is known and the epidemic of this ulcer has simultaneously declined with coronary artery disease in the United States in the past 40 years. In addition, *H. pylori* has been detected in atherosclerotic plaques. These observations suggested causal relationships between the two, possibly due to intensified inflammatory stress, dyslipidemia, arterial stiffness, and other factors such as aging, smoking, poor socio-economic status, and high salt intake. In a review, Xu et al. [15] presented evidence for and against a causal relationship between *H. pylori* infection and atherosclerosis.

Multifactorial Causation

A single factor such as stress and anxiety can trigger an acute response such as myocardial infarction, but many other factors should be present to provide a fertile base. Thus, myocardial infarction has a multifactorial etiology. We must reemphasize that most infectious diseases have univariate etiology (i.e., one agent that causes the infection), although in this case also host susceptibility is an important contributor. Most chronic diseases are clearly multifactorial. Each individual factor makes a specific contribution that could be either independent of other factors or could act in conjunction. Models such as the usual regression and logistic regression help to assess the independent effect as well as the joint effect.

Example 11.7: Multiple Causation of Sudden Infant Death Syndrome (SIDS)

It is generally known that no single factor ordains an infant for death. SIDS generally spares the neonatal period and peaks between 2 and 3 months of age. In an excellent review of causes, Guntheroth and Spiers [16] underscore the multifactorial causation:

- Placenta previa, abruptio placentae, and excessive bleeding during pregnancy in otherwise healthy women can cause severe maternal anemia. This can cause prenatal hypoxia damage to the brainstem, leading to SIDS
- Astrogliosis and neurotransmitter changes
- Reduction in muscarinic cholinergic receptor level
- Hypoplasia of the arcuate nucleus
- Congenital anomalies
- Prenatal hypoxia or ischemia.

Thus a web of multiple causations can be woven for SIDS. Note that these factors are mostly interrelated.

11.4.2 Validation of the Findings

Analysis of data and the results so obtained sometimes is not enough. The scientific community also wants evidence that the results are valid. While validity of measurements (Chapter 6) is a prerequisite for valid results, the statistical methods and models derived also need to be validated.

Validity of Estimates, Statistical Methods, Models, and Scoring Systems

The validity of a statistical method is its ability to provide a correct inference as evidenced by the data. This is mostly assessed by the validity of the underlying assumptions, as already discussed. However, in isolated cases, there may be gross deviations. For example, some use RR for OR, and vice versa. The term validity is also used for **statistical analysis** where, for example, it becomes invalid when a wrong computer command is used while running a statistical package. An invalid design command for computation while using a statistical package will result in an error message in some cases, but in many others the package will give you an output that is not what you want. This can easily happen for a hierarchical design or designs with random effects where computer commands require sufficient expertise. These computer commands require some training and understanding of implications of different commands.

The extent of validity of **statistical models** is evaluated on two criteria: (i) their biological plausibility that says that a possible mechanism should be available that links the outcome with the inputs as stipulated in the model; and (ii) their ability to correctly explain or predict the underlying phenomenon. Because models by their very nature represent simplified versions of the actual process, they are not expected to be 100% valid. In case a model is for predicting a dichotomous or polytomous outcome, percent correctly classified is an accepted measure of validity. For example, the Dimodent equation that uses measurements of certain teeth was able to correctly identify sex in 78.7% of cases in a Lebanese population [17]. This quantifies the validity of this equation in that population, but the validity could be different in some other population.

For an ordinal outcome, the **C-statistic** that measures the area under an ROC curve can used to quantify the validity. For diagnosis of ovarian tumor as benign, borderline, primary invasive, and metastatic on the basis of a risk prediction model, the value of the C-statistic was found to be between 0.57 and 0.64 in external validation for Belgium [18]. On a 0–1 scale, this value is not particularly high to inspire confidence about this model. For a continuous outcome, a predictive model is valid when the mean of residuals (predicted – observed) is close to zero. This is easy to achieve, for example, in regression, by suitably choosing the intercept. In this case, validity can also be assessed by percent correctly predicted, although the primary consideration in such models is the reliability measured by the variance of the residuals instead of the validity. The validity of many outcome models is assessed in terms of biological plausibility, as stated earlier, and their ability to serve their intended purpose.

A large number of scoring systems have been developed for use in the practice of medicine and for research. They are primarily used for gradation of severity (e.g., **APACHE score**) and secondarily for diagnosis. The validity of severity scores is assessed in terms of correct prediction of prognosis, and of diagnostic scores in terms of correct classification of patients into diseased and nondiseased. For example, the authors of APACHE-II found that prediction of survival or hospital death by this score is correct in 85% of cases admitted to critical care in U.S. hospitals [19]. This is the index of validity of this score. The risk of malignancy index has a diagnostic sensitivity of 85% and specificity of 97% for ovarian cancer [20]. These two are the indices of validity in this case. If you have developed a scoring system in your research, examine its validity for that particular use. Using sensitivity and specificity as indicators of diagnostic efficacy is an example of their invalid use; instead, predictivities should be used.

Validity of Results and Conclusions

Validity of results and conclusions can be divided into two broad categories: (1) **internal validity** that pertains to the validity of the information available after the study; and (2) **external validity** that pertains to their generalizability to the target population. Internal validity depends on the use of proper methods on the one hand and consistency of different results on the other. If alcohol intake is positively associated with liver disease in a segment of the population, and it is also observed that mine workers take more alcohol, you should get the result that liver diseases are more common in mine workers. If this is not so in a sample, and no reason can be identified for this inconsistency, the results are not internally valid, and suspicion arises about the method of collection of the data or their analysis. Maybe the subjects gave the wrong information or confounding was not properly accounted for in the analysis.

Another method to check internal validity is to check the results on the subsample of your sample. You can divide the sample into two parts. Derive results from one and test them on the other. There are other methods such as **jackknife** and **bootstrap** that drop some observations and check the results on the remaining.

External validity depends mostly on adequacy of the subjects for a particular generalization. A representative sample is a definite help for validity of results of descriptive studies, but that is not a prerequisite for analytical studies. Some results based on subjects available

100 years ago remain valid for the present population, for example, smoking causes lung cancer is the conclusion derived from a study of people decades ago, but is also valid for the present population. Cause–effect types of relationships generally transcend time and population, as mentioned earlier. A second factor affecting external validity is correctness of the information obtained from study subjects. Remember that wrong information cannot lead to the right conclusions, howsoever immaculate the analysis might be. Thirdly, it also depends on proper choice of variables and indicators for differentially assessing antecedents and outcomes.

External validity is also established by studying another sample from the same population or from another similar population. If the results reasonably replicate, they are accepted for generalization.

11.5 Statistical Fallacies

Data analysis can always be geared to serve an ulterior motive, but our concern in this chapter is with interpretation and particularly reporting. Statistical fallacies in reporting are quite common. Fallacies do not stop becoming fallacies because they are repeated so often. Some of these occur inadvertently, such as clicking a wrong button, but some could be deliberate. A medical researcher is expected to show wisdom and avoid both. For details on various kinds of statistical fallacies, see Indrayan and Malhotra [1].

11.5.1 Cherry-Picking the Statistical Indices

Statistical results can be manipulated by suitably picking the statistical indices. The following are simple examples. Some of these have been cited earlier.

Mean or Proportion

Depending upon preference, the results can be provided in terms of mean of BP levels or in terms of prevalence of hypertension, in terms of Hb level or in terms of anemia, in terms of plasma glucose level or in terms of diabetes. No such name is available for a measurement such as total lung capacity but this can be categorized (in l) as low (< 4.00), medium (4.0– 5.99), and high (≥6.00). All quantitative measurements can be converted to qualities. The summary measure for quantities generally is mean and for qualities is proportion. Which one should be used in a research report?

Means can lead to a different conclusion from the one reached by proportions. This provides a leeway to the investigator to try out both, and report the one that suits a particular hypothesis. In addition, for anemia, for example, various categories can be tried – <11 g/dL, <10 g/dL, or <9 g/dL – and the one that looks "favorable" can be adopted. Thus, the report may not truly reflect the findings. Our statistical advice is to stick to the original metric measurements and not convert them into categories. This is more exact and removes subjectivity in devising categories. When categories are essential, state them beforehand, preferably at the time of writing the protocol, and justify those categories. Do not change them later unless there are strong reasons to do so.

Misuse of Percentages

If six out of eight patients respond to a new treatment, is it proper to say that the response rate is 75%? What about stating one out of two as 50%? Isn't it preposterous to call zero out of one nil and one out of one complete? These are extreme examples but illustrate that percentages based on small n can be misleading. Generally, no percentage should be stated when n is less than 30.

While assessing gestational age for 300 births, if 60 women do not know the date of their last menstrual period, the percentage of births with gestation, say, 32–34 weeks should be calculated out of 240 and not 300. This is quite obvious, yet many present percentages with a wrong denominator.

Linkage of hypertension with A, B, O blood groups has not been investigated much. If the distribution in a sample of hypertensives is A, 15%; B, 40%; AB, 25%; and O, 20% it would be naive to conclude that hypertension is predominant in the B group. These percentages should be compared with the blood group distribution in the target population to come to any such conclusion.

Summary measures such as mean and proportion, when based on the aggregated data, can be deceptive. They could mask or aggravate the variation present in subgroups. We illustrate this for percentages in Example 11.8.

Example 11.8: Percentages Based on Aggregated Data Can Mask Subgroup Variations

Consider case-fatality in cancer patients in a general hospital and a cancer hospital:

Stage of Cancer	General Hospital			Cancer Hospital		
	n	Deaths	Case-Fatality (%)	n	Deaths	Case-Fatality (%)
Stages I and II	150	30	20.0	50	10	20.0
Stages III and IV	50	30	60.0	250	80	32.0
Total	200	60	30.0	300	90	30.0

Both hospitals have the same case-fatality in aggregate, but actually the cancer hospital is receiving patients predominantly in advanced stages. In them, its performance is markedly better: 32% case-fatality in the cancer hospital against 60% in the general hospital. If only the aggregate percentage is reported, this distinction is lost. It is for such discrepancies that standardization is advocated.

Another fallacy occurs in stating too many decimal places. Percentage of 3 out of 35 can be stated to as many decimal places as one wishes. The tendency in medical literature is to use excessive decimals. The rule is as follows. Use one decimal place if $n < 100$, two if $100 \leq n < 1000$, three if $1000 \leq n < 10,000$, etc. Mean and sd should be stated one decimal more than the accuracy of the original values. This retains accuracy without sounding too precarious. If uric acid is measured in mg/dL to one decimal such as 3.3 and 4.5, the mean and the sd should be stated with two decimals. For mean and sd of total lipids, one decimal is enough because the measurement is in integers. The correlation coefficient is conventionally stated to two decimal places.

There are exceptions to these rules. Sometimes it is considered neat to state all the results with the same number of decimals, even when they are based on different n, or even when different measurements have different accuracies. Another concept is **significant digits**.

Zeroes immediately after a decimal are not counted. Thus, 0.0032 has two significant digits and 0.32 also has two significant digits. It would be unfair to state 0.0032 as 0.00 when the system of two decimal places is religiously followed for uniformity.

11.5.2 Fallacious Interpretation

Statistics is not everybody's cup of tea. While calculations can be done by a computer, interpretation of statistical results requires skill. Whereas a large number of examples of inadequate interpretation can be cited, the following illustrates what can go wrong.

Inadequate Interpretation

Many medical researchers are much too keen to look at the difference or gain in medical parameters after treatment compared to values before treatment. In their keenness, they forget that a gain of 3 g/dL in Hb level over pretreatment value 8 g/dL has a different meaning than the same gain over the pretreatment value of 12 g/dL. It is relatively easy to effect a rise over lower Hb values than over higher values.

Another common misinterpretation is considering mere association or correlation as an evidence of cause–effect. This was discussed earlier.

Misuse of P-Values

Scientists debate about the validity of the conventional cutoff 0.05 for P-values. The opinion is growing to use CIs instead of P-values, although CIs too require a fixed confidence level such as 95%. But there is no escape in some situations and a level has to be fixed to assess statistical significance. Certainly no magic happens at 0.05. A safe rule is to interpret P between 0.04 and 0.06 with caution and conclude that further work is needed. This is the same kind of precaution that is always taken for patients with borderline values. In any case, do not take P-values too seriously. They must be complemented by common sense. The P-value is only the probability of a type I statistical error. Other statistical and nonstatistical errors cannot be ignored.

Many examples can be cited from the medical literature when more than one statistical test is done on the same data, each at level 0.05, without realizing that this inflates the total error rate. There are statistical methods such as Bonferroni and Tukey that should be used in such cases to control the chance of error to the specified level.

As stated earlier, statistical inference is applicable only to random samples. The basic purpose is that the sample is representative of a defined target population and generalizability is intact. Many articles use tests of significance on nonrandom samples with an ill-defined target population. Before extrapolating results to a larger group, ensure that the sample in the study is representative of that larger group. The implications of most medical findings is in managing future cases. Thus, examine how the conclusion will be applicable to future cases and of what type. Write the discussion in your paper accordingly.

Misuse of Statistical Tools

Misuse of percentages and P-values has already been discussed. Figure 11.1 illustrates how a graph can be manipulated to show a large variation as small. The graph shows a 1*SD variation whereas in actual practice the variation generally goes up to 3*SD.

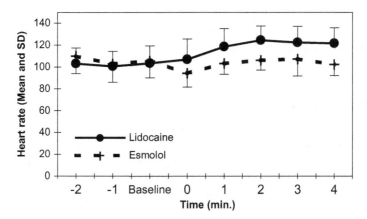

FIGURE 11.1
Variation shown by 1*sd, whereas it generally goes up to 3*sd.

Most graphs do not fully represent the sample size. A mean or percentage based on $n = 3$ is shown in the same way as one based on $n = 50$. Even if n is stated in the graph, perhaps the perception and cognition received from the graph still remain the same.

Looking for linearity when the relationship is clearly nonlinear can damage the results. Ignoring assumptions such as a Gaussian form of distribution, independence of observations, and uniform variance can produce results of doubtful quality.

Statistical packages are also misused. Data are overanalyzed to investigate aspects that were not part of the protocol. Such analysis is not prohibited, but fallacy arises when they are packaged as an original investigation, suppressing the fact that they are incidental findings. The results of such an analysis should be stated as tentative for the purpose of generating a hypothesis rather than for testing it.

Data Dredging

All-round availability of computers and software has made it easier to re-analyze data after dropping some inconvenient observations. This misuse is called data dredging. Editors and reviewers would rarely be able to detect this because a finished report may not contain any such evidence.

Computer technology has surged ahead at a fast rate, but the understanding of statistical methods among medical professionals has not kept that pace. As a result, some researchers use a **black-box approach** to analyze the data. They just grind it through a statistical package without worrying about the applicability of those methods to their data set. Statistical software provides the power to researchers to analyze without accompanying wisdom. They may use regression where ANCOVA is needed, use nonparametric methods where parametric methods are required, use a nonlinear approach where linear is required, develop a model with eight variables when only four were enough, and such other misuses. Our advice is to involve a biostatistician right from the beginning and use their expertise where needed. They will help to improve both the design and analysis, but cannot be expected to resurrect a badly designed study [21]. Beware, though, that the biostatistician may not be able to fully comprehend the medical implications of the results and thus may not be able to provide ideal advice. A frequent interaction between the biostatistician and the researcher helps each to understand the other better. Also realize that good biostatisticians are scarce. Ensure that the biostatistician has adequate knowledge of statistical methods and knows which software is best for a particular application. If time permits, cross-validate your analysis using two different software programs.

11.5.3 Statistical Errors Can Cause Many Deaths

You know that medical errors in terms of misdiagnosis, missed diagnosis, negligent care, treatment errors, prognostic misjudgment, and so forth, can cause misery and death. For this reason, medical professionals are rigorously trained for many years before they are licensed. Yet errors do occur.

Compare this with statistical errors. There are two types: (1) errors that are known and acknowledged, such as type I and type II errors; and (2) errors that occur due to lack of expertise and carelessness. Not many realize that a genuine type I error means an ineffective regimen is proclaimed effective and many deaths can occur due to this error. Similarly, a type II error means an effective treatment is denied to patients, and this also can cause deaths as lives that could be saved are not.

More serious are errors due to negligence, as illustrated in the preceding paragraphs. Uncounted deaths occur due to wrong conclusions arrived at by inappropriate analysis and inaccurate data [22]. These go unnoticed. This can happen with fully trained statistical professionals. However, there is a large number of researchers who have little or no expertise and training in statistical analysis. With the ready availability of statistical software, anybody and everybody can think of themselves as statistical experts and do the analysis. Whereas medical professionals are trained for endless years in the business of saving lives and reducing suffering, neither statisticians nor medical researchers are trained with the same rigor. Medical biostatistics too is in the business of saving lives and reducing suffering, but few realize this to be so.

References

1. Indrayan A, Malhotra RK. Medical Biostatistics, Fourth Edition. Chapman & Hall/CRC Press, 2018.
2. Wong CA, Scavone BM, Peaceman AM, et al. The risk of cesarean delivery with neuraxial analgesia given early versus late in labor. N Engl J Med 2005;352:655–665. www.ncbi.nlm.nih.gov/pubmed/15716559
3. Ra JS, Kim HS, Jeong YH. Associated factors of ischemic heart disease identified among post-menopausal women. Osong Public Health Res Perspect 2019 Apr;10(2):56–63. www.ncbi.nlm.nih.gov/pubmed/31065531
4. Sterne J. Commentary: Null points – Has interpretation of significance tests improved? Int J Epidemiol 2003;32:693–694. https://academic.oup.com/ije/article/32/5/693/665698
5. Feinstein AR. Clinical Biostatistics. CV Mosby, 1977:p11.
6. Lang J, Rothman K, Cann C. That confounded *P*-value. Epidemiology 1998;9:28. https://insights.ovid.com/pubmed?pmid=9430261
7. Ryan TP. Sample Size Determination and Power. Wiley, 2013.
8. Freiman JA. The importance of beta, the type II error, and sample size in the design and interpretation of the randomized control trial: A survey of 71 "negative" trials. New Engl J Med 1978;299:690–695. www.nejm.org/doi/full/10.1056/NEJM197809282991304?url_ver=Z39.88–2003&rfr_id=ori%3Arid%3Acrossref.org&rfr_dat=cr_pub%3Dpubmed

9. Dimick JB, Diener-West M, Lipsett PA. Negative results of randomized clinical trials published in the surgical literature: Equivalency or error? Arch Surg 2001;136:796–800. https://jamanetwork.com/journals/jamasurgery/fullarticle/391750

10. Taddei F, Falcinelli C, Balistreri L, et al. Left–right differences in the proximal femur's strength of post-menopausal women: Multicentric finite element study. Osteoporos Int 2016;27(4):1519–1528. www.ncbi.nlm.nih.gov/pmc/articles/PMC5908234/

11. Vittinghoff E, Glidden DV, Shiboski SC, et al. Regression Methods in Biostatistics: Linear, Logistic, Survival, and Repeated Measures Model, Second Edition. Springer, 2012.

12. Pang T, Huang L, Deng Y, et al. Logistic regression analysis of conventional ultrasonography, strain elastosonography, and contrast-enhanced ultrasound characteristics for the differentiation of benign and malignant thyroid nodules. PLoS One 2017;12(12):e0188987. www.ncbi.nlm.nih.gov/pmc/articles/PMC5724846/

13. Indrayan A, Holt MP. Concise Encyclopedia of Biostatistics for Medical Professionals. Chapman & Hall/CRC Press, 2016.

14. Doi SAR, Williams GM (Eds.). Methods of Clinical Epidemiology. Springer, 2012.

15. Xu Z, Li J, Wang H, et al. *Helicobacter pylori* infection and atherosclerosis: Is there a causal relationship? Eur J Clin Microbiol Infect Dis 2017 Dec;36(12):2293–2301. https://link.springer.com/article/10.1007%2Fs10096-017-3054-0

16. Guntheroth WG, Spiers PS. The triple risk hypotheses in sudden infant death syndrome. Pediatrics 2002;110:e64. https://pediatrics.aappublications.org/content/110/5/e64.long

17. Ayoub F, Cassia A, Chartouni S, et al. Applicability of the Dimodent equation of sex prediction in a Lebanese population sample. J Forensic Odontostomatol 2007 Dec;25(2):36–39. www.iofos.eu/Journals/JFOS%20Dec07/ayoub%20article.pdf

18. Van Calster B, Valentin L, Van Holsbeke C, et al. Polytomous diagnosis of ovarian tumors as benign, borderline, primary invasive or metastatic: Development and validation of standard and kernel-based risk prediction models. BMC Med Res Methodol 2010 Oct 20;10:96. www.ncbi.nlm.nih.gov/pmc/articles/PMC2988009/

19. Knaus WA, Draper EA, Wagnwer DP, et al. APACHE II: A severity of disease classification system. Crit Care Med 1985; 13:818–829. www.ncbi.nlm.nih.gov/pubmed/3928249

20. Jacobs I, Oram D, Fairbanks J, et al. A risk of malignancy index incorporating CA 125, ultrasound and menopausal status for the accurate preoperative diagnosis of ovarian cancer. Br J Obstet Gynaecol 1990 Oct;97(10):922–929. www.ncbi.nlm.nih.gov/pubmed/2223684

21. Hall GM (Ed.). How to Write a Paper. Byword Publishers, 1996.

22. Indrayan A. Statistical fallacies and errors can also jeopardize life and health of many. Indian J Med Res 2018;146:677–679. www.ncbi.nlm.nih.gov/pmc/articles/PMC6396556/

12

Writing a Thesis or a Paper, and Oral Presentation

After toiling hard to complete a research study, it is time to share the excitement. Let the world know what has been or could not be achieved. Regardless of the results, you have a duty to disseminate the findings to other researchers, policy makers, clinicians, and patients so that they can use them in their decision making. No research is complete unless it is read, discussed, and evaluated. Its dissemination could be in a conference through PowerPoint or any other kind of presentation, but most medical research studies culminate in a written report that could take the form of a paper, a thesis, a dissertation, or a fully fledged project report. Successful researchers are skillful biomedical communicators too and they celebrate their research. Medical schools generally marginalize presentation skills and many emerging researchers find effective presentation a difficult proposition. While experienced writers will have their own style and format, the guidelines in this chapter may be helpful to graduate students in overcoming the challenges they initially face in writing a thesis or a paper for publication.

Section 12.1 discusses the general principles of effective writing. The actual contents of a paper or a thesis in terms of what to write and how to write from the beginning to the end are presented in Section 12.2 to Section 12.4. Section 12.5 discusses oral or poster presentation in a conference. Reporting ethics, including plagiarism, are separately discussed in the next chapter. That chapter also contains our advice on the peer-review process followed by most journals. We use a generic term "report" in these chapters for all kinds of written communication such as a paper, thesis, dissertation, and project report. Some of the advice given here is the same as provided earlier for preparing a protocol.

Before starting to write, it is expected that you would appraise the evidence provided by the research and assess its quality by taking into consideration the relevance and applicability of the results and conclusions in a practical setting. You should be convinced yourself about the utility and quality of the research before you set out to convince others. Adopt the ATOM model: *accept* uncertainty, be *thoughtful*, be *open*, be *modest*.

12.1 Effective Scientific Writing

The written document is the predominant mode of communication of medical research. More than 30,000 medical journals thrive around the world on this type of communication. In addition, scores of theses, dissertations, and project reports are prepared every year. The following are some guidelines on the style of preparing a written communication on medical research, particularly for a paper to be sent to a journal for publication.

Reports based on original data or review articles are the backbone of medical research. However, other forms of written communication, such as descriptive articles, clinical practice guidelines, opinions and commentaries, letters, news, and conference reports, are also published by many journals. In addition, there are other modes of publication to communicate your ideas. For example, if your work is a voluminous and in-depth coverage of a specialized topic, you can publish a monograph yourself or as part of a series published by your institution. Think of publishing your work or its summary on a suitable website, including your own. Many institutions provide a page for each member of staff on their website where you can place your work. This will show up in a Google search for anybody to access. There are other dedicated websites also that will accept your work for publication. In addition, there are many pre-publication archiving sites such as the Collection Of Biostatistics Research Archive (COBRA) maintained by Berkeley Electronic Press. Researchers across the world download articles of their choice from such websites.

Manuscript writing is both an art and a science. Scientific writing reflects a creative process, but it is time consuming and often a daunting task [1]. Imagination is required in putting thoughts together in an interesting and lively manner, and a systematic step-by-step approach is required to achieve coherence. The writing should enable the reader to find a way through a labyrinth of ideas by following a thread of thought. The manuscript should be able to organize any chaos and emphasize relevant ideas while discarding irrelevant ones.

The style of writing is as important as the statement of facts. The basic ingredient is that a manuscript should be effective in conveying the meaning. Put yourself in the position of an indifferent reader and write in a manner that communicates effectively – scientific writing sans digression which calls for focused exposition. In any case, the message in any research presentation must be new and original to evince interest. The text must contain all the details of the decision you took at every step, such as the choice of topic, specification of the objectives, identification of variables, method of their operationalization, choice of instruments, control of bias, structure of design, sample size and its justification, method of assessing data quality, and statistical methods. See the next few sections of this chapter for the actual contents of each section of a paper.

12.1.1 Text Style

The text of a communication should be as short as possible without compromising the quality of exposition. Brevity is a virtue that should not be compromised. Do not expect editors and reviewers to devote time to suggesting specific cuts. Examine your manuscript at least three times and delete any superfluous or duplicate material detected each time. Also plug appropriate words and sentences where holes are detected.

The writing process can be frustrating for beginners and difficult for many others. If so, perhaps the best course is to begin writing whatever comes to mind and edit it later. The finished manuscript must follow a logical sequence. Organize it in a manner such that your enthusiasm and confidence in the work are clearly visible. Although scientific writing is not storytelling, a narrative format with events flowing from previous occurrences may be more reader-friendly. Weave it nicely so that paragraphs and sections present a coherent picture. Be prepared to do brainstorming to achieve clarity where needed. Use a judicious mix of text, tables, figures, and bullets to break the monotony. Do not use pompous language as is used in some literary writings, but do not shy away from using punchy words that convey meaning forcefully. Use proper words in their proper place. Although figures of speech and idioms are not favored in scientific writing, sometimes they can provide a very apt description. Always quest for the right words and phrases and do not use inappropriate words or controversial vocabulary. Request that your colleagues and supervisors read the manuscript and provide feedback, and do not take their critique personally. We have found that leaving a manuscript in a drawer for a couple of weeks, and then self-reviewing, is very effective in detecting both technical and language deficiencies.

Science is complex, but it needs to be explained in a manner that can be understood by a reader. The writer must understand what the reader needs, and the style should be such that the reader accurately perceives what the author has in mind [2]. The keyword for this is articulation. The following guidelines might help.

1. Use titles and subtitles to identify the contents. In a thesis, you may like to number each paragraph to make it easier to refer back and forth in the text. Do not have unlinked ideas in the same paragraph. Each paragraph must have at least two sentences.
2. The text description must match the numbers and percentages given in accompanying tables or figures. Editors and other assessors are not kind about such discrepancies.
3. Check that there are no contradictions. Some repetition is allowed if necessary in context, but not much.
4. A written scientific communication is formal prose. Thus, colloquial language should be avoided. Words with uncertain meanings, such as "soon," "a lot of," "something like," and "seem" should be replaced by their exact counterparts as much as possible. For example, instead of "soon," specify how many hours or how many days. Also avoid terms such as "very," "extremely," and "enormous." These terms are fine for books but not for research papers.
5. Avoid unnecessary phrases such as "It is interesting to note that ..." or, "We showed that ..." In a paper, see if sentences in the beginning and at the end of long paragraphs can be deleted.
6. Avoid nontechnical use of technical terms such as "normal," "significant," "interaction," and "correlation." They might confuse the reader.
7. In a paper, particularly, in place of saying that a comparison is shown in Table X, say, for example, that cases had higher body mass index on average (Table X).

Explain all abbreviations when used for the first time. Do not use too many abbreviations and try to restrict yourself to the popularly known ones.

12.1.2 Tables

Tables are powerful tools to display the data in an intelligible and precise format. They tend to condense and summarize the information and sometimes are able to communicate the intricacies better than text. The reader is able to explore the data for several combinations of comparisons. Tables give structure to the answer and provide concrete evidence as a large set of summary statistics can be recorded. However, they can be a source of confusion too when not properly drawn. Some tips on how to prepare various types of tables are given in Chapter 10. Tables containing numbers and percentage of subjects in different categories have a very different format compared with tables containing statistical results (such as odds ratios [ORs], confidence intervals [CIs], or P-values). Percentages should be based on appropriate totals, as described earlier in Chapter 10. The number of subjects in each group should be mentioned, preferably in the column heading. Ensure that the numbers in different tables are consistent with one another. Specify the unit of each measurement.

Data on groups to be compared should be in columns in a table. For example, if the objective is to compare cases with controls, data on cases should be in one column and those on controls in the adjacent column. If the comparison is of males with females, data on these two groups should be in columns (and not two rows). When two or more tables present results on the same set of variables, the order of variables should be the same.

Tables on statistical significance should contain exact P-values that give more insight to the reader than just saying $P < 0.05$ or $P > 0.05$ or significant/not significant. However, $P < 0.001$ is fine because any further accuracy would rarely affect the tenor of the results. Customarily only two or three decimal places are used in values of P. Many texts use lower-case p, but capital P is preferable because lower-case p is used to denote proportion in the sample. When feasible, also give the name of the statistical test on which the P-value is based, but there is no need to give the value of the test statistic such as t, F, and χ^2 in a paper unless required by the journal. On the other hand, in a thesis, it is desirable that these test statistic values are also given along with the df where relevant. State the CIs wherever applicable because they delineate the reliability of the estimates.

Sometimes it is not feasible to explain all column and row headings in a proper manner, or sometimes numbers are inconsistent and require additional explanation. For readers to understand the table in one shot, add footnotes to the table where necessary. You may also have to explain abbreviations in a footnote. For these and other details regarding content, structure, and style of tables, see Section 10.4.2. All tables must be consecutively numbered according to the sequence of their appearance in the text and they must be placed close to the relevant text.

12.1.3 Illustrations

Photos, graphs, and charts sometimes make a tremendous visual impact that text fails to accomplish. Carefully examine when it would be more effective to insert an illustration instead of text. If they do not add to clarity, they are not worth including in the report. Line drawings are sometimes very effective in depicting complex relationships among quantitative variables. For qualitative data, tables may be better.

Only an appropriate diagram for your data as described in Chapter 10 should be drawn. Do not draw a bar diagram where a pie chart is more appropriate (e.g., for proportions), or where a line diagram is more appropriate (e.g., for trend). The bar chart is a versatile diagram, but it is overused too. Use scatter diagrams sparingly only for showing special features such as regression, outliers, and differential variance. In most situations, stating the correlation coefficient in the text or a table would suffice.

A diagram should be self-contained for independent reading without reference to the text. The title, labels, and legend should be clear and appropriately placed. The title should be brief yet descriptive of the illustration. The size of the labels and legends should be proportional to the size of the diagram keeping in mind that it could be drastically reduced at the time of printing in a journal, and use uniform lettering and sizing as much as possible. Try to provide direct labels to categories, lines, and all other features, to make legends redundant. Fonts and symbols should be big enough to remain legible after reduction. Diagrams and drawings must be high resolution (at least 600 dpi). Avoid color graphs, but they may be acceptable if necessary to clarify the details.

No hard-and-fast rules are set, but it is rare for a medical paper to contain more than three diagrams. And it is rare for a medical thesis to have only three. A thesis may contain

10–15 illustrations, including photographs. Use them sparingly in a paper but generously in a thesis, although not as repetition of tables or text. For accurate description of results, use tables instead of graphs because the numbers in tables can be written to decimal places that cannot be so accurately depicted in a graph. Graphs are good for depicting patterns but not exact values. The graph of values 2.1–16.0 may look similar to that for values 2.0–15.8.

Each figure must be referred to in the text. It must be placed as close as possible to the text that gives the first reference to that figure. Try to ensure that the reader does not have to flip the page either way to see the figure. Number the illustrations according to their sequence in the text.

Photographs should be absolutely clear on glossy paper, generally of size 15×10 cm. If they are of patients, it is essential to obtain written permission for use. Even then suppress the identity by covering eyes and other distinguishing features. Digitally enhanced images (computed tomography [CT], magnetic resonance imaging [MRI], ultrasound images, etc.) should be clearly identified as digitally processed, and indicate the method of digital enhancement. They should be sharp and glossy prints for proper reproduction. Photomicrographs should have internal scale markers. Mention the method of staining in photomicrographs. If colors are essential, ask the journal about the format for submission of color illustrations. Some journals charge heavily for color reproductions. In a thesis, dissertation, or report, use color photographs liberally as long as they are not repetitious, and are relevant to the text.

12.1.4 Format of a Manuscript (IMRaD)

An important resource for manuscript preparation, particularly for journals, is the Uniform Requirements [3] of the International Committee of Medical Journal Editors representing more than 500 journals around the world. This committee is popularly known as the **Vancouver Group**. In addition, consult websites of popular journals such as *Lancet* and the *Journal of the American Medical Association*. They also discuss many issues not covered in this chapter, such as writing a case report, a letter, an editorial, practice guidelines, news items, and book reviews. Some of the ideas presented in this chapter are based on these sources, and restricted mostly to reporting research results in the form of an original article.

If your research is complex, consider if the results can be reported in two or three or more separate papers that are nearly independent of one another such that the overlap is not substantial. In this case, always acknowledge the previously reported results.

For the primary medical research that we are discussing in this book, it is customary to divide the report into the Introduction, Methods, Results, and Discussion **(IMRaD)** format. If an Abstract is also included, this becomes AIMRaD. Whereas most papers published in medical journals follow this format, theses may choose to follow a topic-by-topic approach. In a thesis, the results can be described in multiple chapters. For research on kidney transplants, for example, these chapters can have titles such as "Choice of Donors," "Preparation of Recipients," "Surgical Procedure," and "Post-Surgical Management." Theses are sometimes apportioned later into two or three papers for publication in medical journals, where again the IMRaD format would be required.

In a 4000-word article, which is sometimes considered standard for a research paper, the Introduction would generally occupy 500 words, Methods 1500 words, Results nearly 1000 words, and Discussion another 1000 words. Note that the Results section does not occupy much space and the most important is the Methods section.

Subsequent sections in this chapter give details of what each component of a research report is expected to contain, and how to prepare a good manuscript. Consider them as guidelines only. Consult the Instructions for Authors of the concerned journal for papers, or university guidelines for theses and dissertations. Go to a reputed medical library and see some successful theses. For help in writing a thesis and dissertation, also refer to Joyner et al. [4]. For papers, see a series of articles by Peh and Ng [5]. However, remember that good writers are not born but made. Writing skills can be honed with practice. Do not worry if your first draft is terrible – most of us had done so. Prepare your first draft as early as you can – even possibly before the results are known – so that you can anticipate the problems. Plan for several revisions, and notice how the manuscript improves.

IMRaD is only for the main body of a paper. There are always some preliminaries such as title and authors, and end features such as acknowledgments and references. All of these are important components in their own right and deserve careful consideration. A brief description of the guidelines is given in Box 12.1 and the details are explained in the next few sections.

12.2 Preliminaries of a Manuscript

Whether the target of the paper is a journal, of which there is a variety of hues from no takers to worldwide circulation, or thesis examiners who could be from local to international, the preliminaries of a manuscript make the biggest impact and determine its ability to attract attention.

12.2.1 Title

We discussed title earlier in the context of protocol or thesis but now concentrate on title of a paper. Some of these are a repeat of what we mentioned earlier. The title is probably the most important component of a paper. This is the first part of the manuscript seen by the editor and reviewer, and provides a first impression of the work. Although a report is referenced by, the name of the authors, its utility in a particular context is evaluated by the title. Thus the title should be carefully worded: specific enough to describe the focus and lively enough to generate interest. It should grab the attention of the reader and should be appealing. The title should be concise yet sufficiently informative for a reader to anticipate the contents.

Specificity in Title

The title "Obesity and Diabetes" is concise but fails to convey the subject matter. It is not informative. The title "Contribution of Obesity to Development of Diabetes in the Elderly" describes the research adequately. As much as possible, keep the keywords in front. Thus, "Gender Differentials in Obesity Contribution to Diabetes" is preferable to "Contribution of Obesity to Diabetes in Males and Females."

It is a good idea to mention in the title itself that it is a randomized controlled trial, prospective study, case–control study, or whatever. This helps the reader to grasp the essentials of the methodology you followed. Note that the locale of the study almost invariably appears in the title, particularly for an epidemiological study – sometimes even the year of the study is important, particularly when the conclusions are not generalizable to other years.

BOX 12.1 GUIDELINES FOR CONTENTS OF A MANUSCRIPT OF A PAPER

Preliminaries

Title: Concise (generally not exceeding 15 words) yet informative.

Authors: Only those who have substantially contributed and are prepared to take public responsibility for the contents. Identify the corresponding author if there are several authors.

Keywords: List about 5–6 keywords for indexing purposes to enable researchers to retrieve the paper from a database.

Abstract: Generally structured into Purpose, Background, Methods, Results, and Conclusion; lucid, stand-alone, and containing all salient features of the study yet not exceeding 300 words (consult the journal's instructions).

Main Text (IMRaD)

Introduction: Rationale of the study and what new is expected to be achieved: research questions, objectives, and hypothesis.

Methods: Why the study was done in that particular manner, including comments on validity and reliability of the results that these methods are expected to generate.

Results: Select the derivations that focus on the stated objectives; make judicious use of tables and illustrations for precision and impact, respectively, without duplication.

and

Discussion: Implication of the results in light of the existing knowledge and resolution of conflict, if any; conclusion based on evidence along with the limitations; keep opinions and comments separate from the discussion on evidence-based results.

End Features

Acknowledgments: Thank those who contributed but not enough to qualify as author.

Key Messages: Two or three messages in a box that highlight the achievements of the study.

Contribution of the Authors: This describes each author's contribution to the research and confirms that each has contributed significantly.

Funding: Mention the sources of funding of the research. If there is none, mention that explicitly.

Conflict of Interest: Declare any conflict of interest, or clearly state that there is none.

References: Preferably in Vancouver format, and restrict the list to the minimum needed to substantiate the statements made in the text.

Appendix: Highly technical or specialized text, not of much interest to the general reader.

Long titles are boring, but do not sacrifice accuracy for brevity. Titles beginning with "A Study of …" is a waste of words. Avoid an overly general title and avoid abbreviations. Sometimes a subtitle is a useful adjunct to increase specificity.

The title should also serve the interest of its target audience. For example, for a general practitioner audience such as of the *British Medical Journal*, the title should focus on the applicability of your research, whereas for a superspecialty journal, the emphasis could be on technical aspects. The latter might need a slightly longer title to be able to describe the technical content of the research.

Types of Titles of a Paper

Many types of titles are in vogue. The first emphasizes the investigation and second states the main result. The title "A Case–Control Study of Influence of Early Life Factors on Adult Mortality in Country ABC" states what has been investigated and how, without indicating the result. This provokes curiosity. In a question format, this can be stated as "Do Early Life Factors Influence Adult Mortality in Country ABC?" You could be provocative if the research warrants, but do not sensationalize the title. In an answer format, this could be worded as "Childhood Obesity in Low-Birthweight Babies Reduces Life Expectancy: A Case–Control Study in Country ABC." This is a positive statement and describes the main result of the study. No firm evidence is available to indicate which format makes the biggest impact on readers. In our opinion, the last one – the answer format – is most informative and capable of enticing a person to read the article if they are interested in that topic. Choose the format you consider most exciting for the target audience. For further details, see USC Libraries Research Guides at *http://libguides.usc.edu/writingguide/title*. These guidelines apply to medical research also.

Thesis Title

The focus of the discussion in the preceding paragraph is on papers for publication in a scientific journal. The title for a graduate thesis or a doctoral dissertation is usually decided before the investigation is conducted, and certainly way before the results are available, and it cannot be changed at the time of writing. Therefore, the title for these endeavors can never be in an answer format. Precisely because no latitude is available, there is a tendency in some quarters to propose a nonspecific umbrella type of thesis topic that can incorporate variation in the investigation. An example is "A Study of Occlusion of Left Main Coronary Artery." Such nonspecification can occur for two reasons. One, to be able to incorporate various facets of the problem that emerge later, which indeed could be a legitimate reason for a graduate thesis, but the second reason could be the lack of clarity about the specifics of the proposed investigation. Guard against the latter. Examiners and other reviewers are smart enough to detect this lapse.

Title Page

In a thesis, the title page contains the name of the candidate and supervisors, possibly their academic qualifications (optional) and their affiliation with regard to their unit or department. In any case, the name of the department and the university comes at the bottom. In a medical graduate thesis, the title page also contains a phrase saying "In partial fulfillment of the requirement of the degree of Doctor of Medicine/Master of Surgery." The year of submission is also mentioned.

After the title page in a thesis comes the certificate that says that the work is genuine and carried out by the student himself/herself. This must be signed to make you accountable for any fraud discovered later. Some universities require that this be authenticated by the chief supervisor and even the head of the institution.

Then is the Acknowledgment page where you express gratitude to your supervisors and others who helped in your endeavors, including patients and laboratory/nursing staff. A thesis also contains a table of contents with page numbers for each chapter and each section. Examiners look at this critically to find where to go for a particular explanation.

For a paper for publication too, many journals require a title page with the affiliations of all authors, the address of the corresponding author (including email address), keywords, and possibly a running title. The full title is at the top in any case. Sometimes the word count is required and sometimes also the number of tables and figures. Consult the Instructions to Authors of the journal to get a clear idea of what is required.

Authors should use a standardized name for all their papers. Do not write Abhaya Indrayan in one paper and A. Indrayan in another. If such different or abbreviated names are used, computer search and indexing services may count them separately.

12.2.2 Authorship Credits

The practice "I give your name and you give mine" as author is absolutely unethical for any research, and certainly for medical research. Reputed researchers do not allow their name to be associated with work to which they have not sufficiently contributed. Only those individuals can be authors who have substantially contributed to *all* of the following: (i) conception or design; (ii) acquisition of data or their analysis and interpretation; and (iii) drafting or revising the report for its intellectual content. These requirements are slightly different from the Vancouver guidelines. Each author must take public responsibility for their contribution and at least one author should be identified who takes responsibility for the integrity of the whole work. Generally, this would be the same as the corresponding author. Those who have participated only in collection of data, those who have provided support as part of their duty such as those who carried out radiological or laboratory investigations that they are expected to do anyway, those who have helped only in acquiring funding, or those who have been merely general supervisors cannot claim to be the authors. Thus, authorship inflation is not allowed. Also, no person contributing significantly should be omitted, however "junior" they are. Usurping the work of the disadvantaged and the vulnerable gives rise to **ghost authorship**. This is considered gross misconduct. To avoid such instances, some journals now require a signed declaration that specifies the contribution of each author. The term ghost authorship is also used for those hired for this purpose such as medical writers. They can be acknowledged. If a medical writer makes a substantial contribution to the various stages of a project, they can qualify to be an author.

In addition, it is common to have guest or honorary authorship. The tendency to give the name of the head of a unit or a department just to secure his or her "blessing" is abhorred in scientific circles. They make no real contribution and do not meet the Vancouver criteria of authorship. Sometimes this is done to improve the prospect of publication because the name of a high-profile expert appears among the authors. The requirement is that all authors must be familiar with the entire manuscript and should accept public responsibility for its contents. None of them can say later when a deficiency is detected that the other author is responsible for that error. This in a way underscores the need to limit the number of authors to a few who are really eligible. Papers based on complex study and multicentric study can have a large number of authors if all of them have contributed and accept responsibility for the contents. Possibly because of increased complexity, papers in medical journals with a higher number of authors are steeply increasing.

No guidelines are available to name the first author. The authors themselves decide the order of authorship. It is natural to expect, however, that the one who has contributed most, or has been the driving force all through the research endeavor, would be the first author. But they must qualify to be an author first before being named as first author. For issues such as group authorship, consult the Uniform Requirements [3].

The question of authorship for a thesis or dissertation cannot be debated. The author has to be the candidate themselves. However, it is also necessary in this case that the candidate has actively participated in conception and design, has collected and analyzed the data themselves, and has drafted the report. Thesis supervisors can help in the interpretation of results, and may critically review the manuscript. A doctoral dissertation is mainly a candidate's enterprise whereas a master's thesis draws substantially from the intellectual resources of the supervisors. Remember that the objective of a master's thesis is training in research methodology rather than research itself, but a doctoral dissertation is expected to describe frank research.

The report of a research project is prepared by the principal and co-investigators, and they can claim to be the authors. However, it may be necessary to comply with the requirements of the funding agency, if any, in this case.

12.2.3 Keywords

Many medical journals require that 3–6 keywords are identified for indexing purposes. The best resource for choosing keywords is the Medical Subject Heading (MeSH) list on MedLine. Think of words that users would use to locate your research. Prefer popular words over sparingly used words. In any case, they must adequately describe the contents of the paper. A combination of two or more words is often a better variant than an orphaned word. "Randomized controlled trial" is much better than "clinical trial" and "randomization" separately.

12.2.4 Abstract and Summary

The abstract in a paper and the summary in a thesis are the first substantive material encountered by a reader – therefore, they must be impressive, such that they contain all the essentials and explain the complete research well in a nutshell.

Abstract in a Paper

Almost all medical journals require that an abstract not exceeding 300 words – sometimes only 150 words – is prepared that contains all salient features of the study. The abstract is an exercise in précis writing where brevity and clarity are required. Decide if it is easier to write the abstract in the beginning before the full paper as this can crystallize thoughts in some cases and provide the framework for the report. In this case, go back after writing the full paper and improve the abstract if new thoughts emerge.

The abstract contains the essence of the work in an intelligible, informative, and interesting manner. It should emphasize new and important aspects of the study. Where helpful, include hard data, but they should be in the simplest of statistical terms. The tendency of most journals is to structure the abstract under the headings Purpose, Background,

Methods, Results, and Conclusions. Sometimes Limitations are also added. Each of these headings contains two or three sentences, and together should be able to describe the entire research in a coherent manner. These are concise statements of the details described in the next section in this chapter under each of these headings. All parts of the abstract must be consistent with the main text.

Do not repeat the title of the study in the abstract. It begins with the rationale to justify the study. Then objectives or questions are precisely stated, including a priori hypotheses. In the design, state for a trial that it is a randomized controlled trial or nonrandomized controlled trial; placebo-controlled or controlled for existing treatment; any blinding; matching criteria if used; crossover, before–after, up-and-down strategy; and other such aspects. For evaluation of a medical test, state any available gold standard, and how your test compares with this. For an observational study, specify if it is case–control, prospective, or cross-sectional. For modeling, mention training sample and validation sample. Specify that the study setting is community, primary care, referral center, private clinic, ambulatory care, hospital clinic, admitted patients, records, or any other. Briefly state the eligibility criteria for the subjects. State whether random sampling was adopted or consecutive, referred, volunteer, or if a convenience sample was drawn. Also state what exactly the intervention was and how long it continued. List the important outcome measures. State CIs, correlation, statistical significance, the effect size you considered clinically important, number needed to treat, sensitivity/specificity and predictivity along with the prevalence, and other such indicators. At the end, state both negative and positive conclusions with their practical implications. This list looks long but you will discover after some practice that precise and focused statements are not all that difficult to make. All these are the same, as shortly discussed in detail for different sections of a thesis or a paper. Hardly ever, if at all, does an abstract contain any table or graph or references. It should not contain anything that is not included in the main body of the manuscript. Avoid abbreviations unless you are using the same term three or more times.

The abstract appears as such in indexing services such as PubMed and Excerpta Medica. Many evaluate the worth of a paper on the basis of the abstract. Also, it serves as the gateway for the paper. Many times, the abstract itself is considered enough to provide the required information: it should accurately reflect the contents of your paper. Thus, it should be written as a stand-alone text for independent reading. That is, it should make sense without reference to the main text. Only those readers who find from the abstract that the full paper could be useful would look for the full paper. Thus, prepare an abstract in a manner that can persuade the reader to read the full paper. This does not mean leaving holes: only that the abstract should indicate that it is a good research that needs to be looked into in greater detail.

Summary of a Thesis

A thesis summary is generally more detailed than an abstract in a paper and may run to 1000 words. The basic structure is the same, with headings such as Purpose, Methods, Results, and Conclusion, but here you have the opportunity to give more details. Tables and graphs are generally not allowed in this case also. Make sure that the summary contains enough details to convince the reader and the examiner that you have made sincere efforts to achieve the objectives set out earlier and sampling and nonsampling errors are under control. Limitations are an integral part of the summary of a thesis because this research is conducted under the constraints of time and resources. State them without hesitation.

12.3 Main Body of the Report

As already stated, it is customary to prepare a medical research report in the IMRaD format. This is a suitable format for publication in a scientific journal, and quite often is also used for a graduate thesis. For details of how to write a paper in the IMRaD format and beyond, see Jenicek [6]. Our general advice is not to shy away from using "I" or "we" in a research report. This usage conveys the right message that it is your work and you own up, not just to the credit for the good work but also for any gaps. This also helps in building up direct sentences instead of convoluted ones.

12.3.1 Writing a Suitable Introduction

No problem arises in thin air. Begin the manuscript by describing how the problem arose: What was the context or the background? This could be the extension of a previous work, difficulties faced in managing a public health problem, controversies appearing in the literature, unpleasant clinical experience of managing a specific type of patient, deficiency noted at the time of teaching, bottleneck observed in carrying out research, or any such context. In other words, include information about epidemiology, clinical relevance, and current practice regarding the topic. Keep the focus on the local area but do not ignore the international perspective. Emphasize if the research concerns a neglected topic.

Quote important literature if needed to expose any lacunae in knowledge, but do not include a full review. Prefer the recent and most relevant references for this purpose. Reserve a full review for the discussion section but ensure that up-to-date information is given in the introduction. The introduction section should take the reader from what is known to what is not known and arouse the reader's curiosityr. Explain the significance and rationale of the work, and demonstrate that the work being reported is new, and it is needed. Build a logical case and specify the conceptual framework. Then specify the questions under investigation clearly and concisely, and describe their importance. The problem should be clearly articulated, and the objectives stated in precise and evaluable terms. They should be worded in a specific and focused manner. Identify the important antecedent and outcome variables, and the relationships under study. State any hypothesis under test: also that this was a pre-planned hypothesis or was formulated during or after collection of the data. Specify the subjects of your study and describe the general research strategy but not the details.

In short, the introduction should contain a convincing statement about issues and should formulate the rationale for those issues. This should convince the reader that you have thought about the topic thoroughly and have presented a tight case.

It is sometimes helpful to give a preview of the principal results in the introduction to guide the reader through the paper. Do not make sweeping claims and do not give data or full results because that can dissuade the reader from going further. A short introduction is preferred in a paper to a lengthy discourse because a longer introduction tends to lose focus, but the introduction section in a thesis can be as long as every other chapter.

If you are having difficulty starting with the introduction, try to write the results section first and then return to the introduction.

12.3.2 Explaining Materials and Methods

The suitability of a study for publication largely depends on the quality of its Materials and Methods section rather than on results and conclusions. We will come to the material later, which is mostly in terms of the subjects of the study, and give priority to the methods in this section.

The credibility of a research study depends to a great extent on the appropriate methodology. Describe it as accurately as possible: not the planned one but the one that was actually followed. Consult the protocol because that can provide substantial help in preparing the methods section. The focus should be on describing why this study was done in that particular way. Specifically, include in this section the setting in which the study was carried out, the types of groups of cases and controls studied, and the design adopted, with justification of each of these aspects. If your Materials and Methods section is long, divide it into subsections, such as Subjects, Measurements, Data Collation, Statistical Methods, and any other relevant subtitle.

Specify the setting. The setting could be a general community, a primary health center, a referral or a general hospital (inpatients or outpatients), a private clinic, or any such facility. This helps readers to determine the applicability of the results to their own setting. If the source of data is records, specify that clearly. Also describe the steps taken to preserve the quality of the study. Use the past tense except when describing the contents of the present paper.

All applicable elements of design as enumerated in Box 3.1 in Chapter 3 should be stated. State whether the study is prospective, retrospective, or cross-sectional if observational; or therapeutic, prophylactic, diagnostic, or screening if a trial. Describe the design in detail using Figure 3.1 in Chapter 3 as a guide. Justify the choice of controls and state the matching criteria if applicable. Layout, such as crossover or repeated measures, and one-way, two-way, and factorial, should be specified. Actual implementation of the intricacies, such as randomization, blinding, and matching, should be fully explained. If the study involves medical predictions, describe the validation methods used. The reader should understand all potential sources of bias and how they were controlled. Sometimes a diagram of flow of research helps to achieve clarity. As always, the Methods section should be precise yet should provide details for anyone to repeat the investigation for confirmation. Do not commit methodological overkill. There is no need to mention those basic methods that a reader is expected to know but state new methods fully; for others, just give references. The reader should be convinced that the methodology is adequate to ensure reasonable reliability and validity of conclusions. Mention ethical issues and the clearance you have obtained.

Subjects of the Study

This is the material part of the study. For this, define your unit of the study. This could be a patient with chronic kidney disease, a child with bronchiolitis, a pregnant woman at primigravida, a healthy person aged 65 years or more, or any such subject. Mention inclusion and exclusion criteria and justify them.

Identify the setting (hospital admissions, outpatient department patients, patients detected in screening, a community, or any other) again and state how eligible subjects were identified. If possible, give a count of the number of units in the "population" and then come to the sample.

State what groups were covered and why that many subjects were studied in each group, and the period of recruitment. State the statistical power if applicable and justify the difference you considered medically important to calculate the power. Describe how the subjects were selected – whether any of the standard statistical random methods were used, or consecutive cases, or volunteers, or any others included. In the case of nonrandom selection, state how your subjects are still representative of the target population. The percentage of subjects who dropped out on their own decision should be stated separately from those who had to be withdrawn because of adverse effects. Clearly mention the consent taken and how it was obtained.

Intervention and Instrumentation

Fully specify the intervention, if any, including dosage and duration. For drugs and chemicals, include their generic name, route of administration, and any other relevant information. If you have to write the commercial name, write it in parentheses. Explain ethical considerations related to the intervention. State the mechanism of follow-up and its duration, clearly specifying the censoring (incomplete observations such as dropouts) if any. Any deviation from protocol and its reasons should be highlighted.

Specify the instrumentation and provide references that describe them. Give details of any new or modified method or apparatus used, including its testing, and justify the deviation, if any, you made from standard practice. Give as much detail as necessary for the reader to replicate the study. Demonstrate that your instrument is valid and reliable, and that you were able to properly use the instruments.

Data Collation

Clearly define antecedent and outcome measures including diagnostic criteria, and establish their relevance to the study objectives. Explain how you operationalized the research variables. Give sources of data and provide the method of assessment for each variable. If you have used categories such as mild, moderate, and serious, clearly specify how such categorization was derived. Categories are not desirable for continuous quantitative variables, but if used, give reasons such as easy interpretation, and explain the rationale. If scores are used, give complete methodology or a reference to the source that describes it fully. Also comment on the validity and reliability of the scoring system. If your research is on developing a scoring system, provide details of its theoretical justification and state how you plan to assess its adequacy. State the time points when the information was elicited or recorded.

Identify the confounders and state how they were tackled. Limitations of the data collection methods should be stated without inhibition including how these limitations might affect the results. Such a statement would tell the readers that you are aware of these gaps, and would help them to evaluate the utility of results more realistically in the context of their own setting.

Also state the possibilities you envisioned of contamination in the data and how this was resolved. This should include the remedial steps taken for handling missing data and outliers, if any. The second distinct possibility is error in measurement. This occurs all the time, but must remain within tolerance limits. The report must indicate to the reader that you were alive to such errors and were able to manage them with proper instrumentation and adequate handling. If multiple observers or raters are used, include how they were trained for standardized readings and how interrater reliability was assessed. For your own safety, raise a red flag at the time of drafting a report whenever you find the possibility of sloppiness and resolve this adequately in the final draft.

Statistical Methods

State the statistical methods you used to analyze the data in sufficient detail to permit replication. Explain how these methods are appropriate for the kind of data in hand, and how they will achieve the stated objectives of research. The procedures must conform to the research design, and the models and hypotheses you began with. Present appropriate indicators that have medical meaning such as effect size. In addition, state the methods you used to control confounding bias, and describe the methods you used to examine subgroups and interactions. Cite references if the method is not well known. Avoid giving the formula unless the paper is on methodology. If notations are being used, explain them. State the confidence level for the estimates you have generated wherever applicable. Whereas 95% confidence tends to be accepted without question, any other level is expected to be accompanied by its justification. The trend now is to avoid use of the term statistical significance on the basis of a level of significance such as 0.05 but to provide exact *P*-values. Describe any validation method you used such as sensitivity analysis but do not include results here. Specify the computer package used.

12.3.3 Describing the Results

The results section of the report states what has been found and mirrors your research questions. It should include findings on everything that you stated in the introduction and clearly establish the relevance of your methodology. Maintain the integrity of the manuscript by stating the results in an upright manner and state not just the truth but the whole truth. For example, do not gloss over risks and side effects of an intervention under test. Trust that the scientific community is appreciative of frank statements about negative results as much as positive results. All negative results are not failures – they save other workers from treading the same path. If there are failures, their frank admission elevates the confidence of the reviewers and readers, and increases the credence of results; it gives an impression that the authors are not trying to hide something. Do not suppress findings that contradict or do not support your hypothesis. The scientific community is moving to a paradigm to report a study irrespective of the result. The result may be positive or negative, but the important point is that a correct question was investigated, appropriate methodology was followed, and the results were properly interpreted.

Strive for clarity in describing the results. Coherence is the keyword. Opinions based on hunches or preferences, anecdotes, experience, impressions, or conflicting evidence should be avoided in the results section. All results must be evidence based: fully supported by data, and any inconsistency in findings based on diverse evidence must be explained. Use technical terms such as "normal" and "significant" with care.

All relevant analysis must be available before the results section is finalized. Limit the results to the facts as revealed by the data, but translate your data to the medical context with statistical results as supplements [7]. Do not try to extrapolate or generalize in the results section and do not discuss the results in this section. Do that in the Discussion section with a proper explanation. While a statement such as the difference between the treatment group and the control group is statistically significant, or one treatment gives a significantly higher value than another is appropriate for the results section, the statement that a treatment should be preferred should be part of the Discussion or Conclusion.

The trouble with most studies is that they end up with a huge amount of data. You would probably analyze and interpret a wide range of data during the research study. The data may all be interesting, but describe in your results section only those that address the research question. Examine if some of your material is better placed in an appendix without interrupting the flow of text. The mantra is to provide a holistic picture by integrating various results and presenting them fully. Do not ignore any serendipitous, unexpected, incidental, or accidental results, but use these to set the tone for future investigation. Such results can be important. Fleming's discovery of penicillin was based on an accidental result. Also see Example 12.1.

Example 12.1: An Accidental Finding on the Possible Role of Vitamin E in Lowering Prostate Risk

Chase [8] reports about a study designed to test beta-carotene for preventing lung tumors in Finnish smokers. The study found that the substance instead increased the risk of cancer, but it accidentally also revealed that vitamin E could lower the risk of prostate cancer and hyperplasia. Trials were later done to test vitamin E and selenium as preventatives.

Conversely, sometimes a mass of good data is available but time or expertise is not available to exploit it fully. This can particularly happen at the time of writing a graduate thesis for which sufficiently advanced action was not taken and it is to be submitted by a particular deadline. This is dangerous because hurrying can lead to incomplete, even wrong, conclusions.

The first sentence of each paragraph of the results section should indicate the contents – the point addressed or the question answered. Within each paragraph, state the most important result first and then the less important ones afterward. All the information within the paragraph must be related. Also, do not emphasize data per se but rather their interpretation. Start with descriptive results and move to the analytical aspects later. The results should narrate a story that makes sense without looking at the tables and graphs, and strive for continuity and flow. This means that tables and graphs should be referred to parenthetically while describing their interpretation. For example, do not write that "comparison of treatment efficacy in different groups is given in Figure X or Table Y" but write that "treatment A was 10% more effective than treatment B (Figure X) and this difference is statistically significant ($P = 0.003$) (Table Y)." Focus on the take-home message emanating from the results without imputing any opinion.

A thesis, dissertation, and full report obviously will contain results in much more detail with explanation of nitty-gritty of the entire data. State also about the data collected but not analyzed, and give reasons for not doing so. The results in such reports should be comprehensive to cover all aspects of the problem. However, research papers for journals are considerably briefer.

We have already discussed tables and illustrations such as graphs and diagrams in Chapter 10. Follow those rules in the results section of your manuscript.

Describe the Baseline of the Subjects

Begin the results section with the number of subjects actually studied at each stage of study – how many were potentially eligible, how many were actually examined for eligibility, how many were actually found eligible, how many were recruited for the study, how many dropped out and data were available on how many subjects, how many were excluded from analysis for reasons such as outlying or wrong values, and how many were actually analyzed in each group. A flow diagram such as prescribed by CONSORT (Chapter 13) may be helpful. Give reasons for dropouts at each stage.

Next, describe the basic characteristics of subjects – their demographic (age, sex, rural/urban, etc.), social and clinical features, separately for cases and controls.

In the case of clinical trials and other experiments, demonstrate that the test and the control groups were comparable to begin with. Also indicate that not many dropped out of the study. If they did, show that the results are still unbiased. Report the adverse effects of the intervention and consider prognostic factors where relevant. Mention any additional intervention that had to be done in some cases because of their condition, and describe how it has not affected the validity of results.

Statistical Results

All mean values for quantitative measurements must be accompanied by the corresponding standard deviations (SDs). Do not give standard error because that can mask the interindividual variation. Give CIs where appropriate. State the name of the statistical test at the time of giving the *P*-value. Give the exact *P*-value without using threshold such as 0.05. (However, such a threshold will be required for interpreting the result, such as whether a particular variable is worth including in a regression, and to decide about whether one treatment is better than the other when no other objective information is available for this decision.) There is no need to give the actual values of chi-square, t, F, etc., obtained for your data, and the degrees of freedom also are not needed for a paper but are needed for a thesis. All these tests must have been mentioned in the methods section. While stating percentages for categorical data, do not forget to mention the absolute number also because the percentages based on small n can be very deceptive. Also see the guidelines for statistical reporting in Chapter 13.

Do not use symbols, formulas, and equations in a medical paper unless absolutely necessary. Some statistical results such as for analysis of covariance (ANCOVA) and multiple comparisons in analysis of variance (ANOVA) can be difficult to communicate. Software outputs may be voluminous and you may have to devote substantial time to filtering the results of substance. To put them into an intelligible table can be challenging. Thus, there is a tendency to report such results insufficiently. Even reviewers sometimes ignore this deficiency. Seek help from a statistical facility if you face difficulty. Keep the following points in mind.

1. Pay special attention to any sign of flawed data analysis. An appropriate method for the type of data should be used that gives the results exactly matching with the objective.
2. Do not confuse statistical significance with medical significance. First, statistical significance can be high (*P*-value really small) due to exceedingly large n even when the actual difference is small. Second, conversely, nonsignificance can be due to lack of power (small n). For a statistically not significant difference, do not say no difference was found. A discussion is ongoing about whether the term "significance" should be used at all in the results.
3. Exercise caution in reporting results with marginal statistical significance such as with $P = 0.06$. Using a strict level of 0.005 looks like you are being unfair to marginal cases.

Statistical reporting also depends on the design. For a case–control study, report the number found exposed in the two groups, OR, CI, and statistical significance. Give both unadjusted and adjusted ORs for the exposure of interest as well as for all the covariates and confounders. For cohort studies, include the number with positive and negative outcomes, relative risk, and their CI – again, unadjusted as well as adjusted. For trials, report about efficacy, use-effectiveness, side effects, any unusual cases, and any other such significant findings.

If you have investigated the robustness of your results by validation sample, sensitivity, or uncertainty analysis, provide the findings and explain the discrepancies, if any.

12.3.4 Discussion of Findings and Conclusion

The Discussion section is an intelligent exercise in logic, brevity, and clarity. It places findings in the context of present knowledge and current clinical practice and health care. Generally, this is the most useful part of a thesis or paper that helps readers to understand the implications of the findings. This elaborates how the results fit into the larger theory you initially proposed. The language must be clear, precise, and unambiguous. It should have a clear link with the Introduction section.

Argumentation in discussion can be exciting both for the authors as well as for the readers. It allows readers to grasp the real relevance and utility of results in medical care, health policies, or evaluation programs [9]. For the authors, the discussion sometimes helps them rediscover the intricacies of the phenomenon that were possibly obscure earlier. Thus, an argumentative discussion can be a useful exercise. See Jenicek [9] for details of how to write a Discussion section in medical articles and what it should contain. The same principles apply to a thesis and longer reports as well – just in more detail.

Even the best evidence can be lost in a poor argument. What argument is a good argument? This requires critical thinking which can be learned and the cornerstone of this is logic. A good argument contains a claim or proposition that must arise from infallible reasoning based on critically appraised evidence with qualifiers and exceptions. The qualifier must be convincing and the argument should not look like a maneuver [10].

Discuss Your Results

Begin the discussion with the medical context and then bring in the significance of your main findings. Recapitulate the findings without repeating the data. Emphasize the new or important findings without exaggerating. Discuss how your results support or do not support the original hypothesis. If the result is on expected lines, explain the need to carry out the investigation in the first place. Do not introduce a new result that was not presented in the results section. Explain how the statistical significance of your results might be real and not due to errors of measurements, confounding factors, or other biases. Explain what the results mean and how they are biologically plausible – their implication for the practice of medicine – and relate them to the objectives of the study. If the effect of your intervention is small, explain how this might still be valid and useful. Comment on the statistical power of your study and establish the reliability of the new findings so that there is no suspicion. Discuss the robustness of results to minor variations in the underlying procedures and convince the reader that the results are trustworthy. Comment on the generalizability and practical significance, free from your own perception bias. Defend the design of the study, but do not feel shy of describing the limitations and shortcomings of the design. Remain alive to the epistemic gaps. Thus, say what you want to say about the results of your study but provide credible evidence. If there is any accidental finding, explain how it may have arisen. Put forth a new hypothesis if it looks plausible. Lateral thinking out of the box is always an asset. Also discuss the statistically not significant results if they are interesting.

Whether a small paper or a big report, never mix comments with facts. Opinions should be clearly stated as opinions. Personal perspective is important, but do not mix it with data-based results.

Remember that statistical terms such as OR, CI, regression coefficients, and P-values are not directly interpretable for application in medical practice. They need to be transformed to everyday medical language that a practitioner can understand. Remember also that the immediate users of your research are the practitioners who deal with healthy and unhealthy people.

Do not forget to mention the limitations of your study. No result has universal applicability. Failure to report limitations suggests arrogance, or that the authors do not know about them. Your report should not give an iota of an inkling that there is any attempt to mislead the reader.

Compare Your Results

Compare your results with those of other researchers, particularly of known or respectable groups working on that topic. Analyze the literature critically without bias. (If you are reproducing all or a part of somebody else's figure or table in this process, you may have to ask for permission.) Resolve any conflict by providing credible reasons. Argue why your results are convincing and integrate them with present knowledge. When relevant to your work, gently but firmly indicate the deficiencies in the work of others such as their faulty design, inadequate analysis, and wrong interpretation, but this rebuttal must be fully supported by evidence. Also, acknowledge the excellence of others when noticed.

Conclusion

Distinguish between statistical results and scientific conclusion. The latter considers other evidence also – medical context, biological plausibility, present knowledge, clinical experience, and other such relevant considerations. You should explain the mechanism of how the conclusion emerged from the results as well as the collateral knowledge. The conclusion is based on the strength of the evidence of your study and other studies.

Produce a succinct conclusion and discuss its generalizability. It must be a warranted conclusion based on the evidence discussed earlier in the report. Link it to the objectives of the study. Justification of the conclusion should be fully articulated. Do not over-interpret the results and give full consideration to the multiplicity of analyses, findings of others, and limitations of your study. State if the conclusion corroborates or contradicts the original hypothesis and attach the appropriate degree of uncertainty about the final claim. Do not make tall claims – be modest and accept uncertainty.

Instead of restating the findings, emphasize the operative part of these findings. Very clearly state how they add to present knowledge, or how the results have contributed to the progress of science. Describe any future perspective without being arrogant. For practical implications, include recommendations where appropriate. For interventions, for example, the conclusion could be that it is sufficiently effective, or that it is promising but requires further investigation, or that adequate efficacy could not be established. The conclusion may also highlight the trade-offs between benefits and adverse effects. The benefits could be in terms of better efficacy or in terms of reduced cost or increased convenience. The adverse aspects could be side effects, cost, and inconvenience. Common errors in reaching conclusions are: (i) interpreting lack of evidence for an effect as evidence of no effect, or not statistically significant as not different; (ii) ignoring warning signs of negative effect; (iii) reaching beyond the evidence by imputing own judgment; and (iv) stating that more research is needed without specifying what specific research is needed and why.

Discussion in a Thesis

The discussion chapter in a graduate thesis should be divided into subheadings so that disparate ideas on different subtopics are not mixed. In a long report or a dissertation, a chapter may be devoted to each subtopic. In that case, results and discussion on that topic would be together in that chapter. Because critical thinking is more important than data in a doctoral dissertation, the discussion section has a very special place in a dissertation. Use this section to demonstrate that concepts are getting precedence over results because that is what is expected in a dissertation.

12.4 End Features of a Report

IMRaD is for the main body of a paper, but there still remains substantial writing under the headings of Acknowledgments, Key Messages, References, and others as required by the journal. Guidelines on this segment are as follows.

12.4.1 Acknowledgment Ethics

Primary medical research is essentially a team effort, but not all members of the team may qualify to be authors. They are thanked in the acknowledgment section for their contribution. People providing purely laboratory assistance, statistical assistance, data collection assistance, patient care assistance, editing help, clinical assistance, and so forth, particularly outside their routine duty, come into this category. The help of scientific advisers, persons who critically reviewed the manuscript, and departmental heads who provided general support should also be acknowledged. If you have received a data set from somebody, acknowledge this properly. All financial or material support must also be acknowledged, including grant and contract numbers, and fellowships, if any. There is no need to be over-enthusiastic about acknowledging help, or acknowledging merely to serve vested interests. Example 12.2 illustrates what can go wrong even with this benign aspect of the paper.

Example 12.2: Embarrassing Acknowledgment

Chatfield [11] describes receiving a copy of an offprint acknowledging his statistical advice provided 3 years earlier on a trial that could not find a significant difference between low-level laser therapy for rheumatoid arthritis of finger joints and placebo. He had not seen the paper in either draft or final form. The paper had some inappropriate graphs. Perhaps the refereeing process also bypassed statistical content because the name of a (reputed) statistician appeared in the acknowledgments!

Instances of the type described in Example 12.2 are not uncommon. We have found ourselves in a spot many times because of the "generosity" of authors in acknowledging our help without our knowledge. They misquoted our interpretation, even mentioned out of context a statistical procedure that was used for some other analysis. We now ask for an undertaking from our clients that they not acknowledge our help without our approval. Many journals require that written permission be obtained from those acknowledged. The Vancouver Group also endorses this requirement. If the acknowledged persons want to see the manuscript, show it to them so that they can check that you have rightly written about them.

12.4.2 Key Messages

An information explosion has forced the development of new methods to keep abreast of new developments without devoting too much time. Many journals are now switching to provide key messages in a box to summarize the salient features of the study in a few bulleted points. This certainly looks like a welcome development, and seems very friendly not only to readers but also to the reviewers and editors of journals who need to evaluate each paper for its technical worth and space in the journal. If you are clear about what was done and what was the main result, it will not be difficult to write the key messages of your report.

The key message box generally contains one bulleted sentence on each of: (i) what is already known; (ii) what the research adds; (iii) what methodology was adopted; and (iv) what are the limitations. Each message should be complete in itself. The box containing key messages is not necessarily placed at the end in a printed paper, but it is customary to place it at the end of the manuscript at the time of writing. Considering the importance and utility of these messages, it would not be surprising if over time they receive precedence even over the abstract.

12.4.3 References

References may be the least noticed aspect of a scientific manuscript but their proper use brings authority, credibility and precision to scientific manuscripts. The reference section is an important part of a scientific manuscript because references acknowledge the work of other researchers that allowed you to formulate your hypothesis and enable readers of your article to locate those works. At some point, another researcher may reference your article, which allows the field to grow [12].

Selection of References

As stated earlier, the literature cited in the paper and thesis should preferably be recent and directly relevant to your work. If you have a choice, select the ones that are easily accessible to the reader, such as free full-text articles in PubMed. Some critical readers will like to see the work you have cited and the availability of free full-text helps. At the other extreme are conference abstracts, which are difficult to access. As much as possible, avoid citing such abstracts. Also, such abstracts generally contain rudimentary and insufficient information.

Avoid citing papers under preparation or under communication, personal communications, and such other soft material. If you must, take the written permission of the authors of such communications. Also, avoid references cited by others as they may be inaccurate. If you have to, state "cited by ...." Be careful about retracted papers. These can be searched for by typing "Retracted publication" [pt] in the search box of PubMed, where [pt] stands for publication type. As much as possible, avoid references from newspapers, clippings, and magazines.

Except for reviews and meta-analyses, it is not considered expedient to cite a large number of references. In place of a comprehensive list, a few representative papers, possibly on different segments of the population or from different areas, should be cited. Prefer references from well-known peer-reviewed journals or internationally acclaimed reports such as from the World Health Organization. The original of the referenced material should have been seen by at least one of the authors.

The selection should be judicious. Also do not cite many references for a general statement. For example, saying that "there are a large number of studies on homocysteine level related to coronary heart disease (1–20)" does not impress anybody. Make it more specific, such as "ethnic groups in different countries with a higher rate of myocardial infarction have been found with elevated level of homocysteine level (1–3)." Also there is no need to give references for well-known facts such as hypertension is related to obesity, and dietary factors are important precursors for colon cancer. Any statement that could be looked at with suspicion should be accompanied by the reference (or the data) to provide authenticity.

Technology has advanced and references are not restricted these days to print format. A large number of medical journals are published online with no print version. In addition, you can cite the website of professional associations or other academic organizations. Use *doi* (digital object identifier) to cite such a reference. For this, mention the date of your last access because the contents of websites can change quickly.

Format of References

The **Vancouver format** requires that references in the text be cited by consecutive numbers in the order they appear in the text, and listed at the end by these numbers. They must be cited immediately after the idea, in the middle of the sentence if needed, and not necessarily at the end of the sentence. An increasing number of journals are switching to this format. The other format is to cite the reference in the text by the name of the authors (only the last name of the first author, followed by et al. if there are three or more) and the year of publication in parentheses. Consult the Instructions for Authors of the journal to which the manuscript is being sent for consideration and follow those instructions.

The Vancouver style of preparing the list of references is gaining universal acceptance in medical literature. Indexing services such as PubMed were already following nearly the same format. This format says that the authors' last name be written first followed by the first letter of the initial and middle name without full stop (.) sign, using a comma in between the names of the authors. Then write the title of the article. Next is the name of the journal with year of publication, followed by semicolon, volume number followed by colon, and first and last page number of the journal with a dash in between. There are slight changes for citing a book, a chapter in a book, the proceedings of a conference, a conference abstract, a report, a website, and so forth. See the Uniform Requirements [3] for details, or follow the instructions of the journal concerned. It is customary to use PubMed abbreviations for name of the journals. If the journal is not indexed, try to abbreviate according to the PubMed principles. If you are not confident, a safe bet is to spell out the full name of the journal. For examples of references in the Vancouver format, see the list at the end of this chapter.

Inaccuracies in references are common. You may like to check and recheck each reference for the spelling of the name of authors, any missed word in the title of the articles, year of publication, page numbers, and so on. Some journals check the accuracy of the cited references. To avoid errors, it is best to use software such as ProCite and Reference Manager. The next best thing to do is to copy and paste the citation from PubMed and other electronic resources and rearrange in the Vancouver format. The trend now is to provide the weblink so that the reader can access the referenced article with a click.

Bibliography

The bibliography is different from the list of references. References are those that are cited in the text. There may be other articles and material related to the topic but not cited in the manuscript. These may be of interest to readers if they wish to go into the depths of that topic. Most journals do not want a bibliography – they restrict to the cited references only – a bibliography could be a useful adjunct to a thesis, particularly a doctoral dissertation. For these, the thesis supervisor is the best guide to suggest which publications to include in a bibliography.

12.4.4 Contribution of Authors and Conflict of Interest

Many journals now want a statement about the contribution of each author. State what specific contribution was made by each in conceptualizing the problem, designing the study, guidance on how to proceed, collection of data, collation of data and analysis, interpretation of the results, collecting the references, preparing the draft, review and revision of the manuscript, and approval of the same. This statement makes it clear who is responsible for which part of the work and whether each qualifies to be an author. Also, separately state if there is any conflict of interest. This occurs when any author has any kind of relationship with other organizations, and if this relationship can influence any aspect of the research, particularly the results. This is expected to be fully disclosed.

12.4.5 Appendix

Technical matters, not of sufficient interest to the general audience, but of interest to specialists, who want to know the details, go into the appendix. Medical journals tend to relegate mathematical content of a paper to an appendix. Where needed, detailed tables can be provided in the appendix with new identifying numbers. In the case of a thesis and dissertation, consent form, data collection form, and other such material go into the appendix. When the study is small, the entire data set can be appended.

12.5 Oral Presentation

An oral presentation is different from a written communication because it is a personal interface, and the audience does not have the chance to re-read if anything is not clear. Besides content, the effectiveness of an oral presentation depends mostly on speaking style and, to some extent, on visual aids such as slides. These aids are discussed later in this section.

An oral presentation is generally delivered from a podium and could be in the form of a seminar, which is more interactive with the audience, or a lecture where the audience is passive although questions can be asked. For research results, most oral presentations are made in a conference. This could be either a plenary lecture of 30 minutes to an hour before a big audience, an invited talk of 15–20 minutes to a medium-sized audience, or a contributory paper of nearly 10 minutes to a smaller audience. The other, now very popular, format of conference presentation is poster. We discuss oral presentation first and then talk about poster in this section.

12.5.1 Essentials of Effective Presentation

While research capabilities are important, communicating them in an effective manner is also important. Thus, presentation is one of those skills that a researcher must acquire. A presentation is a fast and potentially effective method of bringing people together to think, appreciate, and review the results. It allows immediate interaction between all the participants and the presenter.

Remember that the primary objective of presentation is not transmission but reception. Thus, the audience is the focus. An extremely good presentation may fail if the audience is not able to capture its essence. An effective communication is the one whose message is understood and remembered.

The human mind has segments that work like the cache, RAM, and hard disk of a computer where immediate, mid-term, and long-term thoughts are stored. A presentation should be sharp so as to pierce the mental fog and be able to hold the attention of the audience long enough to be stored at a strategic location in their mind. A good presentation has not only content and structure but also packaging with a human element.

For some, speaking to an audience may top the worst fear. Your body can go into overdrive with release of adrenaline and cortisol, and you notice butterflies in your stomach. They will easily fly away as you begin and provide words to your thoughts. Set the theme early in your presentation so that the audience knows what to expect. Think of what you would like in a presentation if you were in the audience and establish rapport by pretending to be one of them. Try to keep the audience engaged by phrases, small anecdotes, and questions and inviting participation if that is allowed in the format of the organizers.

Remember that most audiences are on your side and they want you to succeed. Translate this into reality by carefully delivering the end. It should be packed with a punch that summarizes your research. Let it come unexpectedly so that the audience does not switch off before your punch line.

The best part is that all this can be acquired by practice. All you need is to pick up the finer nuances of making a good presentation, practice hard, learn from feedback, and practice more.

Speaking

Some people have a natural talent but others can acquire speaking skills by following simple rules. Realize that a talk follows a much more informal format than a written paper. A conversational style in oral presentation can be very effective in communicating ideas. Strike a chord with your audience by captivating them on the emotional front. Try to include an anecdote or two that can infuse life into the presentation. Understand your audience and address them. Keep the audience in good humor. If you are not good at this, do some practice.

Maintain eye contact with the audience and throw words at them, only occasionally directing to the chair and the rapporteur, but never into the air and nowhere. Avoid concentrating on the screen or computer, although this has to be consulted off and on. Throw smiles at different segments of the audience at different times with eye contact as though they are with you. Your audience will be staring at you and your facial expressions should convey that you are relaxed and comfortable.

Your posture also conveys your thought processes. Use it as a tool to reinforce support with the audience. Speak at a slow pace, particularly if there are non-English-speaking persons in the audience, but not at the cost of flow of delivery. Some "ums" and "errs" are not harmful, but too many are distracting. Lower or raise your pitch according to the emphasis. A presentation at a uniform pitch can quickly put some to sleep. Use pauses and repeat critical information. Do not worry too much about syntax and grammar as long as you are able to put across the ideas. If needed, pose questions and provide answers. Tailor the contents to the composition of the audience with regard to the mix of expertise.

A good strategy for oral presentations is to repeat the key points: tell what you are going to tell (the plan of your talk in brief), tell in detail according to the available time what you want to say, and summarize what you have said. The first part and the last part should match. Such repetition reinforces the essence of the research. We have largely followed this system in this book.

Practice does make perfect sense. Present the talk in your department before delivering it at a conference. In addition to practice, this will provide a feeling of the time needed for the presentation and critical feedback from a friendly audience can help improve the talk.

Structure

It is obvious that a 10-minute talk cannot cover as much as a 30-minute talk. Try not to pack too much into a short time: just give the gist of the work and encourage the audience to read the full paper, or prepare a handout for distribution. Omit the review of literature except for one or two references when essential. Abbreviate the methodology rather than the results. Plan properly so that you do not overshoot your time. Remember to spare some time for a question–answer session as this could be the most rewarding time for you to learn more about that topic. An audience loves to have a say. If there are no questions, provoke just one person. Others will follow.

Be prepared for tough questions. When a question is asked, repeat it for the entire audience. Ask the questioner if that is what he or she meant. Respect the questioner no matter how silly the question might look to you. Do not engage in prolonged arguments: instead, suggest a chat after the talk. If you do not know the answer, do not apologize but only offer to get back to them later, or suggest resources, or even ask the audience for suggestions.

An oral presentation is almost invariably more effective when accompanied by visual aids such as slides. Some tips on how to prepare these are given next. Use illustrations to replace or supplement the text wherever appropriate. Diagrams, photographs, and cartoons can be very effective in oral presentations when sparingly used. Decide how you will fill the interludes between the slides so that continuity is maintained.

Also establish links as you go from one idea to another. At the end, gratefully acknowledge the help received from others.

BOX 12.2   FORMAT OF A SLIDE PRESENTATION

- Never fill slides with verbatim sentences. They kill interest and convey the message that you lack confidence. Only points or keywords should be written, but small sentences can be helpful in asserting a point.
- Write large: Title in, say, 40-point font and text in 24-point. Do not include more than eight lines of text in one slide – preferably six lines or less. Cramming too much material into one slide reduces its intelligibility – and consequently compromises its effectiveness in communication. The slides should not be tiresome to read.
- Headings should be in bold letters and centered, whereas the remaining text should be left-aligned in upper- and lowercase as usual. Sans serif fonts such as Arial, Helvetica, and Tahoma may be preferable to serif fonts such as Times, Antiqua, and Courier. Avoid fancy fonts.
- Check slides for spelling mistakes and grammar. Proof read them with care after making a printout.
- PowerPoint has special features for text formatting such as blink, fade, descend, spin, bounce, and float. They can be effectively used to place emphasis and to make the presentation interesting, but do not overdo it. Plain slides are generally preferred. For details of how to use PowerPoint, see Grech [13].
- When needed, divide the slide into two columns – one to carry table, photo, graph, and other illustrations, and the second to carry its text message. If the facility for simultaneous presentation of two slides is available, use it effectively for this purpose.
- Wherever possible, prefer a graph over a table. A table is difficult for the audience to decipher. If you have to have a table, devote extra time to explaining its contents.
- The background and color of the text are debatable, but our experience suggests that a plain white background with text in blue or black does a neat job.
- Contrast between colors of the text and background must be maintained. Titles can be in color, such as scarlet. Use a uniform color scheme and a consistent format.

Presentation Aids

A major aid these days is the PowerPoint presentation. This can be augmented by inserting voice, but that is seldom done. Videos can also be presented as an adjunct to your oral presentation. Transparencies for overheads are becoming outdated, but they have excellent features because you can write and explain as on a whiteboard.

Aids such as slides for projection serve two purposes. First, they keep the talk focused and coherent all through the presentation, and second, they attract the attention of the audience, who may otherwise become distracted. Simple rules for preparing these aids are given in Box 12.2.

Remember that an excellent design of slides cannot make up for deficiency in contents. Like a beautiful container, a good slide format can fool once, but the lasting impression is provided by the thought process exhibited by the content. The purpose of slides is not so much to provide talking points to the presenter but to provide an understanding to the audience of your research. Verbal and visual aids should be coherently integrated to provide a solid picture to the audience. Consider the following points.

1. Start preparing early, and give yourself enough time to revise and improve the presentation. Rehearse it well.
2. Give a mock presentation within your institution/department, invite comments, and improve your slides.
3. Keep a backup of your presentation in another pen drive.
4. Visit the presentation room in advance and acquaint yourself with gadgets such as overhead projector, slide projector, LCD projector, computer, pointer, and projection screen. Apprise yourself about their operation, particularly of those that you may have to handle as a speaker. Play your presentation and check that color and symbols do not change. Sort all problems before presentation: never point out arrangement deficiencies in the talk.
5. Use slides only to reinforce a point. Depend mostly on your memory and knowledge to speak. Too many slides can spoil rather than help. Generally not more than one slide per minute of presentation is recommended. Perhaps one slide per minute is ideal. For a small 10-minute presentation, the distribution of slides can be as follows: Title and your name – one slide; Background of research – one slide; Purpose/hypothesis – one slide; Methods – two slides; Results – two or three slides; Conclusion – one slide.
6. Make sure you do not obstruct the view of the audience.
7. Make effective use of the pointer while speaking. If a pointer is not available, you can use a mouse cursor to point to the text of interest.
8. Allow some lead time (a few seconds) between slides at the time of presentation for the audience to read the content.

Dissertation Defense

Most universities want a public defense of a doctoral (PhD) dissertation. The audience generally would be faculty and upcoming and outgoing students. There may be some other experts and examiners from other institutions and organizations. Generally, only those attend who are interested in the topic. It is an oral presentation by the candidate followed by a grueling question–answer session. Hopefully you have attended such defense yourself as a doctoral student and have apprised yourself of the format.

Discuss your presentation with the colleagues and teachers in advance and get their feedback. Address their concerns in the presentation. Opposing views may come up and it is helpful to identify them and prepare in advance how they will be resolved.

Remember that your adviser is your ally. Although a dissertation is mostly the work of the student, the adviser also has a stake. They are expected to keep the research on track. Thus, take their help in preparing the defense and ensure their full support before, during, and after the presentation.

A good research study empowers science and not the candidate. Thus, do not emphasize the lessons you learned, but emphasize the gains of your work to science. Show that the research was adequately planned and meticulously executed. Sometimes the process of research takes precedence over the utility of results. Therefore, spend time in explaining the methodology. At any point in time, do not be defensive about your defense. A vigorous presentation with full preparation is the key to facing the audience successfully.

12.5.2 Poster Presentation

Because of an exponential increase in presenters despite a steep increase in the number of conferences, only a few get the opportunity to make an oral presentation. Many, particularly graduate students, are assigned to make a poster presentation. Perhaps you will present more posters in your initial career than oral presentations. The presenter is expected to stand by the poster at specified timings and explain it to whosoever cares to show interest. There is no captive audience, but a poster presentation provides a unique opportunity for one-to-one interaction with the selected interested audience who are attracted by the poster.

A standard practice in conferences these days is to provide a space (e.g., boards), approximately 4×5 feet in size for contributors to display a poster on their work. The poster size is nearly 3×4 feet.

The contents of a poster are slightly more than of an abstract but certainly much less than a full paper. Perhaps one or two tables or graphs can be included in the results section, and one or two references can be cited. Such a facility is generally not available in an abstract. Otherwise the structure is the same as of an abstract and the same guidelines apply. Abstract contents have been discussed earlier in this chapter.

Although a poster can be prepared on, say, six pages of size A4 that are easy to carry when traveling, there is an increasing tendency to prepare it as one big poster in the literal sense. Modern technology easily allows printing of 3-foot wide paper to as much length as needed. Generally the length of a poster is 4 feet. Really large fonts can be used for titles and subtitles, and slightly smaller ones for text. The title should be readable from a distance of 9 feet and text should be readable from a distance of 3–6 feet. Large fonts also correctly prevent you cramming too much information in a poster.

The format of a poster greatly depends on the type of audience. The format would be different when the target group is specialists rather than students. Since as a poster audience is not captive as in an oral presentation, the poster must have a format that can attract attention, otherwise it will be ignored. It should be able to "sell" just like an advertising billboard. One tool is the large font size, as mentioned in the preceding paragraph, and the second is layout. Try different layouts and select the one that looks most effective. Guidelines for this are in the next paragraph. A format that can do the "talking" is preferred. Third is the choice of different fonts and colors. Do not overuse them. Consistency helps to retain attention. Perhaps two types of fonts (one for headings and the other for text) each in two colors (e.g., black and navy blue) on a light brown or light gray background that contrasts are appropriate. You may like to try a scarlet heading and black text in light gray boxes. Fourth is that the poster should be error-free. Any error in content or spelling can be embarrassing because you are standing by the poster. Fifth is introducing an element of sensationalism to arouse interest and possibly controversy to catch the limelight. Many would disagree with this for a scientific presentation.

Layout of a Poster

The title at the top should not be lengthy and should fit in one line in a large font. Do not use exclusively capital letters. Leave space on the side for your institutional logo. A logo looks good, provides authenticity, and brings your institution into focus. Sometimes your institution attracts the attention of viewers.

Divide your poster into sections and clearly demarcate them by thick lines in a light color. These sections could be Purpose, Background, Methods, Results, Conclusion, References, and Acknowledgments. You may like to have any other structure. This structure should be recognizable from a distance.

Think of including a map showing the location of your study, or a photograph of your hospital or the activity of the study. One or two graphs can be very attractive. All the illustrations may look better on one side rather than in the center.

Be consistent in font size and color so that the viewer knows that they are looking at similar things. For example, all sectional headings should be of the same size and color, and all graph headings should be of the same size and color but different from sectional headings. Tables and graphs can have a light background. Font sizes should be proportionate to their importance and not unduly large or small. Use of underlined text should be rare, if at all, because it causes clutter.

Sufficient blank space between the text and illustrations helps viewers to get a balanced view. Cluttered posters are generally ignored by viewers. One horizontal line should not generally contain more than 10 words for viewers to remain focused. Consider having a few copies of the poster or a summary of your research in A4 size to hand out to anyone who is interested. You may also want to include your address or email address at the bottom in case someone needs to approach you.

References

1. Hoogenboom BJ, Manske RC. How to write a scientific article. Int J Sports Phys Ther 2012 Oct;7(5):50–57. www.ncbi.nlm.nih.gov/pmc/articles/PMC3474301/pdf/ijspt-07-512.pdf
2. Gopen GD, Swan JA. The science of scientific writing. Am Scientist 1990;78:550–558. https://cseweb.ucsd.edu/~swanson/papers/science-of-writing.pdf
3. Uniform Requirements. Uniform Requirements for Manuscripts Submitted to Biomedical Journals. International Committee of Medical Journal Editors. www.icmje.org – last accessed 19 April 2019.
4. Joyner RL, Rouse WA, Gladthorn AA. Writing the Winning Dissertation: A Step-by-Step Guide, Fourth Edition. Corwin Press, 2018.
5. Peh WCG, Ng KH. Effective medical writing: Pointers to getting your article published. Singapore Med J (i) Basic structure and type of scientific papers, 2008;49:522–524. (ii) Peh WCG, Ng KH. Title and title page, 2008;49:607–608. (iii) Ng KH, Peh WCG. Writing the materials and methods, 2008;49:856–858. (iv) Ng KH, Peh WCG. Writing the results, 2008;49:967–968. (v) Ng KH, Peh WCG. Preparing effective tables, 2009;50:117–118. www.crc.gov.my/wp.../1_10_Preparing_a_manuscript_for_submission.pdf
6. Jenicek M. Writing, Reading, and Understanding in Modern Health Sciences. Routledge, 2014.
7. Turbek SP, Chock TM, Donahue K, et al. Scientific writing made easy: A step-by-step guide to undergraduate writing in the biological sciences. Bull Ecol Soc Am 2016;97(4):417–426. https://esajournals.onlinelibrary.wiley.com/doi/epdf/10.1002/bes2.1258
8. Chase M. Cancer prevention, at a price. Wall St J 2003 (June 24). www.usrf.org/news/070703_finasteride/WSJ.comcancerprevention.html
9. Jenicek M. How to read, understand, and write "Discussion" sections in medical articles: An exercise in critical thinking. Med Sci Monit 2006;12:SR28–SR36. www.medscimonit.com/download/index/idArt/451279
10. Jenicek M. Towards evidence-based critical thinking medicine? Uses of best evidence in flawless argumentations. Med Sci Monit 2006;12:RA149–RA153. www.medscimonit.com/download/index/idArt/452871
11. Chatfield C. Confession of a pragmatic statistician. Statistician 2002;51 (Part 1):1–20. http://citeseerx.ist.psu.edu/viewdoc/download?doi=10.1.1.93.3273&rep=rep1&type=pdf
12. Foote M. Why references: Giving credit and growing the field. Chest 2007;132:344–346. https://journal.chestnet.org/article/S0012-3692(15)35722-6/fulltext
13. Grech V. WASP (Write A Scientific Paper): Optimisation of PowerPoint presentation and skills. Early Hum Dev 2018;125;53–56. www.sciencedirect.com/science/article/abs/pii/S0378378218304043

13

Reporting Guidelines

A large number of guidelines are available for reporting of various kinds of studies. There is one for clinical trials, called CONSORT, one for observational studies, called STROBE, and one for diagnostic accuracy studies, called STARD. In addition, for statistical reporting, we have SAMPL guidelines because many authors falter on statistical reporting and are unable to properly draft their thesis or paper despite doing good work. We discuss all these guidelines in this chapter so that you do not have to face inconvenient questions when the research is reported for publication in a reputed journal, or when a thesis is examined.

All these guidelines and much more are available on the EQUATOR network [1]. This is regularly updated as and when the guidelines are revised. It is a good idea to consult the latest version at this website. The existing guidelines are as follows.

13.1 Guidelines for Reporting of Clinical Trials (CONSORT Statement)

The CONsolidated Standards Of Reporting of Trials (CONSORT) statement prescribes the format in which a trial should be reported. The objective is to provide complete details to the reader about the plan and execution of the trial so that the reader him-/herself can make judgment about the validity of the results. The statement is periodically revised to reflect new realizations about such reporting. It was developed in 1996 and revised in 2001 and 2010.

The basic premise of CONSORT is that it is important to properly report a clinical trial to the community after so much resources have been spent on its planning and execution. A good trial such as a randomized controlled trial must also be reported in a format that could be appreciated by readers. The features of the CONSORT statement are the same as generally known, namely, the report of the trial should indicate why the study was undertaken, including scientific background and explanation of rationale, structured review of all pertinent literature not leaving out the opposite view, selection of subjects and sample size, allocation of subjects and blinding, baseline data, transparency regarding analytic methods including for missing data, noncompliance, and similar other details [2]. Though the principles are widely known, many researchers were not as comprehensive in their reporting – thus the need to develop such a standard format.

To help minimize confusion and promote clarity in reporting the methods and results, the CONSORT statement comprises a 25-item checklist and a flow diagram (Figure 13.1).

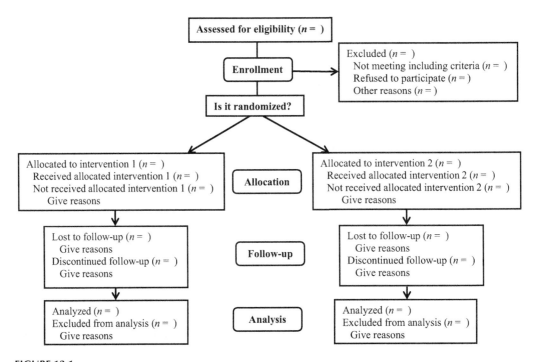

FIGURE 13.1

Flowchart of CONSORT statement – one of the interventions could be control. (Schulz KF, Altman DG, Moher D. CONSORT 2010 statement: Updated guidelines for reporting parallel group randomized trial. BMJ 2010;340:c332. www.bmj.com/content/340/bmj.c332 [2].)

This list ensures clear and transparent reporting of key elements of clinical trials. However, there are some deficiencies. As of 2018, the flow diagram does not include information on blinding, although it contains information on randomization. Moreover, there is no exclusive mention of the number of cases actually followed up, although this can be deduced. CONSORT guidelines do not require much information on statistical methods. The statement outlines the minimum requirement and one can always supplement to make reporting more complete and accurate.

13.2 Reporting of Observational Studies (STROBE Statement)

STrengthening of Reporting of OBservational studies in Epidemiology (STROBE) is a guideline for fully reporting the results from an observational study. This contains a checklist of 22 items (Table 13.1) on the contents of the article and on the results of observational studies, and is endorsed by a large number of biomedical journals. Some points are separate for prospective, retrospective, and case–control studies and others are common for all observational studies. For example, for cohort studies, one item is "summarize follow-up time (e.g., average and total amount)," which is not required for other studies.

The statement requires that scientific background and rationale for the study should be clearly stated and requires a cautious overall interpretation of results considering the

TABLE 13.1

STROBE Statement – Checklist of Items That Should Be Included in Reports of Observational Studies

Section	Item no.	Recommendation
Title and abstract	1	(*a*) Indicate the study's design with a commonly used term in the title or the abstract
		(*b*) Provide in the abstract an informative and balanced summary of what was done and what was found
Introduction		
Background/rationale	2	Explain the scientific background and rationale for the investigation being reported
Objectives	3	State specific objectives, including any pre-specified hypotheses
Methods		
Study design	4	Present key elements of study design early in the paper
Setting	5	Describe the setting, locations, and relevant dates, including periods of recruitment, exposure, follow-up, and data collection
Participants	6	(a) Independent Groups
		Cohort study: Give the eligibility criteria, and the sources and methods of selection of participants. Describe methods of follow-up
		Case–control study: Give the eligibility criteria, and the sources and methods of case ascertainment and control selection. Give the rationale for the choice of cases and controls
		Cross-sectional study: Give the eligibility criteria, and the sources and methods of selection of participants
		(b) Matched Groups
		Cohort study: Give matching criteria and number of exposed and unexposed
		Case–control study: Give matching criteria and the number of controls per case
Variables	7	Clearly define all outcomes, exposures, predictors, potential confounders, and effect modifiers. Give diagnostic criteria, if applicable
Data sources/ measurement	8*	For each variable of interest, give sources of data and details of methods of assessment (measurement). Describe comparability of assessment methods if there is more than one group
Bias	9	Describe any efforts to address potential sources of bias
Study size	10	Explain how the study size was arrived at
Quantitative variables	11	Explain how quantitative variables were handled in the analyses. If applicable, describe which groupings were chosen and why
Statistical methods	12	(*a*) Describe all statistical methods, including those used to control for confounding
		(*b*) Describe any methods used to examine subgroups and interactions
		(*c*) Explain how missing data were addressed
		(*d*) *Cohort study*: If applicable, explain how loss to follow-up was addressed
		Case–control study: If applicable, explain how matching of cases and controls was addressed
		Cross-sectional study: If applicable, describe analytical methods taking account of sampling strategy
		(*e*) Describe any sensitivity analyses
Results		
Participants	13*	(*a*) Report numbers of individuals at each stage of study, e.g., numbers potentially eligible, examined for eligibility, confirmed eligible, included in the study, completing follow-up, and analyzed
		(*b*) Give reasons for nonparticipation at each stage
		(*c*) Consider use of a flow diagram

Continued

TABLE 13.1

STROBE Statement – Checklist of Items That Should Be Included in Reports of Observational Studies (*Continued*)

Section	Item no.	Recommendation
Descriptive data	14*	(*a*) Give characteristics of study participants (e.g., demographic, clinical, social) and information on exposures and potential confounders (*b*) Indicate number of participants with missing data for each variable of interest (*c*) *Cohort study*: Summarize follow-up time (e.g., average and total amount)
Outcome data	15*	*Cohort study*: Report numbers of outcome events or summary measures over time *Case–control study*: Report numbers in each exposure category, or summary measures of exposure *Cross-sectional study*: Report numbers of outcome events or summary measures
Main results	16	(*a*) Give unadjusted estimates and, if applicable, confounder-adjusted estimates and their precision (e.g., 95% confidence interval). Make clear which confounders were adjusted for and why they were included (*b*) Report category boundaries when continuous variables were categorized (*c*) If relevant, consider translating estimates of relative risk into absolute risk for a meaningful time period
Other analyses	17	Report other analyses done, e.g., analyses of subgroups and interactions, and sensitivity analyses
Discussion		
Key results	18	Summarize key results with reference to study objectives
Limitations	19	Discuss limitations of the study, taking into account sources of potential bias or imprecision. Discuss both direction and magnitude of any potential bias
Interpretation	20	Give a cautious overall interpretation of results considering objectives, limitations, multiplicity of analyses, results from similar studies, and other relevant evidence
Generalizability	21	Discuss the generalizability (external validity) of the study results
Other information		
Funding	22	Give the source of funding and the role of the funders for the present study and, if applicable, for the original study on which the present article is based

Source: STROBE Statement. www.strobe-statement.org/index.php?id=available-checklists – last accessed 15 January 2019.

*Give information separately for cases and controls in case–control studies and, if applicable, for exposed and unexposed groups in cohort and cross-sectional studies.

objectives, limitations, multiplicity of analyses, results from similar studies, and other relevant evidence. A discussion of the existing external evidence is particularly important for studies reporting a small increase in risk.

As of now, STROBE does not specifically require that new findings be put into context by conducting a systematic review of other similar studies. This obviously would be a positive feature as "this could alert us about consistency of findings, allow exploration of sources of heterogeneity and would ensure, in the same way as it does for randomized trials, that research effort is not spent on rediscovering the same finding again" [3]. For details and the latest on STROBE, see STROBE Statement [3].

13.3 Reporting of Diagnostic Accuracy Studies (STARD Statement)

The acronym for STatement for Reporting studies of Diagnostic Accuracy, STARD consists of a checklist of 30 items and a flowchart that authors can use to ensure that all relevant information is present in their report on research on the diagnostic accuracy of a medical test [4]. This is one of the resources to improve reporting of diagnostic accuracy studies, and is in realization that complete and informative reporting can only lead to better decisions in health care.

Medical tests are quite commonly used in clinical settings to provide a certain degree of assurance and to confirm the diagnosis for a disease or any other health condition. The term medical test is generic and refers to any method of obtaining additional information on the patient, and includes not just laboratory and imaging tests but also history and examination. Thus, it can include only the signs and symptoms. These tests help in initiating a treatment and in deciding when to modify or stop the treatment. However, the problem is that these tests rarely, if ever, provide infallible results, and the validity of the results depends on a host of factors such as condition of the patient, method of administering the test, inherent qualities of the test, quality of reagents, care in following the recommended procedure, and other such considerations.

Whenever a new test is developed (call it an index test), it is expected that its performance will be evaluated against the existing procedure and its superiority or equivalence would be established. This can be either in terms of validity as measured by sensitivity and specificity (or predictivities) against a reference standard or could be efficiency in terms of convenience, cost, and time. The test is tried on a series of subjects and the results are reported. It has been observed that sometimes this reporting is incomplete and the reader is not able to comprehend all aspects. The STARD statement is an attempt to standardize reporting so that nothing is missed and all steps of the study are properly described. Its first version appeared in 2003. The latest version (2015) is given in Table 13.2 and the flowchart is depicted in Figure 13.2 [4].

Ever since the STARD statement was issued, it has been increasingly used to report diagnostic studies, and the reporting quality seems to be improving [5]. Cheung et al. [6] used this format to report assessment of breast specimens with or without calcifications for diagnosing malignancy and atypia for mammographic breast microcalcifications without mass, and Alcoba et al. [7] used it to report the results of their study on proadrenomedullin and copeptin in pediatric pneumonia.

13.4 Guidelines for Reporting of Statistical Methods (Revised SAMPL Statement)

Whereas the previous three guidelines are for the specific design of the study, the SAMPL statement is applicable to all empirical research. Much of the clarity in the reporting of such research comes from clear statements about how the data were collected, what analysis was done and how, why that particular analysis was right for the problem in hand, and how the conclusion was drawn. The description of the intricate statistical methods is admittedly challenging, but errors have been observed in basic methods. Generally, these basic methods are used by clinicians without the help of a competent biostatistician, and they sometimes falter. The errors frequently go unnoticed by readers. Sometimes these errors can blow up into an enormous mis-statement that can jeopardize the life and health of many people over the course of time [8].

TABLE 13.2
STARD Statement

Section and topic	Item no.*	Details
Title or Abstract		
	1	Identification as a study of diagnostic accuracy using at least one measure of accuracy (such as sensitivity/specificity, predictive values, or area under the curve)
Abstract		
	2	Structured summary of study design, methods, results, and conclusions
Introduction		
	3	Scientific and clinical background, including the intended use and clinical role of the index test
	4	Study objectives and hypotheses
Methods		
Study design	5	Whether data collection was planned before the index test and reference standard were performed before (prospective study) or after (retrospective study)
Participants	6	Eligibility criteria
	7	On what basis potentially eligible participants were identified (such as symptoms, results from previous tests, inclusion in registry)
	8	Where and when potentially eligible participants were identified (setting, location, and dates)
	9	Whether participants formed a consecutive, random, or convenience series
Test methods	10a	Index test, in sufficient detail to allow replication
	10b	Reference standard, in sufficient detail to allow replication
	11	Rationale for choosing the reference standard (if alternatives exist)
	12a	Definition of and rationale for test positivity cutoffs or result categories of the index test, distinguishing pre-specified from exploratory
	12b	Definition of and rationale for test positivity cutoffs or result categories of the reference standard, distinguishing pre-specified from exploratory
	13a	Whether clinical information and reference standard results were available to the performers or readers of the index test
	13b	Whether clinical information and index test results were available to the assessors of the reference standard
Analysis	14	Methods for estimating or comparing measures of diagnostic accuracy
	15	How indeterminate index test or reference standard results were handled
	16	How missing data on the index test and reference standard were handled
	17	Any analyses of variability in diagnostic accuracy, distinguishing pre-specified from exploratory
Results		
Participants	18	Intended sample size and how it was determined
	19	Flow of participants, using a diagram (Figure 13.2)
	20	Baseline demographic and clinical characteristics of participants
	21a	Distribution of severity of disease in those with the target condition
	21b	Distribution of alternative diagnoses in those without the target condition
	22	Time interval and any clinical interventions between index test and reference standard
Test results	23	Cross-tabulation of the index test results (or their distribution) by the results of the reference standard
	24	Estimates of diagnostic accuracy and their precision (such as 95% confidence intervals)
	25	Any adverse events from performing the index test or the reference standard
Discussion		
	26	Study limitations, including sources of potential bias, statistical uncertainty, and generalizability
	27	Implications for practice, including the intended use and clinical role of the index test

Continued

TABLE 13.2

STARD Statement (*Continued*)

Section and topic	Item no.*	Details
Other information		
	28	Registration number and name of registry
	29	Where the full study protocol can be accessed
	30	Sources of funding and other support; role of funders

Source: Bossuyt PM, Reitsma JB, Bruns DE, et al. STARD 2015: An updated list of essential items for reporting diagnostic accuracy studies. BMJ 2015;351:h5527. www.bmj.com/content/351/bmj.h5527.

*At the start of each item row, authors should specify the page number of the manuscript where the item can be found.

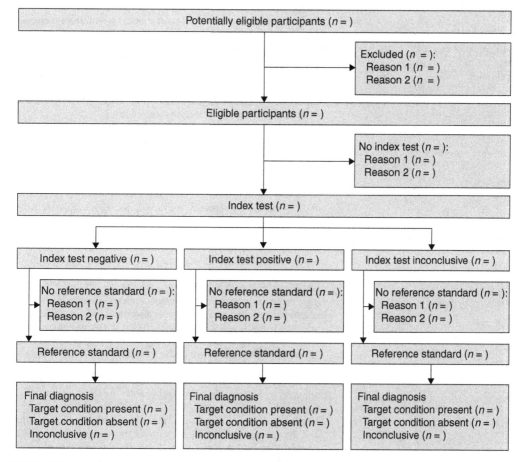

FIGURE 13.2

STARD flowchart. (Bossuyt PM, Reitsma JB, Bruns DE, et al. STARD 2015: An updated list of essential items for reporting diagnostic accuracy studies. BMJ 2015;351:h5527. www.bmj.com/content/351/bmj.h5527 [4].)

TABLE 13.3

Revised Guidelines for Reporting Basic Statistical Methods

Topic	Item no.	Details
Subjects under study	1	Identify the target population, state the method of selection of the sample, sample size, groups, and group sizes, state how many were missing values and outliers with reasons, and comment on the representativeness of the sample available for analysis
Variables under study	2	State all the variables on which the data were collected and identify the ones on which the present analysis is based along with the unit of measurement of each and describe the validity of the measurement method. For reporting, if needed, give categories of continuous data and the number of subjects in each category. If helpful, give histogram and comment on the distribution pattern
Descriptive summaries	3	Summarize the data: give mean (SD) or median (IQR) of each continuous variable depending upon the Gaussian or (highly) skewed distribution, respectively (do not use SE here), and percentages for qualitative data. All should be with the appropriate degree of decimal accuracy*
Modification of raw data	4	Describe transformation, if any, with justification, including scores, rates, and ratios (such as BMI)
Hypothesis	5	State all the hypotheses, keeping the objectives in view; include the minimum effect to be considered as clinically important if applicable with its justification. For equivalence and noninferiority studies, give the maximum equivalence margin
Main method of analysis	6	Describe the data analysis methods in light of the study design, confirm the underlying assumptions, justify the parametric and nonparametric methods used for different variables. Give reference or explain the methods not in common use. State the software used
Estimation	7	For the descriptive part of the study, provide an estimate of the effect size with the confidence interval. The effect can be in terms of difference between means or proportions, odds ratio, correlation coefficient, phi coefficient, or any other
Tests of statistical hypothesis	8	Give the name of each test and its exact P-value. For $P < 0.001$, state with less than sign. Report any adjustment made for multiple comparisons. Indicate whether the test is one-tailed or two-tailed with the reasons thereof. Avoid the term statistical significance based on cutoff such as 0.05
Regression analysis	9	Describe the purpose of the regression analysis, identify the response (outcome) and regressor (antecedent) variables with their selection process, assess collinearity, report the regression equation with its adequacy such as R^2 for quantitative and generalized R^2 for logistic regression, and P-value for each regression coefficient with the associated confidence interval. Comment on the randomness of the residuals. For logistic regression, give the unadjusted and adjusted odds ratios. Specify whether and how the model was validated
Survival analysis	10	Describe the purpose of the survival analysis, identify the beginning and the endpoint for the duration under study, specify censoring, name the survival analysis method with the confirmation of the assumptions, give the survival curve and median survival time with the confidence interval, discuss the points of inflexion, if any, specify the method used for comparing two or more survival curves, and give exact P-value

Continued

TABLE 13.3

Revised Guidelines for Reporting Basic Statistical Methods (*Continued*)

Topic	Item no.	Details
* Decimal accuracy (rounded) as follows:		
For percentages		One decimal place if $n < 100$ and two decimal places for $n \geq 100$
For mean and SD		One decimal place more than the original values. If BMI is in integers, use one decimal place for mean BMI and SD of BMI. If Hb level is measured to one decimal place, mean Hb level and SD of Hb level should have two decimal places
For correlation coefficient		Generally two decimal places
For odds ratio, relative risk, and hazard ratio		Generally two decimal places
For *P*-values		Exact *P*-values to three decimal places and not as $P < 0.05$ or $P \geq 0.05$ (for extremely small values, write $P < 0.001$)

BMI, body mass index; Hb, hemoglobin; IQR, interquartile range; SD, standard deviation; SE, standard error.

In view of statistical concerns as mentioned above, Lang and Altman [9] presented a set of guidelines for reporting of statistical aspects of the paper. The authors admit that these guidelines are limited to the most common statistical analyses, but consider them sufficient to prevent most reporting deficiencies. The guiding principles are that the statistical methods should be described with sufficient detail for knowledgeable readers to verify the reported results if the data are provided to them. The second principle is to report the descriptive statistics from which other indicators such as relative risk and odds ratio are derived. Table 13.3 contains our version of the summary of these guidelines. This version is different from what the authors described and is suitably revised in format and content. Further refinement and fine tuning are in progress [10]. These guidelines are only for basic statistical methods and advanced methods such as Cox regression, cluster analysis, and multivariate analysis of variance (MANOVA) are excluded in the hope that a qualified biostatistician will be involved when such advanced methods are used.

References

1. EQUATOR Network. Enhancing QUAlity and Transparency Of health Research. www.equator-network.org/reporting-guidelines – last accessed 9 January 2019.
2. Schulz KF, Altman DG, Moher D. CONSORT 2010 statement: Updated guidelines for reporting parallel group randomized trial. BMJ 2010;340:c332. www.bmj.com/content/340/bmj.c332
3. STROBE Statement. www.strobe-statement.org/index.php?id=available-checklists – last accessed 15 January 2019.
4. Bossuyt PM, Reitsma JB, Bruns DE, et al. STARD 2015: An updated list of essential items for reporting diagnostic accuracy studies. BMJ 2015;351:h5527. www.bmj.com/content/351/bmj.h5527
5. Selman TJ, Morris RK, Zamora J, et al. The quality of reporting of primary test accuracy studies in obstetrics and gynaecology: Application of the STARD criteria. BMC Women's Health 2011;11:8. www.ncbi.nlm.nih.gov/pmc/articles/PMC3072919/
6. Cheung YC, Juan YH, Ueng SH, et al. Assessment of breast specimens with or without calcifications in diagnosing malignant and atypia for mammographic breast microcalcifications

without mass: A STARD-compliant diagnostic accuracy article. Medicine (Baltimore) 2015 Oct;94(42):e1832. www.ncbi.nlm.nih.gov/pmc/articles/PMC4620838/

7.   Alcoba G, Manzano S, Lacroix L, et al. Proadrenomedullin and copeptin in pediatric pneumonia: A prospective diagnostic accuracy study. BMC Infect Dis 2015 Aug 19;15:347. www.ncbi.nlm.nih.gov/pmc/articles/PMC4543464/

8.   Indrayan A. Statistical fallacies and errors can also jeopardize life and health of many. Indian J Med Res 2018;148:677–679. www.ijmr.org.in/text.asp?2018/148/6/677/252165

9.   Lang T, Altman D. Basic statistical reporting for articles published in clinical medical journals: The SAMPL guidelines. In: Smart P, Maisonneuve H, Polderman A (Eds.). Science Editors' Handbook. European Association of Science Editors, 2013.

10. Indrayan A. Guidelines for reporting of basic statistical methods in biomedical journals: revised SAMPL statement. In press.

14

Reporting Ethics and Peer Reviews

Ethics is conforming to the standards of conduct. In the context of medical research, it has several facets. Research ethics is in terms of sufficient reasons to start a new investigation and using an appropriate design, including adequate sample size, so that the efforts do not go waste and there is no unnecessary exposure to the subjects. This was discussed in Chapter 8. Concern for the welfare of study subjects was expressed in Chapter 2. Now we discuss reporting ethics in this chapter. Some of this too has already been discussed. For example, advice on truthful reporting of results without inhibition even if they are negative has already been given. Negative results can also be useful for future researchers in learning lessons. Acknowledging the limitations and shortcomings of the investigation has also been emphasized. Also we mentioned earlier unbiased review of the literature, not precluding opposite or variant views. After all this, some aspects of reporting ethics still remain undiscussed. These include duplication and plagiarism, copyright and permission, conflict of interest, and peer review. In short, reporting ethics is about increasing the integrity of the report, as summarized in Box 14.1.

BOX 14.1   REPORTING ETHICS

- A duplicate publication based on already reported data is unethical unless it is a translation into another language, or written for another audience with altered focus. In this case, acknowledge the original publication and give reference.
- Stealing the results or ideas of somebody else without acknowledgment is plagiarism. This is misconduct and deserves to be punished.
- Reproducing a small part of a text, one figure, one table, and so on, from a publication is allowed when the credit is cited and written permission is obtained.
- Clearly state financial, personal, or professional conflicts that have the potential to influence your findings, even if they are not actually influenced.
- Respect peer review. Such a review is standard practice in all scientific research.
- Do not misreport your findings and do not suppress inconvenient results. In other words, do not restrict your paper to the favorable results. Truthfully describe the limitations of your research.
- Do not deviate from the protocol. If the circumstances make it necessary to deviate, record the reason, and explain why it was necessary. Also state how this deviation will affect the results.

Among many negative things talked about in this chapter about what not to do, we begin with a positive note on what to do. Ethics requires that your paper, when sent to the editor, is accompanied by a proper covering letter. Hopefully you have selected a journal that has a decent chance of accepting your paper. Subsequent sections are on duplicate publications, misreporting, and conflict of interest.

Covering Letter

When sending a manuscript for publication, it is generally necessary for it to be accompanied by a covering letter. Although a simple sentence saying that the enclosed manuscript may be considered for publication works, editors generally like to know what this paper is about and why you have chosen that journal. Thus, try writing a paragraph containing this information. Include information on your previous publications and presentations based on the same work, if any. Some journals would want to see a copy of this material to decide on the suitability of the submitted paper. Also mention the number of tables and illustrations enclosed.

Some journals provide a pre-submission checklist that you need to complete. If you have not been able to follow the journal's instructions fully, give reasons why a particular instruction could not be followed. All this will help expeditious processing. Some journals require the signatures of all the authors with specification of exact contribution of each author. This sometimes goes into the body of the paper instead of the covering letter. If not included in the text, mention conflict of interest in the covering letter. See later in this chapter for details of this conflict.

14.1 Duplication

Distinguish between two kinds of duplication. The first is duplication of your own previous report, and the second is copying others. The second is called plagiarism.

14.1.1 Duplicate Publication

Preparing three papers on different aspects of a work is not necessarily duplication, even if the data are same. If the research has three distinct conclusions, each can be reported separately in a journal focused on that aspect. The expectation in this case, however, is that each paper will contain a reference to the previous or concurrent publications on that data. A full paper based on an abstract or conference presentation earlier is also not considered duplication. Brief results reported in a clinical trial registry are also not duplication when a full paper on this trial is prepared. Two publications based on the same data written in different languages or for different audiences are also acceptable as long as the original publication is acknowledged and the purpose of this new publication is clarified. A publication on assessing clinical agreement was first printed in a statistical journal [1] and repeated in *Lancet* [2] with altered focus for medical professionals. This is not considered duplication. What, then, is a duplicate publication? Clear guidelines are yet to emerge, but the following discussion may help.

Two papers on the same aspect of the same data possibly with differing titles in different journals is duplication. Sometimes cosmetic changes in presentation or in data content (e.g., add one more variable to the five analyzed earlier or add a few more subjects) are made to escape detection. Two papers with substantial overlap of results on the same or nearly the same data is also considered duplication. These occur mostly to falsely inflate the curriculum vitae of the author. While working on pancreatic cancer, we detected two papers in the PubMed database by Gold [3] and Gold and Goldin [4] with identical titles and a substantially similar abstract. Both occupy 25 pages of the respective journal. Two articles by Patel et al. [5,6] in different journals also have identical titles and essentially the same abstract. We do not know what transpired, but in such a case it is necessary to inform the editor about the previous publication.

Preliminary reporting to media, other agencies, and a letter to the editor also come under this category. The editor decides whether to publish or not each case on its merit. If the previous publication is suppressed and this "misconduct" is detected later, the journal may denounce the authors publicly and that can bring disrepute to the author and the institution or funding agency. The editor may also notify the institution or the funding agency regarding this misconduct and this can jeopardize the author's job. Never ever try to do this.

Instances of duplicate publication of the type mentioned in one of the preceding paragraphs are rare, but another misconduct, of redundant publication, goes on quite frequently. This occurs when the paper substantially overlaps with another paper. The *British Medical Journal* considers that overlap of more than 10% is the threshold to be on guard and examine another paper for its content before deciding on publication. Adding a few cases or a few more investigations or a slightly different set of variables comes into this category. Such papers unnecessarily increase the load on readers and journals and should not be published. Journal editors are still grappling with the kind of response they should make against redundant papers. Publishing first on a website and then in print is also unethical. However, preprints or monographs do not fall into this category.

In the same vein, simultaneous submission of a paper to two or more journals is also unethical. Journals also have the right to penalize the author for this misconduct. The penalty could be not considering any future paper from that author and informing the author's employer about this misconduct.

14.1.2 Plagiarism

Plagiarism is representing the results, figures, ideas, and words of others as your own. This is cheating and abhorred more than duplicate publication. All public documents such as publications in journals are for use by anyone, but the requirement is that the source must be acknowledged so that proper credit is given where due. Verbatim sentences of others should be in quotations with references. If you want to avoid quotation marks, paraphrase in your own words without changing the meaning. For this, read and understand the source material then put it away and express the idea in your words. Because the idea still belongs to somebody else, the reference of the source document should be cited. The whole idea is to respect others' intellectual property just as you would like yours to be respected. However, there is no need to cite references for statements of common knowledge. When saying that lack of exercise and high calorie intake contribute to obesity, there is no need to cite the reference even if it belongs to someone else.

Another dangerous trend now catching on in some countries, particularly with graduate theses, is the copy–paste "technology." Collect six previous theses on the topic similar to your research, identify sentences and paragraphs that you can incorporate, and copy and paste them into your thesis. This certainly does not help in the way of your talent, and a smart examiner will spot such handiwork. This may still get "rewarded" if the examiner chooses to remain silent for an ulterior motive, but there is the chance of being punished too. In any case, this sets up terrible guilty feelings when you become a thesis supervisor and your students do the same.

14.1.3 Copyright and Permissions

Quoting a sentence or two, or borrowing ideas from a cited reference, is one thing, but reproducing a full paragraph or a figure or a photograph is another. The latter raises the issue of copyright and permissions.

Almost all formal publications – journals, books, and reports – are copyrighted these days. They clearly mention in the beginning that any kind of reproduction in full or in part is not allowed without the written permission of the authority vesting copyright, otherwise legal action can be taken. This, however, does not forbid anyone from making photocopies of a few pages for personal reading, but no part can be copied for commercial purposes.

Reproducing material from some other publication requires written permission. Permission is indeed granted in scientific pursuits but many publishers charge a fee. This could be exorbitant for some authors. Experience suggests that if it is a question of reproducing a small part, such as one figure or one table, and the inability to pay is shown, the publishers are benevolent for academic and scientific purposes and may waive the fee in such cases. Do not hesitate to contact the publisher or the copyright owner for permission. The responsibility for obtaining the permission lies with the author.

Most journals want the copyright of the paper to be transferred to the journal before publishing a paper. Consider the implications, such as in obtaining patents, before the rights are transferred. If the patents are already obtained, inform the editor. There is an ongoing debate regarding granting copyright to publishers for the writings of authors. Perhaps authors as individuals feel insecure in enforcing copyright whereas publishers have the resources to protect the copyright. One view is that authors should have the right to distribute their work. Open access has loosened the hold of publishers. In any case, realize that the publisher has the copyright for the writing you did but the work or the result continues to be your own, and the authors are generally allowed to share and self-archive rights.

14.2 Conflicts and Reviews

If the attitude or behavior of a research worker tends to get affected because of extraneous considerations, assume that there is some conflict of interest. Generally, self-interest is the cause of such conflicts. These arise mostly because of financial considerations, but can arise due to personal or professional considerations as well. These conflicts can undermine public trust in medical research.

14.2.1 Conflict of Interest

These can be categorized into financial conflicts, and personal and professional conflicts.

Financial Conflicts

A funding agency naturally expects that the research sponsored by it will at least do it no harm, if not further its interest. If the funding agency happens to be a company in the business of promoting a drug, device, or any other intervention, and the research findings go against that product, how can this conflict be resolved? Integrity of research is maintained by truthfully reporting what is found, and not being influenced by such extraneous considerations. The trend now is not to accept a research proposal with potential conflict of interest even if the work is not actually affected. Research workers should not have any link with the company whose product is being researched, and certainly should not have a stake in that company. Accepting a consultancy or honorarium from such a company is also considered to be an adverse factor and such "inducements" also should not be accepted in the near future after the research is over, because that too can serve as a motivation to influence the findings. The influence can be indirect in designing, conducting the investigation, data analysis, and interpretation, and not just in reporting. Even when there are no financial interests, researchers do benefit when their hypothesis is validated. This can help to attract more grants or may help the researcher secure promotion. This, of course, is allowed.

Personal and Professional Conflicts

The results of a study can go against the results of your seniors or against a reputed research worker. To avoid conflict with them, you may have to delete certain parts of the findings or try to modify them. Conflict can also arise at the time of peer review when the reviewer happens to have a connection with the company of the researched product or with the researcher. If the paper is from a competitor of a reviewer, the review could be biased (see Section 14.2.2). Such conflicts can arise at the editor level as well.

The author would not know about conflicts occurring at the level of reviewer or editor, but all other known or perceived conflicts should be disclosed at the time of submission of the manuscript to a journal. Merely disclosing conflicts does not make them allowable. Explain how your findings are not compromised because of any such extraneous consideration. The editor will decide whether the integrity of the research is maintained or not, and publish accordingly. They may also decide to publish conflict disclosures for the benefit of readers. Disclosing a conflict of interest does not necessarily reduce the worth of the report and it does not imply dishonesty either. In contrast, this disclosure can enhance the credibility of the authors.

Reporting Conflict of Interest

The previous paragraph included a brief discussion on reporting conflict of interest of the authors. Most medical journals require that any such conflict be reported upfront. For financial conflicts, report the sources of support, including sponsor and the role of the sponsoring organization in the study design, selection of the objects, collection of data, analysis, interpretation, drafting the manuscript, and the choice of journal. The author should explicitly declare whether any such involvement occurred or not.

For personal and professional conflicts, the journal may require authors to state what kind of access they had to the study data, and that there was no interference from any external person or agency.

14.2.2 Peer Review

Skepticism in science is a regular feature and fair criticism is welcome. Unbiased and independent assessment of all research by colleagues is considered an integral part of the scientific process. Peer review is the process of appraisal by experts regarding the contents of each section of the report. A graduate thesis is examined and graded according to its contents and presentation, whereas doctoral students may be asked to defend their dissertation in an open professional presentation with examiners making up the audience. A question–answer session exposes the weaknesses and strengths of the work. A project report is also frequently sent for review before being accepted. Such reviews do not fall into the classical "conflict of interest" slot, but we include them here because they too can lead to conflicting postures. The reviewer may dislike the methodology or may question the validity of the conclusion, and the author can steadfastly refuse to accept the suggestions. Arguments and explanations are the only way of resolving these conflicts.

Review Process in Journals

All reputed professional journals, particularly in medical sciences, follow the system of peer review of articles submitted to them for publication. This helps them to get a fair assessment of the scientific merit of articles. The journals generally keep a database of subject matter experts after judicious selection. The reviewers, are initially asked if there is any conflict of interest that can bias their review. The review is supposed to be factual and completely free of bias, although that cannot be said for all reviews.

The review process helps editors to decide the suitability for publishing the work. This is considered an important quality control measure, and may help in improving the accuracy and clarity of published research. The editor looks at the paper and may decide to reject it outright without sending it for review. Only those papers that look worthwhile on first reading are sent for review. Some journals approach three or four reviewers but the standard is two. This job requires considerable time from reviewers, but they are generally not paid. They are not part of the editorial staff either. Many do this thankless job willingly in the interest of science, possibly considering it as a sign of recognition of their professional maturity. Perhaps it is a pleasure to review somebody else's work, and to comment on its strengths and weaknesses. The reviewers are forbidden to use the process to further their own interests in any manner.

When submitting a paper for publication, be prepared to receive comments, some of which may not be compliments, and shortcomings in the methods and flaws in the results may be highlighted. It is better to foresee them and prepare the manuscript accordingly. The peer review process can be very rewarding because the suggestions received can increase the value of the report. There is another view, though. Little evidence exists of the effectiveness of peer review, but considerable evidence exists of its deficiencies. This view arises from its failure at detecting some frauds [7].

The dominant system earlier followed was masking of authors and institutions by deleting the first page of the manuscript containing this information. This system is on the decline. Perhaps editors have found that most reviewers are unbiased, and knowledge of the name of the authors and institution does not affect the tone of review. Even when the names of the authors and their affiliation are removed from the manuscript, the contents of the paper, such as the topic, the source of subjects, and the methodology, can still provide hints about the identity of the authors. Thus, bias in some cases cannot be ruled out, although this would be rare. Nevertheless, a review can be highly subjective in isolated cases.

Some journals require that the study data are publicly available – a condition to which many authors would be reluctant to agree. Some journals may even want to repeat the analysis by an independent biostatistician. Almost all medical journals of repute try to get a rigorous biostatistical review. It is good practice to keep the data and the analysis in record for, say, 10 years so that any subsequent questions that arise can be answered.

Beware of **predatory journals** that accept and publish almost any paper for a fee. Whereas some of these are fair in charging a fee, as they provide open access and do not get revenue, many are pseudo-journals that exist to make money. Most such journals may claim peer review but may not be actually doing so. These are not indexed either by reputable indexing services such as MedLine. Some authors publish in such journals to add to their list of publications and further their career, but whether it really helps is not known.

Review of Thesis

Many graduate theses across the world are accepted with or without raising a question. That may have compromised their quality. In some cases, the examiner may not be fully satisfied, may even be fully dissatisfied, but does not want to be perceived as a tough person or as the one trying to spoil the career of a student. Raising queries and rejecting a thesis involve a lot of work that many examiners want to avoid, and involve threat to his or her examinership in future. Thus, the flaws in graduate theses rarely come to the fore.

The situation with doctoral dissertations is not that dismal, although that also requires raising the present standard. Some examiners are strict and ask for revisions where necessary, but some are relaxed. Caution is exercised both by the student and by the adviser to produce a work that can be professionally defended.

Responding to the Reviews

As opposed to theses, perhaps not more than 10% of papers sent to good journals are accepted as submitted. Many are rejected for various reasons – mostly for not meeting the standard set by the journal. Most articles are referred back to the authors for revision, sometimes with inconvenient questions, but also offering suggestions that tend to improve the quality of the paper. Sometimes the suggested revision may be intractable, in which case the authors can try another journal.

Sometimes a paper is rejected without assigning any reason. This could be painful, but a good manuscript can be rejected if it does not fit into the scope of the journal. It is to obviate this that we suggested that your covering letter should include why you selected that journal. Do not lose heart in the case of rejection. There are instances when a paper was accepted after being rejected by eight journals [8]. Many journals give reasons for rejection, including but not limited to that the research is only repetitive or just confirmatory with no new findings, or it has poor design, unclear hypothesis, poor presentation, or any such gross deficiency. Brood over the reasons coolly and examine what you can do to alleviate the deficiency. Remove the deficiency as much as possible and submit to another journal. If you have sincerely carried out a research study, be assured that the paper will be accepted by one or the other journal. Many journals remain on the hunt for suitable manuscripts.

Quite often the paper is returned with comments from one, two or even three reviewers that help you revise the manuscript. You must carefully read all the comments and prepare a detailed point-by-point reply. Do not ignore any comment even if it looks trivial because that can delay acceptance. Some suggested changes may not be to your liking. Explain the changes you have made in the manuscript in response to each comment, and also explain if you find that changes as per any comment will not be appropriate. Do not worry if your response is long. For those comments that look appropriate to you, express gratitude to the reviewer for pointing them out. Some journals require that changes in the manuscript be made in "track changes" mode.

Experience suggests that it is expedient to comply with the comments of the reviewers and modify your manuscript accordingly instead of raising a counter-argument. If you feel strongly about a comment, give a polite explanation why it is not appropriate, or cannot be complied with, and cite supportive evidence. See if your writing lacks clarity, which led to this kind of comment. Merely giving an explanation in reply to the comments is not enough: the text of the manuscript should also be changed accordingly so that it reflects the reply. Each comment must be individually attended to. Get help from the other authors if you have others for the paper. Do not be disappointed if the paper is not accepted even after complying with all the suggestions. This can happen, although it is rare.

Some journals may not provide comments and only ask you to reduce the size of the paper because they have space limitations. Think critically regarding which part of the text, which table, and which figure can be safely deleted without altering the essential content. Do so with discretion, because continuity and flow have to be maintained and no vital information should be lost.

Sometimes there is a conflict in the comments themselves. One reviewer may ask to delete some portion and the other may say that the portion is good. One reviewer may also provide conflicting advice – for example, to cut short the paper and to add some explanation. Make the best of such conflicts without raising controversy.

Although the decision to accept or reject is supposed to be based entirely on the scientific merit of the paper, the editors are not above the board either. They are perceived to be in a tremendously advantageous position. Perhaps there is no author who has no grievances against one editor or another. British and American journals are sometimes accused of being biased, although they claim to bend over backward to accept quality papers from developing countries. Some journals (e.g., *Lancet*) have appointed an ombudsman for redressal of grievances. You can file an appeal if you feel strongly about unfair rejection or any such occurrence. Journals are supposed to clearly state the process of appeals and have a system for redressal.

14.3 Confidentiality and Misreporting

We have discussed ethics in conducting medical research earlier in Chapter 2 and the present chapter is on ethics to be followed in *reporting* of research findings. While confidentiality was discussed there, this needs to be reemphasized in the context of reporting. Misreporting is in any case is a serious issue globally.

14.3.1 Confidentiality

In the context of publishing research, the question of confidentiality arises at least at two levels. First is the respect for privacy of patients or subjects. No information that can identify any individual should be part of your manuscript. The names certainly cannot be revealed, but things like photos and pedigrees should be sufficiently masked. Only in cases where necessary for scientific reasons can this identity be revealed with the full and expressed consent of the person concerned. This consent should be free of any duress or pressure.

The second is at the level of the authors and reviewers. All reviews must respect the confidentiality of the authors and the names of the reviewers also are not disclosed. Authors have the right not to be discussed for their work unless it is published. Reviewers cannot take advantage of their privilege of knowing the contents before publication. Nonetheless, the confidentiality of the authors can be breached in a rare case of fraud, when established, with respect to subjects, methods, statistical misappropriation, and other such lapses. This brings us to misreporting.

14.3.2 Misreporting

Scientific misconduct in terms of misreporting can go unnoticed in subtle ways. This is manipulating the results and includes bogus research. This not only impedes the progress of science but also sometimes misleads. All such instances must be reported and investigated when noticed. Researchers are not supposed to keep silent or sweep it under the carpet. Whistle-blowers are generally protected in all countries.

Result Manipulation

This can occur in one or more of the following ways.

1. Changing the endpoint or outcome of interest from, say, death to complication or vice versa when results for the planned outcome fail to meet the expectations of the investigator. This can also be in terms of looking at 1-year outcome in place of a 2-year outcome as originally planned, or any such deviation
2. Presenting the results groupwise instead of combined, or vice versa, when such transposition helps to provide findings in support of the investigator's hypothesis
3. Presenting results for a subgroup of patients, pretending that other groups were not there
4. Presenting univariate (unadjusted) results when the objective was to present results adjusted for confounders
5. Presenting results for proportions when averages fail to serve the hypothesis of the investigator, or vice versa; or using proportion where odds ratio should be used
6. Arbitrary merging of categories of data to provide specific results
7. Altering or omitting part of the data to manufacture the results

These are examples of the avenues that can be misused to cook up the desired results. Some will select part of the data to get "evidence" in support of their hypothesis. There is a famous saying that if someone searches hard enough, part of the data can be located that would support almost any hypothesis. The difficulty is that such misreporting is hard to detect in a finished report, and can go unnoticed for a long time. It is up to you to be true to yourself and science, and report the full facts. Correctly reported results replicate well and endure while incorrectly reported results are soon forgotten. They may help to improve your career résumé, but at a substantial cost to science. A true doctor would never do this.

Misreporting includes both intentional and unintentional lapses. The unintentional could be due to carelessness or honest errors. The latter could be due to miscoding, miscalculation, or inadequate method of statistical analysis. Honest deviation from the design or subjective deviations in those aspects which were not thought of earlier at the time of protocol also are not misconduct. According to the publication guidelines, a correction can be published if these errors do not change the essential results. Otherwise, the paper may have to be retracted or republished. Whereas substantial deviation can occur from established medical practice due to new research with the wrong results that can adversely affect many patients, Indrayan [9] has pleaded that benign aspects such as wrong statistical methods can produce results that can jeopardize health and life of many persons. This further underscores the need to be careful about reporting of research results. Intentional errors, in all cases, are inexcusable.

Fanelli [10] reported that nearly 2% of scientists admitted to have fabricated, falsified, or modified data or results at least once in their career, and up to 38% admitted other questionable research practices.

Having said all that, there might be valid reasons in rare cases to report part of the findings. These could be that you merged categories or groups as these had small numbers, discovered an interesting finding for a specific subgroup, found that the data for a particular group are erroneous – not properly collected, or any such reason. In such cases, explain what happened and why only part of the results is being reported. The keyword is the intention of the researcher to commit the misconduct. If it is established as being unintentional, it can probably be excused.

Bogus Research

At the extreme is research based on fake data. No or very little data are collected and the major part is imputed at will to get the desired results. This is fraud, to say the least, and puts the reputation at stake not only of the researcher and institution but of the whole country. Fraud in the context of research is falsification, fabrication, or deception. This can prove to be a setback to the research endeavors or detrimental to science. Many patients may be affected and some may even be victims of death when wrong results are used for treatment. Persons reporting such research can be severely punished by their employer. If the results have wider implications, even the police can take action. Known frauds may be just the tip of the iceberg as most of them remain unknown.

14.4 The Last Word

Medical researchers have a tall order of producing a worthwhile result when uncertainties are numerous and many are insurmountable. The core of success lies in being able to identify the sources of uncertainties and using a methodology that can take care of most of them. Time spent in developing the proposal is well spent. Do not shy away from working hard at that stage. Constantly remind yourself about the identification and management of medical uncertainties.

Credibility of research mostly depends on sound methodology rather than on results. The objective is to reach reliable and valid conclusions that are verifiable by repeating the investigation. Check that all known epistemic and aleatory uncertainties have been tackled, and the design has taken care of various sources of known bias. Those that creep in despite the best design should be dealt with at the analysis stage. If this is achieved to the satisfaction of all concerned, consider that the research has attained a high quality.

Do not succumb to the pressure of producing quantity at the expense of quality. A lengthy list of publications may give some mileage in the beginning but ultimately a reputation cannot be built on shoddy research. Haste at the expense of care cannot pay. Most employments, promotions, and recognitions are based on, say, the five best publications rather than the full list. In some instances, an extremely long list of low-quality publications is disliked rather than appreciated. Thus, resist the temptation to publish or present research that you know is substandard. Quality work gives immense satisfaction that sloppy work cannot provide.

In the end, we must emphasize that there is no alternative to common sense. Tools such as protocol, design, and statistical analysis are only aids to carry out research in a systematic manner. They must only complement common sense and not replace it.

References

1. Altman DG, Bland JM. Measurement in medicine: The analysis of method comparison studies. Statistician 1983; 32:307–317. http://people.stat.sfu.ca/~raltman/stat300/AltmanBland.pdf
2. Bland JM, Altman DG. Statistical methods for assessing agreement between two methods of clinical measurement. Lancet 1986;i:307–310. www-users.york.ac.uk/~mb55/meas/ba.pdf
3. Gold EB. Epidemiology of and risk factors for pancreatic cancer. Surg Clin North Am 1995;75:819–843. www.ncbi.nlm.nih.gov/pubmed/7660248
4. Gold EB, Goldin SB. Epidemiology of and risk factors for pancreatic cancer. Surg Oncol Clin N Am 1998;7:67–91. www.sciencedirect.com/science/article/pii/S0039610916467307
5. Patel SV, Hodge DO, Bourne WM. Corneal endothelium and postoperative outcomes 15 years after penetrating keratoplasty. Trans Am Ophthalmol Soc 2004;102:57–65. www.ncbi.nlm.nih.gov/pmc/articles/PMC1280087/
6. Patel SV, Hodge DO, Bourne WM. Corneal endothelium and postoperative outcomes 15 years after penetrating keratoplasty. Am J Ophthalmol 2005;139:311–319. www.ncbi.nlm.nih.gov/pubmed/15733993
7. Smith R. The Trouble with Medical Journals. Royal Society of Medicine Press, 2006.
8. Cummings P, Rivara FP. Responding to reviewers' comments on submitted articles. Arch Pediatr Adolesc Med 2002;156:105–107. https://jamanetwork.com/journals/jamapediatrics/article-abstract/191489
9. Indrayan A. Statistical fallacies and errors can jeopardize life and health of many. Indian J Med Res 2018;148:677–679. www.ijmr.org.in/text.asp?2018/148/6/677/252165
10. Fanelli D. How many scientists fabricate and falsify research: A systematic review and meta-analysis of survey data. PLoS One 2009;4(5):e5738/ https://journals.plos.org/plosone/article?id=10.1371/journal.pone.0005738

Index

Printed in the United States
by Baker & Taylor Publisher Services